Laying the Foundations

Laying the Foundations

Manual of the British Museum Iraq Scheme
Archaeological Training Programme

Edited by John MacGinnis and Sebastien Rey

with contributions by

Duygu Camurcuoğlu, Claudia Da Lanca, Amy Drago, Rand Eppich, Jamie Fraser,
Alberto Giannese, Elisa Girotto, Guy Hazell, Ewout Koek, John MacGinnis,
Kate Morton, Sebastien Rey, Mary Shepperson, St John Simpson, Joanna Skwiercz,
Mathilde Touillon-Ricci and Faith Vardy

ARCHAEOPRESS ARCHAEOLOGY

ARCHAEOPRESS PUBLISHING LTD
Summertown Pavilion
18–24 Middle Way
Summertown
Oxford OX2 7LG

www.archaeopress.com

ISBN 978-1-80327-140-8
ISBN 978-1-80327-141-5 (e-Pdf)

This book is available direct from Archaeopress or from our website www.archaeopress.com

Contents

Foreword

In 2014, at the height of the monstrous damage and destruction wreaked upon archaeological sites, monuments and museums in Iraq at the hands of Daesh (the so-called Islamic State), and with the support of Neil MacGregor, the then Director of the British Museum, I devised a programme of training for colleagues in Iraq that would allow them to confront the challenges of the aftermath of this affront to their cultural heritage. Known originally as the 'Iraq Emergency Heritage Management Training Scheme', but more recently as just 'the Iraq Scheme', it attracted the attention and support of the British Government's Department of Culture, Media and Sport (DCMS), and the British Museum was fortunate in receiving a substantial grant to finance the project. Between 2015 and 2020, we welcomed a total of 50 employees of Iraq's State Board of Antiquities and Heritage (SBAH), both men and women, to the British Museum where, in groups of six to eight at a time, they received state-of-the-art training in all aspects of field archaeology from some of the world's leading practitioners.

But field archaeology, by definition, is not a theoretical undertaking – it is a practical discipline. For this reason, from the outset, the Iraq Scheme employed two senior archaeologists, not only to supervise the UK training programme and act as mentors for the Iraqi participants, but to direct major excavation projects in Iraq where the participants would put into practice what they had learned in the classroom. For the benefit of our Iraqi colleagues it was essential that these excavations were not merely 'training digs' but fully developed research projects to which the participants would contribute in every aspect, from field operations to publication.

So it was that sites were selected in what were then seen as 'safe' (Daesh-free) areas of Iraq. In the North in Iraqi Kurdistan, John MacGinnis, an experienced field archaeologist who had previously worked on numerous projects in the Kurdish Region of Iraq, chose a small group of threatened sites disposed around the north-eastern shore of Lake Dokan. In southern Iraq, Sebastien Rey, similarly experienced from his work at Tello, the immensely important Sumerian site of Girsu, and for which he already held the excavation permit, chose to continue his operations and incorporate the training activities there. Both directors assembled formidable dig teams, populated with many of the same experts who had provided the training in London. By this means it was possible to construct a comprehensive programme for our participants which combined the teaching of hands-on excavation skills with the sophisticated techniques available to modern archaeology, such as MultiStation 3D surveying, geophysical mapping, geographical information systems, photogrammetry and the use of drones and satellite imagery.

Both of the excavation projects have produced scientific results that have been highly significant and, in some cases, spectacular. They have been achieved, in no short measure, through the dedicated and enthusiastic engagement of our Iraqi participants, and the fruits of their contributions will be seen in the numerous publications that have appeared, or will appear in due course.

The result of the overall project has been to substantially build capacity within SBAH by adding a cohort of more than fifty highly trained practitioners to an already well-established nucleus of experienced Iraqi field archaeologists. This contribution, involving professionals in every province of Iraq, will be an enduring legacy of the Iraq Scheme.

The other legacy of the Scheme is this manual. It would have been a tragic waste if the wealth of expertise gathered for the Iraq Scheme had not been captured and preserved, to be drawn upon by future archaeologists, students and those concerned with the protection and preservation of cultural heritage. I am indebted to John MacGinnis for taking the initiative to do just that, and by bringing together those experts responsible for the training scheme, for producing a comprehensive and authoritative guide to the nuts and bolts of conducting archaeological fieldwork. Although based on our work in Iraq, the principles are applicable to projects throughout the Middle East and beyond. The following pages cover every aspect of archaeological fieldwork from conception and initiation to execution, post-excavation analysis and publication, with additional sections on reconstruction and site management. A very important intention from the outset was to ensure

Group 5 at the British Museum

that the manual should be fully accessible to our Iraqi colleagues, an aim achieved by the Arabic and Kurdish translations which accompany this English version.

My thanks go, of course, to all those involved in the manual, but especially to St John Simpson, John MacGinnis, Sebastien Rey, Suzy Minett and Claudia Da Lanca, who have edited and shaped the contributions into a coherent whole. Special thanks are also due to the State Board of Antiquities and Heritage in Baghdad, the General Directorate of Antiquities of Kurdistan, the UK's Department of Culture, Media and Sport and our outstanding Iraqi participants, without all of whose enthusiastic involvement the Iraq Scheme could not have been such a stunning success.

Jonathan N Tubb
Director of the Iraq Scheme and Keeper of the Department of the Middle East at the British Museum

Preface

The compilation of this manual has been a long and rewarding process running hand-in-hand with the training of the Iraq Scheme delivered in the UK at the British Museum and in Iraq at the two excavations initiated for this purpose. There is a huge amount to learn in archaeology, and it would be impossible to cover every single aspect of the profession. Rather, our aim has been to provide a framework of the key components needed for a field programme. The emphasis is on practicality – the basic skills and approaches at the core of an excavation project. We are well aware that other people might have written a different text with differing emphases – of course, they are welcome to do so! As Diakonoff famously said, there are as many conceptions of Sumerian grammar as there are Sumerologists, and the same is true of archaeological field methodology. We have striven to find a balance between the many competing approaches to recording and post-excavation processing. A guiding principal has been to produce a work of genuine practical use to our Iraqi colleagues working in the field, to which end the production of the openly available translations into Arabic and Kurdish has been a fundamental objective from the outset.

Group 7 of the archaeologists participating in the Iraq Scheme

The list of people to thank is vast, but we must start with the commitment of the Government of the United Kingdom which has made this endeavour possible, and in particular the members of the Department of Digital, Culture, Media and Sport who have steered the project through its many challenges: Tracy Crouch, John Glenn and Michael Ellis, successive Ministers at the Department, together with Rebecca Clutterbuck, Ritvik Deo, Harriet Hoffler, Dominic Lake, Keith Nichol, Joseph Rowlands, Giles Smith, Lucien Smith and Kate Snelson. We are likewise grateful to Tim Loughton MP, Tom Tugendhat MP, Nick Abbott, Jaimie Bowden, Tim Clayden, Simon Hayes, David Livingstone, Marc Owen, David O'Toole, Tim Purbrick and Stephen Spittle. Nor can we fail to record our appreciation for the support from the top levels of the British Museum, from the Trustees, the Chairman George Osborne and his predecessor Sir Richard Lambert, the Director Hartwig Fischer, and the Deputy Directors Jonathan Williams and Chris Yates, as well as the many other staff listed further below.

The Iraq Scheme has from the beginning been a collaborative venture with the State Board of Antiquities and Heritage in Baghdad and the General Directorate of Antiquities of Kurdistan. We express our

Group 2 on a visit to the London Mithras Temple

deep gratitude to Laith Majeed Hussein, Director General of the State Board, as well as his predecessors in this office, and also to the many previous and current SBAH officials in Baghdad who have provided much appreciated help and support, including Haider Abd al-Wahed al-Mamori, Saleem Khalaf Anaeed, Mohammad Saleh, Mahdi Ali Raheem, Mohammad Sabri, Adil Jabour Diwan, Ahmad Kamel, Hussain Ali Habib, as well as to the new director of excavations, Ali Shalgam; and to Kaify Mustafa Ali, Director General of Antiquities of Kurdistan, his predecessor Abubakr Othman Zainadin (Mala Awat), Barzan Baiz Ismael, Director of Antiquities of Raparin, Kamal Raheem Rashid, Director of Antiquities of Sulaimaniya, and Hashim Hama Abdullah, Director of the Sulaimaniya Museum.

The work at Tello, ancient Girsu, would not have been possible without the determination, guidance and help of the project's Deputy Director, Fatma Yassir Husain; of Qais Hussein Rashid, former Deputy Tourism and Antiquities Minister, who was instrumental in the launch and early delivery of the Iraq Scheme; of the SBAH office in Nasiriya (Thi Qar province) and its Director Amer Abdul Razzaq and his predecessors Thaer Queen Amjad Nahma Shabib; of Colonel Fuad Karim Abdullah, former commanding officer of the Nasiriya Archaeology Police, and its new commander General Shaker Hilal, as well as the whole archaeological police force, who ensured the security and well-being of the expedition in southern Iraq; and of the archaeologists of the Nasiriya office, and especially the inspectors who participated in the different seasons carried out at Tello: Karar Abde Kwali, Abd al-Hadi Kraydi Jabr, Ahmad Khadim, Abbas Saheb, Saad Ali Danoun, Abd al-Hassan Maktouf Sayah, Aqeel Sfayyih, Mohammad Sahdi, Mohamad Ali Khalaf and Hiba Sabah. The contribution of the SBAH guards and the hundred or so friends and colleagues from Nasriya and its environs who have worked with us at the site has been absolutely central. Last but not least, a special word of thanks to Amir Doshi, who translated the annual reports on the seasons at Tello into Arabic, as well as for his work on translating this manual. To all of these we extend our profound gratitude.

In Kurdistan we were privileged to receive the support and encouragement of Sasan Othman Awni Habib, Minister of Municipalities and Tourism; Amal Jalal, the Head of the General Board of Tourism; Jihan Sindi, Advisor at the Presidency of the Council of Ministers; Kaify Mustafa Ali,

Director General of Antiquities of Kurdistan, and his predecessor Abubakr Othman Zainadin (Mala Awat); Barzan Baiz Ismael, Director of Antiquities of Raparin; Kamal Raheem Rashid, Director of Antiquities of Sulaimaniya; Hashim Hama Abdullah, Director of the Sulaimaniya Museum; Dr Abdullah Khorsheed, Director of the Iraqi Institute for the Conservation of Antiquities and Heritage; Hiwa Qarani Abdulla, Governor of Raparin; Hussain Mohammed Ibrahim, mayor of Rania; General Hassan Swara, head of Rania Police; Hazhar Mohammed Bapir, the head of local Security (Asaish); Dr Mufaq Khalid Ibrahim, President of Raparin University; our representatives, Sami Jamil Hamarashid, Halkawt Qadir Omer and Awaz Jihad Hedan; Ismail Mohamed Ali, who helped us with his huge local knowledge; Ramazan Qadir Ismael and his family, who kept us well-fed in an orderly house; and to all the many local men and women who participated in the work. A special word of thanks goes to Halala Aki Omer, who translated for our training sessions in Rania into both Arabic and Kurdish, and to Dilshad Abdul-Mutalib Mustafa, who translated this manual into Sorani Kurdish.

Group 4 in the Great Court of the British Museum

In London we owe an enormous debt to His Excellency Dr Salih Husain Ali Al-Tamimi, former Ambassador of the Republic of Iraq to the Court of St. James, and his successor His Excellency Mr Mohammad Jaafar Mohammad Bakr Al-Sadr, for facilitating the progress of the Iraq Scheme in every way, supported by their unfailingly helpful staff at the Iraqi Embassy, including Wael Al-Robaaie, Nazar Mirjan Mohammed, Sufyan Abbas, Razaq Al-Mashkoor, Dr Hassan Al-Alak, Mushtaq Sultani, Atheer Alsaedy, Aseel Mirza and Hamailok Dizayee; to Dr Ghassan Saddawi, Iraqi Consul General, and his predecessor Mr Mushtaq Sultani, together with Mostafa Al-Hassani and all the staff of the Iraqi Consulate; and to Karwan Jamal Tahir, High Representative of the Kurdistan Regional Government to the United Kingdom, together with Legaa Firas, Khasro Ajgayi and all the staff of the Kurdish delegation.

We are similarly grateful for the support of Stephen Hickey, British Ambassador to the Republic of Iraq, his predecessors Frank Baker and Jonathan Wilks, and all the staff at the British Embassy in Baghdad; and to David Hunt, British Consul in Erbil, his predecessors James Thornton, Angus McKee and Martyn Warr, and to all the staff of the Consulate. We are also deeply indebted to Brian Brivati, David Fairbank, Nick Jariwalla, Ghassan Jawad, Paul Kramer, Eileen Laca, James Rickard and Hayley Williams for their assistance with visa applications, both for our Iraqi colleagues coming to the UK and British Museum staff travelling to Iraq.

The London-based component of the training provided a very wide-ranging introduction to the theory and practice of cultural heritage management, as well as an introduction to key archaeological concepts and technical skills. We owe an immense debt of gratitude to the huge number of individuals who taught sessions in the course of this training. From within the British Museum this included Wendy Adamson, David Agar, Stefka Bargazova, Gemma Barlow, Mark Bates, Gareth Brereton, Megan Bristow, Duygu Camurcuoğlu, Caroline Cartwright, Sarah Collins, Vesta Curtis, Claudia Da Lanca, Sophie Dave, Andrew David, Simon Denham, Valeria Di Tommaso, Tony Doubleday, Adrian Doyle, Amy Drago, Joanne Dyer, Nicola Elvin, Irving Finkel, Sally Fletcher, James Fraser, Christos Gerontinis, Alberto Giannese, Darwin Goodridge, Bill Greenwood, Angela Grimshaw, Hannah Gwyther, Carine Harmand, Nathan Harrison, Duncan Hook, Dudley Hubbard, Imran Javed, Judy Joseph, Brian Kerr, Zeina Klink-Hoppe, Dimitra Kountiou, Lawrence Leason, Benedict Leigh, Michael Lewis, Denise Ling, Kevin Lovelock, Janine Marsh, Rocio Mayol, Andrew Meek, Amandine Merat, Suzy Minett, Kate Morton, Laura Phillips, Venetia Porter, Shezza Rashwan, Philippa Ryan, Niki Savvides, Margaret Sax, Antony Simpson, St John Simpson, Michela Spataro, Rebecca Stacey, Ruth Stone, Jo-Anne Sunderland, Tracey Sweek, Nigel Tallis, Jonathan Taylor, Roberta Tomber, Mathilde Touillon-Ricci, Jonathan Tubb, Julia Tugwell, Rosalind Wade-Haddon, Quanyu Wang, Emma Webb, Derek Welsby, Harriet White, Craig Williams, John Williams, Jonathan Williams, Barbara Wills, Hannah Woodley, Adele Wright and Holly Wright.

And we also owe an equal debt to the many external colleagues who taught sessions either in the scope of the London training or on visits to their host institutions: Mark Altaweel, Steve Aucott, Nick Bateman, Graeme Barker, Andrew Bevan, Paul Bennett, Robert Bewley, Andrew Brown, Sheena Browne, Stephen Bull, Paul Bryan, Felicity Cobbing, Darren Crimes, John Darlington, David Divers, Mike Dunn, Emma Dwyer, Rand Eppich, Peter Guillery, Cordelia Hall, Andrew Hann, Mahmoud Hawari, Teresa Heady, Tricia Hillas, Sophie Jackson, Nicola Kalimeris, Brian Kerr, Heather Knight, Nineb Lamassu, Dan Laurence, Liz Jones, Matthew Law, Fiona Macalister, Steve Macaulay, John MacDermot, Roger Matthews, Wendy Matthews, Iain McCaig, Debbie Miles-Williams, Henry Owen-John, Andreas Pantazatos, Graham Philip, Leigh Reuss-Daters, Bijan Rouhani, Andrew Skellern, Nigel Smee, Stephen Spittle, John Stewart, Dani Tagen, Richard Thomas, Kathy Tubb, Faith Vardy, Angela White and Marek Ziebart.

A very special thanks goes to Peter Dinshaw, who expertly translated the highly technical language of a broad range of specialised subjects, materially contributing to the effective delivery of the training; and also to Annabel Jackson, our external evaluator, whose monitoring and feedback was likewise immeasurably beneficial.

The Iraq Scheme has benefitted from the truly extraordinary resources of the British Museum, with the support and expertise of a very wide range of staff beyond those who taught modules of the training. While this list cannot possibly be comprehensive, we would like to express our thanks to Mohamed Ahmed, Philip Baxter, Dean Baylis, Jill Beardon, Nabilah Begum, Mica Benjamin-

Group 6 in the forecourt the British Museum

Mannix, David Bilson, Hannah Boulton, Anna Buelow, Gladser Carvalho, Wei Kiat Chen, Jill Cook, Anna Cottle, Glenn Cumiskey, Graham Dunkley, Melissa East, Joe Edwards, Nicola Elvin, Joanna Fernandes, Iain Fishpool, Achilleas Fontivero, Laurie Frey, Valentina Gasperini, Fleur Gatineau, Nick Harris, Carl Heron, Peter Higgs, Amy Hitchcock, Rebecca Horton, Ruth Jones, Abida Kassam, Ivor Kerslake, Thomas Kiely, Janet Larkin, Nicholas Lee, Mhairi Letcher, Celia Lloyd-Davidson, Joanna Mackle, Antonio Marin Fabra, Henrietta Martin-Fisher, Freddie Matthews, Emma Meekings, Claire Messenger, Martin Meyler, Sunil Mir, Thorsten Oppert, Georgi Parpulov, Steven Pasquale, Beth Penny, Laura Phillips, Jane Portal, Nadja Race, Imma Ramos, Tansy Ratcliffe-James, Lee Roberts, Seonaid Rogers, Harriet Rose, Sarah Saunders, Sophie Shepherd, Allison Siegenthaler, Bryony Smith, Sandra Smith, Suzi Smith, Sophie Stead, Shakira Stevens, Fahmida Suleman, Michael Tame, Jonathan Teer, Olivia Threlkeld, Bradley Timms, Sian Toogood, Russell Torrance, Lucy Wallace, Tania Watkins, Jane Whittaker, Jonah Wilberg, Hilary Williams, Evelyn Wood and Angela Wright.

We would like to say a particular thanks to the following who have contributed chapters to this manual: to Mary Shepperson for the sections on laying out trenches, use of the dumpy level, drawing plans and sections, and Harris matrices; to Mathilde Touillon-Ricci for the sections on databases and registration; to Guy Hazell and James Fraser for the section on surveying with a total/multi station, and to James Fraser again and Ricardo Cabral for the section on the use of drones; to Kate Morton, Faith Vardy and Claudia Da Lanca for the section on the illustration of small finds; to Elisa Girotto for the section on the illustration of ceramics; to Duygu Camurcuoğlu, Amy Drago, Ewout Koek and Joanna Skwiercz for the section on conservation; and to Rand Eppich for the section on photogrammetry. We would, additionally, like to thank the following who have contributed on specific aspects and, in many cases, also generously granted the right to use the images which they provided: Tomáš Chabr, Petra Creamer, David Filipský, Peter Miglus, Sophie Mills, Daniele Morandi Bonacossi, Karel Novaček, Gwil Owen, Rocco Palermo, Leesa Vere-Stevens and Jason Ur.

At the very heart of this enterprise have been the Iraqi and Kurdish colleagues who participated in the field training after first completing the London-based component of the course. It has been an immense privilege to work with such talented and dedicated individuals. Their experiences, insights and inputs have been an inspiration. And so we would like to express our warm gratitude to: (Group 1) Faleh Ghadawi Noman Almuturb, Hayder Isan Abdulrasool, Hemin Naman Kawes, Kovan Ihsan Yaseen, Mohammed Jasem Abd al-Elayawi, Tareq Khaleel Othman Al-Salihi; (Group 2) Adil Amin Sharif, Ali al-Hmeda, Halkawt Omer, Jabbar Libawi, Saad Jassim Hamoodi al-Khazraji, Zaid Saadallah; (Group 3) Nawzad Abdullatif Abdulkarim Al-Jaf, Dilshad Abdul-Mutalib Mustafa, Mehdi Ali el-Rahim, Ali Kamel Ghazal, Zahed Mohammed Eleywi, Toufik Abd Mohamed Muthuan, Osama Muhammad Khorshit, Qasem Rashid Hamid; (Group 4) Anas Abdalsattar Zaidan Zaidan, Birnadet Hanna Matti Al Maslob, Estabraq Ghazi Younus Alzuabidi, Nadia Suhail Mohamedbsher Al-Ghadhanfri, Nadia Fadhil Saleem Saleem, Rana Bashar Saleh Saleh, Rana Zuheir Ibrahim Naati, Zinah Naziyah Abdulrazzaq Alabdali; (Group 5) Awaz Jihad Ghedan, Diman Sadraldin Mohammed Ali, Sara Sulaiman Younis Younis, Ahlam Jabbar Ali Al-Kareem, Suad Obaid Hussein Yasari, Dhuha Dheyaa Sabeeh Sabeeh; (Group 6) Ahmad Smail Hamad Ameen, Awder Nasralddin Hamasalim, Aymen Jasim Mohammed, Hayder Mohammed Ali Abdulhussen, Ihsan Lafta Enad Al-Ghanimi, Ali Ahmed Abdulateef Al-Tameemi, Mhmood Mohsin Hachim Al-Saedi, Saad Ahmed Abed Abed; (Group 7) Ethar Qasim Mashkoor Al-Agoobee, Faeza Mohammed Jumaah Al-Rubaye, Hadeel Miri Jumaah Jumaah, Majida Hatif Dawood Battah, Muntaha Adheem Kadhim Al-Shuwaili, Saya Halko Fattah Agha, Valentina Abdulrahman Ali Ali and Zinah Mohammed Abdullah Abdullah; (Group 8) Ala`a Karim Da`ach, Ahmed Abdullah Dahham Al-Mamoori, Ahmed Ibrahim Salmami, Fouad Dalil Mahmood, Karwan Ismael Awrahman, Taher Queen Aneed; and (Group 9) Hero Hassan Khidhr, Zhakaw Pirot Rasul, Halala Saleh Ahmed, Hiba Sabah Muter, Huda Nassir Abd Mosa, Noorah Ahmed Hantosh, Ranya Mohammed Abdul Wahid, Taisser Mahmud Hame and Tufoof Mohammed Dahham.

Carrying out archaeological fieldwork in Iraq is very demanding. We owe an incalculable debt to the members of the excavation teams who worked for protracted periods under often difficult conditions in order to share their own skills and expertise in a spirit of international co-operation: at Tello, Fatma Yassir Husain (Deputy Director), Sila Akman, Eleanor Atkins, Dita Auzina, Stefka Bargazova, Anthony Baxter, Gareth Brereton, Helene Canaud, Angelo Di Michele, John Darlington, Ella Egberts, Charlotte Faiers, Caterina Fantoni, Adam Fraser, James Fraser, Andrew Ginns, Elisa Girotto, Tina Greenfield, Cordelia Hall, Luke Jarvis, Jaafar Jotheri, John MacDermot, Hilary McDonald, Ashley Pooley, Uxue Rambla-Eguilaz, Thea Rogerson, Joanna Skwiercz, Dani Tagen, Jon Taylor, Ebru Torun, Faith Vardy and Lisa Yeomans; and in Rania, Barzan Baiz Ismael, Sami Jamil Hamarashid, Halkawt Omer, Awaz Jihad Hedan, Mustafa Ahmad, Bahzad Mohammed, Fidaa Almehho, Fereidoun Fayaq, Stefano Bertoldi, Gemma Barlow, Julie Bessenay, Megan Bristow, Ricardo Cabral, Jan Čibera, Raghdah Dagher, Claudia Da Lanca, Liam Devlin, Amanda Dusting, Maria Gajewska, Alberto Giannese, Tina Greenfield, Guy Hazell, Floor Huisman, Achilles Iasonos, David Kertai, Hero Hassan Khidr, Ewout Koek, Ben Leigh, Tom Lyons, Timothy Matney, Andy

Miller, Sophia Mills, Suzy Minett, Kate Morton, Sandra Mularczyk, Mathilde Mura, Virág Pabeschitz, Andrew Petersen, Stephen Porter, Lucas Proctor, Morgan Revels, Sarah Ritchie, Saleh Salimi, Alice Salvador, Christoph Schmidhuber, Mary Shepperson, Ruth Stone, Mathilde Touillon-Ricci, Necmi Yaşar, Ramazan Qadir Ismael, Charly Vallance, Craig Williams and Zozik Sabah Noori.

We would like to express our very great thanks to David Davison, Ben Heaney and all the staff of Archaeopress, both for seeing through the publication of this printed version of the manual and for providing open-source access to the PDFs of the English, Arabic and Kurdish versions on the Archaeopress website.

Group 3 outside the British Museum

Last but absolutely not least, it is our deepest pleasure to thank our colleagues in the Iraq Scheme Core Team: Angie Grimshaw, whose knowledge, practicality and common sense has been a linchpin from the outset; Gemma Barlow, Megan Bristow, Claudia Da Lanca, Suzy Minett and Ruth Stone, at the helm of the project management, without whose seemingly fathomless abilities, unlimited patience and unfailing assistance none of this could have ever been achieved; St John Simpson, Deputy Director of the Iraq Scheme, whose immense knowledge of the archaeology of the near east (and beyond), equally comprehensive mastery in negotiating the pitfalls of institutional and government procedures and protocols, unrivalled feeling for the material artefact, and wry good humour have held us in awe; and, lastly, our esteemed leader, Jonathan Tubb, Keeper of the Department of the Middle East and Director of the Iraq Scheme, whose vast archaeological experience in the Middle East guided his vision and determination in bringing the Iraq Scheme into existence, and the leadership with which he has led it, with ceaseless humour and encouragement, through its many evolutions. It has been a privilege to work with you.

To all the above we extend our profound gratitude.

John MacGinnis
Sebastien Rey

Chapter 1

Initiating a Field Project

Initiating an archaeological field project is an exciting, yet challenging, prospect for an archaeologist. Our job is the recovery, preservation and interpretation of the past through its material remains, and the contribution from field projects has been, and continues to be, immense. Of course, excavation is one part of this – but it is only one part. This has always been true. In the case of Iraq, the earliest excavations were accompanied, and indeed preceded, by evaluation of written sources and mapping projects. The range of methods now available to modern archaeologists is very extensive – study of documentary sources, regional and topographical survey, remote sensing through overhead imagery and geophysical prospection, surface collection and, finally, excavation. These methods go hand in hand. It will be evident that a huge amount can be learnt without putting a trowel in the ground. And when an excavation does take place, as many of these

Figure 1.1 The Season 4 team in Rania

approaches as possible should be combined to form an integrated picture of the site – ideally even before the digging begins.

Nowadays, nobody digs just for the sake of digging. Excavation is, by its nature, destructive. It should only be undertaken with careful consideration and the justification should be clear. Sometimes this is in response to a threat, such as dam construction, road construction, urban expansion or agricultural attrition – the list is not exhaustive, and applies to every part of the world. In these cases, the aim is to recover as much information as possible before a site is destroyed. In other cases, excavations are initiated as part of a research programme of a department of antiquities, museum or university. But in all cases, it is important that the project takes place within the framework of a clear research agenda. The starting point may be an archaeological or historical period of obvious importance – or indeed which forms a gap in the record of a region – and a focus on one or more aspects which will contribute to our understanding of the past.

To get the most meaningful results, archaeologists need to arm and prepare themselves with probing questions. What led to this occupation or that expansion? Why is evidence for this period lacking? How was this society or community organised? How did it relate to larger political units? How was rule maintained? What was the subsistence strategy? How was this shaped by the environment? Our raw materials are the remains of buildings, deposits, artefacts and eco-factual data. We interrogate this material. Our task is to tease out an eloquent response from these mute remains. Approaching a site or a landscape with such questions allows the archaeologist to design a project so that the recovered material can help to provide answers. This may be more evident in the case of research excavations. But it is equally, or even more, important with rescue excavations, where the opportunity to address such issues is limited and hard choices will, inevitably, have to be made about what to prioritise. In the following pages we take a look at the components that can constitute a programme of archaeological field investigation – the many techniques for non-invasive research, as well as the techniques and methodology for carrying out stratigraphic excavation.

Field staff

Running an excavation is a complex business involving bringing together a team with many skills, who can between them deliver the repertoire of expertise demanded by modern archaeological practice.

Director

The director needs to be an experienced field archaeologist familiar with working in the local conditions and with the archaeology of the region, and able to handle the logistical challenges of an archaeological excavation. The latter includes setting up the dig house and excavation, hiring workmen, working with the representatives of the State Board of Antiquities & Heritage (or equivalent), managing the budget, writing reports, and dealing with the many other issues that emerge during a field season.

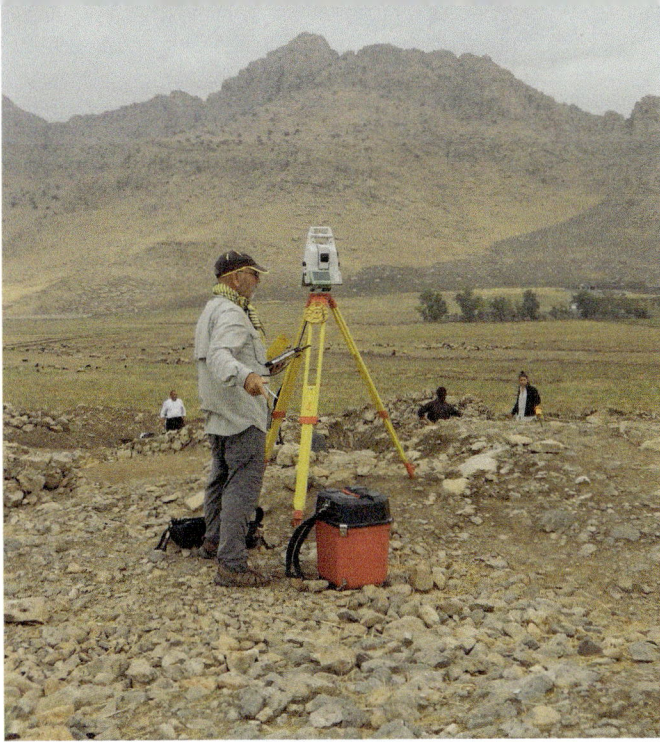

▲ Figure 1.2 Modern survey methods can integrate all the various sets of spatial data generated by the fieldwork

Surveyor

The capacity for accurate electronic survey is at the heart of any field project as it provides the framework for setting up the field operation, the recording of results and the processed output for the final record. To achieve this, a trained surveyor is required, familiar with and adept at using a total station and/or multi station to carry out tasks such as topographic surveys; marking out transects for surface surveys and grids for geophysical prospection; integrating and geo-referencing data from satellite imagery, drone imagery and geophysical mapping; laying out excavation trenches; planning the excavated remains (in collaboration with the site supervisors), producing orthophotos as required; processing the data and distributing output imagery to the site supervisors and director, as required.

Archaeological supervisors

The project will need experienced field archaeologists familiar with the local archaeology and living and working conditions of an excavation. They will also need to be adept at the full range of skills pertaining to excavation fieldwork – actual excavation with pick, trowel and brush; understanding stratigraphy, excavating by context and maintaining proper context recording; maintaining a written record with sketch plans and daily logs; taking environmental samples; keeping a photographic record of the progress of the excavation; drawing plans and sections; and, back in the dig house, entering context information into the database;

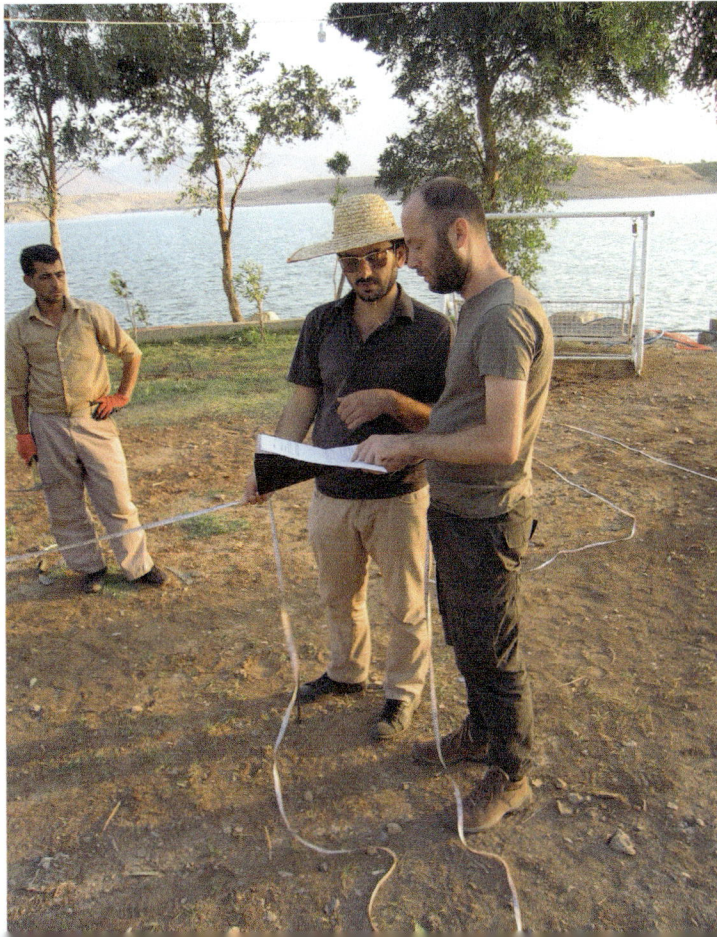

► Figure 1.3 Site supervisors discussing laying out a trench

downloading, labelling and archiving site photographs; writing weekly and final reports on the areas under their direction; digitising plans and sections; and, as necessary, assisting with other tasks such as flotation, processing ceramics and small finds, and so on.

Registrar/Database manager

It is essential for a major excavation project to have a well-designed and functioning database. At a minimum, this should have sections for recording stratigraphic contexts (with photographs) and for small finds and environmental samples. These are separate sections, but they can, and should be, linked. In addition to this, the database could have other sections for recording ceramics, epigraphic finds and so on, and again, linked to the stratigraphic record. The database therefore forms the centre of the excavation record. In the field it enables the efficient tracking of ceramics, small finds and environmental or other samples as they move between registrar, conservator, ceramicist, photographer, illustrator and others, and allows these specialists to add their contributions. During the post-excavation phase a properly functioning database enormously facilitates the process of writing up. The structure of the database and the creation of the programme need to be carefully planned prior to the commencement of work. Therefore the database manager will be needed to design and create the database, set it up in the excavation house and deliver it via an internal Wi-Fi system; instruct and assist field staff in its use; monitor functioning through the season, solving problems as they arise; maintain regular (or continuous) back-up of the data; create catalogues of samples and small finds; and ensure that the project is in possession of a full set of records at the end of the season. For an operation of any size it is highly desirable that the project has a full-time member of staff dedicated to this. In practice, it works well for the database manager to also be responsible for registering small finds and samples as they come in from the field, ensuring that they are registered and then sent to the conservator, photographer, illustrator and other specialists, as required.

Figure 1.4
The systematic registration of finds, contexts and other data lays the foundations for the process of research and writing up

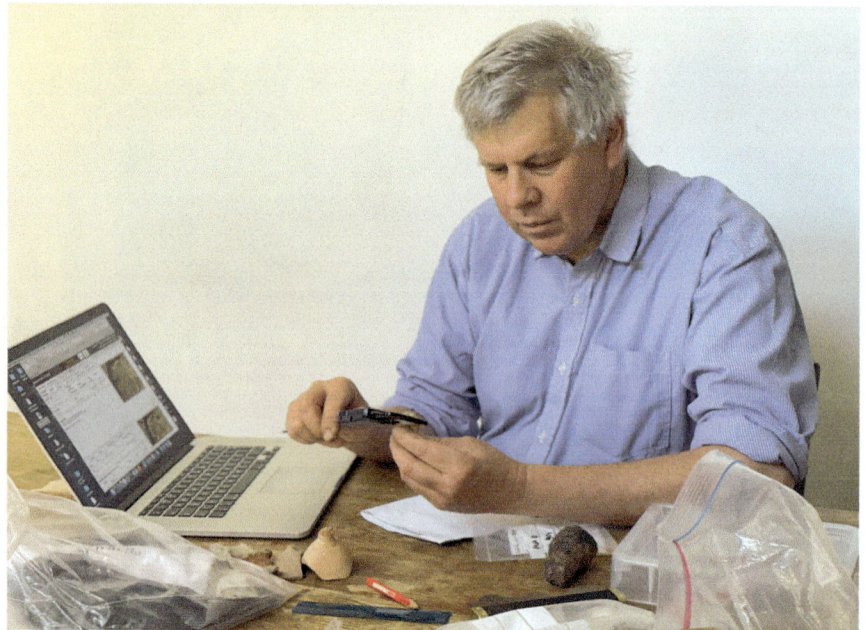

Ceramicist

Excavations generate huge amounts of ceramics. Keeping on top of this is a massive task. The job of the ceramicist entails supervising the material coming in from the field and processing it, from washing and initial sorting through to recording and successive levels of analysis – examining production methods, establishing typologies, working out dating and function, and so on. The ceramicist needs to be in constant dialogue with the director and archaeologists on-

Figure 1.5 In addition to their use for dating, ceramics can help us understand the function of different parts of a building or site, as well as shedding light on social and economic organisation

site, feeding information back to them on the dating of deposits, room function and so on. Every project will need at least one ceramicist, and very often more than one, or at least one or more assistants to the ceramicist.

Conservator

Every excavation should have a trained professional conservator. The tasks will include lifting fragile objects on-site, stabilising them in the laboratory, ensuring that they are ready to be handled by the photographer and illustrator, restoring them, preparing them for transport to a museum or storage magazine, and preparing them for museum display. To achieve all of this, the conservator will need to advise on and co-operate in the creation of a conservation field laboratory equipped with the appropriate equipment and chemicals. Depending on the size of the operation, or the particular requirements (such as removing wall paintings), more than one conservator may be required.

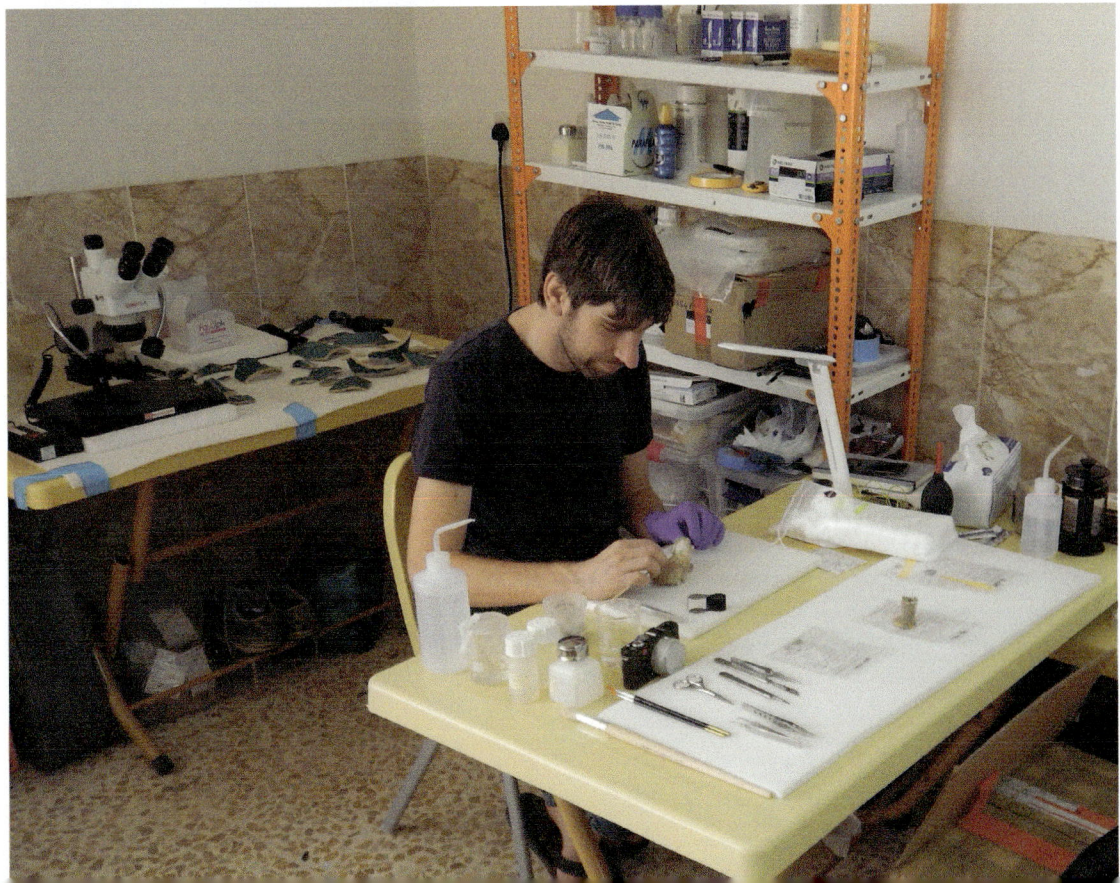

Figure 1.6 A well-equipped conservation studio is essential for the proper treatment of small finds

Photographer

The photographic archive is a core part of the excavation record. On any project with a significant volume of finds, the project needs the skills of a dedicated photographer to create a full photographic record of the small finds and key ceramics. In the case of large-scale projects this will often be a full-time member of staff. Additionally, while day-to-day photographs of the excavation in progress can be taken by the excavators, having a professional photographer to take final photographs of the excavations for publication can be hugely beneficial.

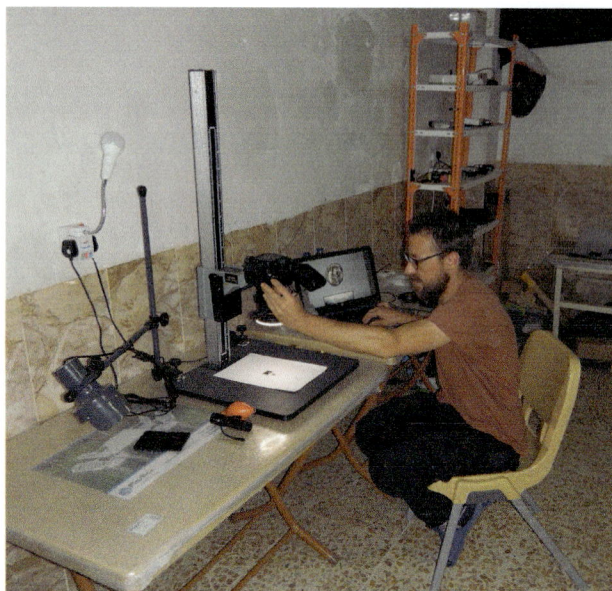

Figure 1.7 Every small find needs to be photographed

Illustrator

The illustration of small finds is another key part of the excavation record. If there is a large number of finds it is best to have a professional illustrator to do this. With certain classes of artefact (e.g. coins, sculpture) the illustration should, if possible, be done in consultation with relevant specialists. Depending on arrangements, and the quantity of material, illustrators may also assist the ceramicist in the illustration of ceramics. On larger projects it may be desirable to have more than one illustrator.

Archaeobotanist

Archaeobotanical remains constitute a highly important element of the material generated by excavations. There will be very few sites which, properly managed, do not yield significant archaeobotanic data. Every site needs a protocol for archaeobotanical recovery, including

Figure 1.8 Illustrator at work on a ceramic drawing which will in due course be digitised for publication

Figure 1.9 Flotation of soils samples is used to recover archaeobotanic remains (the 'light fraction'), as well as microdebris of other materials such as ceramics and stone ('the heavy fraction')

both a sampling strategy and a procedure for flotation. To achieve this, a trained archaeobotanist is needed to design and implement the programme of flotation for recovering archaeobotanical remains and study the material recovered. Whether the archaeobotanist needs to be present on site for the full length of the excavation season will depend on the volume of material generated, and also on whether or not it is possible to study the material in a laboratory elsewhere. See further details in the section on environmental sampling below.

Archaeozoologist

Likewise, the archaeozoological remains constitute an important element of the excavation material. While hand selection of larger bones is one part of the recovery process, the project needs a protocol for recovery of archaeozoological remains based on a consistent sampling strategy supported by dry sieving and flotation. Hand recovery alone will miss smaller diagnostic elements (such as bird or fish bones or milk teeth), cannot be easily quantified, and leads to interpretation biased in favour of larger mammals. An archaeozoologist is required both to design and implement such a programme and to study the material recovered. Whether the archaeozoologist needs to be present on-site for the full length of the excavation season will depend on the volume of material generated, and also on whether or not it is possible to study the material in a laboratory elsewhere. See further details in the section on environmental sampling below.

Physical anthropologist

Most excavations will encounter burials at some stage. The excavation of these can be undertaken by experienced excavators, but it is important that they follow a set procedure of both recording and environmental sampling. The scientific study of the human remains needs to be undertaken by a trained physical anthropologist. The amount of input required will of course depend on the volume of material in question. All stages of this process, from excavation to final resting place, need to be guided by a clear ethical code. See further details in the section on burials below.

▲ Figure 1.10 Archaeozoological analysis can yield a huge amount of data on social, economic and environmental aspects of ancient societies

◄ Figure 1.11 Osteologist examining a human skeleton

▲ Figure 1.12 Epigraphist working on bricks inscribed in cuneiform writing

Epigraphist

If working on a site of an historic period, one or more epigraphists may be required, whether this be for inscriptions in cuneiform, Aramaic, Greek, Arabic, Kurdish or any other language and script.

Other specialists

In addition to this, the input of other specialists may be required according to the nature of the finds. For example, if significant finds of sculpture, seals, ivories or coins are made, you may need to involve specialists in these fields. To understand the processes of site formation and the use of individual spaces you may want to employ specialists in geoarchaeology and/or micromorphology (the microscopic study of sequences of soils and sediments through the analysis of 'thin sections' made from blocks of undisturbed deposits carefully cut out from the excavation). Furthermore, analyses may need to be conducted off-site after the completion of the excavation season. This might include the analysis of charcoal, first of all for species identification and then for radiocarbon dating, and the material analysis of artefacts involving techniques such as X-raying, X-ray fluorescence, scanning electron microscopy, gas chromatography, etc.

▶ Figure 1.13 A well-run kitchen is at the heart of a successful expedition

House staff

It is essential that the project has a dedicated house staff. At minimum this should consist of a cook and a housekeeper. It is not reasonable or efficient to ask the professional team members to take turns cooking. They are exhausted from being in the field, and it takes them away from the proper work which they need to do in the dig house – and they may not know how to cook! Similarly, the project needs a housekeeper to keep the house clean and tidy and to do the laundry – laying these tasks on the professional staff will again only result in detracting them from their proper work, and ensure that these tasks are not properly done. Depending on the size of the expedition, both the cook and the housekeeper may need one or more assistants.

Figure 1.14 The 2019 team at Tello

Chapter 2

Documentary Research

Wherever possible – even with emergency rescue work – every effort should be made to find out what is already known about the site and its environs from previous research prior to the commencement of excavation.

Ancient sources

Are there ancient sources relevant to the site or region under consideration? There will very likely be something! Of course, the first thought goes to cuneiform sources, whether Akkadian or Sumerian (or one of the other languages recorded in cuneiform). If you are working at one of the major Sumerian or Assyrian or Babylonian cities, you may find a wealth of material relating to the history, topography, demography, economy, political affiliation, social organisation, natural history and many other aspects of the ancient milieu. And even at a smaller site you should be able to find some handles to help understand its place and function in the historical sequence.

► Figure 2.1 Sir Henry Rawlinson working on a cuneiform inscription

It is also important to remember the 'Classical' – Greek and Latin – authors such as Herodotus, Diodorus Siculus, Pliny, Berossus and others – these can be informative with regard to the first millennium BC and early first millennium AD. These may relate to all of the areas of interest listed above, as well as recording traditions of folk tales current in their times.

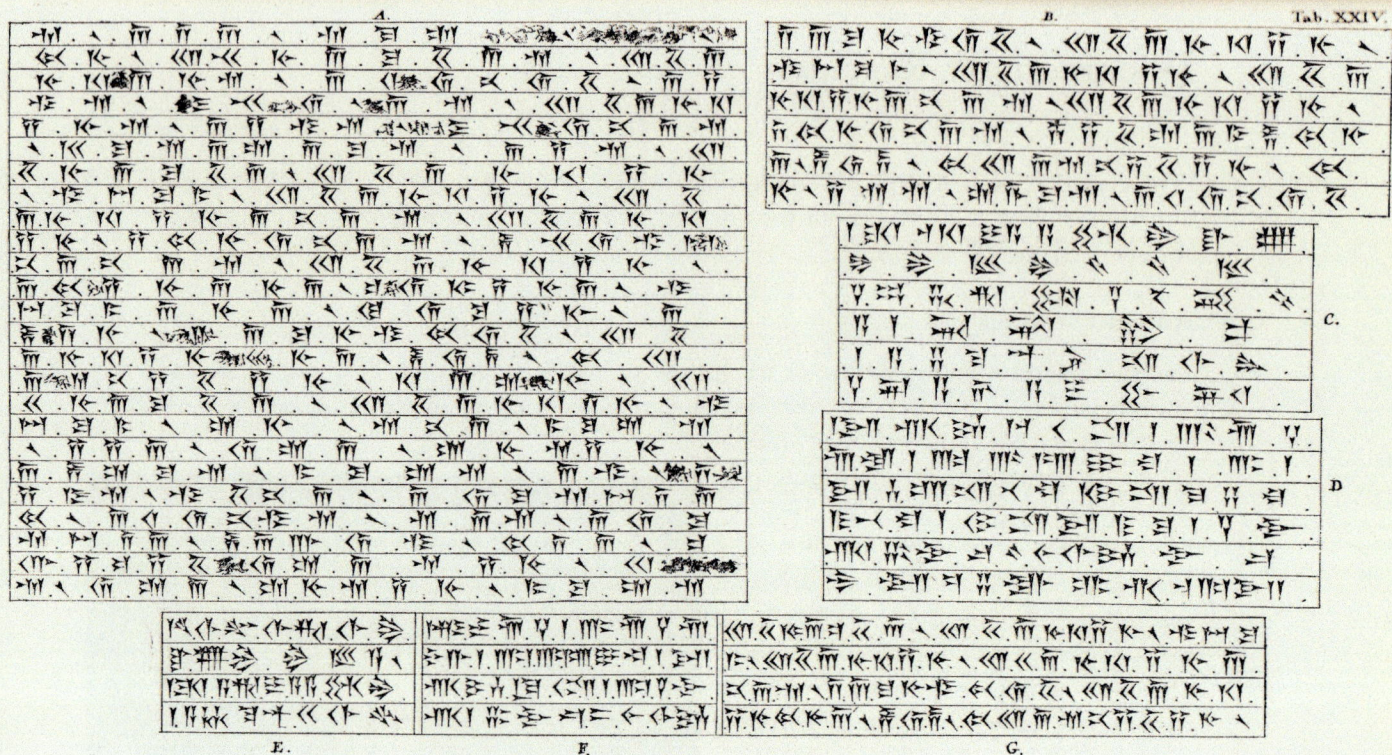

Figure 2.2
Copy of an
Old Persian
inscription
by Carsten
Niebuhr

Travellers' accounts

The accounts of travellers, scholars and historians may be of interest and contain information relating to a site. These include Arabic and Kurdish sources from the Middle Ages and later, as well as accounts of western travellers and explorers from the eighteenth century onwards. The list is huge, but mention should at least be made of Ibn al-Jawzi, Ibn Battuta and al-Muqaddasi and the *Sharafnama* of Sharaf Khani Batlisi. Moving on to the eighteenth century, the expedition commissioned by king Frederick V of Denmark to explore 'Arabia Felix'- the Arabian Peninsula – is famous. The expedition, which suffered many setbacks, eventually visited Egypt, Sinai and Yemen on the way out, and Iran, Iraq and Syria on the way back. The results were published by Carsten Niebuhr, the only member of the expedition to survive, on his return in *Beschreibung von Arabien* (1772) and *Reisebeschreibung nach Arabien und andern umliegender Ländern* (1774 and 1778). Alongside descriptions of topography, natural history, architecture and languages, Niebuhr's copies of cuneiform inscriptions from Persepolis – which we now know to be written in Old Persian – played a decisive role in the decipherment of cuneiform writing. He also made many interesting observations about sites and life in Iraq.

Turning to the nineteenth century, while much has been written about such pioneers as Claudius Rich, Paul Emile Botta, Austen Henry Layard and William Kennett Loftus, there are other less well-known individuals whose works deserve to be better known. One such figure is Robert Mignan, a British officer who, while serving with the East India Company in Basra, travelled extensively through Iraq and Kurdistan (and further afield), forming a deep interest in the antiquities of the land. He published the results of his explorations in two works, *Travels in Chaldaea: Including a Journey from Bussorah to Bagdad, Hillah, and Babylon* (1829) and *A Winter Journey Through Russia, the Caucasian Alps, and Georgia: Thence Across Mount Zagros by the Pass of Xenophon and the Ten Thousand Greeks, into Koordistaun* (1839). Mention should also be made of William Ainsworth who, after serving as surgeon and geologist on the expedition of General Francis Chesney mapping the course of the Euphrates, went on to travel extensively in the Near East, including Mesopotamia. Ainsworth published numerous accounts of his travels and observations – *Researches in Assyria, Babylonia, and Chaldea* (1838), *Travels and Researches in Asia Minor, Mesopotamia, Chaldaea, and Armenia* (1842) and *Travels in the Track of the Ten Thousand Greeks* (1844). There are many other accounts left by travellers, missionaries and political officers who also provide useful descriptions of the landscape, natural history, local customs and antiquities of both southern and northern Iraq. For Kurdistan, two important modern works to mention are Hussen Huzny Mukuriany, *The History of the Soran Emirate* (1931) and Muhamad Amin Zaki Bag, *The Brief History of Kurdish and Kurdistan* (1935).

Numismatics

When working with sites dating from the Achaemenid period onwards, the evidence of numismatics (coins) is likely to be important. Coins can be useful not only for the evidence they give on dating or coin circulation, but, particularly with lesser-known kingdoms, can also give information of fundamental importance on the evolution and history of the polity. This is, for

Figure 2.3
Hellenistic coin
from Qalatga
Darband

example, true of the Hellenistic-Parthian kingdoms of Adiabene and Characene. It is accordingly important to be aware if there is numismatic evidence relating to the area of research, whether in published sources or in unpublished material in museums. That said, it is important to be aware of the pitfalls of using coins in dating, whether excavated or collected from the surface of a site. For one thing, coins may stay in circulation for long periods of time, particularly if they are made of an intrinsically valuable material like gold or silver (which is why these materials are hoarded and valued by weight). Low-denomination coins of copper alloy or similar metal usually last in circulation for shorter periods of time, but that may also depend on the amount of money in use. Coins may also have been dislodged from their original archaeological context by animal and root action. A golden rule is that a site or context should never be dated by single coins, and in every case should be checked against the dating offered by the pottery or absolute means such as radiocarbon dates.

Site reports

Finally, you will want to thoroughly familiarise yourself with the reports of any previous work at a site. This not only includes published reports, as you may also have access to unpublished reports kept in museums or offices of the State Board, or other archives outside the country. Such reports will detail the discoveries – architectural and artefactual – of previous work, and help form an understanding of the site as a whole. A good site report will not only describe the results of the fieldwork but will also put these in a historical context and discuss how the findings relate to – and may even contradict – our understanding from the results of previous investigations and from historical sources. Furthermore, appreciation of previous fieldwork results will help shape the focus of the research when returning to a site, raising new questions to address the implications of what was (and was not) found and the many issues which form the fabric of a fully developed research agenda (see previous chapter). This might lead to resuming excavation in areas of previous investigations and/or opening up entirely new areas. A special word can be said about using old site plans. You will certainly, as a minimum, want to show the locations of earlier trenches on your own maps of the site, and may want to incorporate detailed plans of architecture previously exposed. It is easy to do this digitally. Old site plans can be scanned and uploaded for digitisation into a graphics programme such as Adobe Illustrator and/or a GIS system.

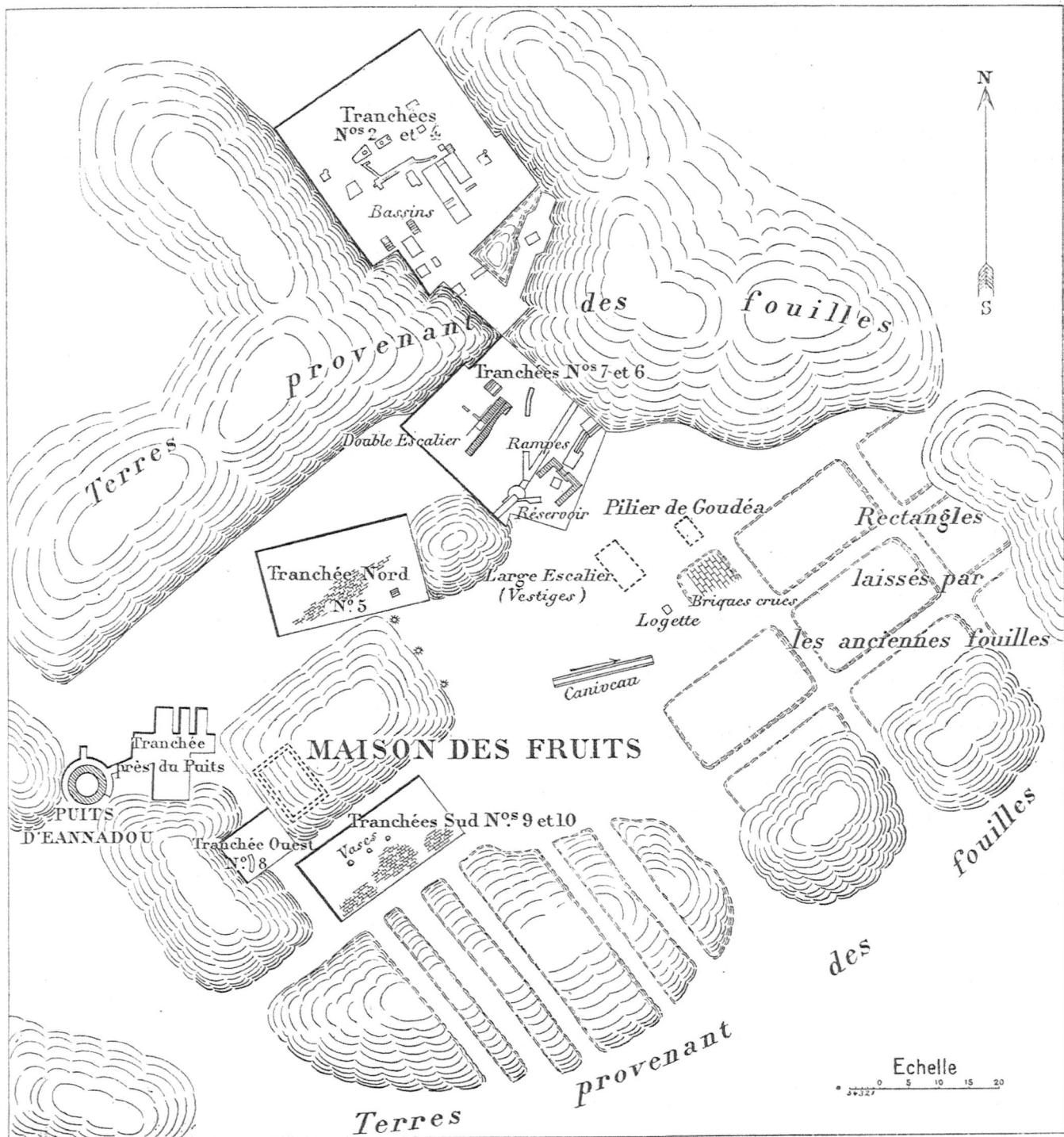

Figure 2.4 Old
site plan of Tello
by de Sarzec

Inside figure:

N
S

Tranchées
Nᵒˢ 2 et 4

Bassins

des   fouilles

Tranchées Nᵒˢ 7 et 6

provenant

Double Escalier

Rampes

Terres

Réservoir

Pilier de Goudéa

Rectangles

Tranchée Nord
Nᵒ 5

Large Escalier
(Vestiges)

Briques crues

laissés par

Logette

les anciennes fouilles

Caniveau

Tranchée
près du Puits

MAISON DES FRUITS

PUITS
D'EANNADOU

Tranchée Ouest
Nᵒ 8

Tranchées Sud Nᵒˢ 9 et 10

Vases

fouilles

des

provenant

Echelle
0 5 10 15 20

Terres   provenant

Chapter 3
Regional Survey

Regional survey is at the heart of archaeological exploration. It is the means for carrying out the basic research of a landscape, establishing the inventory of sites in a region, and by doing so working towards an understanding of the relationship of human occupation to the geographical setting, settlement patterns and changes through time. The first archaeological surveys in Iraq can be traced back to the nineteenth century. A notable figure in this context is Felix Jones who, having started by carrying on the survey of the Euphrates commenced by Captain Henry Lynch, went on to survey the Tigris as far as the confluence with the Hamrin, the old bed of the Tigris up to Opis, the course of the Nahrwan canal and the area between the Tigris and the Upper Zab; numerous archaeological sites were documented in the course of these surveys – his maps of Nineveh and Nimrud and their surroundings are particularly famous. In southern Iraq, an equally important series of maps was made by Bewsher and Selby in the 1860s, and theirs are particularly useful for showing the pre-modern types of land use and courses of the waterways.

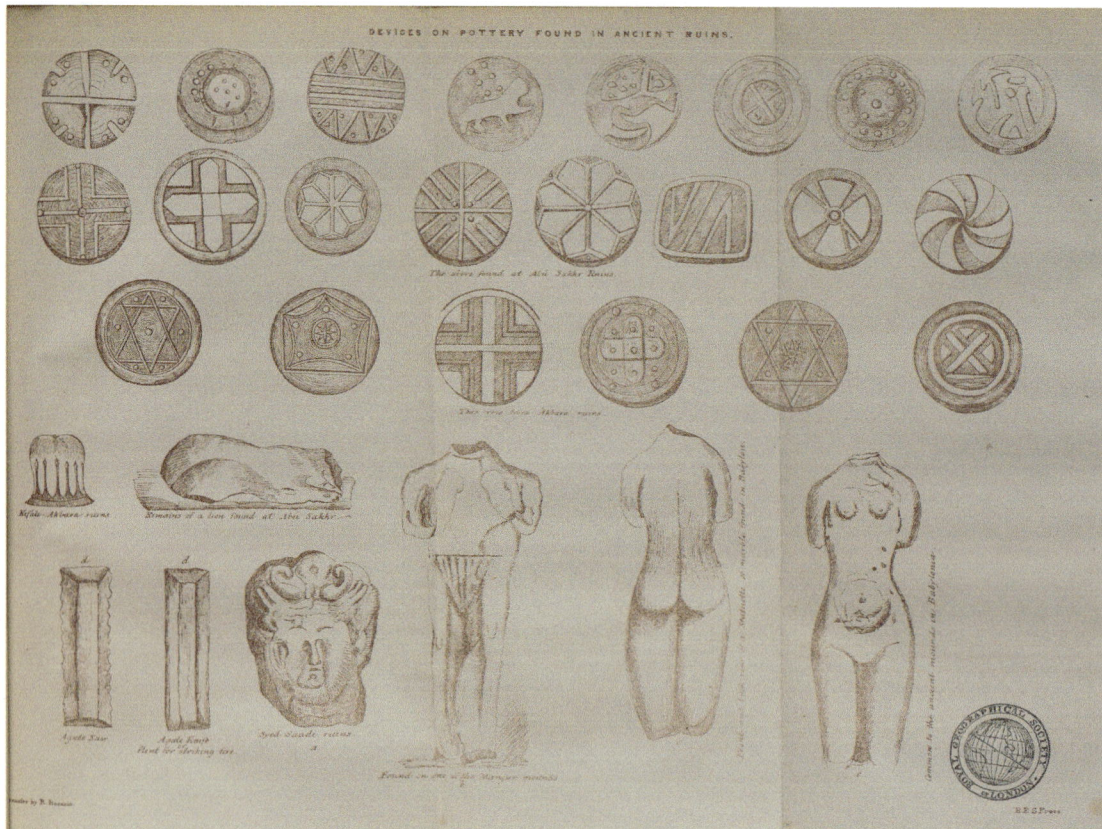

Figure 3.1 Artefacts collected from ancient ruins by Felix Jones during his survey work

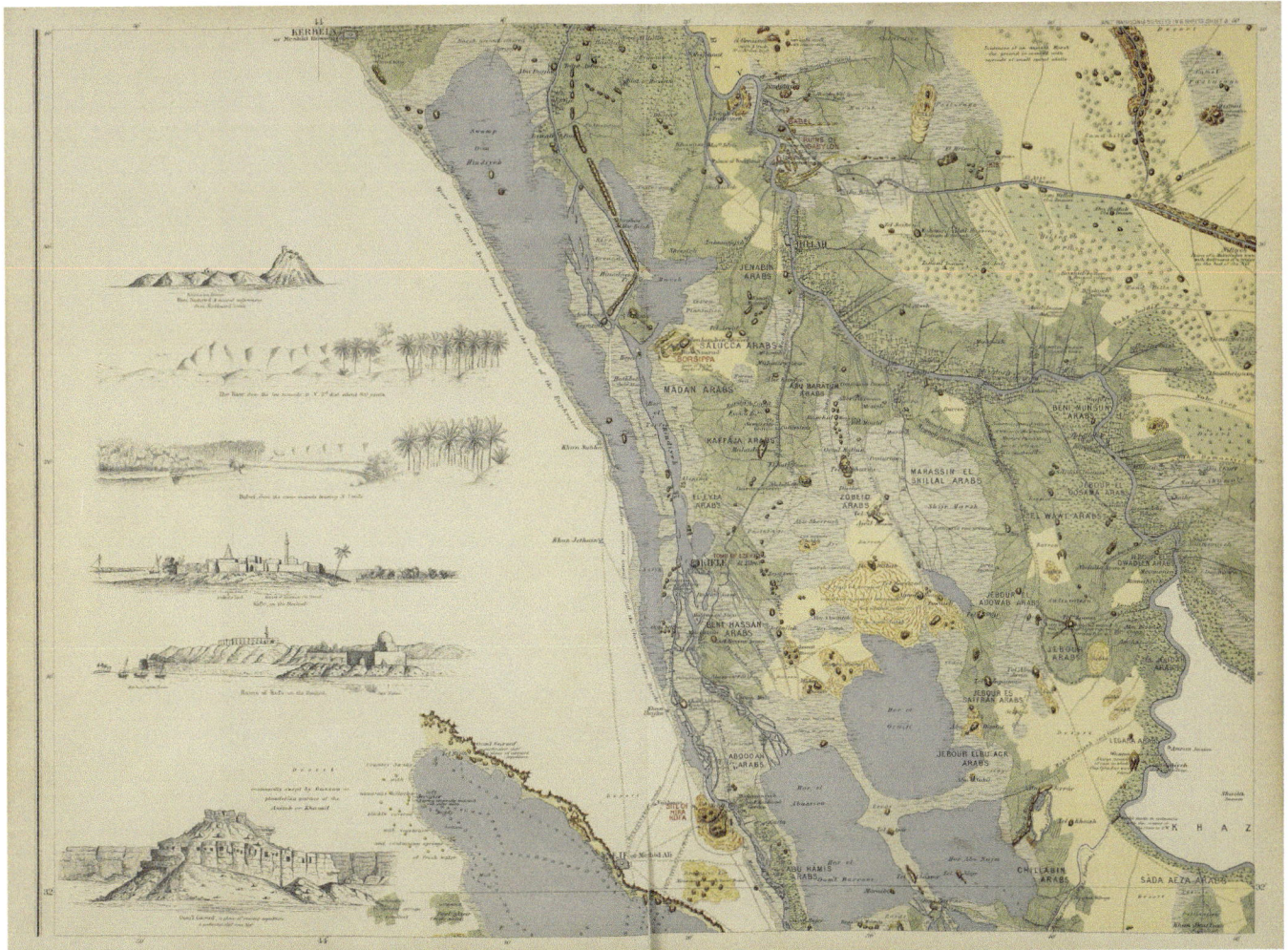

Figure 3.2 Map from the survey by Brewsher and Selby showing Babylon and Borsippa

In the early years of the twentieth century Gaston Cros conducted systematic reconnaissance of the environs of Tello by horseback in order to investigate the ancient city's place in the landscape. Like Jones, Cros was a trained military surveyor, and he had carried out several topographical surveys of the Sahara Desert. Upon his arrival in the southern Mesopotamian floodplain of Iraq, he applied his knowledge and skills as a trained surveyor to map out the site of Tello and its surroundings, making accurate maps of his itineraries and the sites he visited, and paying attention to pottery and other surface finds. This was not the only such attempt, as the American Wolfe Expedition, led by William Hayes Ward, also tried to explore sites in this region, but the problem both faced was lack of good dating of the pottery they were finding. This is always true: a survey is only as good as the person's knowledge of the pottery, and the results always have to be compared with excavated assemblages, and periodically re-assessed.

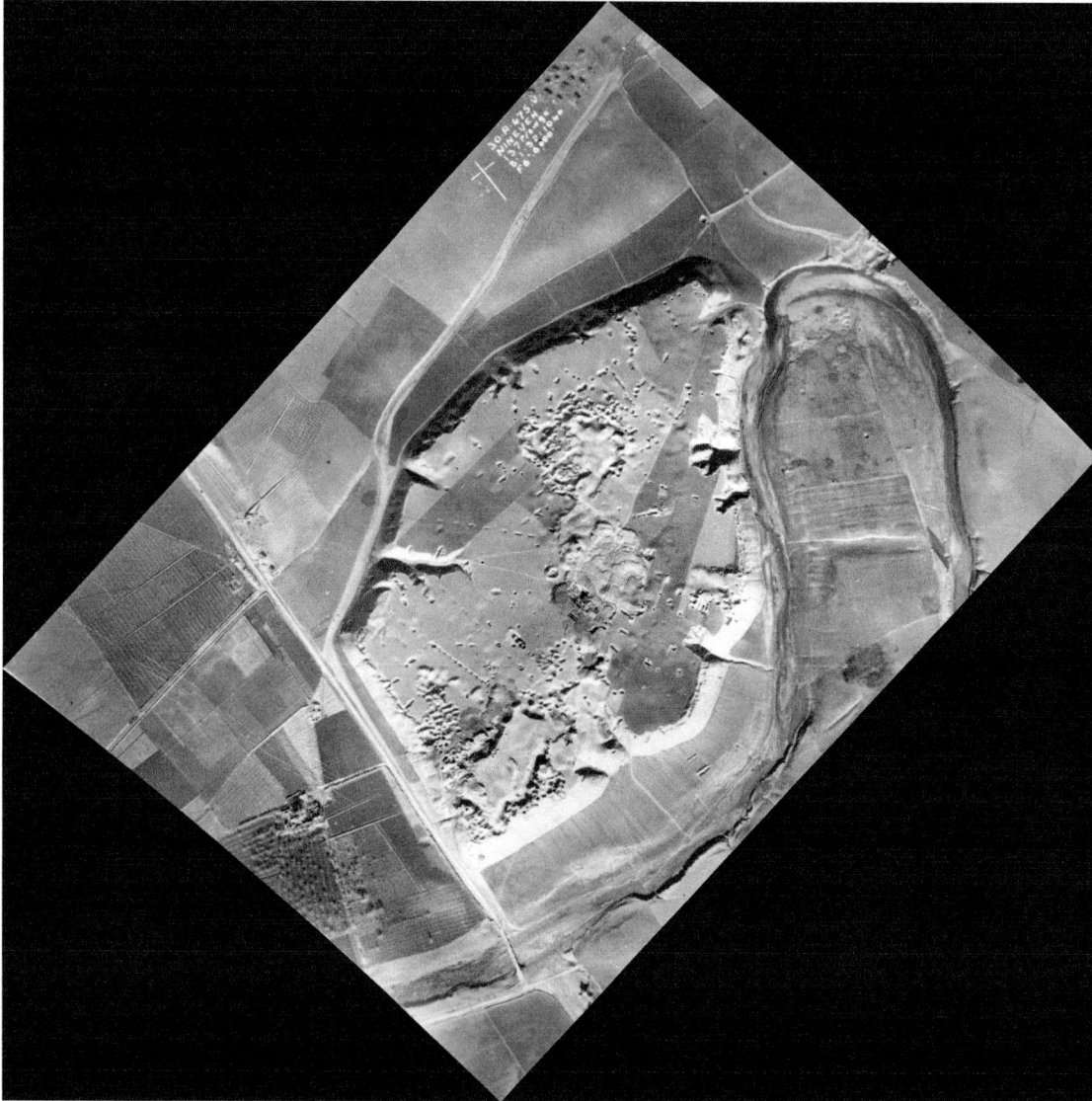

Figure 3.3
1933 Royal
Air Force
photograph
of the mound
of Kouyunjik
(Nineveh)

The concept of regional survey as a distinct component in archaeological fieldwork began to gather pace in the 1930s with surveys carried out by Max Mallowan in the Habur (1934), Thorkild Jacobsen in the Diyala (1936–7) and Seton Lloyd and Gerald Reitlinger in Sinjar (1938). The use of military observation balloons in the First World War revealed the extent of the Abbasid city at Samarra for the first time, and RAF aerial photographs began to reveal other new details, including important sites such as Seleucia and Hatra. This led to Fr Antoine Poidebard making many aerial surveys of his own over Syria, Aurel Stein doing the same in northern Iraq, and Eric Schmidt in parts of Iran. They revealed many details of ancient sites, but in most cases they were unable to land easily, so many of their sites could not be dated at the time and some of their interpretations over Roman frontier systems, for instance, are questionable. The period after World War II saw a steady rise in interest in the landscape outside the great cities, ranging from exploratory tours to formal surveys.

Another major development in the twentieth century has been the archaeological exploration carried out in advance of major dam projects. Dam rescue archaeology began in Egypt at the beginning of the twentieth century. In the 1960s the salvage campaign in advance of the Aswan High Dam became well-known internationally. Following World War II the holding of salvage campaigns in advance of major dams spread to Syria, Iraq, Turkey and, to a lesser extent, other countries such as Iran. These were models of international collaboration, and the starting point of field experience for many archaeologists. While it is not possible to list every such attempt, mention should be made of the important Iraqi initiatives carried out to record archaeological landscapes in advance of dam projects. This started with the survey undertaken in the context of the Dokan Dam salvage campaign in the late 1950s, which paved the way for the subsequent salvage campaigns undertaken as part of the Hamrin, Haditha and Eski Mosul dam projects. It is important to remember that Iraq has some of the most extensive experience in this area. Alongside this, other major achievements were the publication by the Directorate General of Antiquities of the *Archaeological Map of Iraq* (1967) and the *Atlas of Archaeological Sites in Iraq* (1975).

Figure 3.4 The submergence of Tell Abu Dhahir, one of the largest multi-period tells in the northern part of the Eski Mosul dam reservoir, and previously excavated by the University of Mosul and the British Archaeological Expedition to Iraq

Figure 3.5
The 1967
Archaeological
Map of Iraq

Very important are the regional surveys carried out by Robert McCormick Adams from the late 1950s to the 1970s. His work was inspired by that of Jacobsen and he surveyed large areas of the Diyala and central regions of southern Iraq as far as Uruk. These surveys set out to reconstruct the patterns of ancient occupation in the Mesopotamian floodplain by an approach which integrated, for the first time, the mapping of sites, water courses and other large-scale archaeological features visible in the landscape with the collection of surface materials, together with geomorphological, environmental, ethnographic and historical data, as well as, in due course, data from aerial (and later satellite) imagery. The approach was extended further still by Thorkild Jacobsen in his Girsu Survey (1969), which integrated the survey data with textual evidence relating to the landscape such as villages and waterways from the Early Dynastic period. These surveys were truly ground-breaking because they completely shifted the research agenda from the urban focus on temples, palaces and tablets to the countryside – in Adams' word's 'the rural settlements and irrigation agriculture that produced and sustained the city'. For example, the Uruk Regional Survey, conducted jointly by Adams and Hans Nissen, was able through analysis of settlement hierarchy to show how the sustained growth of proto-historical settlements paved the way for the rapid growth of the first urban centres at the expense of rural sites, many of which then disappeared – a landscape of mega-cities that 'burn out' villages. Furthermore, these surveys were pioneering in the context of the development of archaeological method more generally, beyond the bounds of Mesopotamia. The famous volumes which came out of these endeavours – *Land Behind Baghdad* (1965), *The Uruk Countryside* (1972) and *Heartland of Cities* (1981) – are formative landmarks in Near Eastern archaeology and cornerstones which assumed a significance in the worldwide development of the discipline. However, each has major drawbacks, as was noted at the time of their publication. The biggest is that the publications do not record the types of pottery that were found at each site: not only does this prevent control, but as the datings of many types have now been re-assessed (a continual process), it impossible to re-interpret the results. The books therefore remain classics, but deeply flawed and frustrating to use.

▶ Figure 3.6 Robert Adams' pioneering work revolutionised the practice of landscape survey

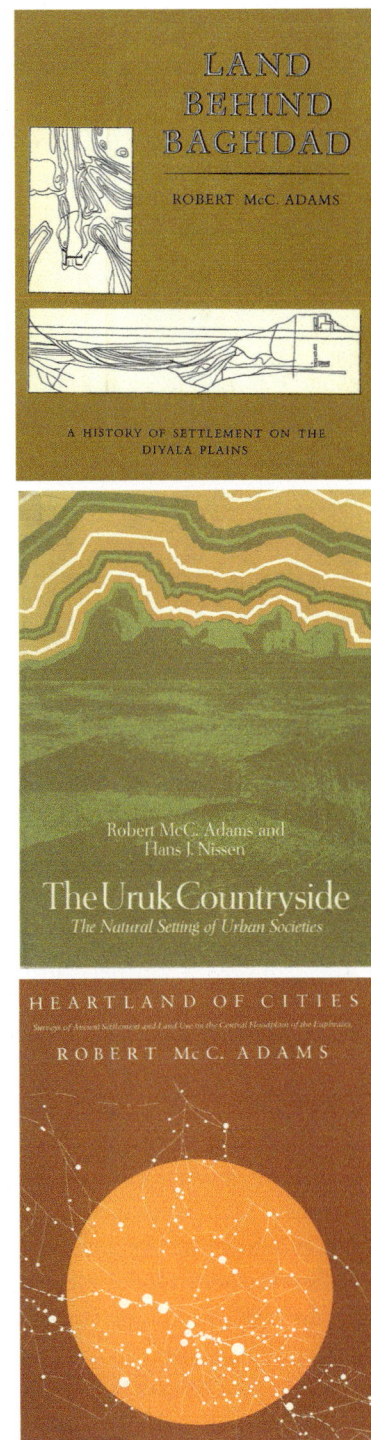

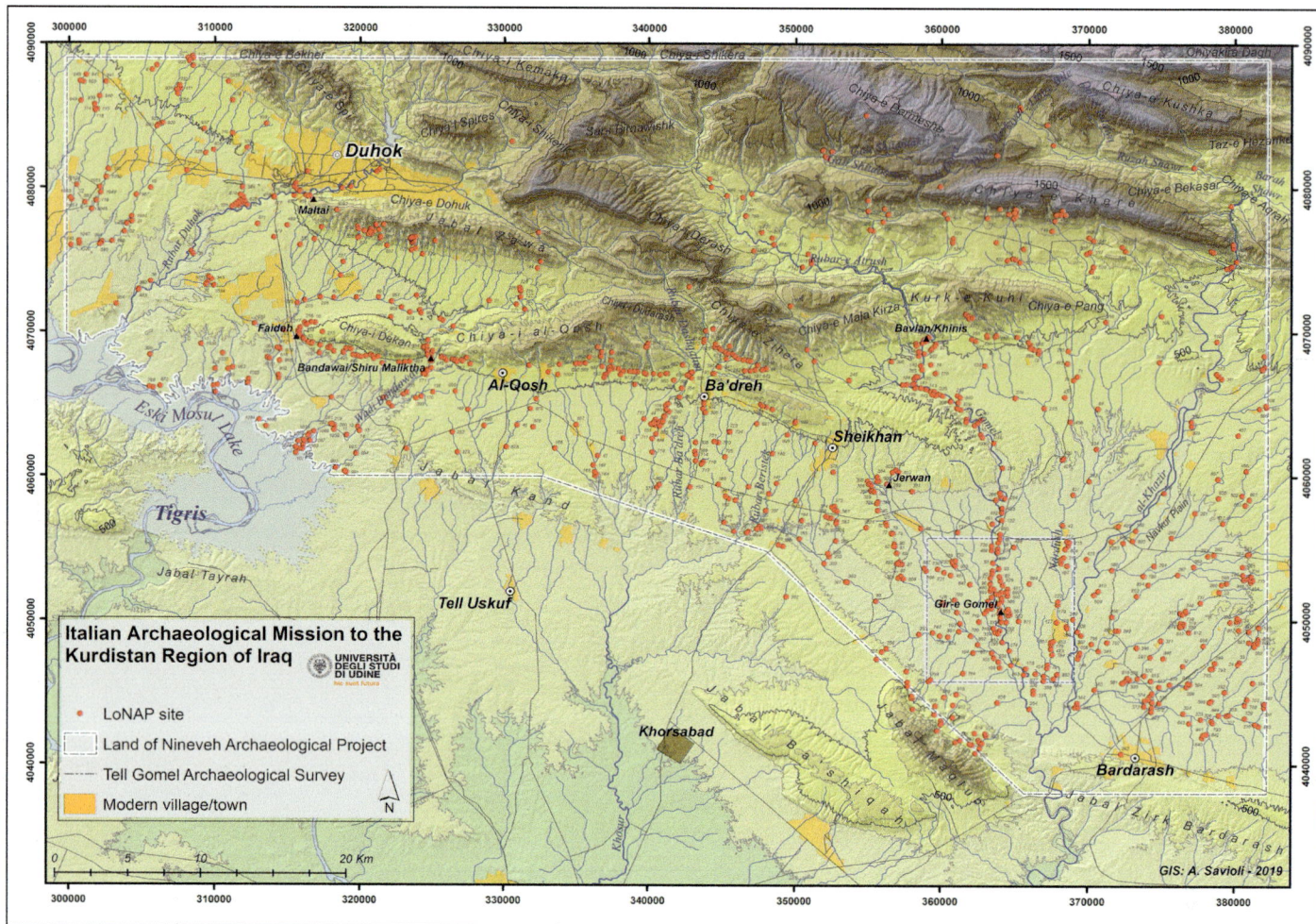

Figure 3.7
Survey map
from the Land
of Nineveh
Archaeological
Project (courtesy
Prof. Daniele
Morandi
Bonacossi)

Other surveys were made in the Kish area by McGuire Gibson and by Georges Roux in the Hor al-Hammar region: the Kish survey revealed how unreliable Adams' Akkad Survey was, and Roux's survey pointed to the existence of sites in the marsh region which contradicted the idea that these had always been swamps. The significance of this has only recently been shown by more recent Iraqi surveys after the draining of these relatively recent wetlands.

In the twenty-first century archaeological landscape research has entered a new phase. Most obviously this is characterised by the use of satellite imagery (see following chapter), but the full revolution in the field comes from a combination of three factors: the integrated use of satellite imagery, electronic survey equipment and computer processing. A pioneer in this field was the late Tony Wilkinson, who argued that once properly geo-rectified and scrutinised, aerial or satellite datasets permit highly detailed and accurate mapping, and as a result significantly enhance earlier or modern surface reconnaissance. A major impetus came with the declassification of the American spy satellite CORONA programme, an amazing resource for Near Eastern archaeology.

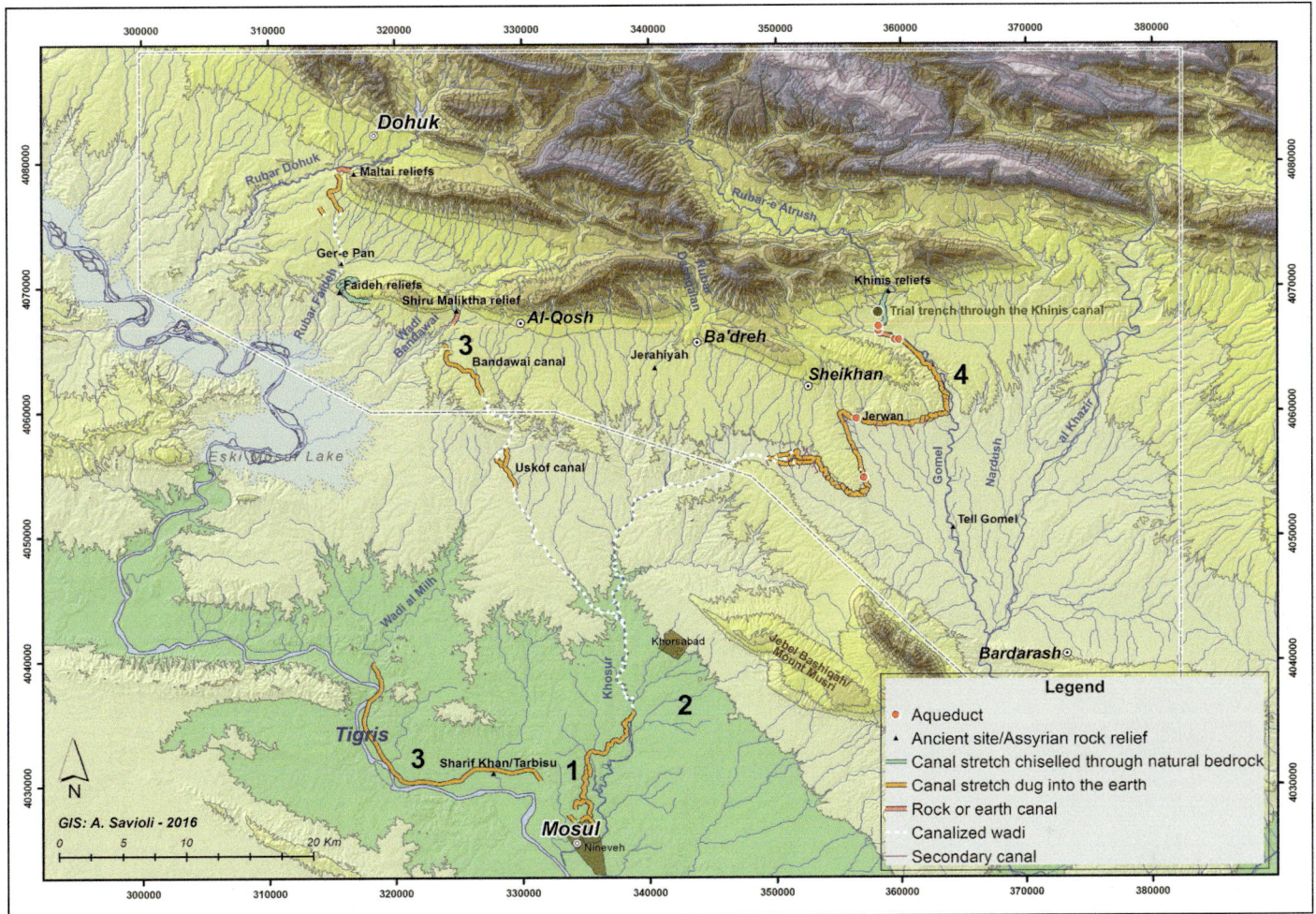

Figure 3.8 Survey map from the Land of Nineveh Archaeological Project showing the line of Assyrian canals (courtesy Prof. Daniele Morandi Bonacossi)

More recently declassified satellite programmes now provide much higher resolution imagery and much of this is now freely available as it is integrated into Bing and Google satellite maps. The combination of these tools is very powerful, allowing a coverage of huge areas with georeferenced data in a manner which in earlier times was simply not possible. Even so, this approach is not totally comprehensive, and there are caveats – satellite data can be less revealing with regard to mountainous or heavily farmed regions, for example. And alongside this the need to study data from previous surveys and excavation reports remains very important, as does the time-honoured practice of walking the fields, inspecting sites on the ground, collecting and dating the pottery closely and seeking information from local inhabitants. Unfortunately, it is not always possible to do this. Purely satellite-based surveys are weak on interpretation and run into the same pitfalls as the pioneering aerial surveys by Poidebard and Stein (see above). But when using all the available approaches surveys can map the archaeological inventory in a systematic manner, and do so in a way which feeds directly into the analysis of the exploitation of natural topography and natural resources, spatial organization and shifts in settlement patterns over time.

Chapter 4

Satellite Imagery

In this chapter we will review some of the most used satellite images in landscape archaeology in Iraq, highlight the importance of ground-truthing techniques to confirm the identification of archaeological features detectable from space, and present a step-by-step tutorial using the freely-accessible online CORONA Atlas.

Figure 4.1
HEXAGON
Satellite image
of the site of
Nimrud

Satellite imagery and remote sensing techniques are an increasingly important component of the technical and methodological tool-set available in archaeological research. As outlined in the preceding chapter, in Iraq they have been an essential part of the pioneering landscape work carried out from the 1960s onwards. By the early 1980s, large-scale images were available for broad-brush reconstructions of ancient watercourses. For example, in his *Heartland of Cities: Surveys of Ancient Settlement and Land Use on the Central Floodplain of the Euphrates*, published in 1981, Adams used LANDSAT images to derive an interpretive map plan of ancient levees in southern Iraq.

For archaeologists, a major step forward came in the 1990s with the declassification and release of historic CORONA imagery. These were cheap, easily bought, and allowed for a comparison of landscapes as they were in the 1960s and 1970s and as they are now. For much of the Middle East, these early images have proved invaluable as many of the areas have since undergone massive change through agricultural, industrial, urban and infrastructure development. From the beginning of the twenty-first century, higher resolution imagery has become available from several commercial ventures such as QUICKBIRD and others. These all have a much improved spatial resolution (pixel size) and spectral resolution (band coverage of the electro-magnetic spectrum) than CORONA imagery. They are, however, expensive, and put the archaeologist in the awkward position of not knowing whether the image will give meaningful data for a site until it has been bought. Fortunately, both the CORONA imagery and the data of the Shuttle Radar Topography Mission (SRTM) are now available easily and at no cost.

The analysis and interpretation of satellite images have led to the identification of countless archaeological sites and elements of ancient infrastructures such as roads, canals and off-take channels. A word of caution needs to be expressed, though. Interpretation of features in images is not always easy, and the fact that it is 'remote' sensing, not undertaken on location, introduces a certain degree of uncertainty. Accordingly, it is important that analysis of satellite imagery is backed up by robust control – 'ground-truthing' – which is to say on the ground inspection, dating of the surface pottery, perhaps extending to the carrying out of targeted small-scale excavations to verify interpretation. Such a methodology mitigates the risks of misinterpreting data from remote sensing by introducing a procedure for testing the correlation between features appearing in a satellite image and different material remains and morphological features on the ground.

CORONA imagery

CORONA images are derived from a United States intelligence satellite programme which operated from 1959 to 1972. In 1995 the imagery was declassified by the American Government, and the data has been publicly available since 1998. These images can be searched and ordered via the internet through the United States Geological Survey website or downloaded for free from the Arkansas University website (see below). CORONA images are particularly useful for the reconstruction of ancient landscapes because they provide a valuable archival record of many surface features that have since been destroyed or obscured by urban development or large-scale

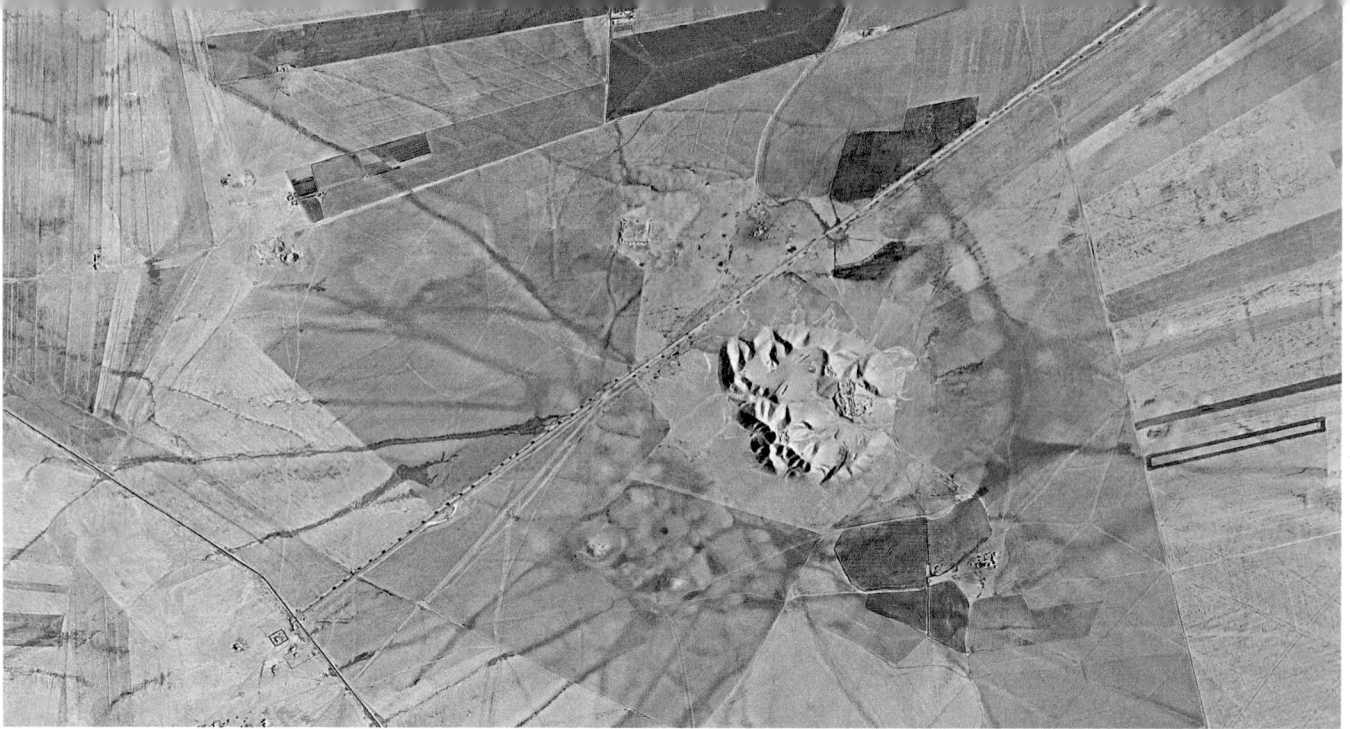

agricultural projects. The imagery is produced from high-resolution photography taken with panchromatic film (black and white film sensitive to all wavelengths of the visible spectrum). Many natural surface features can be clearly identified in CORONA images because of the high spatial resolution of the imagery. The best ground resolution for the different CORONA missions is from 2 to 13 m.

▲ Figure 4.2 CORONA image of Tell Brak

QUICKBIRD imagery

DigitalGlobe is a company founded in 1994 that provides high-resolution satellite images to governments and commercial users, including Google. In 2009 it started to sell QuickBird satellite images to the public. The Imagery is very high resolution – 61 cm resolution for panchromatic data and 1.61–2.44 m for multispectral data. In 2007, the Iraqi Government purchased QuickBird images of the whole of the country taken in 2006 with a 0.6m resolution in natural colour. QuickBird imagery has proven to be useful in both verifying results from the interpretation of data from

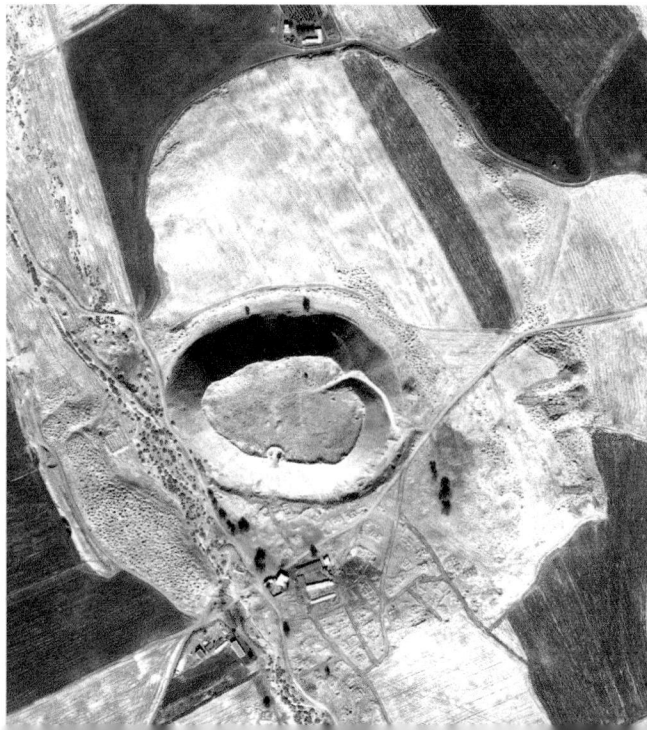

◀ Figure 4.3 Quickbird image of the site of Bakr Awa

other satellite programmes and for locating potential geomorphological features that cannot be easily distinguished in other imagery.

Digital Elevation Model topography (SRTM and ASTER)

A Digital Elevation Model (DEM) is a digital three-dimensional topographic modelling of the surface of the earth based on radar mapping or stereographic processing of data.

SRTM

The data of the Shuttle Radar Topography Mission (SRTM) was generated by a radar system on board the Space Shuttle Endeavor in 2000, with the objective of producing elevation data for the globe over latitudes between 56^0 S and 60^0 N. Imagery is available for Iraq at 90 m resolution (pixel size), and it can be freely downloaded. The SRTM data is organised into 'tiles' each covering the area between set latitudes and longitudes. The easiest way to get the data is to go to 'SRTM Tile Grabber' website (https://dwtkns.com/srtm/) and simply click on and download the tiles you need. For more on downloading SRTM tiles, see the section on QGIS below.

Figure 4.4
Digital elevation
Model from
SRTM data

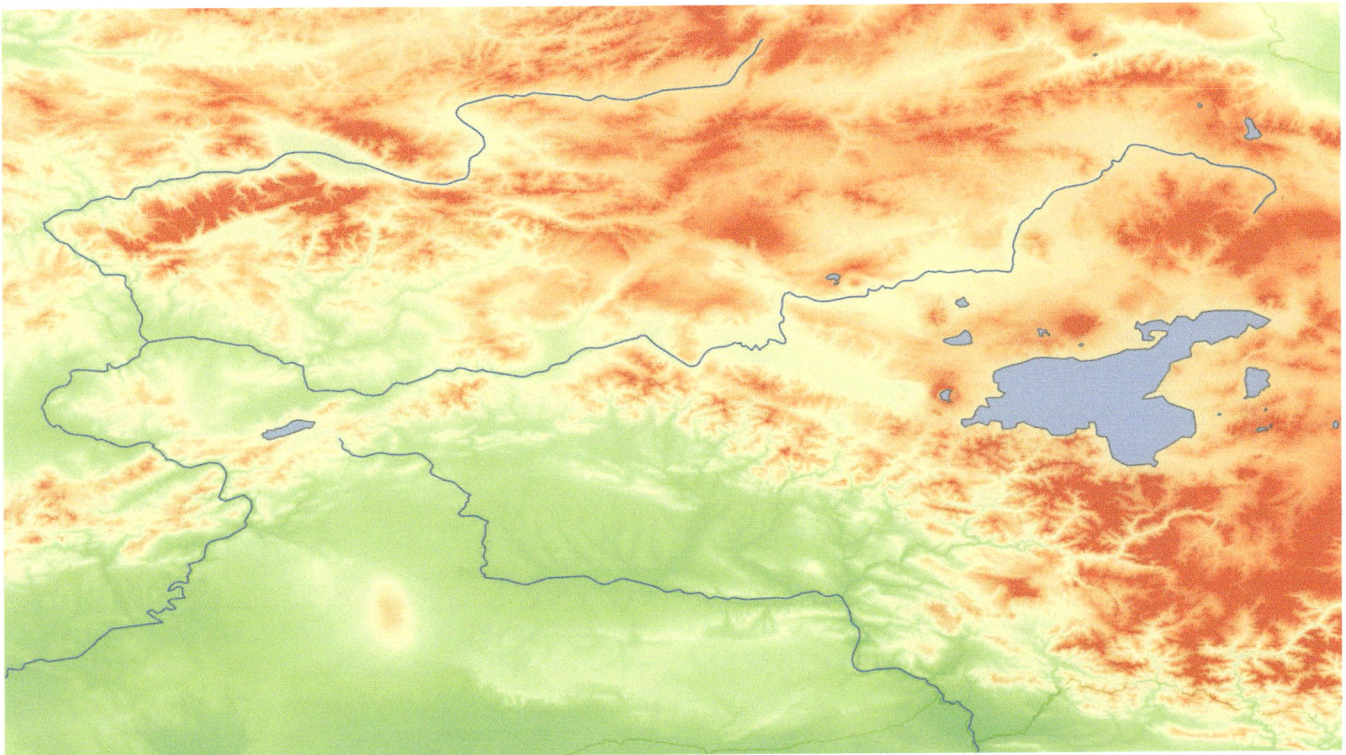

ASTER

The data of the ASTER (Advanced Spaceborne Thermal Emission and Reflection Radiometer) satellite system data has a pixel size of 15 m covering 14 spectral bands, from the visible to the thermal infrared wavelengths. A stereo viewing capability has made it possible to create digital elevation models (DEMs), which are now also available (referred to as ASTER GDEM). Most archaeological features in the Mesopotamian floodplain have a relatively high topographic elevation with respect to the surrounding area; this phenomenon can make these features easy to identify in both SRTM and ASTER data. Many ASTER images, including DEMs, are now available free on the USGS Earthexplorer website (it is necessary to first register with NASA Earth Data).

Figure 4.5
Aster image of
Babylon

Ground-truthing

Ground-truthing is essential to pinpoint archaeological features identified on satellite imagery. This has a role to play in both systematic field surveys and excavations. Either way, fieldwork can permit ground-truthing of observations made initially from satellite imagery and digital elevation models, as well as allowing the collection of samples for dating and other analytical techniques.

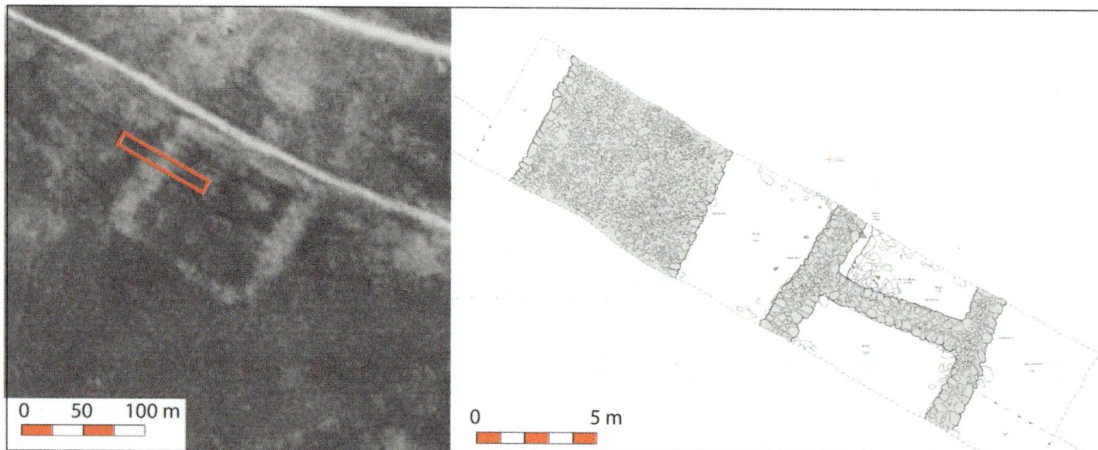

(left) the Corona image of the Parthian fort which ground-truthing trench shown in red, and (right) the results of the excavation, showing the outer wall of the fort and a section of internal architecture.

Figure 4.6
Ground-truthing at the site of Qalatga Darband

In the above image (Fig. 4.6), the CORONA image on the left shows a c. 150 m square feature which was provisionally interpreted as a Parthian fort. The red line indicates the location of a ground-truthing trench, which revealed the foundations of a 6 m wide wall clearly consistent with the interpretation as a fortification. The Parthian date was confirmed by ceramics recovered in the excavation.

CORONA Atlas of the Middle East

https://corona.cast.uark.edu

The CORONA Atlas of the Middle East is a very useful and free online database created by Arkansas University of geo-rectified CORONA imagery. It allows the user to search and download CORONA imagery of archaeological sites in Iraq. Coordinates can be read and there are tools to measure distance and area.

Finding a site

Figure 4.7
Corona Atlas
website –
coverage of the
Middle East

You can manually zoom to a known site or use the 'Zoom to location' option by clicking on the upper left 'Tools' icon and entering the geographic coordinates (latitude, longitude). Alternatively, you can search the name of an archaeological site in the atlas's database.

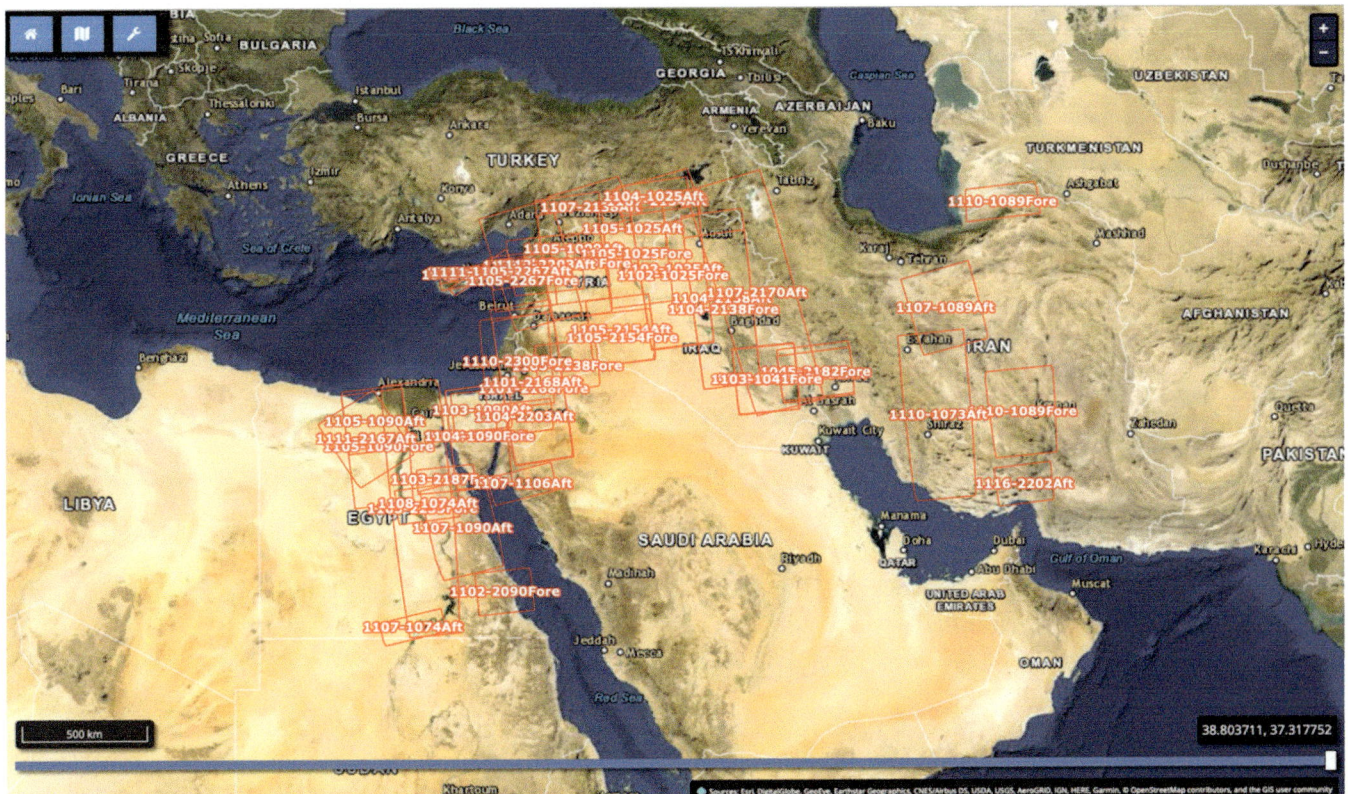

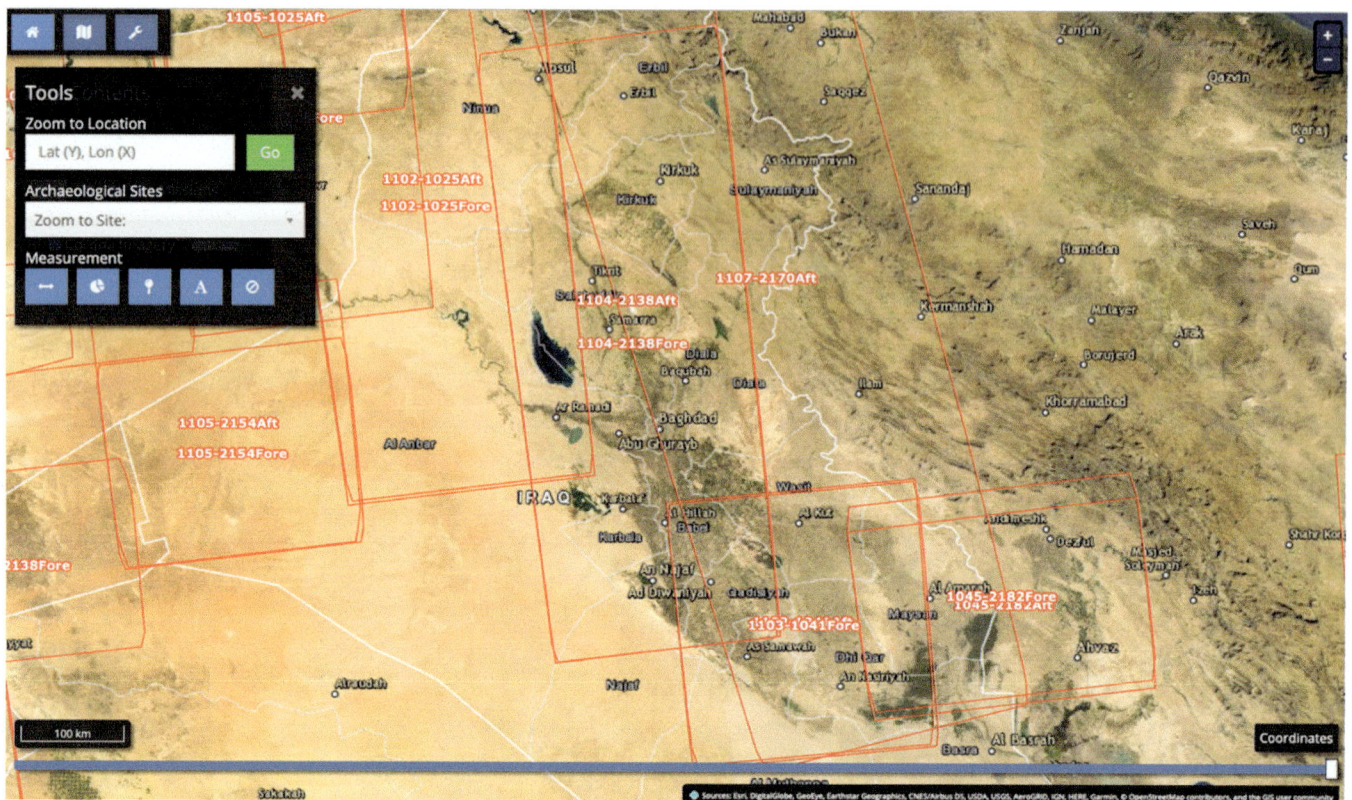

Downloading the CORONA imagery

You can download satellite photographs (listed by the dates of the 'Missions') by clicking on the upper left 'Map Contents' icon. Below the lines for 'Sites' and 'Missions' is a section 'Corona imagery'. Click on the + icon to reveal the list of missions with imagery covering the site in question. To download an image, click on the + icon next to the mission you want and then click on the download icon.

Measuring distance and area

You may want to make measurements on a site. This might be a linear measurement, for example the dimensions of the site or its distance from another location or watercourse. Or it might be an area measurement such as the overall area of the site or of a feature within it. You can measure distance and area by clicking on the 'Tools' icon and then the 'Distance' and 'Area' icons below.

Figure 4.8
Corona Atlas
website –
coverage of
Iraq

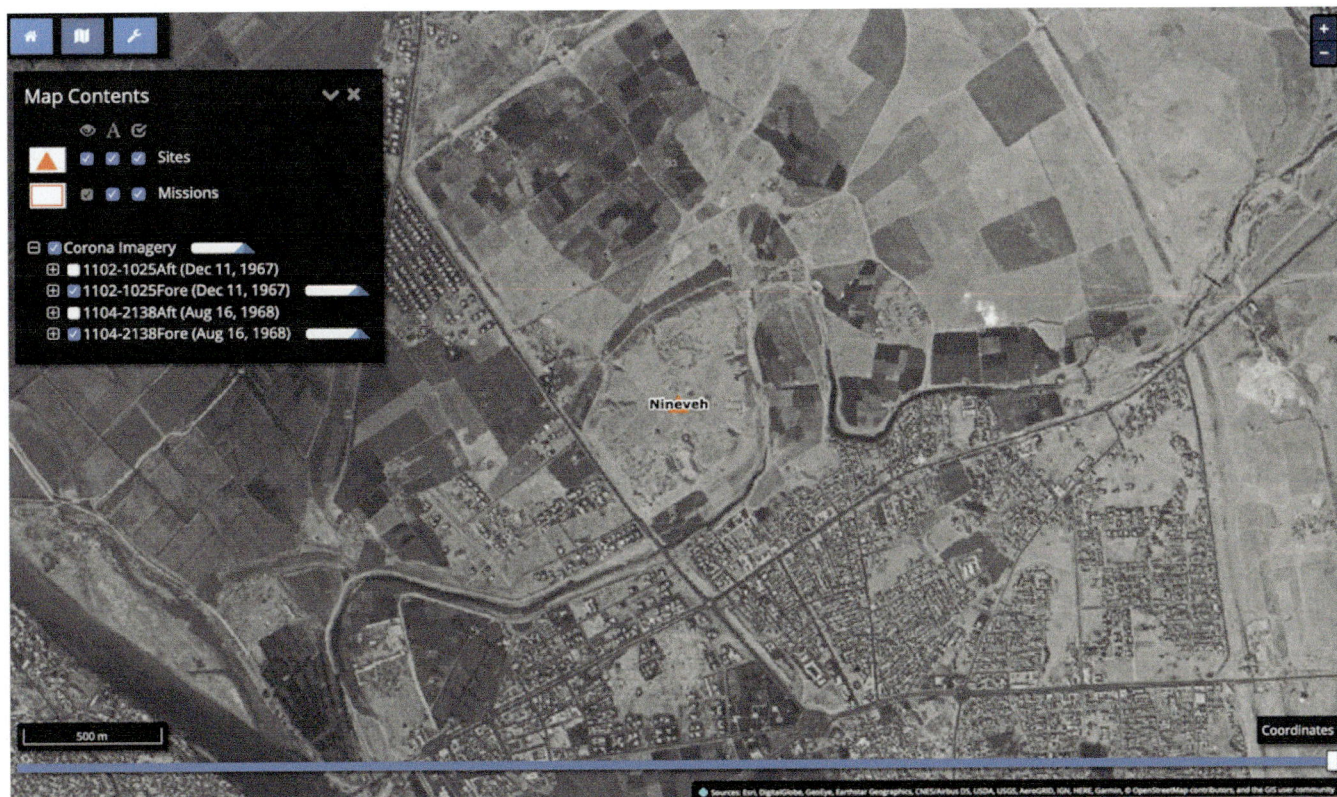

Figure 4.9
Corona Atlas
website – image
of Nineveh with
Map Contents
panel

Coordinates

You can obtain the precise coordinates of any point by clicking on the 'Tools' icon and then the magnifying glass below.

In this example, we have calculated the surface area of the main mound of Nineveh, Kuyunjiq (0.35km²); the length of the city's fortification walls (12.06 km); the distance between the site's western limits and the modern-day Tigris (1.38 km); and we have obtained the coordinates of the central point of the ancient site, as well as of the north-eastern and southeastern corners of the enclosure wall.

Comparing today's archaeological landscape with the 1960s

On the Corona Atlas website, the CORONA imagery always appears on top of modern satellite photographs. At the bottom of the screen there is a blue line with a white rectangle on the far right. You can move the white rectangle towards the left to reveal the modern imagery for comparison.

Figure 4.10
Corona Atlas
website – image
of Nineveh with
Tools panel

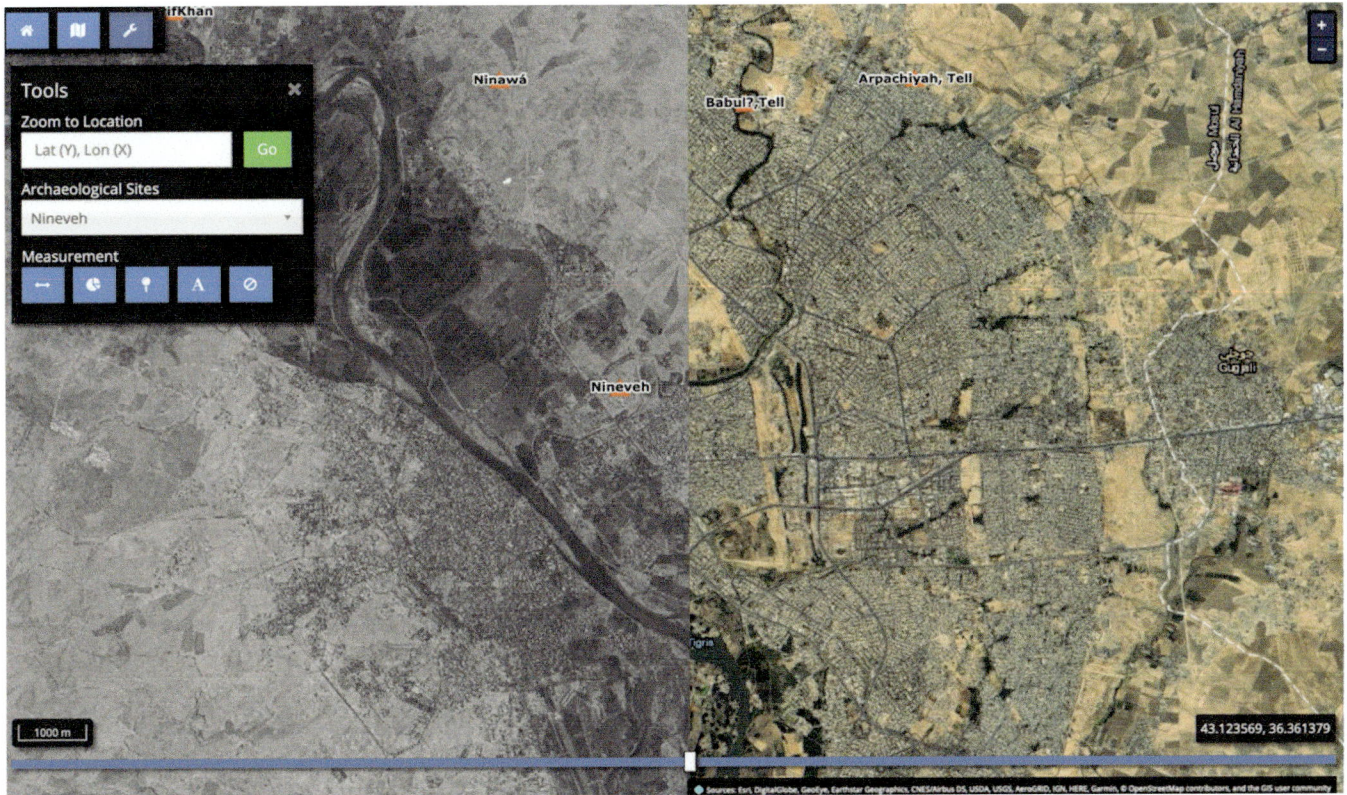

Figure 4.11
Corona Atlas
website – image
of Nineveh
showing historic
and modern
imagery

Chapter 5

Geophysical Prospection

Geophysical prospection refers to the mapping of subsurface remains using a variety of scientific techniques. The use of geophysics is now a standard and indispensable tool in the archaeologist's toolkit, allowing archaeologists to map the layout and components of a site, the internal plan of buildings, and identify specific features such as kilns, fire places, pits and ditches. This data not only feeds into the overall understanding of a site, but can also help identify areas for targeted excavation. Geophysics can also contribute to establishing the limits of preserved archaeology, and help with site protection.

There are several different methods of geophysical prospection. The oldest, and still most common, are magnetometry, resistivity and ground-penetrating radar. More recent are seismology, electrical resistance tomography and microgravimetry. With all methods of geophysics, it is important to understand the local geology and soil conditions, and to have an idea of what sort of features you are looking for or may expect to encounter.

Grids and transects

Most geophysical methods work by measuring along transects, taking measurements at multiple points along a line. With the methods commonly used for area survey (magnetometry, resistivity, ground penetrating radar), this is expanded into a grid consisting of multiple parallel transects. A precursor to any collection of data is therefore laying out the transect or grid – this will normally be the task of the surveyor.

Magnetometry

Magnetometry (or geomagnetic survey) works by detecting tiny variations in the earth's magnetic field caused by the influence of the subsurface remains. The principal goes back to the

Figure 5.1 A geophysical grid

Figure 5.2
Conducting
magnetometry
at Qalatga
Darband

nineteenth century, but in archaeology the method was first used in 1958 in Northamptonshire (England), to locate pottery kilns before road construction. It was known that the kilns existed, but their exact location was not known and the geomagnetic survey succeed in locating them. There is more than one type of equipment for geomagnetic survey. A proton magnetometer works by measuring the absolute magnetic field at individual points. A fluxgate gradiometer takes continuous readings (but results can be more difficult to interpret). Lastly there is magnetic susceptibility, which works by transmitting an electromagnetic signal into the soil: the magnetic susceptibility is affected by human activity, so this method is good for establishing the overall limits of a site and for identifying areas of intensive use, whether domestic or industrial. The depth to which all these methods work is generally up to 2 m.

Magnetometry works best on sites which are roughly single period. It is much less successful on complex mound sites, where the continuous additions and modifications, pits and other features, cut into the remains and greatly obscure the results, often to the point where they are unreadable. The method is good at detecting ferrous metals (not gold, silver, bronze, copper); anything altered by fire (over 700°C), such as hearths, kilns and destruction layers; and features where soil has been disturbed such as pits and ditches. It is very important that the area being surveyed is cleared of metal objects such as nails and bits of agricultural (and military) tools and machinery. The presence of water and gas pipes, cables, fences and well heads all cause problems and it will not be possible to collect meaningful data close to these. The results of magnetometry can often be difficult to interpret. The visualisation of the data can be modified by mathematical filters but, even so, it may be considered optimal to ground-truth the results to be sure of the interpretation.

Resistivity

Resistivity works by measuring the degree of resistance to an electrical current passed between two points. Electricity will pass more easily through wet earth than dry earth, and different soil compositions will have different characteristics for example, stones and stone blocks are very resistant. The technique was first used in 1938 at Williamsburg in Virginia (USA); in England it was first used in 1946 to detect prehistoric ditches at Dorchester (near Oxford). Carrying out resistivity is more time-consuming than magnetometry. The method generally entails measuring out and marking the locations of the probes. It may be necessary to make a small hole for the probe, and even pour water down the holes to increase effectiveness (moist soil conditions will give better results). All of this takes time and will also require at least one additional team member. The area does not need to be cleared of small metal objects on the surface as is the case with magnetometry, nor is the presence of overhead electrical power lines a problem, however the presence of unshielded metal pipes or other large pieces of metal below ground will affect results. Like magnetometry, resistivity works best on sites which are roughly single period. It is much less successful on complex tell sites. The method is good at detecting stone features (walls, pavements, roads) and some hollow features (pits, ditches); generally, due to the greater time involved, resistivity is best used for searching for linear features and the depth to which this method works is generally up to 2 m.

Qalatga Darband
Area 7 - Magnetic Gradiometry
31 October 2018
T. Matney/M. Revels

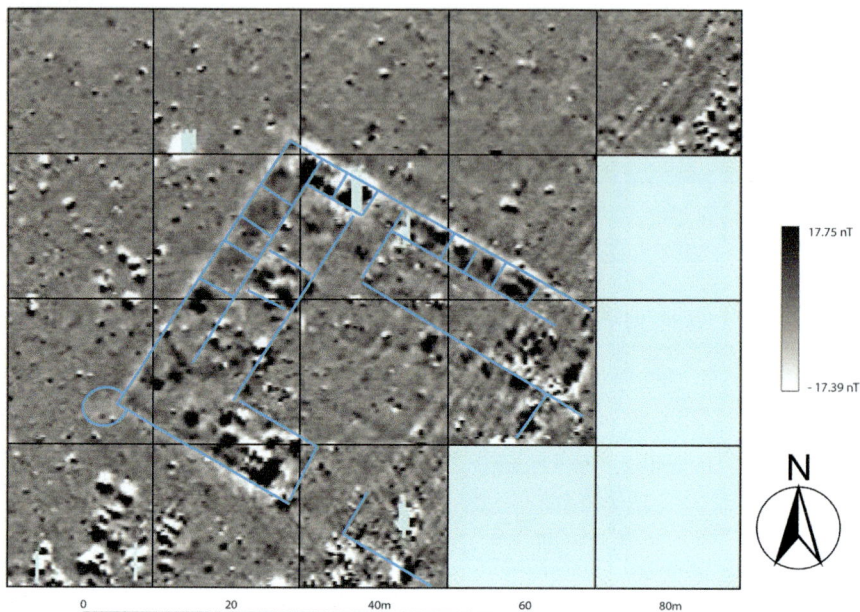

17.75 nT

- 17.39 nT

N

Figure 5.3 Resistivity mapping of a building in the southeastern quadrant at Qalatga Darband

Ground Penetrating Radar

Ground Penetrating Radar (GPR) works by transmitting radar pulses into the ground and measuring the returns. The concept of GPR was first formulated as a tool for geological research in 1910, and the technique was successfully used to measure the thickness of the ice of a glacier in Greenland in 1929. GPR was trialled in archaeology in the 1970s – a famous case was experimenting with the technique to find buried walls at Chaco Canyon in the southwestern United States in 1976. GPR is most effective with dry soil – a significant water presence prevents its use as the radar waves bounce off the water. In archaeology GPR can image

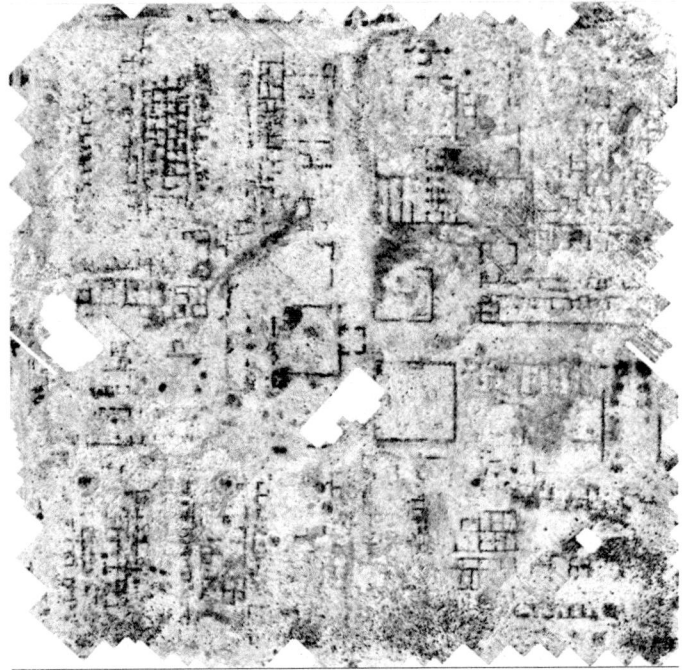

subsurface remains up to 30 m below the ground. It can be good at detecting masonry, major changes in soil characteristics, metal pipes and empty spaces such as tombs, chambers and tunnels.

Microgravimetry

Microgravimetry works by measuring tiny changes in the local gravitational field resulting from material close to the surface of the earth. The method was invented in 1936 and was first used in archaeology in the late 1970s. The equipment works by measuring the acceleration of a mass in a vacuum. Microgravimetry can detect anomalies at depths of over 100 m however, on its own it cannot give a depth estimation. This is due to the fact that an anomalous reading could be a direct result of the presence of a more massive entity relatively distant from the point of measurement or a smaller one nearer by. In practice, microgravimetry can help detect substantial masonry and voids.

Electrical Resistivity Tomography

Electrical Resistivity Tomography (ERT) is an extension of conventional resistivity, but is different in that it is used to image deep profiles across a site rather than mapping the nearer sub-surface remains in a linear or areal form. It produces a two-dimensional vertical section. The concept of ERT has its origins in the 1930s, but it was not utilised in archaeology until the 1990s. ERT works by taking readings along a line (the 'base line'). The depth of imaging depends on the length of the base line – for example, an 80-m base line will image up to 12 m below the surface, a 160-m

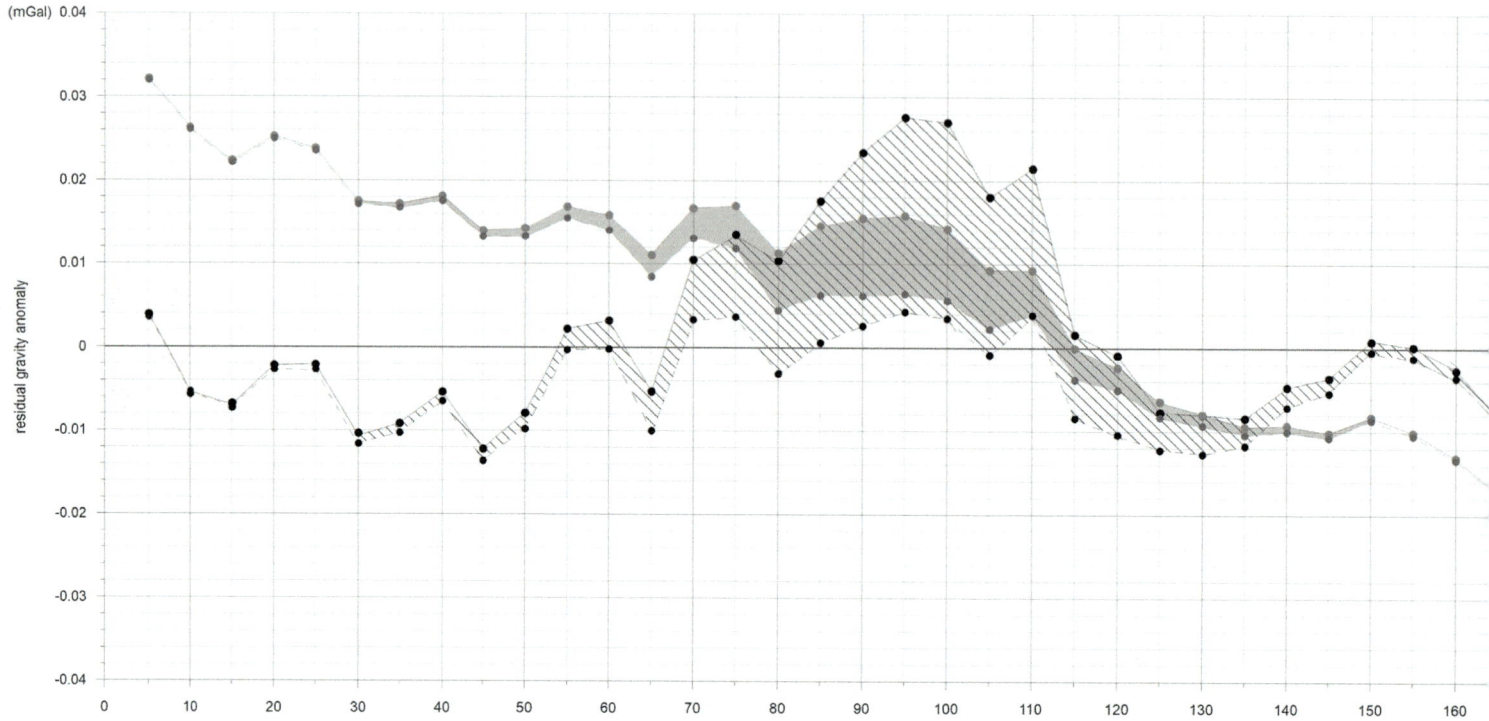

baseline up to 25 m, and a 400-m baseline up to 60 m. The technique can be used to estimate the dimensions and nature of sub-surface targets such as the soil/bedrock interface and the thickness of archaeological strata (as long as they are sufficiently differentiated) and may be able to detect walls, ditches, filled-up channels and empty spaces.

▲ Figure 5.5 Microgravimetry plot from the citadel of Erbil

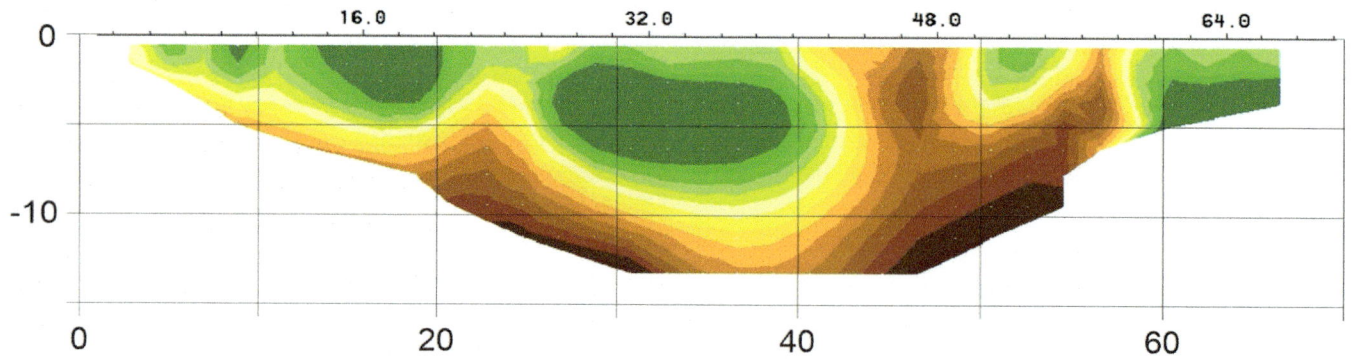

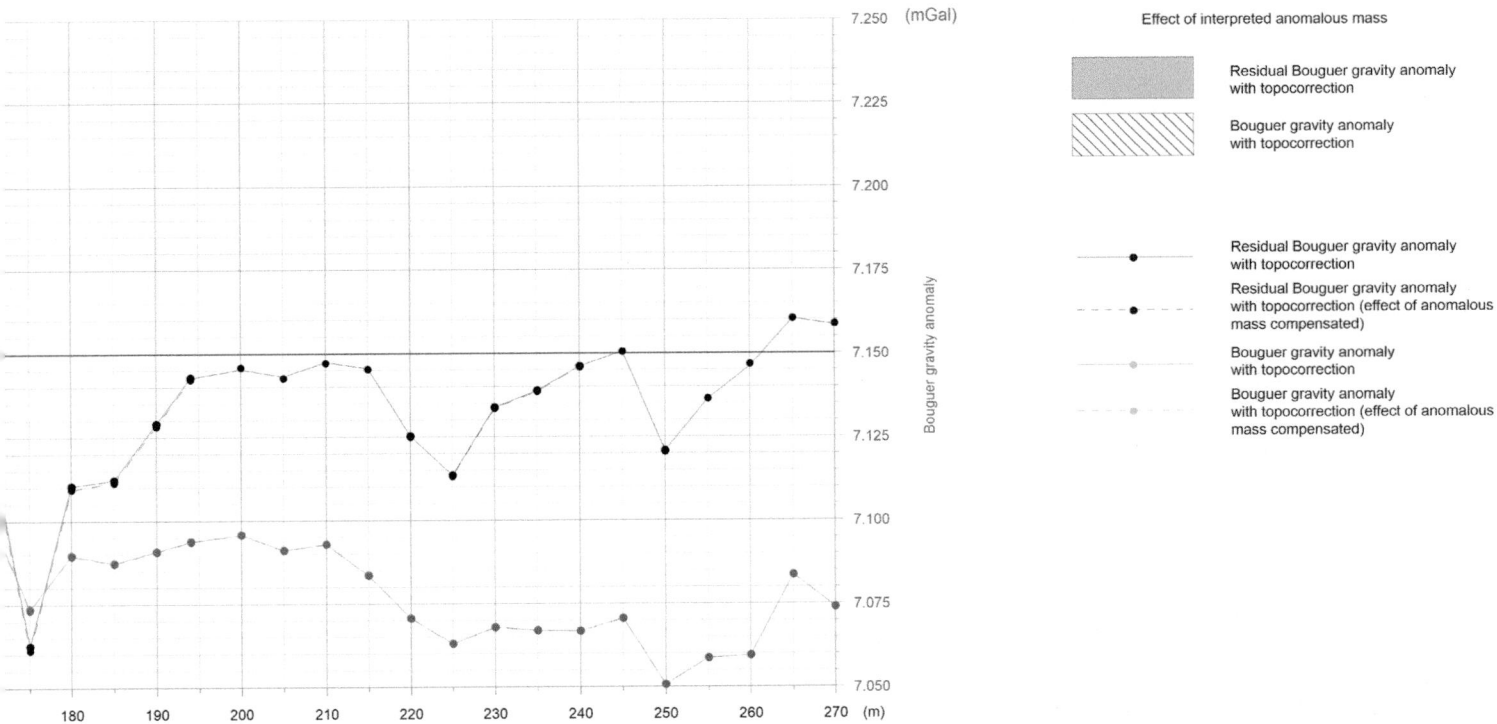

7.250 (mGal)

Effect of interpreted anomalous mass

Residual Bouguer gravity anomaly
with topocorrection

Bouguer gravity anomaly
with topocorrection

Residual Bouguer gravity anomaly
with topocorrection

Residual Bouguer gravity anomaly
with topocorrection (effect of anomalous
mass compensated)

Bouguer gravity anomaly
with topocorrection

Bouguer gravity anomaly
with topocorrection (effect of anomalous
mass compensated)

▲ The area of high readings on the left is thought to correspond to a substantial block of masonry (courtesy Tomáš Chabr, David Filipský and Inset Company, copyright Czech Archaeological Mission in North Iraq and Kurdistan)

◄ Figure 5.6 Electrical Resistivity Tomography plot from the citadel of Erbil (courtesy Tomáš Chabr and Inset Company, copyright Czech Archaeological Mission in North Iraq and Kurdistan)

Shallow Refraction Seismology

The concept of Shallow Refraction Seismology (SRS) goes back to the mid-nineteenth century, when it was proposed as a means of measuring the depths of geological layers, an application in which it stills plays a major role today. The process works by transmitting seismic signals into the ground and measuring the reflection of the seismic waves as they bounce off different features. In geology the waves are created by explosives. In archaeology, where the technique has been applied from the late 1970s, the method is to lay out a transect, placing a metal or plastic plate on the ground with receptors (sensors) at various points along the base line. The plate is struck with a hammer and the seismic reflections are recorded by the sensors. Prospection by this technique can produce imaging down to a depth of around 15–20 m. The method is good for charting major boundaries in underlying stratigraphy (e.g. between clay and sand, or between soil and bedrock), and may also succeed in locating the presence of major anomalies (such as large structures), if they are sufficiently differentiated from the matrix in which they lie.

Refraction tomography, profile velocity section

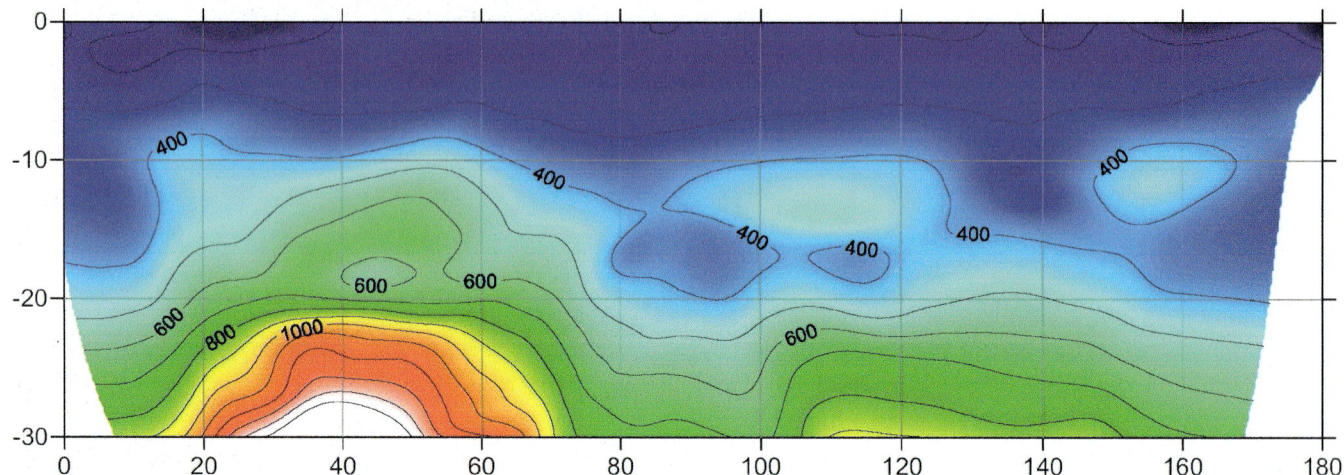

Combining methods

In ideal conditions geophysical prospection can give excellent results, but no single method will image everything. Pyrotechnic installations such as kilns, ovens and hearths, for example, show up very clearly in magnetometry but may be invisible to other methods. Resistivity may miss the pyrotechnic installations, but should show up stone masonry. Both these methods can in any case only image remains down to around 2 m below the surface. Ground penetrating radar can go much deeper and can also detect voids. Ideally, therefore, the plan for geophysical mapping of a site will employ multiple methods – it is quite common to use magnetometry and resistivity and ground penetrating radar all at the same site: the combination of multiple methods will produce an overall understanding of the sub-surface remains which is more varied, more detailed, more reliable and more nuanced. It may also allow for the identification of false anomalies – where an erroneous interpretation suggested by one technique may be corrected or discarded on the basis of data from another technique.

▲ Figure 5.7 Shallow Refraction Seismology from the citadel of Erbil (courtesy Tomáš Chabr and Inset Company, copyright Czech Archaeological Mission in North Iraq and Kurdistan)

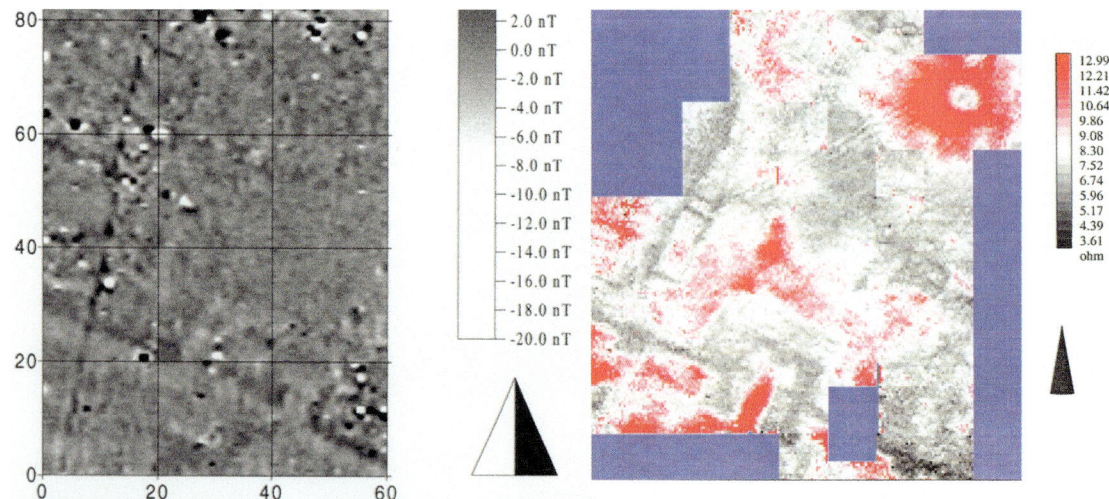

◄ Figure 5.8 Comparison of magnetometry and resistivity surveys at the southern gate at Ziyaret Tepe

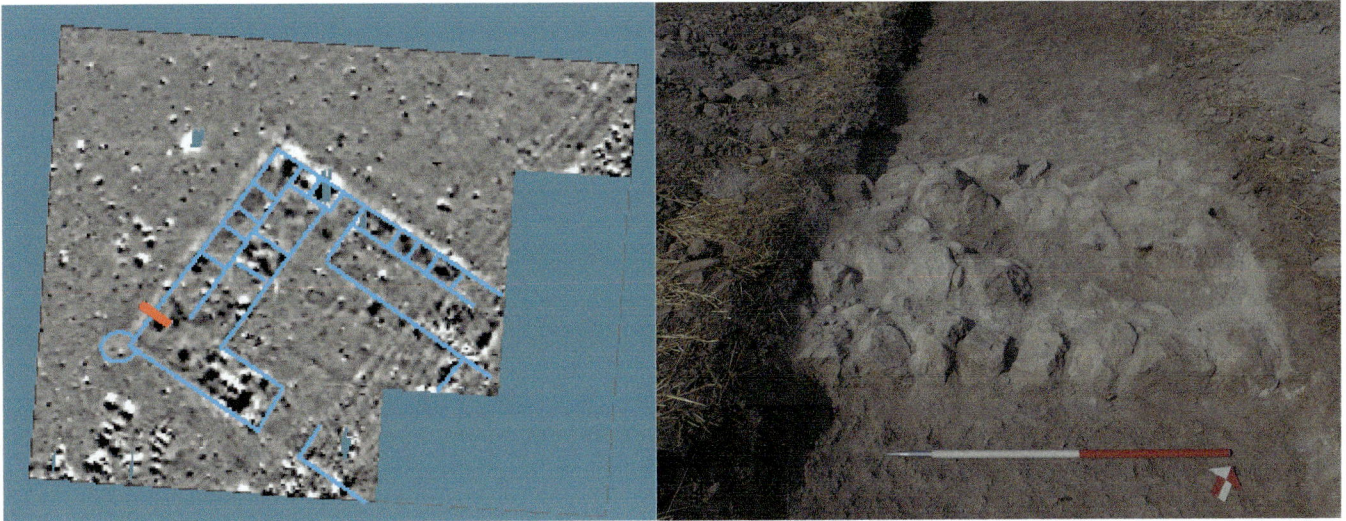

Figure 5.9
Location
and results
of a trench
excavated
at Qalatga
Darband
to ground-truth
the results of
the geophysics
survey

Ground-truthing

Another important practice is 'ground-truthing'. As with satellite imagery, it is optimal to verify the interpretation of a geophysical image by digging a small trench to check the results. In earlier decades this was particularly important with mudbrick architecture, which barely showed up (if at all) in geophysical prospections with the equipment of the time.

Summary of geophysical methods

	types of sites	*features*	*depth*
Magnetometry	open area sites, particularly with a single major occupation near the surface	hearths, kilns, destruction layers, pits, ditches, walls (including mudbrick), ferrous metals, modern cables and pipelines	2 m
Resistivity	open area sites, particularly with a single major occupation near the surface; confined spaces	stone walls (also mud brick walls in good conditions), pavements, roads, pits, ditches	2 m
Ground Penetrating Radar	open areas sites, spaces within confined areas, tells, cemeteries	stone walls, major changes in soil characteristics, empty spaces such as tombs, chambers and tunnels, metal pipes and cables	15 m
Microgravimetry	tells, area sites with substantial structures	major anomalies (such as large structures), pavements, empty spaces, tunnels, mine shafts	30 m
Electrical Resistance Tomography	area sites, tells	major changes in soil characteristics, thickness of archaeological strata, walls, ditches, filled-up channels, empty space	5 m
Shallow Refraction Seismology	tells	major changes in soil characteristics; major anomalies such as large structures, ditches, open spaces, mining areas	2-15 m

Chapter 6

Geographic Information Systems

Figure 6.1
Working on
location maps
in QGIS

A GIS is a framework for gathering, managing and analysing spatial data. GIS applications are now a standard tool in engineering, planning, transport, logistics, military, telecommunications and many other businesses. The combination of computer technology with the precision offered by modern survey instruments coupled to satellite telemetry gives GIS systems an enormous capability to record spatial properties and to relate them to any amount of associated data. A GIS is not just a map, it is a map linked to a database that can record whatever you want to record, at any level of complexity, and present it in visual form.

For archaeologists, the uses of GIS include:

- Creating location maps
- Creating maps of survey data, integrating location of sites with the results of surface collection
- Creating topographical maps of a site, including the location of excavation trenches
- Adding satellite and aerial images
- Adding images from drone flights
- Adding scans of old maps and site plans

- Adding data from geophysical surveys
- Adding a Digital Elevation Model (DEM) – an electronic model of the terrain
- Recording architecture and stratigraphic deposits
- Recording the location of small finds with associated data

A GIS database stores all this information in layers. It is possible to turn layers on and off to only display the data you wish to see at any one point. Moreover, it is possible to analyse the data attached to a layer in 'attribute tables'. For example, if studying survey data, it is possible to look at sites of only a certain size, or only a certain distance from water sources, or only above a certain elevation above sea level, or only of a certain period. If studying finds, you can choose to view only finds of a certain type (coins, figurines, ceramics, etc.), or only from levels of a certain period, or only themselves dating to a certain period, or only of a specified material (bronze, iron, glass, etc.) – whatever corresponds to the particular research question.

The DEM of a landscape can be used to generate 'viewsheds' – what parts of the landscape can be seen from any one point, including adjusting this for time of day. 'Least-cost analysis' can suggest the optimal place for settlements in terms of access to resources, and the easiest route between any places. Comparing DEM models generated at different times can identify changes to the site resulting from site erosion, looting, agricultural encroaching and other factors.

There are many GIS programmes. Two of the most common are ArcGIS and QGIS. ArcGIS is the programme most used by professional surveyors and engineers, however, it is expensive. QGIS on the other hand, which is free, can do everything that most archaeologists require.

In the following pages we give the steps and information you need for creating a basic map in QGIS.

Creating maps in QGIS

It is very important when creating a new map in QGIS to decide where to put the map in your computer and where to store the data (shapefiles, csv's, etc.) and DO NOT MOVE these files from their locations. If you move them, the programme will not be able to find the files and the map will not work. So, first of all, create a folder labelled 'QGIS' or the like and put your raw data into it, and perhaps your maps as well.

* If you cannot find the map after you have opened it (that is, if the space appears empty), click on a layer and go to View – Zoom to Layer.

Creating a new map

To start a new map open QGIS, go to Project and select New.

Name it by going to Project – Save As and giving it a title.

Basic handling – Side panels and Toolbar

The Side panels present the basic information on what is in the map and how it is displayed, while the Toolbar gives some basic tools for viewing and handling the map.

Figure 6.2
QGIS display
showing side
panel and
toolbars

The Side panels

The side panels are presented down the left hand side of the map. The most important is the layers panel, which shows each layer that has been created in the map, its place in the stack, whether it is turned on or off, and an indication of how it is displayed.

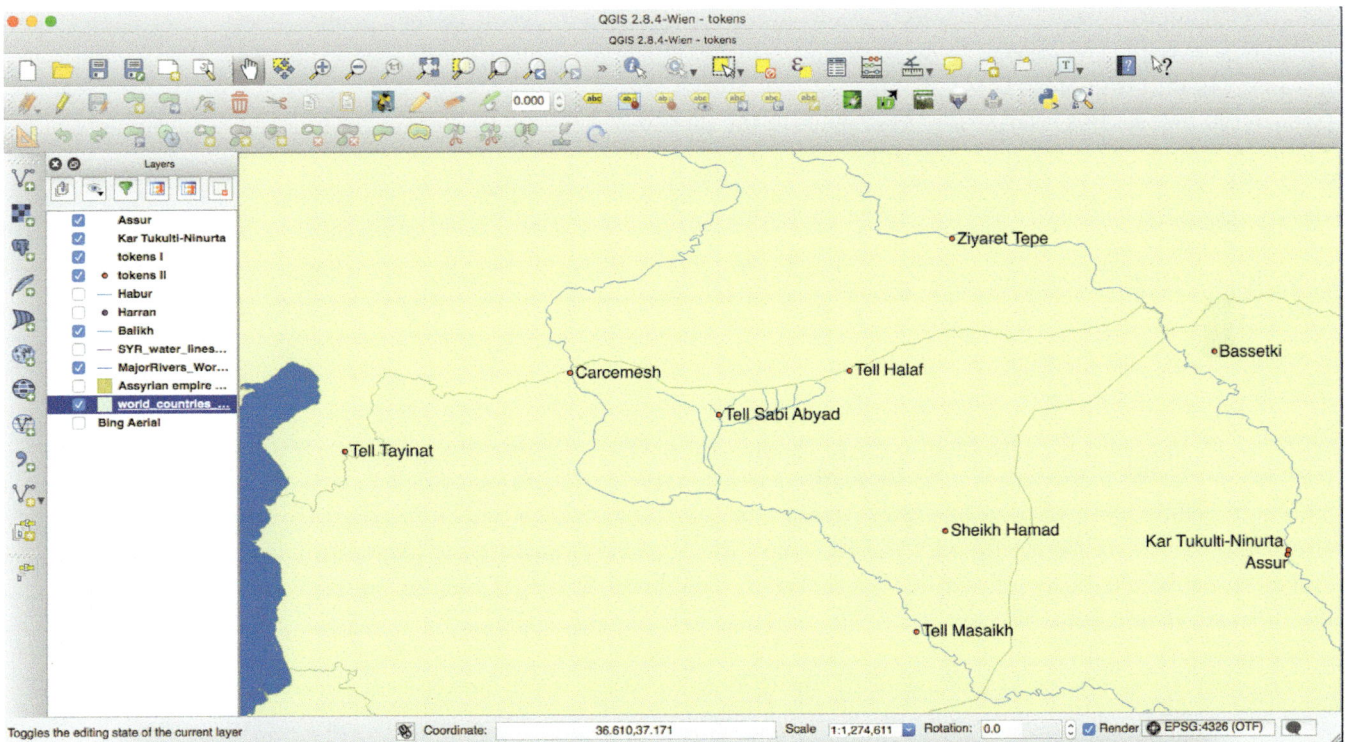

The Toolbar

The toolbar (a horizontal bar running across the top of the map) displays the basic tools for manipulating the map such as moving it around, zooming in or out, and measuring distances, areas and angles. As you learn to use more advanced features, more tools can be displayed.

To change the size of icons and text in the Toolbar

Settings – Options – General – Icon Size

Two important preliminaries

It is essential to decide which Co-ordinate Reference System (CRS) you want to use at the very beginning of the process of creating a map. It is also sensible to set the background colour (which will, for example, become the colour of the oceans and major seas) at the same time.

Co-ordinate Reference System (CRS)

For most general maps, WGS 84 is a very good CRS to use. For maps specific to Iraq, professionals will probably use UTM 38. Assuming we want to use WGS 84, go to Project – Project Properties – CRS – and choose WGS 84.
* If you do not see this listed, type 'WGS 84' into the filter box
* Choose simple 'WGS 84' (not a variant saying UTM)

Background colour

To set the colour of the background click on Project – Project Properties – Background – Background Colour.

Layers

QGIS – in fact, all GIS programmes – work by layers. You will certainly have a layer of a background world map and/or country map, to which you can add as many layers as you like. This can include layers of water features (rivers, lakes, etc.), overlays of satellite data and/or the street map from Google Earth, a Digital Elevation Model, layers showing the location of cities and towns, survey data, geophysical data, excavation data (architecture, extents of archaeological deposits, small finds) and so on.

Layers are viewed in a stack, looking from top to bottom. What is on the top will cover what lies underneath (though it is possible to adjust the opacity of a layer so that you can partially see through it). There are three types of layers which we need to consider: vector layers, raster layers and CSVs. These correspond to vector data, raster data and geographic co-ordinates.

Vector data

Vector data encodes mathematical information to describe a point, line or polygon (two dimensional shapes). Vector data can be made into vector files. Subject to accurate measuring, and errors that may arise switching between different co-ordinate reference systems, these points, lines and polygons can be projected precisely. An important quality is that, no matter at what scale you view the data, or how much you zoom in or out, they retain their definition perfectly.

Vector data is expressed in specific file formats. These come in various forms, but for our purposes we will deal with 'shape files' which have the designation '.shp' at the end. The complete set of associated files may include others, such as .dbf, .prj and .shx. We do not need to know about these specifically, but it is important, when you are downloading vector files from the internet, and you have created a folder for this purpose, to extract all the associated vector files into that folder. For example, if you are downloading an outline map of Iraq, do not just download and store the .shp file, but all the files that are given.

Examples of vector data that can be made into layers are:

Points – the location of fixed survey points, the location of finds, any other point location you wish to record.

Lines – rivers, canals, roads, water and gas pipelines, electricity and telephone lines, fences and borders (if not closed shapes).

Polygons – base maps (of the world, individual countries, provinces, districts), lakes, limits of survey areas, limits of archaeological sites, limits of excavation areas, any two-dimensional feature (e.g. rooms, pavements, walls) in a site.

Raster data

Raster data is essentially pictorial, composed of thousands of tiny squares – 'pixels'. Each square has a colour. It is possible to change the colour, whether when processing the original data or after uploading it into a GIS, but each square can only have one colour at a time – it cannot have a mix of colours. Black and white images are a subset of this. While the pixels are very small, they are discrete, and as you zoom in you will see the image changing from a smooth picture to the colour block of each becoming distinct. We call this pixelisation of the data. Accordingly, a raster image will (hopefully) look smooth at a large scale but – unlike vector data – move to being pixelated as you progressively zoom in. The stage at which this happens depends on the 'resolution' of the data. This is determined by the size of the pixel, and corresponds to the number of 'pixels per square inch', referred to as DPI (or PPI). Examples of raster data that could be uploaded as raster files are photographs (including from aerial and satellite imagery), the results of geophysical surveys, and scans of old maps and site plans.

CSVs

CSVs are files for formatting geographical co-ordinates for point locations. Examples are the locations of villages, towns, cities and archaeological sites. But you can create CSVs for anything for which you have the data – the location of rock reliefs for instance, or wells, or artefacts scattered around a site. The process for making CSVs is explored further below.

Adding vector and raster layers

To add a Vector layer

Either click the V+ icon in the toolbar on the left

or Go to Layer – Add Vector Layer ... browse to the file you want (ending in .shp) ... click on Open then Add then Close.

The layer should now appear on your map, accompanied by a new layer name in the layers panel.

To add a Raster layer

Either click the chequered square with + (below the V+ icon) in the toolbar on the left

or go to Layer – Add Raster Layer

The layer should now appear on your map, accompanied by a new layer name in the layers panel.

Turning layers on and off

Layers can be turned on and off by clicking on the small square box on the left of the layer in the layers panel:

layer turned on

layer turned off

Renaming a layer

To rename a layer, right click on the layer in the layers panel and click on Rename.

To move a layer

You are likely from time to time to want to change the position of the layer in the stack. This can be done by simply clicking on the layer in the layers panel and dragging it up or down.

To delete a layer

To delete a layer, *either* click on the layer in the layers panel and go to Layer – Remove Layer/ Group, *or* right click on the layer and click Remove.

To change the 'Symbology' (appearance) of a layer

Click on the layer in the layers panel then *either* right click *or* click on Layer – Properties – Symbology (or Style). You can change the colour, size, symbol used – in fact every property of how the layer is displayed. To change the opacity, go to Layer – Properties – Style and adjust the bar marked 'Layer transparency'.

Some tips

If the layers panel does not appear to the left of the map

Either go to View – Panels – Layers, *or* right click (or click with two fingers) on the Toolbar at the top – this will give the Toolbox options: select Layers (or Layers Panel).

If the side bar of tools does not appear on the left hand side

Go to View – Toolbars – Manage Layers.

Basic manipulation of a map in QGIS

To move the map on the screen

Click on the white hand in the toolbar

To zoom in or out

Click on the magnifying glasses with a + or −

To go back a step

Click on the magnifying glass with an arrow pointing left.

Adding the world map

The first layer you will want to add is a world map. To do this you will need to download and store the shapefile (and associated data), but before you do that, you need to create a place to save this data.

Create a folder 'World Map'

So, as a first step, inside your QGIS folder create a new folder and call it 'World Map'.

Downloading a suitable shapefile from the internet

You then need to download a suitable shapefile. Googling 'World map shapefile' will give you several options. One good one is the 'Natural Earth shapefile of world countries' – follow that and download the shapefile into your new folder 'World Map'.

Uploading the world map

This data is vector data, so do this by following the process for adding vector layers outlined above.

Adding Iraq water features

Follow the same process as with the world map. You will first need to download and store the relevant shapefiles.

Create a folder 'Iraq Water'

Inside your QGIS folder create a new folder and call it 'Iraq Water'.

Downloading suitable shapefiles from the internet

You then need to download suitable shapefiles. The best place to get these is from Diva-GIS.

Go to Diva-GIS.org

Click on Free Spatial Data then Country Level Data

Choose 'Iraq' for Country and 'Inland water' for Subject [You may need to download Iraq Water Lines (i.e. rivers, canals, streams) and Iraq Water Areas (i.e. lakes) separately; you will see there are other useful options, such as administrative boundaries]

Press OK and then Download

This will download a folder called Iraq Water which contains data on Iraq water lines (i.e. rivers) and areas (i.e. lakes). When this data has downloaded, go to Downloads, find the ZIP folder and click on 'Show in Folder', right click on the ZIP folder in the list, click on Extract All. Click on Browse and browse to the folder 'Iraq Water' you created inside your 'QGIS' folder. Click on Select Folder and click on Extract.

Uploading Iraq Water shapefiles

This data is vector data, so follow the process for adding vector layers outlined above.

Adding place locations – making and uploading CSVs

To add a place location on to the map you need to put the coordinates (in decimal form) into a file called a CSV and upload this into your map. You will thus need to (1) establish the coordinates of the location, (2) convert these into decimal coordinates if necessary, (3) put these coordinates into a CSV file and (4) upload the CSV into your map.

Establishing the coordinates of a location

There are numerous ways you can get the coordinates of a location you are interested in:

Wikipedia

For any major site or town, go to the Wikipedia entry for the site. On the right hand side it will show you the conventional coordinates. Click on this and it will take you to a page which gives you the coordinates in three forms, Conventional, UTM and Digital – you want the digital coordinates.

Google Maps

Put a marker at the location on Google Maps and read off the coordinates.

Google Earth (Pro)

Move the cursor to the location in Google Earth (Pro) and read off the coordinates.

GPS

Establish the coordinates with a GPS device.

Converting conventional coordinates to decimal

Google 'convert degrees to decimal'- this will give you several options: www.fcc.gov is a good one.

Creating a CSV file

Create a folder 'CSVs'

As a first step, inside your QGIS folder create a new folder and call it 'CSVs'.

Creating a CSV

CSVs can be done as either .txt files or Excel files.

(a) Creating a CSV as an Excel document

Open Excel, create a new file, then go to Save As where you need to (i) give the file a name, and (ii) save it as .csv.
* Label the first three columns 'sitename', 'latitude' and 'longitude' ('lat' and 'long' will be OK), then enter the data for the location in the next row.
* Make sure there are no spaces in the cells with the coordinates.
* There is no limit to how many locations you can add – just start a new line for each location.

(b) Creating a CSV as a .txt file

The first line of the file needs to be 'sitename,lat,long'
* Note (i) no spaces after the commas and (ii) 'sitename' needs to be written as one word.

The entry for the site needs to be in the form of the site name followed by the coordinates, e.g. 'Qalatga Darband,36.2133,44.9732' separated by commas with no spaces (you *can* have spaces in the site name, but nowhere else).
* CSV files use decimal coordinates.
* Note that the data in a CSV must be formatted exactly – not only the actual coordinates, but the exact way in which they are written – it is critical not to have any empty spaces in the coordinate entries.

Uploading a CSV file

To add a CSV to a map, go to Layers – Add Layer – Add Delimited Text Layer.

Browse to the file you want and select it.

Tick 'CSV'

In Geometry Definition

– for the X field select 'longitude'

– for the Y field select 'latitude'

Make sure the CRS is 'WGS 84'

Click ADD

Click CLOSE

N.B. while we tend to actually say 'latitude and longitude' in English – and coordinates are often given in that order – in a GIS system longitude will normally be given first (the 'X' coordinate), and latitude second (the 'Y' coordinate).

Your place should now appear as a symbol on your map, accompanied by a new layer in the layers panel.

You may want to change how the location is displayed on the map – such as the size, colour, the symbol itself – to do so, see the entry on Changing Symbology above.

Adding the site name

To show the site name:

Either click on the layer name in the left hand pane and go to Layer – Labelling

or right click on the layer name and go to Properties – Label.

Then tick 'Label this layer with' and select 'Site Name'.

Go to 'Text' to change the size, font, colour, etc. of the text.

Go to 'Placement' to change the positioning of the text:

– select 'Offset from Point' and choose which option you want.

– change the amount of offset by changing the number (for this, it is probably easier to select 'mm' than 'map units').

Measuring distances, areas and angles

Click on the icon near the right-hand side of the toolbar, which will appear as one of the following:

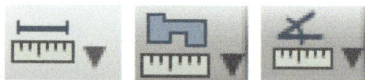

All three are located in the same place. Select the first to measure a linear distance on the map, the second to measure an area, and the third to measure an angle.

To digitise lines/polygons

You may want to copy details from raster images in your map and turn them into digital – that is vector – data. For example, if you have a satellite image uploaded into the map and geo-referenced, you may want to copy the position, course or outline of specific features. You may want to copy the location of a site or a fixed visible landmark, such as a radio mast (points); you may want to trace along the lines of canals, road, rivers, etc. (lines); or you may want to trace out features, such as the area surrounded by a fortification wall, the limit of a site, an area of water and so on (polygons). The same applies to images from geophysical surveys and old site plans from earlier excavations. If you have an ortho-image of a site or an excavation area loaded into your map, you may want to trace the limit of excavation areas and any number of features in the trench.

To create vector files for digitising points, lines and polygons

As with all geo-database files, you first need to decide where you will store the data, so you will need to create a new folder in your QGIS folder. Let us call this folder 'Digitised data'.

Then go to Layer – Create Layer – New Shapefile layer, and tick on 'Point', 'Line' or 'Polygon' according to whether you want to copy/trace a point location, a linear feature or a closed shape.

To make a point

Click on Layer – Create Layer – New Shapefile layer – Point – OK.

Enter a name for the new layer in the dialogue box and choose where you want to save it, then click on Save. The new layer is now created and will show in the Layers panel.

To add a point to this layer, click on the yellow pencil in the tool bar.

Then click on the white star in a yellow square surrounded by three dots.

Then simply click wherever you want to create a point in this new layer. As you will see, you need to give an ID to each point. When you are finished, click on the yellow pencil again – a dialogue box will ask you whether you want to save the changes. Change the symbology by following the notes above.

To make a Line

Click on Layer – Create Layer – New Shapefile layer – Line – OK.

Enter a name for the new layer in the dialogue box and choose where you want to save it, then click on Save. The new layer is now created and will show in the Layers panel.

To add a line to this layer, click on the yellow pencil in the tool bar.

Then click on the V icon with a white star in a yellow square.

To make lines, click wherever you want to start and then at each subsequent point (node) that you want in the line – you can have as many points in a line as you want, and you can have as many lines in the layer as you want. Right click on the final point in each line – as you will see, you need to give an ID to each line. When you are finished, click on the yellow pencil again – a dialogue box will ask you whether you want to save the changes. Change the symbology by following the notes above.

To make a Polygon

Click on Layer – Create Layer – New Shapefile layer – Polygon – OK.

Enter a name for the new layer in the dialogue box and choose where you want to save it, then click on Save. The new layer is now created and will show in the Layers panel.

To add a polygon to this layer, click on the yellow pencil in the tool bar.

Then click on the green lake with a white star in a yellow square.

To make polygons, click wherever you want to create the first point and then each subsequent point you wish to have in the polygon. You can have as many points as you want, and you can have as many polygons in the layer as you want. Right click on the final point in each polygon – as you will see, you need to give an ID to each polygon. When you are finished, click on the yellow pencil again – a dialogue box will ask you whether you want to save the changes. Change the symbology by following the notes above.

Plug-ins

Plug-ins are additional tools that can be used to extend the functionality of the software. They are available as extra features, rather than as part of the core software, in order to reduce the size of the programme. They can cover all manner of geographical and statistical analysis. We will consider two of the more basic ones that you might want to use – Quick Map Services and GPS Tools.

To add a Plugin

Go to Plugins – Manage and Install Plugins.

Quick Map Services

Install the Plugin – go to Plugins – Manage and Install Plugins – select Quick Map Services and click Install Plugin

In the Menu bar, find the icon for Search Quick Map Services (Search QMS) (a globe with a Q)

In the search box type 'Google'

Find Google Satellites and click Add (the 'Add' tab is on the right and may be partially hidden from view)

Find Google Maps and click Add

Find Google Terrain and click Add (you may need to type 'Google Terrain')

Adding GPS data

First, activate the GPS Tools plugin: go to Plugins – Plugin Manager – GPS Tools.

To upload data go to Vector – GPS Tools – Load GPX File, choose your gpx file and select Feature Type as Waypoints.

Exchanging data between QGIS and Google maps

To use a QGIS layer in Google Earth Pro

Save the layer in QGIS as a shapefile by right-clicking on the layer in the layers panel, go to Save As and choose 'Esri shapefile':

– this will save the layer as a .shp file
– of course, choose carefully where you wish to store this file
– make sure the CRS is correct.

To import this into Google Earth Pro, go to File – Import and navigate to the new .shp file

Marking points and digitising lines and polygons in Google Earth Pro and exporting into QGIS

You may want to copy point locations or digitise line or polygons features in Google Earth Pro and import the layers into your QGIS.

To mark points or create polygons in Google Earth Pro

In Google Earth, click on Add Placemark, Add Polygon or Add Path as appropriate and mark the feature you want to copy with the cross-hair square.

When you are finished with each feature, give the layer a name and click OK to save.

The new layer should now appear in the Places panel to the left: right click on the layer, go to Save Place As and choose .kml.

Import the .kml file into QGIS: this is a vector layer, so follow the normal procedure for uploading a vector layer.

Producing an output map

You can either export the map just as you see it on the screen, or compose it into a finished map with its North arrow, scale, labels, etc.

To save a map as you see it on the screen

Go to Project, where there will *either* be an option Save as Image (where you choose JPG, PDF or other option) *or* there will be separate options for (a) Save as Image (where you choose JPG or other option) and (b) Save as PDF.

To compose a map with North Arrow, Scale and Labels

Go to Project – Composer Manager – Add, then type in a name for the new map output.

In the new screen that appears, click on the icon of a scroll and + (normally the fifth icon down) 'Add map'

Next, click and drag a rectangle across the screen to create the area you want the map to fill: when you release the button, the map should now appear in this screen.

To add a North Arrow

Go to Layout – Add Image. Then draw a rectangle – this will activate a dialog box. Look for Search Directories – click on this and then click on the image you want.

To add a normal arrow

Either go to Layout – Add Arrow, *or* click on the Add Arrow box in the left hand sidebar.

To add a Scale

Either go to Layout – Add New Scalebar, *or* click on the Add Scalebar in the left hand sidebar.

To add Labels

Either go to Layout – Add New Label, *or* click on the 'T' (for Text) box in the left hand sidebar.

To Export as a PDF or JPG

To export as a PDF, go to Composer – Export as PDF.

To export as a JPG, go to Composer – Export as Image.

Digital Elevation Models

A digital elevation model (DEM) is a three-dimensional model of the surface terrain. A DEM can be generated by survey by LIDAR (airborne radar) and by photogrammetry using drone images. For regional maps, a very common DEM used in archaeology is based on the data from the Shuttle Radar Topography Mission. The SRTM was an 11-day mission in which the American space shuttle orbited the Earth for 11 days, taking radar readings off the Earth's surface. The resulting data covers from 56^0 S to 60^0 N. The data for the Middle East is available at 90 m resolution – this is good enough for regional maps, but not suitable for fine details.

Acquiring SRTM DEM data and uploading into QGIS

The DEM data from the SRTM is organised into 'tiles', each covering the area within set limits of latitude and longitude.

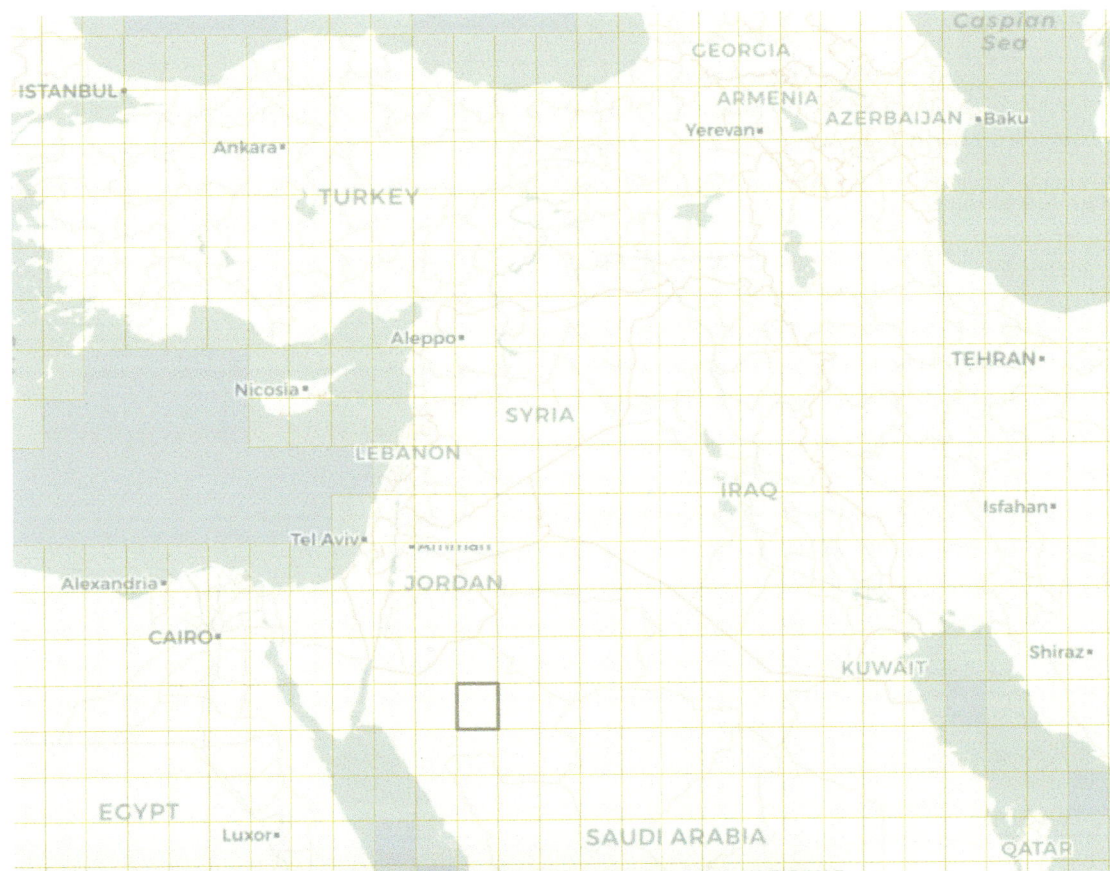

Figure 6.3
SRTM tiles

The easiest way to access data is to use the 'SRTM Tile Grabber'. As you will see, to cover the whole of Iraq you will need seven tiles. To download the data, you simply click on the tile – but as usual, you should first create a folder to save this data in:

Create a folder 'SRTM'

Inside your QGIS folder create a new folder and call it 'SRTM'.

Downloading SRTM tiles

Go to SRTM Tile Grabber and click on the tile you want. This will download a ZIP file. When this data has downloaded, go to Downloads, find the ZIP folder and click on 'Show in Folder', right click on the ZIP folder in the list, and click on Extract All. Click on Browse and browse to the folder 'SRTM' you created inside your 'QGIS' folder. Click on Select Folder and then Extract.

Uploading SRTM tiles

This data is raster data. The file you need is the TIFF file. Fortunately, this comes already geo-referenced! So all you need to do is upload it into QGIS by following the steps for uploading raster files above.

The DEM tile should now appear on your map and in the layers panel to the left.

To change the Symbology of a Digital Elevation Model (DEM) layer

Click on the layer in the window on the left side of the map; go to Properties – Style, then

change Render to 'Single band pseudo-colour'

set the colour scheme, intervals, etc. in the panel to the right

click on Classify

click on Apply

Chapter 7

Survey with Total Station / Multi Station

▶ Figure 7.1
A traditional
theodolite

Archaeologists have long used maps to depict the spatial attributes of archaeological sites. These maps draw on spatial data collected through archaeological survey. The basic principles were developed for survey with **theodolite**, an instrument that measures the angle between two points along both a horizontal and a vertical plane. A plan can be drawn from these readings, or points can be positioned in accordance with an existing plan.

In modern times the theodolite has evolved into the **total station**. A typical total station includes an electronic theodolite to calculate angles to reference points. But unlike the traditional theodolite, a total station can also measure distance using an on-board electronic distance measurement device (EDM). With careful set-up, the use of a total station allows archaeologists to collect spatial data with great accuracy across distances of several hundred metres.

A **multi station** is an instrument that combines a total station with a 3D laser scanner. Its scanning capabilities, used to generate high-resolution digital models, can capture 30,000 points per second.

Figure 7.2
Setting up a
multi station on-
site

Figure 7.3
The reflector
mounted on a
staff

A traditional total station survey requires two people: an operator to control the instrument, and an assistant to move the reflective target from point-to-point. The reflector target is usually a staff with a reflective prism. Total stations can also work in 'reflectorless' mode, recording the return of the laser signal reflected directly back from the object.

The latest models of total and multi stations have a robotic or motorised function that enables the operator to control the instrument from a distance via remote control, eliminating the need for an assistant to hold the staff.

Angle measurement

Most total stations measure angles by means of electro-optical scanning of extremely precise digital barcodes etched on rotating glass cylinders or discs within the instrument. The best quality Total Stations are capable of measuring angles to 0.5 arc-second (i.e. 1/120 of a degree), while standard instruments generally measure angles to 5 or 10 arc-seconds.

Distance measurement

Distance measurement is accomplished with an infrared signal emitted along the instrument's optical path. The laser beam is reflected by the prism reflector or by the object under survey. The pattern in the returning signal is read and interpreted by the computer in the total station. A typical total station can measure up to 1500 m away with an accuracy of about 1.5 mm.

▲ Figure 7.4
Survey using
a multi station
by one person
using the
remote function

Coordinate measurement

To record an unknown point location, a total station requires a direct line of sight. When the instrument is set up over a known point and its orientation is set, it can emit its infrared beam to the reflector positioned over the unknown point. The total station then calculates the coordinate of the unknown point in three dimensions relative to the total station's position. These coordinates are referred to as X, Y and Z (or easting, northing and elevation).

Orientating the instrument

In order to proceed, the instrument needs to know both where it is and how it is oriented with respect to north. To achieve this, it needs to orient itself with respect to two points whose coordinates are known. One of these points can be the set-up location of the instrument, the other being a back-sight. Alternatively, the

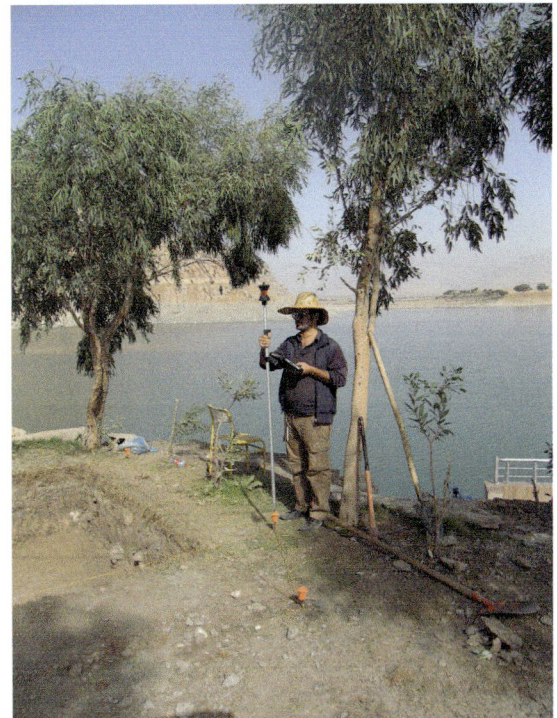

▶ Figure 7.5
Holding a staff
with reflector
over a point

Figure 7.6
Measuring a
static GNSS
point at Usu
Aska

surveyor can also set up a 'free station' (also known as resection) on an unknown location, if they have line of sight to two or more points whose coordinates are known.

Multi Stations and some newer models of Total Stations have the ability to be connected to a Global Navigation Satellite System (GNSS) receiver. These instruments calculate coordinates using GNSS. However, the instrument still needs to orient itself working from a basis of at least two known points. [Some controllers and tablets (and mobile phones) have built-in GNSS receivers, but these are not survey grade and only give accuracy in metres].

It is also possible to set up on a 'false origin' or a local station. This is done by assigning an arbitrary coordinate to the primary datum, such as 1000 m north (X), 1000 m east (Y), and 100 m in elevation (Z). To orientate the machine a back-sight can be placed in a northerly direction – using a compass, for instance – from the machine and set orientation as 0° 0' 0". This method is used when no GNSS data is available at the time of set-up. This 'false origin' system is simple, flexible and allows for the possible expansion of a site map in any direction at a later date. The total station computer also allows data points to be changed as a batch if needed.

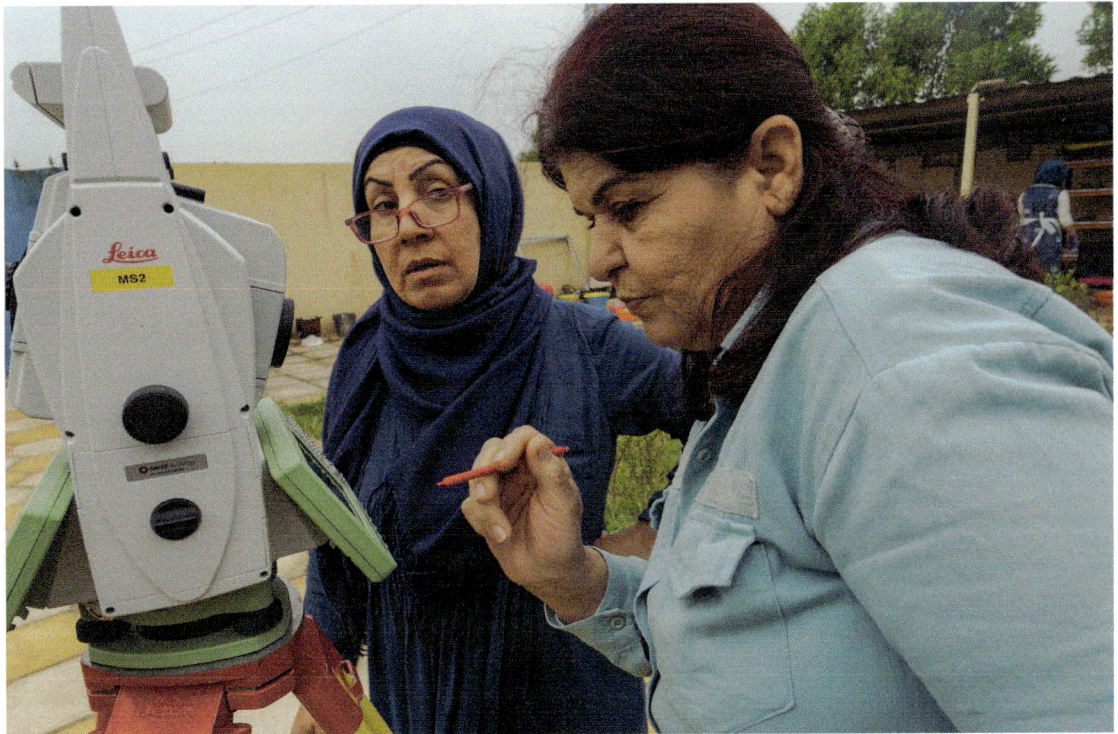

Figure 7.7
Using the
control screen
on a multi
station

Establishing a network of control points

Once the positions of at least two points have been established – whether by GNSS, or with reference to previously unmovable survey points (such as national survey points) – it is possible to establish a network of fixed points with known co-ordinates which serve as the basis for survey operations across the site. These are known as control points, and are typically designated with the prefix STN (for 'station'). The number of control points needed will vary according to the size and morphology of the site: on a small flat site just a few may suffice, but a large site with significant topography is likely to require a considerable number – in all cases, the greater the number of points, the greater the accuracy and flexibility of the system.

Establishing a site grid

The physical characteristics of a given archaeological site will determine how data is collected for a particular map. However, there are some basic features whose use is standard. For example, most surveyors record data using the coordinate mapping function of the total station. This enables the total station to record a range of points that conform to an X, Y, Z coordinate system.

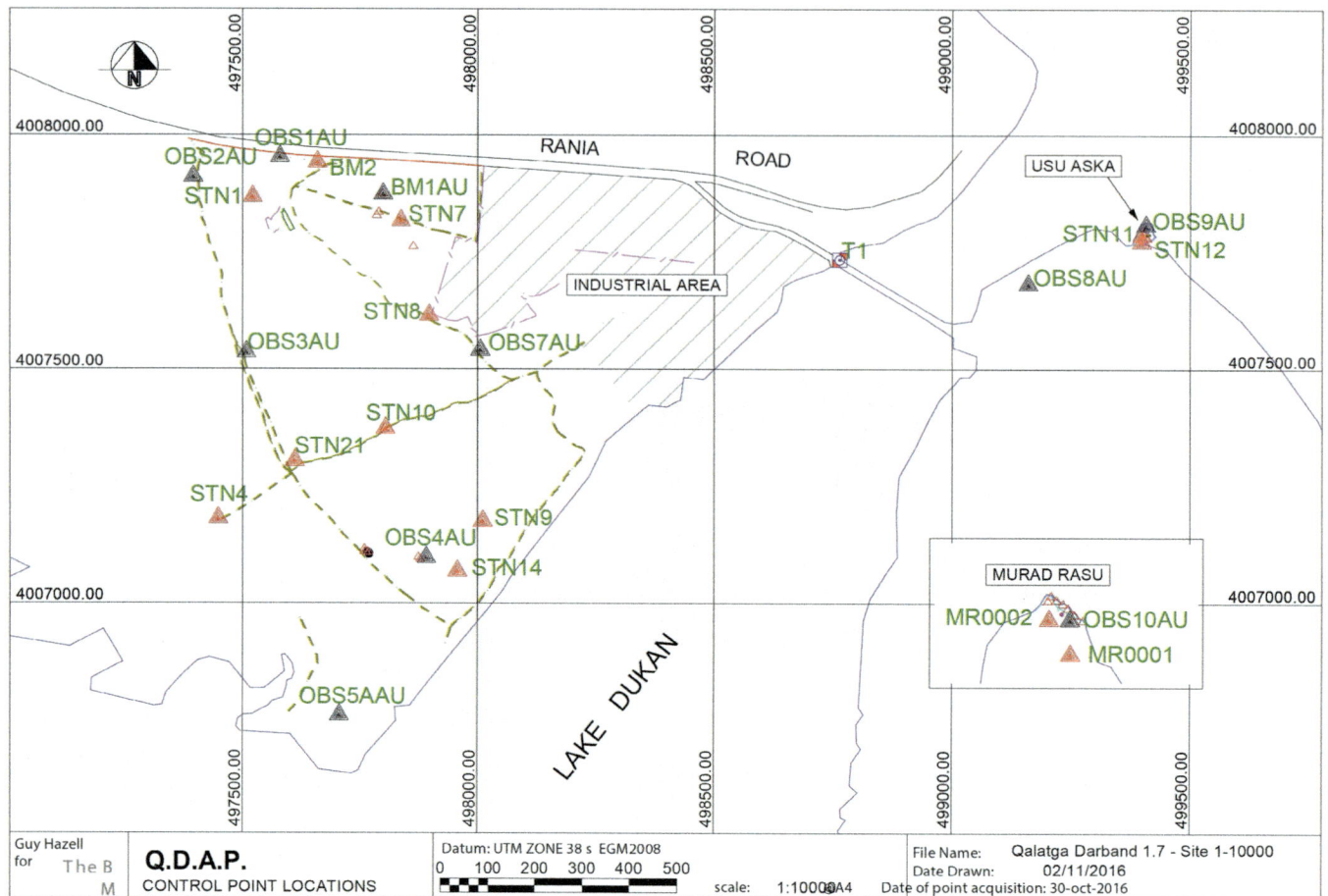

Guy Hazell
for   The B
M

Q.D.A.P.
CONTROL POINT LOCATIONS

Datum: UTM ZONE 38 s EGM2008
0   100   200   300   400   500

scale: 1:10000A4

File Name: Qalatga Darband 1.7 - Site 1-10000
Date Drawn: 02/11/2016
Date of point acquisition: 30-oct-2016

When known points are available

Set up instrument on known point and back-sight to known point for orientation or resection. Use the UTM coordinate numbers to stake out at required distances.

When no known points are available

A local station can be set up using 1000 m E, 1000 m N, 100 m Z and a North orientated back-sight. Then stake out points at 20 m intervals (for instance) 1020E, 1000N then 1040E, 1000N and so on – this will give a row of points on the 1000N alignment then repeat for the 1020N alignment.

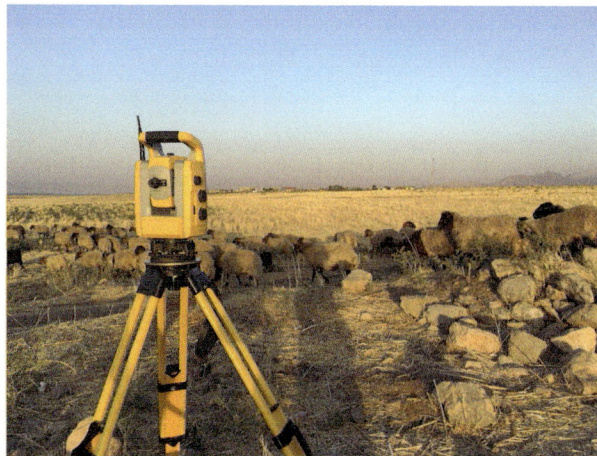

▲ Figure 7.8
The network of control points established for survey operations in the Darband-i Rania

◄ Figure 7.9
Aligning the instrument to a distant antenna

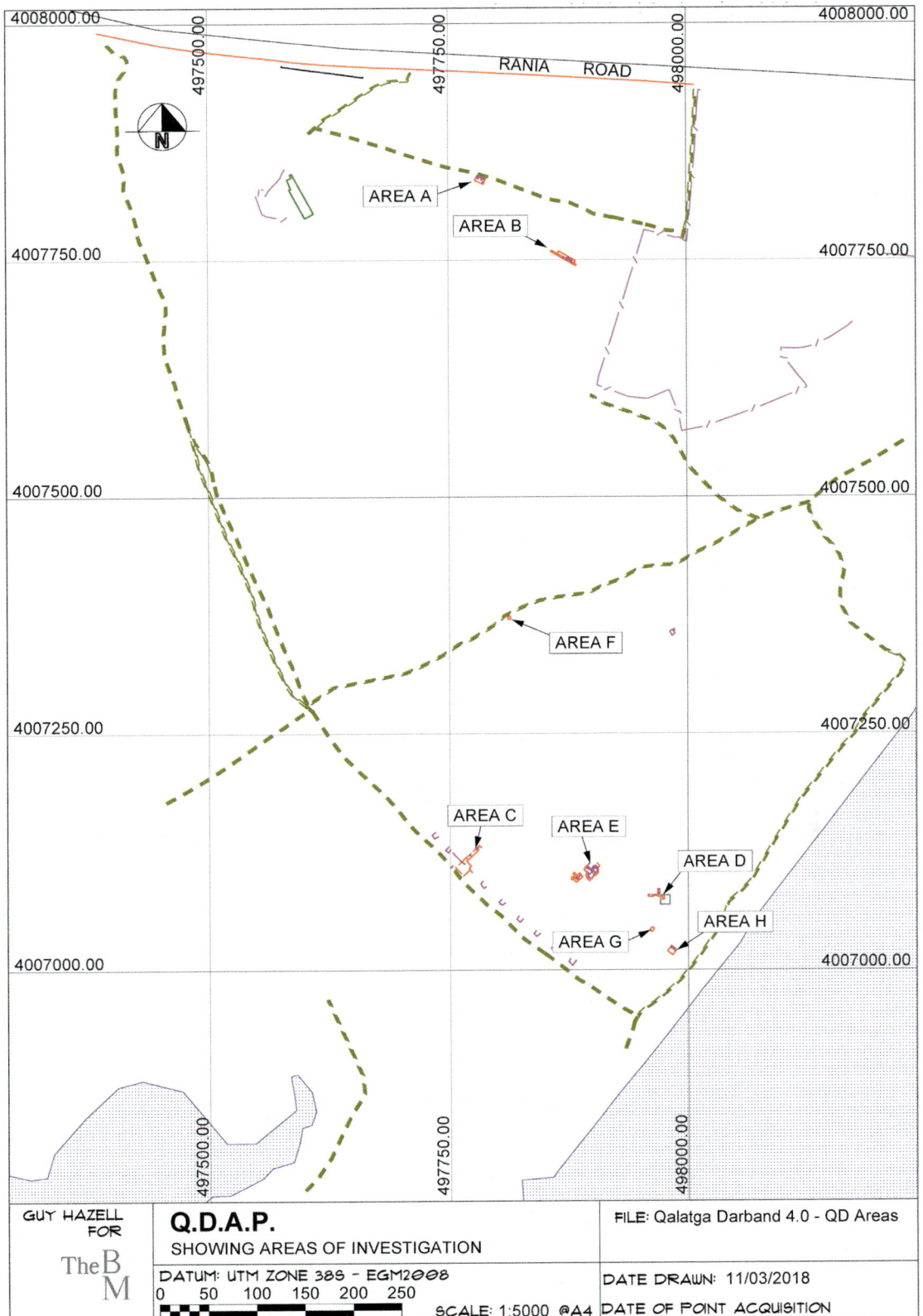

Figure 7.10
Site map
of Qalatga
Darband with
its coordinate
grid

Independent Grid

This is when a grid is needed which is independent of the site grid – for instance, if a room needs to be gridded in 1 m squares, orientated to the room, for use in surface sampling. Use the function 'stakeout to the line'. First, record a point in one corner of the room (A), then another point in the next corner (B); this will form the line A-B. Stake out points along the line at required intervals, then stake out points offset at required intervals for the next rows. Some instruments will need a – (minus) when staking out left of the line A-B.

Although establishing an arbitrary X, Y, Z site grid based on a 'false origin' has many advantages, it is important to integrate this grid within global coordinate systems in order to fix the site in its overall spatial location. Most archaeological maps use the World Geodetic System (WGS). The revised 1984 version (WGS 84) is standard for map-making and satellite navigation systems. WGS 84 is valid for the whole of the globe. However, the world is not flat and this causes irregularities and errors. A more precise coordinate system, tailored to regional zones, is Universal Transverse Mercator (UTM). The UTM system is based on WGS 84, but is a projected coordinate system, effectively flattening out the curve of the globe, devised in a way to minimise distortion for each of the 60 zones, formed by longitudinal strips, into which it is divided. UTM assigns X and Y coordinates according to these zones. For maps specific to Iraq, for example, surveyors will probably use UTM 38.

WGS 84 assigns earth-centred coordinates (X, Y and Z).

A site's elevation in WGS 84 is the height above the mathematically correct ellipsoid. However, since the earth is not a perfect ellipsoid, elevations should be calculated using a geoid (a model of global sea levels used with the GNSS receiver to calculate precise surface elevations).

DGNSS (DGPS) – Surveying with the satellites

GNSS (Global Navigation Satellite System) is the combined data from the American GPS, the Russian GLONASS system, the European Galileo, the Chinese Beidou system, and other regional systems. GNSS has many more satellites to collect data from than just GPS.

DGNSS (differential GNSS) is a method of applying corrections to a roving GNSS receiver. This method uses two GNSS receivers, one set up over a known point (the Base) and the other used to collect new data points (the Rover). As the Base is set up over a known point, any differences it receives from the satellites (due to atmospheric conditions, satellite orbit errors, etc.) can then be sent to the Rover, usually via radio, and adjustments applied at the Rover to correct the errors. The accuracy will depend on the distance between the Base and Rover – 10 km would be a maximum separation. To obtain an accurate position at the Base (if not known) a static position can be recorded.

Figure 7.11
Using a DGNSS
(DGPS) receiver
mounted on a
pole

Used more commonly nowadays is the precise point position (PPP) method. This uses the data from the Continuously Operating Reference Stations (CORS) set up around the world to form a network of reference stations that can then send corrections back to the Rover to adjust its position. The advantage of this method is that only one receiver is needed and the corrections can be sent to the receiver via an internet connection (3G mobile phone is adequate) or via a dedicated corrections satellite directly to the receiver, useful if there is no mobile phone reception.

▶ Figure 7.12a
Topographic
map of the
island at Usu
Aska

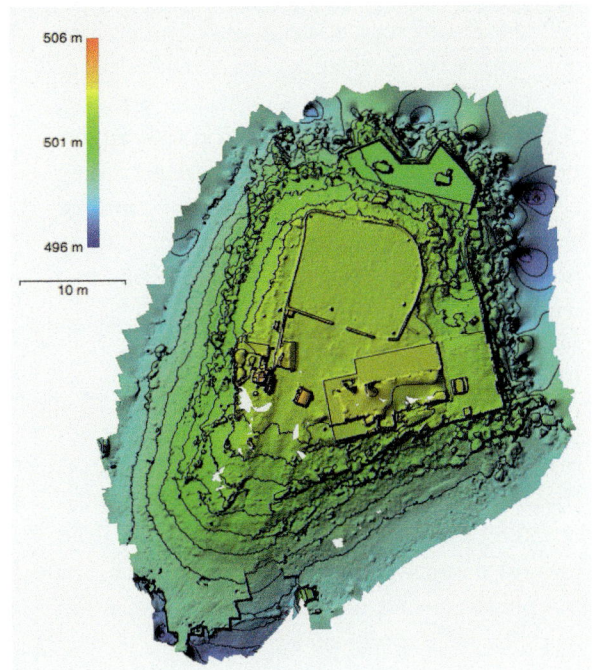

Topographic maps

Most software packages provided by total station manufacturers can create a topographic contour map by extrapolating or interpolating the data points collected in the field. However, the accuracy of the contour map will increase with the number of points collected. When collecting field data for a contour map, it is necessary to collect spot heights from multiple points around the landscape, especially in areas where the elevation changes, such as on slopes, depressions or rises such as spoil piles.

Site maps

Site maps can depict the excavation trenches and the archaeological features they contain, as well as broader site-wide features such as topography and surface remains. By using a coordinate system, it is possible to export the data into geo-spatial analytical systems such as a GIS. The depiction of features such as walls or pits can be visually manipulated in a GIS to produce maps that communicate the site's spatial properties as clearly as possible.

Object distribution maps

Use of a GIS also enables the survey data to be interrogated spatially. For example, if one type of object was recorded as a particular category (for example, inscribed cuneiform cones), then the GIS can map the distribution of this type of object according to its relationship with other data collected from the site, such as walls, cuts and other types of artefacts.

Photogrammetry

When a site is recorded using photogrammetry, it is important to establish the relationship of the photogrammetric model to the site grid. A surveyor will use a total station to establish points around the site that are mapped according to the grid coordinate system. When captured as part of the photogrammetric survey, these points enable the 3D model to be calibrated within the site grid.

Orthoimages

An orthoimage is created by stitching together many photographs overlapped at the same scale. The images can be captured using either a pole-mounted camera or a drone. Once again, fixed ground control points need to be established to optimise the alignment of the images and to help place the survey on larger maps.

Figure 7.12b Taking a mosaic of images for photogrammetry using a pole-mounted camera, with co-ordinated 'targets' (arrowed) used to scale and orientate the 3D point cloud created by the photo array. The orthophoto is then created from the point cloud

▶ Figure 7.13
Orthoimage
of the Assyrian
fortifications at
Usu Aska

The fixed reference points should be secure and visible without detracting from the archaeological features being recorded. These points can be paint marks on fixed features or distinctive pegs placed around the site. Calibrating aerial images with these points enables the production of 3D models, orthoimages and DEMs (Digital Elevation Models) that can be exported into a GIS for analysis.

Multi station laser scanning

Multi stations differ from total stations in their capacity to capture data for 3D modelling using an in-built laser scanner. By scanning along both the horizontal and vertical planes, multi stations can gather high-resolution data of architectural features and monuments that can be used to generate 3D digital models in the data processing stage. As a multi station captures these data within the coordinate system, these 3D models do not need calibration with fixed reference points.

Data processing

Most instruments write the data on to an internal electronic hard-drive or an external data collector, such as a hand-held computer or field logger. When downloaded from the total station onto a computer, software applications compute the data to generate a map of the surveyed area. The newest generation of total stations and all multi stations can also show the map on the instrument's touch-screen immediately after measuring each point.

The process of transforming raw data into a particular mapping format varies between software platforms. Generally, data is initially processed using the software supplied by the instrument's manufacturer, such as Leica or Sokkia. Once the data has been retrieved from the instrument, it can be exported from the instrument's software package into a text file that can be read by standard spreadsheet applications such as Microsoft Excel, or imported directly into a mapping software package such as QGIS or ArcGIS.

Codes

The ease of interpreting and depicting data in the processing stage depends on how the data was classified in the field. It is important to create and maintain a list of standard codes to classify different types of points over the course of a survey. These codes enable the software package to map the data as different layers according to the type of feature surveyed. A typical example might be:

Instrument Code	Category
ARTE	Artefact
BR	Bedrock
CUT	Trench Cut
GRDPT	Grid Point
LEVELS	Spot Levels
LoE	Limit of Excavation
P	Pit
WALL	Wall Edge

Through the process of gridding, three-dimensional (X, Y, Z) data can be used to create different map formats, including contour maps, surface maps, image maps and shaded relief maps. Contour maps, for example, are useful for displaying topographic data in two dimensions, particularly in combination with other site features such as architectural remains or excavation units.

Instrument care

Total Stations and Multi Stations contain sensitive and highly calibrated mechanics. They must be kept stable and as free from dust as possible. Their custom-made cases are robust and designed to withstand standard transportation, including by car or plane. However, when taken out of its case, the instrument should always be held with two hands: one holding the handle at the top, and the other supporting the base plate. The handle should never be released until the instrument has been secured firmly onto the platform of the tripod. The tripod should be set up on firm ground with its legs wide enough to withstand wind. If the instrument is dropped or knocked, then it should be taken to the manufacturer or surveying service to recalibrate the instrument, if required.

Figure 7.14 multi station training at Qaltaga Darband

Chapter 8

GPS

Use of the GPS (etrex 10) to collect points

Turn on by pressing 'light' button

Go to Mark Way Point, and press Done; if you want to label the point this can be done in the Note box

Displaying results

There are many ways of displaying the results. The data needs to be fed into one GIS system or another. There are many options to choose from. We will work with GPS Visualizer and QGIS.

GPS Visualizer

Download points to computer (go to Garmin – GPX – select the Waypoints you want)

Then go to GPS visualizer http://www.gpsvisualizer.com/ browse to and upload the waypoints, choose Output Format – Google Maps, and click on Map It

Save the map as a PDF (File – Export as PDF) [if this does not work, go to Print – PDF – Save as PDF]

To get the raw data, choose Output Format – Plain Text Table

QGIS

You need to have activated the GPS plug-in: when you have opened QGIS go to Plugins – Plugin Manager – GPS Tools

To upload data, go to Vector – GPS – GPS Tools, choose your gpx file and select Feature Type as Waypoints

To save as a jpeg, go Project – Save as Image – JPG

Figure 8.2
Recording a
surface find
using GPS

Google maps

You will first need to register with Google Maps   https://www.google.co.uk/maps

https://www.google.co.uk/maps

Then go to My Maps

Select 'Create New Map'

Click on 'Add Layer'

Click on 'Import' and browse to and select the file

Other websites

Other websites to explore are:

Bing Maps   http://209.118.90.140/MapMartBingMaps/Map.aspx

Earth Explorer   http://earthexplorer.usgs.gov/

Chapter 9

Drones

Drones – also known as UAVs (Unmanned Aerial Vehicles) – are remotely controlled aerial vehicles that can be used for surveying historic buildings, monuments, landscapes and sites. Drones serve as platforms for sensors – most commonly cameras, but this can also include devices such as hyper-spectral imaging units and laser scanners that enable the rapid collection of high-quality aerial data at multiple scales and resolutions. Using these techniques, drone imagery offers the opportunity to view sites and monuments in their wider landscape, to create detailed photographic records, to generate ortho-images for integration into GIS systems and for use in drawing plans, and to produce three-dimensional photogrammetric and terrain models. Drones can also provide dramatic videos for media engagement and other outputs.

Figure 9.1
Preparing for
drone operation

Drones have become standard tools for archaeological field recording. While airborne and satellite data can provide large-scale photographic coverage, closer-range aerial images enable more detailed recording. Until recently, such imagery was commonly captured using cameras attached to tethered platforms such as balloons or kites, or from the ground using poles. In these methods, the operator had limited control over the direction of the camera, and was reliant on the camera's pre-programmed settings. These techniques have been superseded by drones. Their greater precision and control, their flexibility and ease-of-use allow the capture of large amounts of data at high resolutions, typically from 20 to 200 m above the ground. The modern versions are very easy to fly and the skills can be acquired by anyone.

Types of drones

Two types of drones are typically used for heritage-related applications: multi-rotor and fixed-wing platforms. Each platform has different capabilities that determine the type of sensor it can carry. When selecting a platform, it is important to consider which model would best achieve the project objectives.

(A) Multi-rotor system

Multi-rotor platforms are made of a central body with multiple rotors that power propellers to fly and manoeuvre the drone. There are usually four rotors (a quadcopter), but there can be as many as six (a hexacopter) or eight (an octocopter). Multi-rotor drones are more manoeuvrable than fixed-wing systems, making them ideal for surveying and mapping sites.

Advantages
more manoeuvrable
able to hover
can use gyro-stabilised mounts

Disadvantages
shorter battery life and slower flight speed restrict the range of operation
pre-planning of flight routes is not universally supplied
may be prohibited in designated areas where they are a threat to bird life

(B) Fixed-wing systems

Fixed-wing platforms are larger in size, with a wingspan from 60 cm to 2 m across. Fixed-wing drones can fly uninterrupted over long distances. This system is limited in the type and weight of sensor it can carry. Fixed-wing systems are generally used for landscape surveys, and are less suited to recording vertical features such as buildings or monuments, or for the day-to-day recording of sites.

Figure 9.2 A DJI Phantom IV multicopter drone being operated at the site of Tello

Figure 9.3 Launching a fixed wing drone (courtesy Prof. Jason Ur)

Advantages
longer battery life and faster flight speeds allow long-range operations
more accurate GNSS receivers
can cover large areas in pre-programmed strips
can carry better cameras

Disadvantages
less manoeuvrable
cannot hover

In addition to mounting cameras, drones can also carry other types of sensors to record non-visible portions of the electro-magnetic spectrum. Infrared sensors or ultraviolet sensors can detect subtle features that may not be visible to the naked eye. Thermal imaging sensors record heat signatures, which may be able to indicate the presence or absence of buried structures. LiDAR sensors measure reflected laser beams to create high-precision modelling of the surface topography – as LiDAR can penetrate vegetation, drone-mounted LiDAR survey has the potential to investigate even heavily heavily-wooded areas.

Applications of drones in archaeology

Landscape survey

Drones can be used to capture photographs for large-scale landscape survey. Fixed-wing drones are particularly suitable for this purpose. In optimal conditions, current models can cover up to 10 km² a day. Other types of sensors, such as infrared scanners, can help improve the visibility of archaeological features through the detection of crop marks, soil marks or heat signatures. LiDAR can help investigate archaeological landscapes hidden beneath vegetation and woodland. The data captured can be used to create high-resolution images, maps and digital elevation models. The speed and precision of this type of mapping have superseded traditional mapping and survey methodologies used only a few years ago.

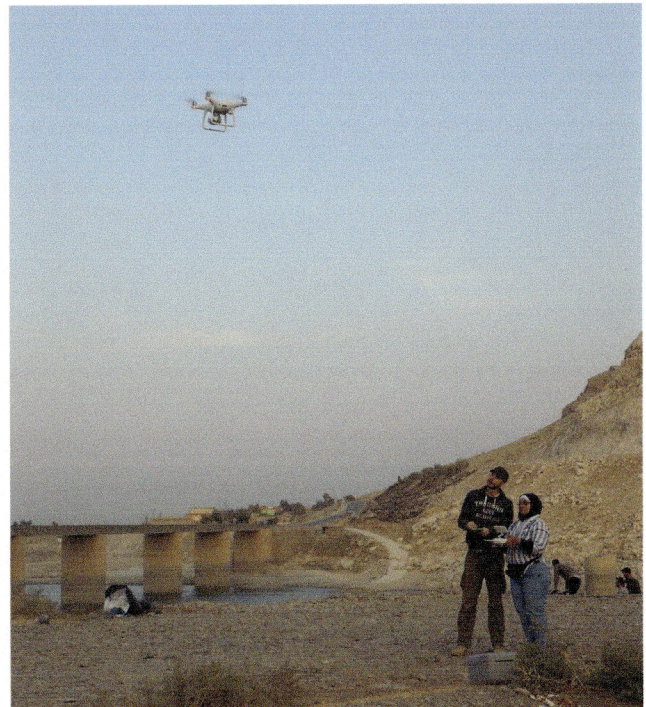

▶ Figure 9.4 Commencing local survey at Usu Aska

Recording monuments

Because of their ability to hover in place, multi-rotor drones are well suited for recording monuments and structures and capturing images from above and from oblique angles (note, though, that some fixed-wing platforms now offer an in-flight 'tilting' function). This particularly applies to recording structures that are not easily accessible, or that contain elements that are inaccessible or hidden from view; for example, remote ruins and rock reliefs. Drones can also fly over to investigate and record areas that are too dangerous to approach. Images taken by drones can help visualise and understand the relationship between monuments and their surrounding landscapes.

Digital Elevation Models

The imagery from drones can be used to create Digital Elevation Models (for more on DEMs, see the sections on Satellite Imagery and GIS above). These are important records and can help understand the morphology, development and use of a site. DEMs can also play a role

Figure 9.5 A drone recording an Assyrian rock relief in the Darband-i Rania (courtesy Prof. Peter Miglus)

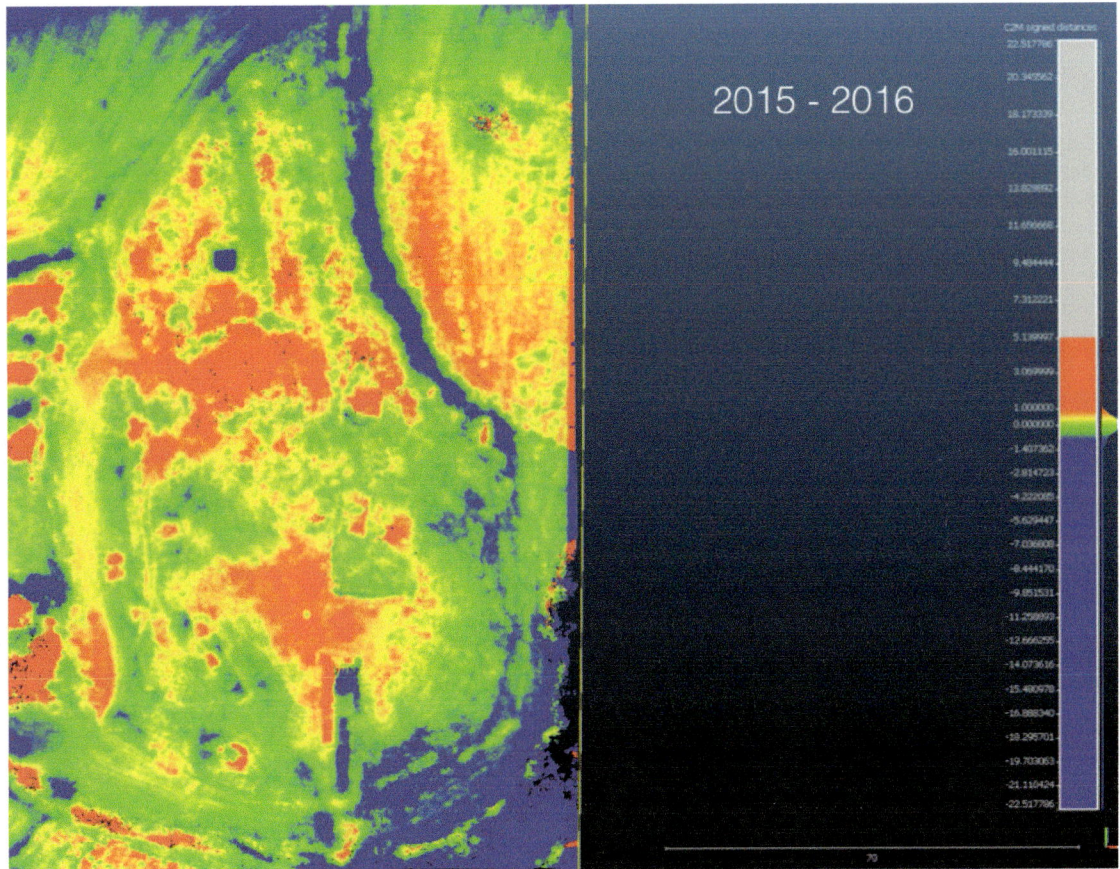

Figure 9.6
Digital Elevation
Model of the
site of Kani
Shai showing
changes in site
morphology
between
autumn 2015
and 2016
(courtesy Dr.
Ricardo Cabral)

in monitoring and assessing landscapes, sites and monuments with respect to conservation and protection. By comparing DEMs generated over time it is possible to map changes to the site and detect damage caused by erosion, construction, agricultural encroachment, looting and other sources of damage.

Ortho-images

An important use of drone imagery is to supply the raw material for the creation of 'ortho-mosaics'. These are generated by a computer from multiple photographs overlapped and stitched together at a single scale to create an image with each point depicted from directly above. Ortho-images have two great advantages: they can be uploaded as a layer into a GIS, and they can be uploaded into a graphics programme such as Adobe Illustrator, allowing for the quick, easy and accurate creation of digitised plans. It is common practice when capturing images for the ortho-mosaic to place markers with unique geometric patterns around the area being recorded; this facilitates the programme in recognising how to stitch the images together.

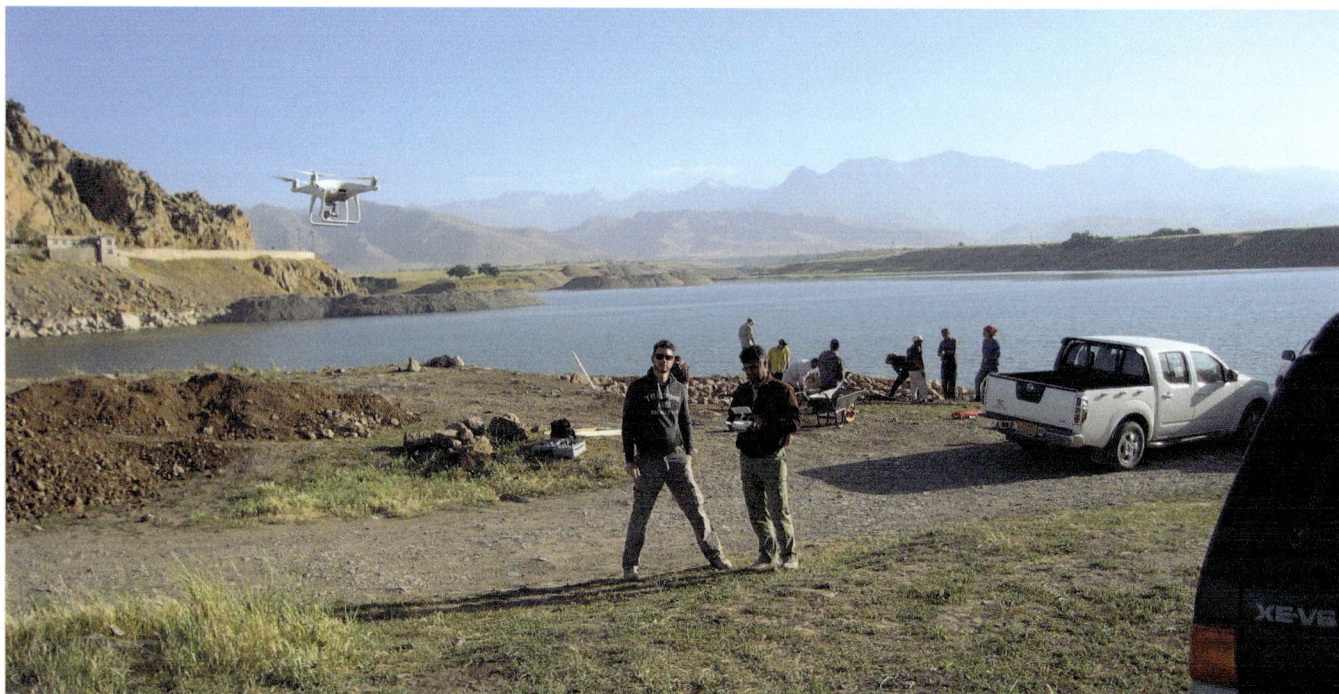

Figure 9.7
Recording the
excavations at
Usu Aska with a
drone

Excavation recording

Multi-rotor drones have become standard tools for recording archaeological excavations. The ease with which drones are launched and their capacity for rapid data collection mean that drones can be used to record different stages of an excavation over the course of a season – even on a daily basis. Of course, an archaeological project using a drone in this way must have the means to store the many large data files that will be produced. Also, as multiple aerial images of the same trench can be confusing, it is important for the person processing the data to liaise closely with the trench supervisor to ensure that phases, contexts and structures are accurately identified and described.

Geo-referencing

For images that will be incorporated into GIS systems it is important that the imagery is geo-referenced. This is achieved by including fixed ground control points in the area being surveyed – these can be obvious points on landmarks (such as the corner of a building or marks painted onto buildings or large rocks), fixed survey points or temporary markers.

False colour imagery

In some cases, particularly where imagery has recorded crop marks or heat signatures, it may be that processing in false colours may show up features that are either obscure or invisible in the raw data.

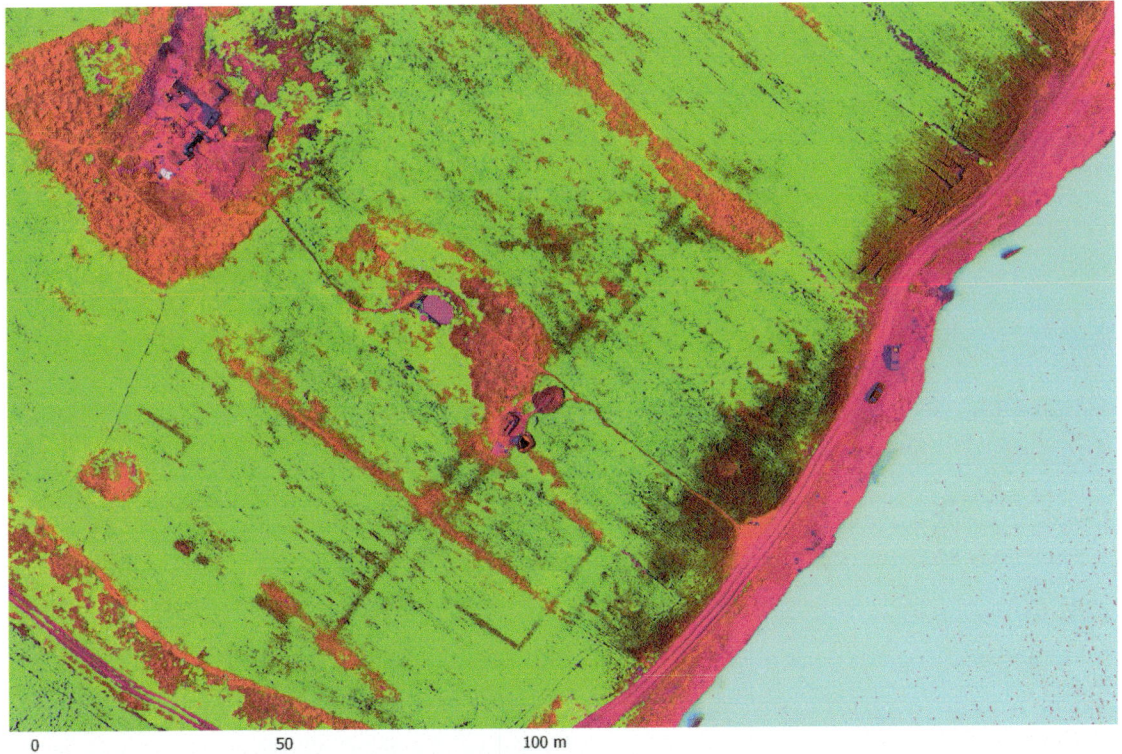

Figure 9.8 False colour image showing lines of walls in the the southern part of Qalatga Darband

0   50   100 m

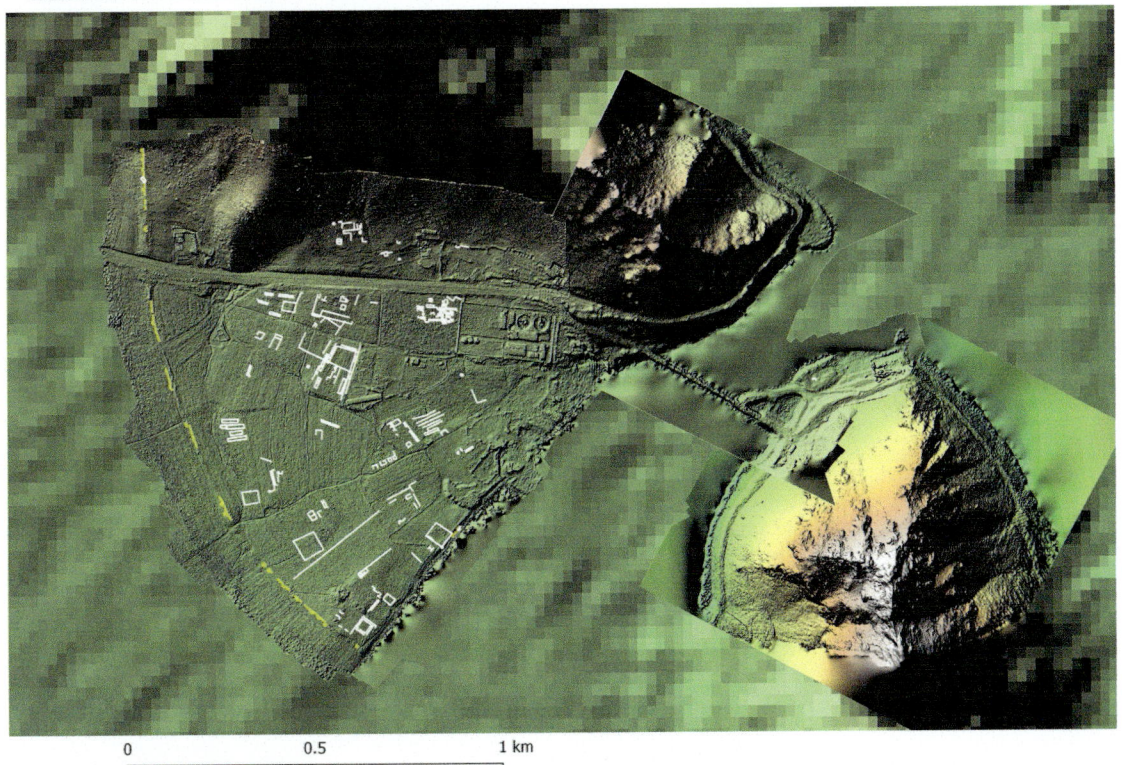

Figure 9.9 Tracings of linear features appearing as crop marks at Qalatga Darband

0   0.5   1 km

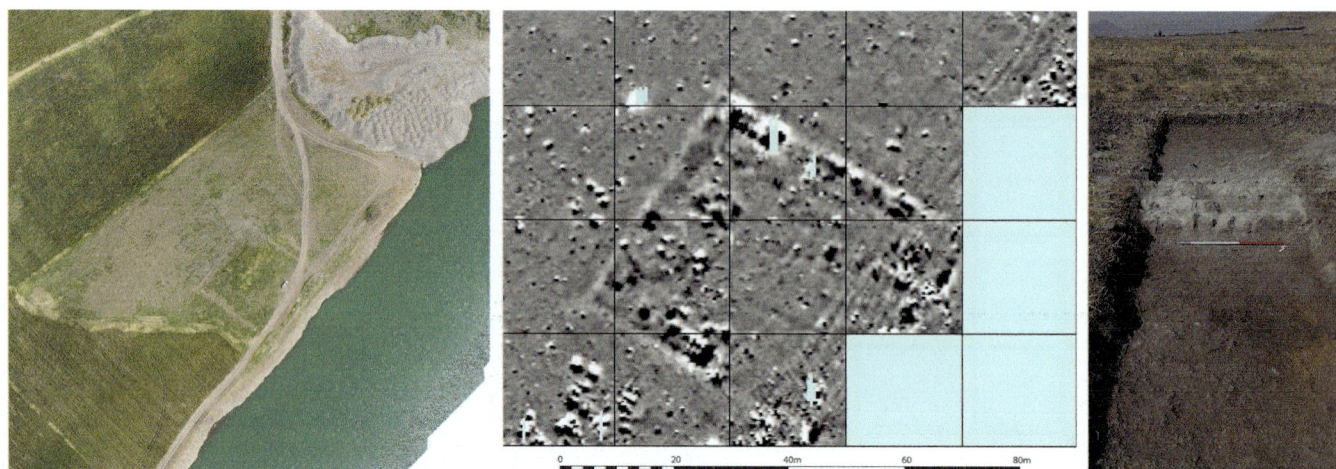

(a) discovered by drone survey, followed up by (b) surveying the area with magnetometry and (c) a ground-truthing trench across one of the wall lines

Figure 9.10 A structure on the southeastern edge of Qalatga Darband

Ground-truthing

As with all remote sensing, there may be features that you can see in the drone imagery that would benefit from ground-truthing. In the image below, a rectilinear feature noticed in the drone imagery at Qalatga Darband, which was not visible either in the satellite image or on the ground, was confirmed firstly by mapping the area with magnetometry and then by laying out a trench for ground-truthing across one of the wall lines.

General considerations

Images acquired by drones should be studied and interpreted by someone with an experienced eye. Therefore, an important part of the process is to visit the site or area before the drone is flown to form a good understanding of the landscape or site prior to analysing the patterns observed from the air. This will also help distinguish between features, for example between tracks and watercourses, which may appear very similar from the air – the wrong interpretation can have a huge effect on the understanding of a site or region.

Weather and lighting

Drones can operate in a range of environments and field settings, such as different lighting and seasonal and land-use conditions. However, strong winds can significantly affect their manoeuvrability, rain can damage the sensors and water droplets can obscure the camera lens. Weather will also determine the quality of the images that the drone can collect. The fundamental

Figure 9.11
Using a
drone in the
landscape

rules of standard photography apply to drone use, as no amount of technical sophistication during the data processing stage can account for poor weather, lighting or composition. Where possible, images for compilation into ortho-images or 3D models should be captured in similar lighting conditions; if acquired over several days, then the drone should be flown at the same time each day to allow for changing shadows, or on cloudy days when no shadows are cast.

Regulations and restrictions

Most countries have regulations concerning drone use. It is important to thoroughly familiarise yourself with the local regulations. Although regulations will vary from country to country, they usually include:

obtaining a permit to operate a drone
restrictions on the weight of drone and camera (or other sensor)
restrictions on the height to which a drone can fly
restricted areas within which drones are forbidden to fly, such as near airspaces, international borders, urban areas, police stations, military installations, and nature reserves

Some tips

Before commencing flying, write a mobile number on the drone in indelible ink – if it gets lost this gives some chance that it can be returned to you.

Do not fly in strong or gusty winds.

Do not try using the drone to lift things.

When flying a drone always keep it in sight and do not fly it above 120 m or further than 4 km away.

Watch out for power lines and other obstacles.

It is critical to keep away from restricted areas such as military and police stations, airports and any other designated infrastructure: while the internal programming should prevent the drone from entering such restricted airspace, it remains the responsibility of the operator to ensure that there is no infringement.

Figure 9.12
Operating the
drone control

Figure 9.13
Drone image of
the site of Tello
(Girsu)

In case of a problem, for example, if you lose sight of the drone or if it is not responding to commands, use the Return-to-Home option to bring it back.

Chapter 10

Database

A functioning and efficient database is at the heart of a well-run project. The database is, at the first level, the repository for all the data generated by the project – contexts, finds, samples, plans and sections, object illustrations, photographs and all manner of associated information relating to the conservation, processing and study of the excavated material. This information is collected by the registrar. But there is more to archaeological registration and documentation than just recording this data. The information recorded becomes meaningful when relationships and links can be established; for example, between finds and contexts. The database is therefore more than just a data repository. By enabling the information to be manipulated and put into perspective, the database is also an essential research tool. An archaeological project database thus has a double purpose: to be used during excavations for information recording, and during post-excavation work for information analysis.

The example above (Fig. 10.1) shows a typical example of the the flow of materials from the field via the hands of the registrar and and on to other specialists. Complicated as it is, this is still a simplification, as other categories of materials (such as chipped stones, glass and slag) might be separated out in the field, and additional specialists might be involved, both for these and for other classes of artefacts such as seals, sculptures and so on.

Figure 10.1 Schematic representation showing the flow of materials from the field into the registrar and onto specialists (solid lines), and the entry of the information generated into the database (dashed lines)

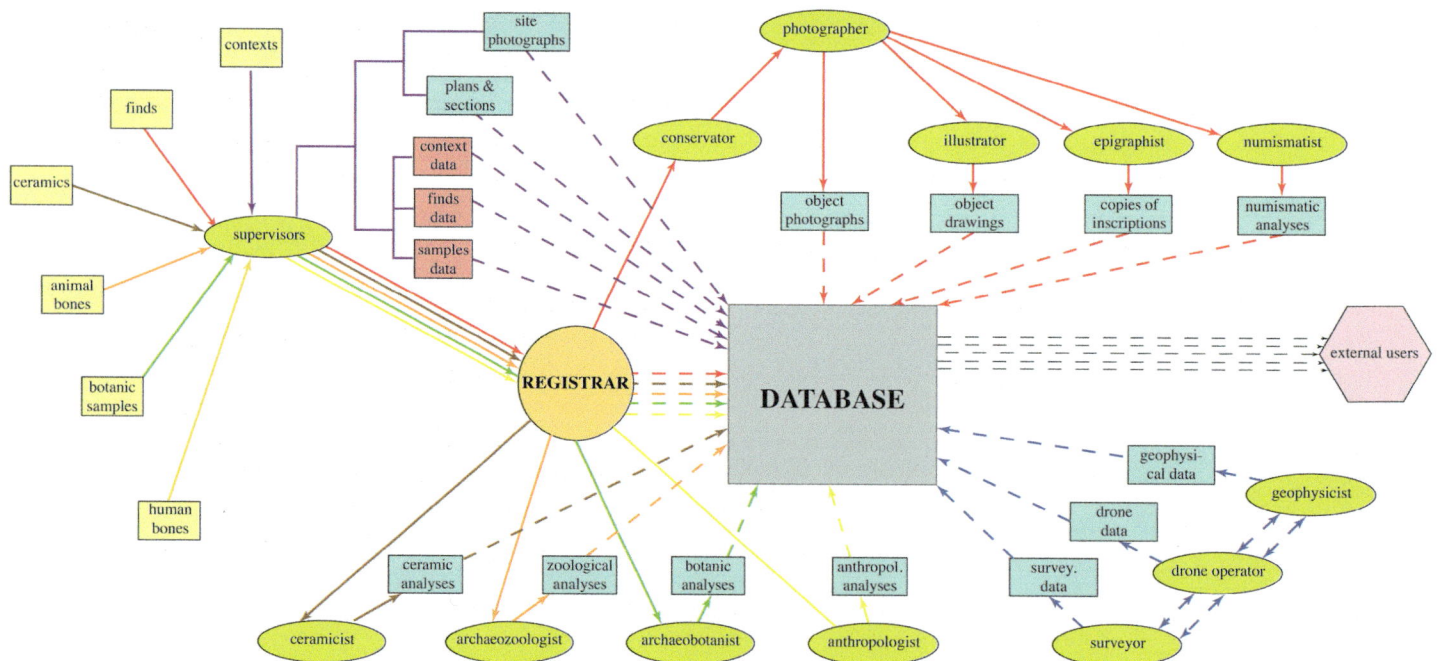

Database design

The database for each project is purpose designed, individually tailored to the requirements of the project in terms of methodology, material to be generated and research objectives. The design of the database should take place prior to the commencement of the fieldwork, so that it is in place and ready for use once excavation begins. Since the scope of each project will determine what is expected from the database, its design should be discussed at the outset between the field director and the registrar.

The main questions to address when designing an archaeological database are:

What information will be recorded?
e.g. finds data, excavations data, photographic images, illustrations, conservation data
How will this information be recorded?
e.g. transcribed from paper-based information, upload of digital information

Who will record information?
e.g. registrar, supervisors, conservator, other specialists

How will the database be delivered during and after the excavations?
e.g. by individual or shared computers? Via a router? Over the internet?

Resources and requirements

Designing a bespoke archaeological database is a substantial task, and time and resources need to be allocated accordingly. Ideally, a qualified database designer should be engaged to carry out the technical aspects of the database design, undertaken in consultation with the field director and the registrar (who may in turn wish to bring in the contributions of other specialists, such as site supervisors and those responsible for conservation, illustration and photography).

The main requirements of database design are to:

- enable accurate, consistent and secure recording of information
- enable relational links between data sections and data points (individual data entries)
- meet the needs of all team members (field director, archaeologists, specialists)

In all events, the database should be comprehensively tested before being launched to ensure that it is fully operational from the first day in the field. It is also important to think about longer term aspects such as technology obsolescence and data legacy in order to settle on a solution which will span the full lifetime of the project (and not just the immediate aftermath of the fieldwork).

Database sections and fields

The database can include any section deemed appropriate to the scope and needs of the project in terms of information recording and analysis. The two core sections are for finds and archaeological contexts. Accessory sections may gravitate around these two core sections to host related digital content such as photographs, illustrations, plans and drawings. Ideally, the database should also include additional sections for other activities such as conservation, ceramic processing, geophysics and other forms of remote sensing, and specialist studies such as epigraphy and numismatics. In any case, each section should be designed in consultation with its main user – the conservator for the conservation section, the epigrapher for the epigraphy section – so that the data fields are perfectly adapted to the nature of the information to be recorded. Below we give examples of the core sections of find registration and archaeological context, with comments on the specifications for data fields, links between data points, and user interface.

Finds registration database section

Information recording in the finds registration section of the database follows the principles outlined in the section on Registration below. Data fields can be configured to ensure that these principles are applied in practice.

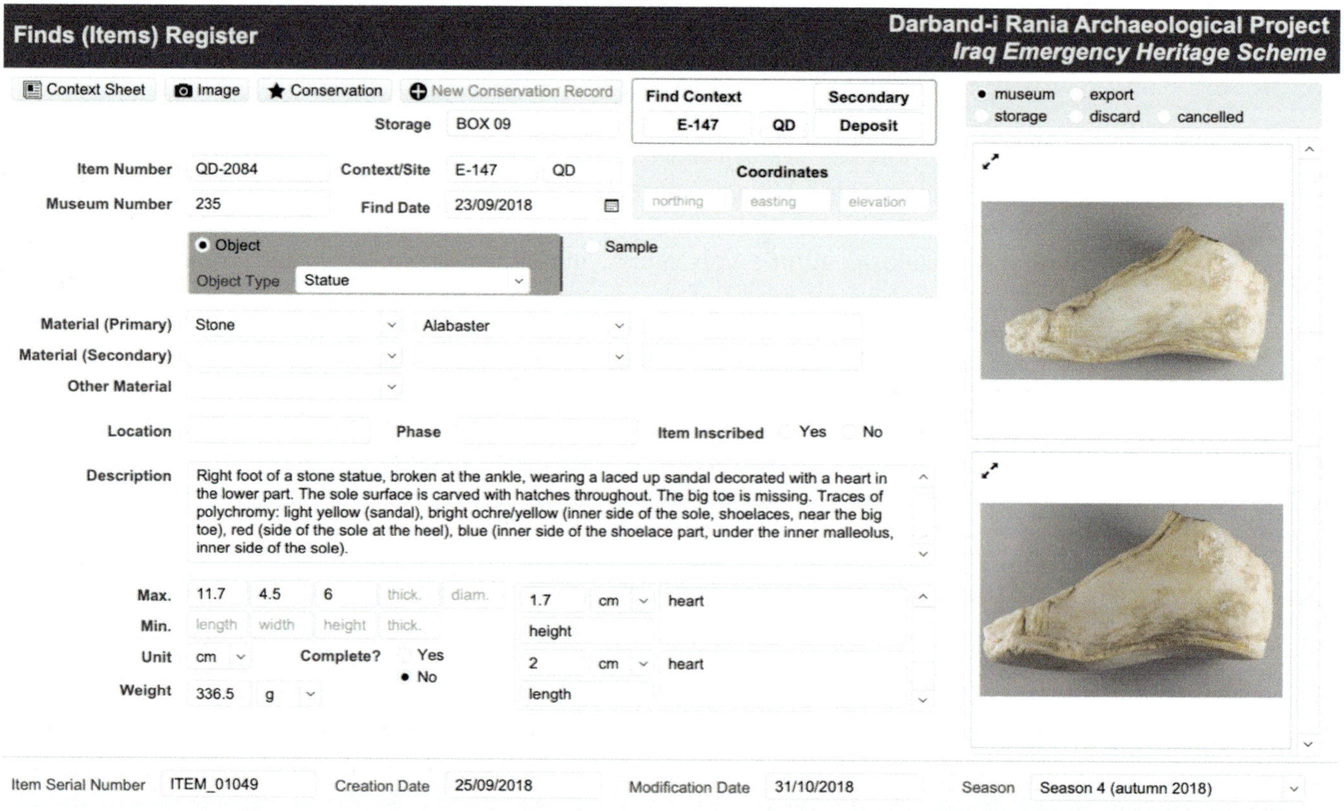

Figure 10.2 Example of a section in a database for finds registration

In the example presented here, all the basic pieces of information – item number (field number), context number, date, find type – are recorded in mandatory fields. When making an entry in the database, a mandatory field cannot be left empty and the user cannot exit the find record without filling out all the mandatory fields. The use of mandatory fields is therefore good practice in order to ensure that all essential information is duly recorded. Note that the item number is recorded in a field that automatically checks whether the number already exists in the database, thereby avoiding duplicate entries. This is essential to ensure that identification numbers remain unique.

To ensure that information is consistently recorded, some fields may be populated through a prepared list of options. In the example presented here, the object typology and material fields allow the user to choose the relevant description from a list of terms presented in a drop-down menu.

Some accessory fields may also automatically record data. Auto-enter fields are useful to date records, and therefore information. Timestamps can be considered for indicating the date of both when a record was created and when it was last modified.

The finds registration section of the database presented here links to other sections, such as archaeological contexts, photographs, digitised drawings and conservation records. The information recorded in these sections is linked to the find registration information by the links established in the relational structure of the database.

Archaeological context database section

The fields in the archaeological contexts section of the database also need to be configured in a way that ensures that the information is recorded consistently and accurately. For example, the field for the unique archaeological context number is mandatory and set to only allow unique values. The contexts section also displays information from other sections of the database. All associated imagery, such as photographs and plans and sections, is displayed in the right-hand side of the screen and listed at the bottom. The user can access each file by simply clicking on it. The relationship between archaeological context and finds, established during the finds registration process, is also displayed on the screen and clickable. The interface gathers related data points and sections in one view, thus providing further insight into the recorded information.

Technical specifications

This section presents the main technical aspects to consider when building, delivering and maintaining a database.

Software

The double purpose of the database of both recording and analysing information will influence what software is chosen to build it. In any case, the mixed nature and the broad scope of the data

Images	**Darband-i Rania Archaeological Project** *Iraq Emergency Heritage Scheme*	Objects/ Samples

Context Sheet	Continuation Sheet	Ceramics	Find & Sort	Season 1 (autumn 2016)

Context Number E-046

Site QD
Area E   Trench

Supervisor VP   **Data Entry**
Start Date 24/10/2016   **End Date** 27/10/2016

Context Type
Deposit

Reliability
Primary   Tertiary   Clear   Mixed
● Secondary   Context Deleted   ● Merging

Context Date

Phase

Room Number 2   **Corridor Number**

Description
Deposits: composition, compaction, inclusions, colour
Structure: material, inclusions, brick sizes, mortar joins, bonding

This context equals
E-049;

Compact clayey deposit above the suprafloor. It contained jar fragments (E-057,E-058 and E-059) and statue fragments. No more roof tiles in the deposit.

Composition: clayey silt with charcoal spots
Compaction: compact
Inclusions: few large stones, few small stones
Colour: dark yellowish brown and black ashy spots.
Very similar deposit to E-047 and E-071, E-087 in the other rooms.

Question: trash deposit or leveling deposit or intended filling?

	Length	Width	Height/Depth	Elevations	
Max	5	5	55	Max Elevation	510.549
Min			45	Min Elevation	509.689
Unit	m	m	cm		

Stratigraphic Relationships *Insert Context and Site*

Is Above	Cuts	Fills	Abuts	Part of	Equals
E-065 QD					E-049 QD
E-067 QD					

Is Below	Cut by	Filled by	Bonds with	Consists of	Associated with
E-034 QD				E-057 QD	E-057 QD
				E-058 QD	E-058 QD
				E-059 QD	E-059 QD

Bulk Finds

X Bone	X Shell			Object/Sample Numbers 🗐 See all		
Chipped stone	Slag	Sieved?	● Yes No	QD-1169	Object	Statue
Glass		Sieve Mesh Size?	Sieve Mesh	QD-1197	Sample	Soil
X Metal				QD-1198	Sample	Charcoal
Modern finds		% Sieved?	100%	QD-1210	Object	Statue
Pottery						

Representations 🗐 See all

Photograph	QD_E-042_E-046_E-048_E	Room 2 overview 2017 spring
Photograph	QD_E-042_E-046_E-048_E	Room 2 overview 2017 spring
Photograph	QD_E-046_7_VP.jpg	Jars
Photograph	QD_E-046_8_VP.jpg	jars
Photograph	QD_E-046_9_VP.jpg	jars

Record Creation Date 04/11/2016   **Record Last Modification Date** 20/09/2018

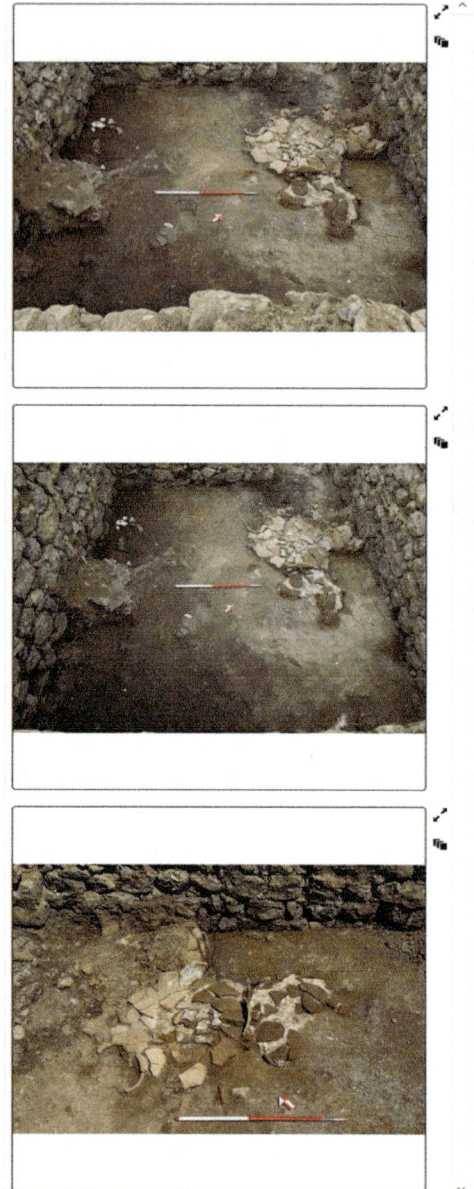

to be recorded (contexts, finds, conservation, photography, etc.) calls for a relational database that can link data sections and points. Other aspects to consider include pricing, support and maintenance, and platform operability.

Figure 10.3 Example of a section in a database for archaeological contexts

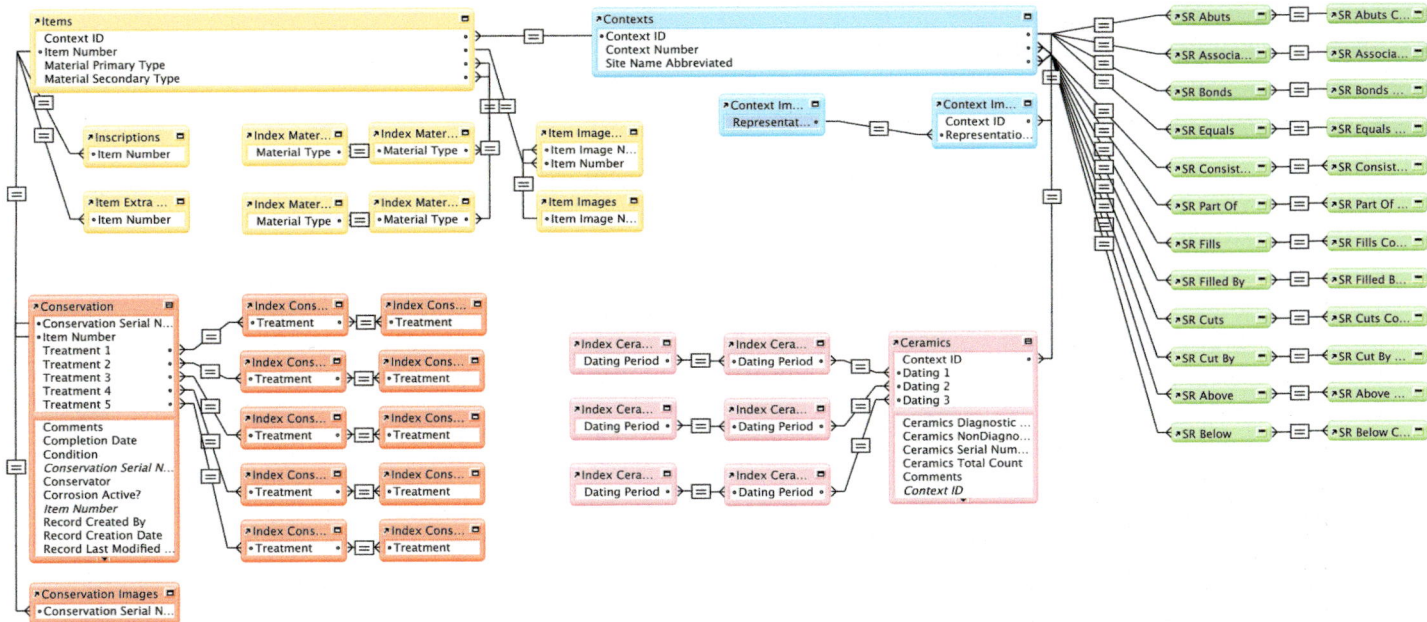

Figure 10.4 Structure of a relational database showing the relationships between data sections

There are a number of relational database programmes available on the market. At the time of writing, the two main programmes are Microsoft Access® (MS Access) and Claris FileMaker® (FileMaker). The two offer similar options, but they differ in that FileMaker is cross-platform, i.e. it can be used on both MacOS and Windows operating systems, whereas MS Access is restricted to Windows systems. FileMaker also has the advantage of offering more flexibility in terms of design (back-end) and user interface (front-end), thus enabling the creation of a bespoke, easy-to-use solution adapted to each project. Note that Microsoft Excel® (Excel) is a spreadsheet programme and not a database. As such, Excel may be used to create lists, but it cannot be used to dynamically link or analyse information.

Database delivery

Alongside designing the core features of the database, its mode of delivery and the hardware necessary to do this should be considered from the outset. Different set-up options can be considered. How to choose the best-suited option depends on the facilities offered in the dig house during excavations and in the office for post-excavation work, on the size of the team, and on whether team members need to use the database simultaneously. In all cases, a single designated computer should be allocated for the exclusive use of hosting the database.

Single computer operation

The database is hosted on a computer with team-members only using this one computer for database access and use. This option is the easiest and the cheapest set-up to implement, but it is also the least flexible and collaborative since it only enables one team member to use the database at any one time. This set-up therefore requires a tight schedule of allocated time slots to access the database and is only suitable for small teams.

Networked provision

The database is delivered on multiple computers through a network and/or server architecture. This set-up is the most flexible, but implementing it requires more technical and hardware resources (whether wired through cables, or wireless through a router) and greater expertise to set up and run. The use of a server may also involve additional costs from the database software provider, e.g. a FileMaker Server licence. As a result, this form of delivery is also more expensive. In a network/server set-up, the database is still hosted on a single dedicated computer, but it can be delivered simultaneously to multiple computers. In practice, this means that team members can access the database as and when they need.

Hardware

Whichever delivery set-up is used poses questions of storage, back-up and power supply. The risk of data loss associated with sudden power cuts can be mitigated by choosing appropriate equipment and accessories. Laptops have built-in batteries that normally enable them to continue operating for a period of up to a few hours in case of power cuts: they should therefore be preferred over desktop computers. Any other electrical equipment without emergency batteries (e.g. the router, hard drives, etc) can be plugged into a dedicated uninterruptible power supply (UPS).

The information recorded in the database needs to be safely stored and backed up. How much storage space is needed should be estimated at the beginning of the database design process and reassessed regularly through the life of the project. Storage capacity should consider both active data (database and associated files) as well as back-up data. Depending on the set-up chosen to deliver the database, active data may be stored on the hosting computer (single computer set-up) or on the hosting server (server set-up). Back-up data should be stored on external hard drives, preferably portable ones with built-in batteries. It is good practice to have separate sets of back-up hard drives: a set to be used in the dig house during the excavations, and a set to be used at the end of the excavations to create an extra safety backup. Keeping in mind that the amount of information to be recorded in the database will grow as the project goes on, including very large numbers of heavy files such as photographs and illustrations, the capacity of the hard drives should be in the range of terabytes (Tb) rather than gigabytes (Gb).

Documentation protocols

Establishing protocols for all aspects of the documentation of an archaeological project is necessary to ensure that information is recorded consistently and fully and safely stored. In practice, documentation protocols fall within the remit of archaeological registration. Accordingly, it normally works very well (and is a common solution) for the registrar and the database manager to be the same person.

Database management

Backing-up the data

The information recorded during the life of the project represents an enormous amount of work from multiple team members. To mitigate the risk of losing data, this information should be backed up regularly and securely. The schedule chosen for doing this should find a balance between frequency and storage capacity: the more frequent the back-up, the more storage space needed. Ideally, during the excavations data should be backed-up every day (preferably after the end of work) and every week (preferably after end of work on the last working day). To make efficient use of storage space, daily back-ups can be kept for up to two weeks and then deleted, while weekly back-ups can be kept for up to a month.

Access

Regardless of the sensitivity of the information stored in the database, it is best practice to control access to the data. This is usually achieved by setting up password-protected user profiles with different levels of access.

The three main levels of access are normally:

full access: access to front-end and back-end use of the database, data entry and query rights, record creation and deletion rights, administration rights. Typically, this level of access would be for the registrar and database manager only.

data entry: access to front-end use of the database, data entry and query rights, record creation and deletion rights. Typically, this level of access would be for team members needing to record information in the database, such as site supervisors, conservators, illustrators, photographers and other specialists.

read-only: access to front-end use of the database, data query rights. Typically, this level of access would be for those users only needing to consult (and not alter or update) the database, such as external researchers.

Beside the levels of access regarding what the user can or cannot do, user profiles also determine which sections of the database can be accessed, and how. Combining levels of access and user profiles helps adapt the database to the needs of team users. For example, the registrar's profile can be set to open the database on the finds page, the conservator's profile to do so on the conservation section, and so on.

Training

The database is a complex infrastructure, but its operation does not have to be complicated. While the original design of the database will ensure ease of use, anyone granted access to the database should be trained beforehand. Systematic training sessions may be offered to all new team members and tailored to each. For example, training for field archaeologists will give more attention to the context-sheet section of the database. In addition to training, it is important that the database manager remains available for any additional support that may be required during and after the excavations. It may also be useful to write practical reference guides to distribute to the team.

Post-excavation access

At the end of each season, the computer hosting the database should travel back with the field director, along with the back-up drives. Access to the database after the excavations have finished, when team members are scattered in different locations, poses technological challenges. For many members of the team the principal requirement may be to have access to the information recorded in the database during the season, i.e. read-only access. The easiest way of providing remote access on a read-only basis may be to create individual clones of the database, either in the original format or as a PDF. More advanced solutions, allowing full remote (and operational) access to team-members are possible, whether delivered through websites or in Cloud-based programmes. Such solutions are, however, expensive and to be implemented require more resources in terms of hardware, expertise, requirements for on-going maintenance, training and trouble-shooting.

Figure 10.5
Pottery in from the field and awaiting registration in the database

Chapter 11

Surface Collection

The collection and analysis of the material present on the surface of a site is a straight-forward but very useful means of gaining an insight into the archaeology below. At the very least this will give you a picture (not necessarily complete) of periods represented at the site, at the best it can allow you to make conclusions about period distribution and the nature of the subsurface remains. In Iraq, the introduction of formal surface collection can be credited to Gaston Cros at the beginning of the twentieth century (see Chapter 3). In the course of his reconnaissances around the site of Tello he collected surface sherds from the sites he visited and compared these with the

Figure 11.1
Surface
collection

pottery known from Tello in order to date them. In the later twentieth century, and particularly after World War II, surface collection emerged as a natural component of site reconnaissance in the context of regional survey. The controlled collection of surface material on sites is a natural development from this.

Before starting on a surface collection it is important to be aware that the collection of surface material constitutes removal of information and a change of the integrity of the site. It is therefore important to be clear what the aim of the collection is, how it will be conducted, recorded, and analysed, and what arrangements will be made for long-term storage of the material. There is also a difference between the collection of surface material in the course of a regional survey and the intensive collection of material from a single site which forms the focus of an excavation project. In the case of regional survey, the primary aim is to collect evidence for the overall occupational history of a site, paying attention to the shape and areas of the site as appropriate. The aim of an intensive survey focused on one site is to establish a much more detailed picture of what can be learnt about the nature and layout of the site from these surface materials. The differences in these objectives affect the nature of the collection: surface collections for sites in a regional survey are likely to be organised over larger units and, unless the amount of surface material is very small, will not aim for total collection. Surface surveys of sites forming the focus of dedicated field projects will be organised by smaller collection units and may well aim for total collection.

Of course the greatest bulk of material found on the surface is almost always going to be pottery. Traditionally this is key for dating, but may have other messages to tell – a scatter of crucible fragments is likely to relate to a metal-production area, a concentration of *pithos* (large jars) fragments probably indicates a storage area, the presence of fineware might be a sign of elite housing, oven fragments hint at an area where food production took place, and so on. Depending on the date of the site, fired bricks may give some indication of date and point to the presence of more important architecture. An area of roof tiles will indicate not just an occupation of Hellenistic/Parthian date, but also the presence of a high-status building. Other finds such as fragments of sculpture, stone bowls, flints, figurines, inscriptions and coins will also be important in interpreting the date and function of the site.

In the case of prehistoric and/or aceramic sites, and other sites where there is a large quantity of artefacts and debitage from the production of artefacts in flint, chert and obsidian, a decision needs to be made about how and how much of this to collect. In this respect, the difference in aims between regional survey and a single site forming the focus of an excavation project is pertinent. A regional survey will want to collect material for identification and dating without

Figure 11.2
Squares
flagged out
for surface
collection at
Tello

stripping the site of its surface data, leaving this intact for a dedicated operation: a restricted collection with attention paid especially to tools and without collecting too much general debitage would be enough. By contrast. a focused field project on a prehistoric site is likely to aim for total collection of sherds (if present) and lithics in small units, such as 10 x 10 m squares: not only will the drop-off in density help establish the site limits, but total collection is necessary as the lithics (and ceramics) need to be washed in order to identify diagnostics that serve as indicators for both dating and the location of specialised activity areas.

There are many different ways of approaching surface collection. Sites can be collected according to a geometric system – for example, a grid or radial lines – or divided up according to their natural topography. Below we give examples of different systems. This list will not be exhaustive, but it does give a good range of possible approaches. The method you choose will depend a lot on the type of site and how much is already known, what your objectives are, and the resources and time available. One thing to stress, though, is that these methods are most applicable to smaller sites and to low-lying sites with open areas. Surface collection is more problematic on large

mounds, where the results can be much more ambiguous due to the burial of older layers sometimes very deeply below the surface, the recycling of materials in brick-making and other factors. Tightly nucleated settlements from earlier periods may be deeply buried below later remains and may present little or nothing in the way of surface traces. Conversely, the recycling of materials on a mound is likely to result in surface material which has been displaced.

Informal collection

Collecting material from the surface of a site without further division or recording: this is the simplest form of collection, but of course the least precise and least informative. It may be suitable when covering many sites in a regional survey, particularly with small or very small sites, but it does not preserve spatial information and is not suitable for the detailed study of an individual site.

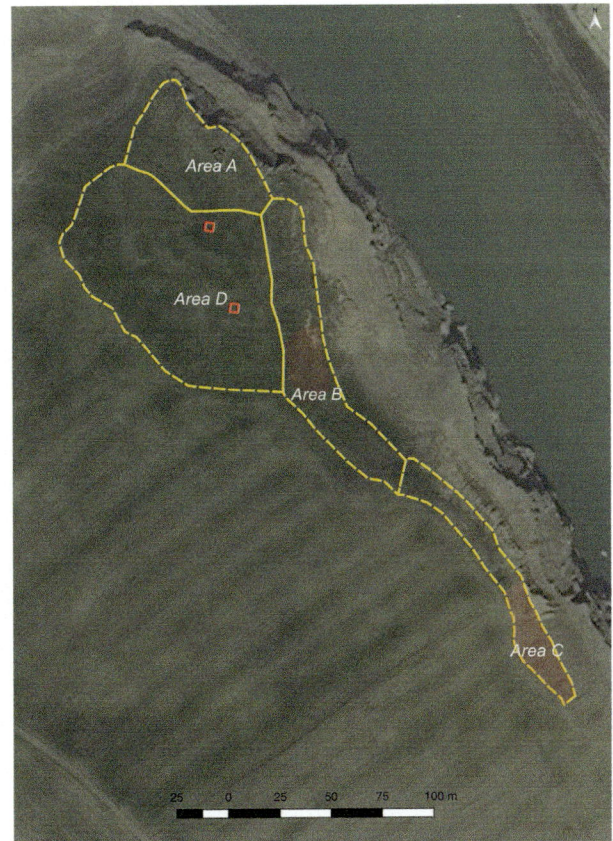

Figure 11.3 Surface collection areas at Murad Rasu determined by natural topography

Natural Topography

This method works by dividing up a site according to its natural topography and other obvious features – for example, the top of a mound, the slopes on different sides, areas in the lower town, fortification walls, ancient canal beds, outlying elevations and so on. It may be that features of the modern landscape, such as streams, roads, fences, farm buildings and electricity and pipe lines, contribute to the delineation of areas. This method requires having or making a map illustrating the different areas. This can be from a local map (if sufficiently detailed), an extract of a satellite image or a plan sketched with the help of some measurements. This method is considerably more useful than informal collection, and can be useful when collecting materials for regional surveys from middle-sized and larger sites.

Grid (total area coverage)

This approach involves creating a grid for the site and collecting material according to this. The laying out of a grid needs to be done by a surveyor. An important decision is the size of the squares collected: for instance, on a small site you might opt for 10 x 10 m squares, on a larger site for 20 x 20 m or even 50 x 50 m squares. The method normally proceeds with people walking in a line across the square, so one factor in the calculations will be the number of people available – it is, for example, possible to walk a 50 x 50 m square in one go if you have enough people, or it could be walked in two 25 m wide strips. The advantage of this method is that it will give you complete coverage with good spatial control. The disadvantage is that it takes a good deal of time to lay out and execute. But it is the optimum method for a detailed and intensive study of small and medium sites.

Grid (sampling)

This approach again involves creating a grid for the site and collecting material according to this. However, in this case, total coverage is not aimed for, but rather the collection of a representative sample. Typically, the sampling might be restricted to just one part of each main grid square (for example, the southwestern corner or the middle of the square), or to alternating squares, or a combination of both. In all cases, the laying out of a grid needs to be done by a surveyor. The method is best suited to medium and large-scale sites. The advantage is that it will give you quicker coverage of a site with good spatial control.

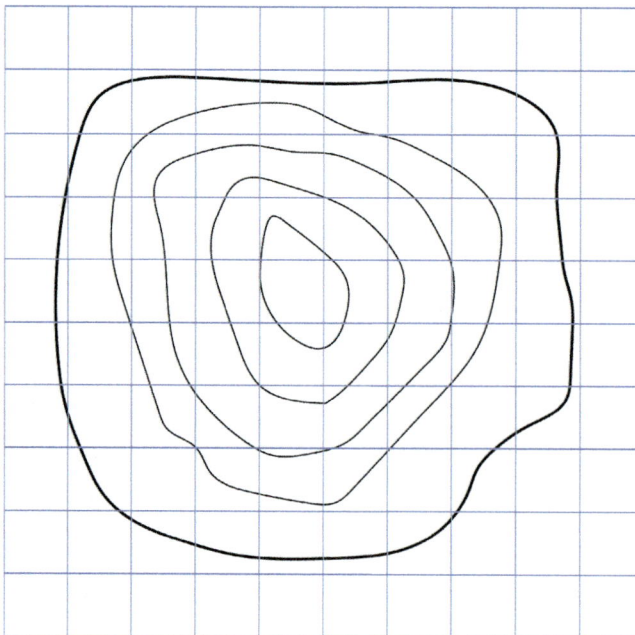

Figure 11.4 Surface collection by grid squares across a site

The fact that it is not total coverage is not necessarily a disadvantage – on large sites a strategy of total collection is very likely to generate a volume of material that is unmanageable, demanding a large allocation of resources without necessarily generating a significantly better understanding of the site. In these circumstances a controlled sampling may well be preferable to total collection. Important decisions are the size of the main grid squares and the sampling strategy. At the site of Qalatga Darband, for example, we had an overall grid of 100 x 100 m squares (laid out by the surveyor), collecting the surface material from a 10 x 10 m square (laid with tapes using Pythagoras's theorem) in the southwestern corner of each of these.

Radial zone collection

In this method a base point is established in the middle of the site and radial lines drawn out from that using string or tapes. It is, of course, possible to lay out these lines using a survey instrument, but this can equally be done with a compass. At the simplest, this might be four lines going north, south, east and west. The surface material is then collected in each sector. This method is quick and easy to set up and may be particularly useful for small, low sites with an obvious centre where time is limited.

Figure 11.5
Two methods
of sampling by
grid: (a) by collecting alternating squares,   (b) by collecting from a restricted zone within each square (in this case the southwestern corner)

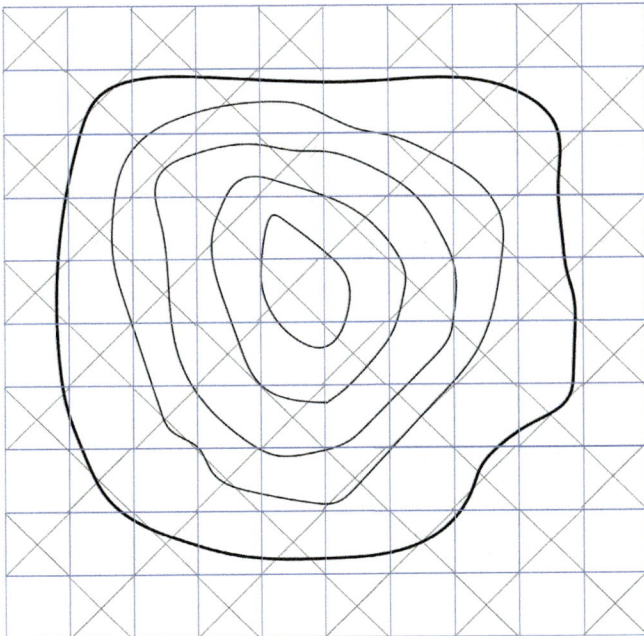

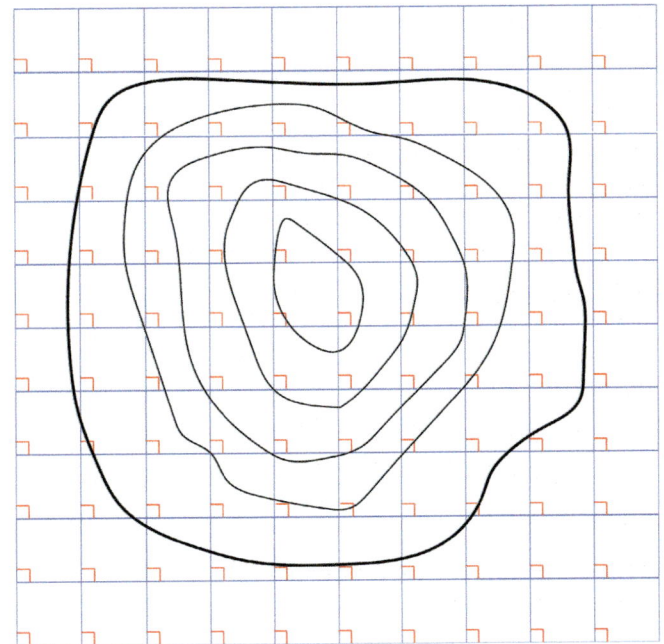

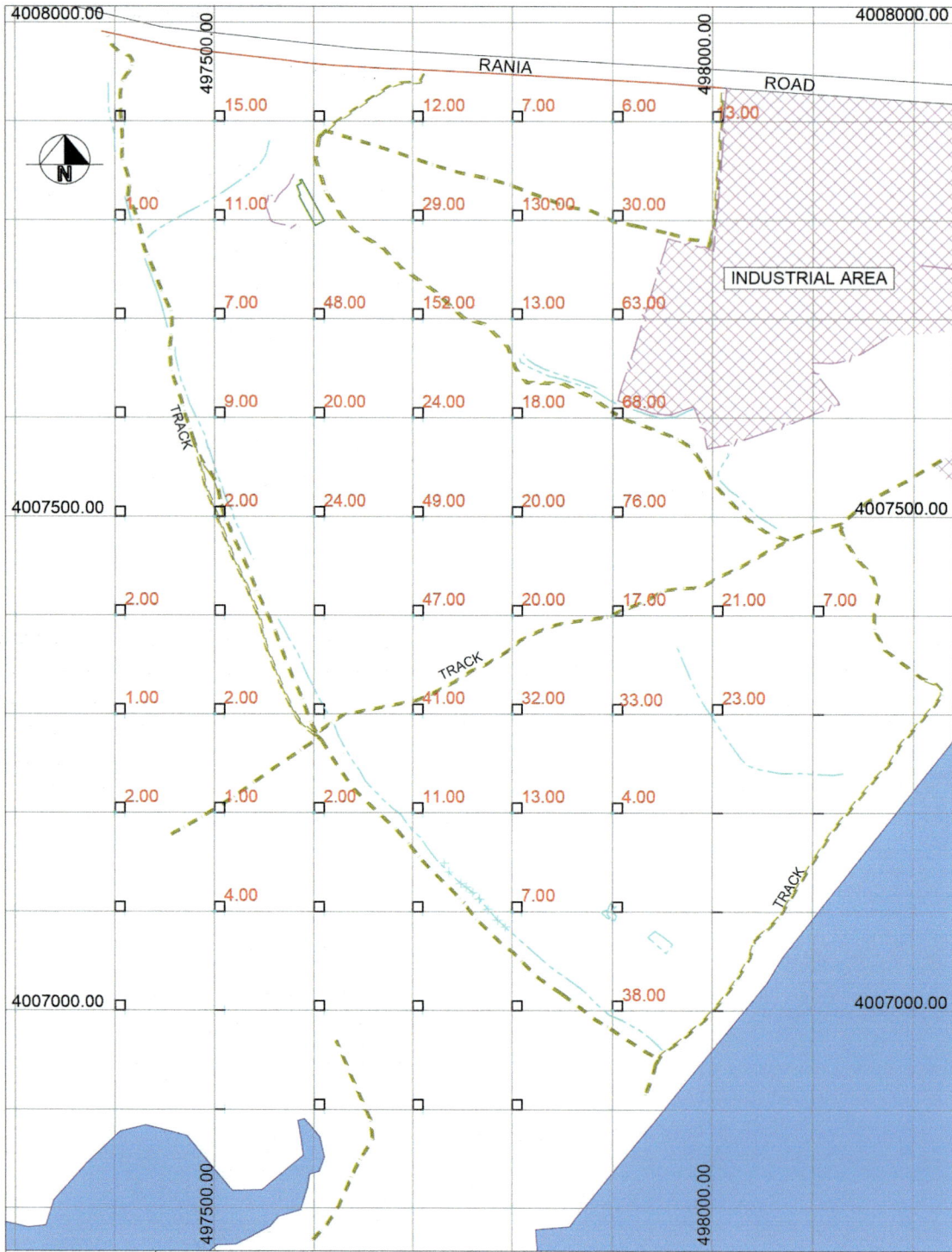

Figure 11.6 Ceramic surface collection at Qalatga Darband, with total collection of material from each 10 x 10 m square in the southwestern corners of the 100 x 100 m squares

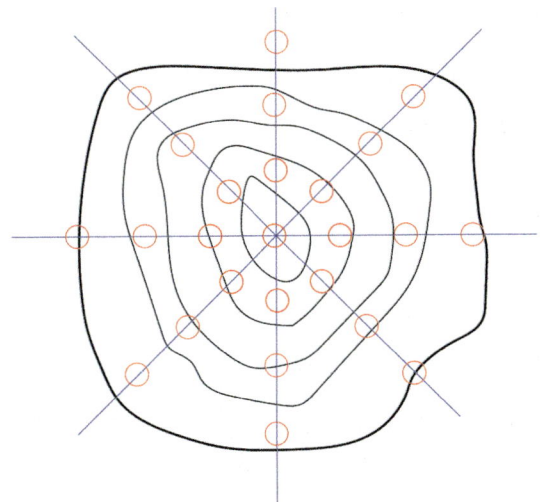

Figure 11.7
Collection by
dividing the
site into radial
zones

Radial controlled sampling

In this method a base point is established in the middle of the site and radial lines (which can once again be fixed using either a survey instrument or compass) are drawn out from the base point using string or tapes, with each line continuing to the limit of the site in that direction. The next stage is to put in pegs at set intervals along each line – perhaps every 25 m or 50 m, according to the size of the site. Surface material is then collected in a circle around the peg (a 2–5 m radius is usual). This method is again quick and easy to set up and is an efficient and effective way to collect a sample of surface material, giving a good spatially-controlled coverage of small and medium-sized sites.

Random allocation

In this method, the site is divided into a grid with the aim of collecting material from a restricted sample of squares chosen mathematically at random. A determination will need to be made of how many squares will be selected and of what size. For example, it might be that the site is divided into 100 squares and 10 of these are selected randomly for collection. The origin of this method is that it is perceived to be more scientific and not relying on bias. It is really only sensible where a more controlled collection is not feasible (perhaps due to the size of the site or constraints of time). The disadvantage of the

► Figure 11.8
Collection
by radial
controlled
sampling

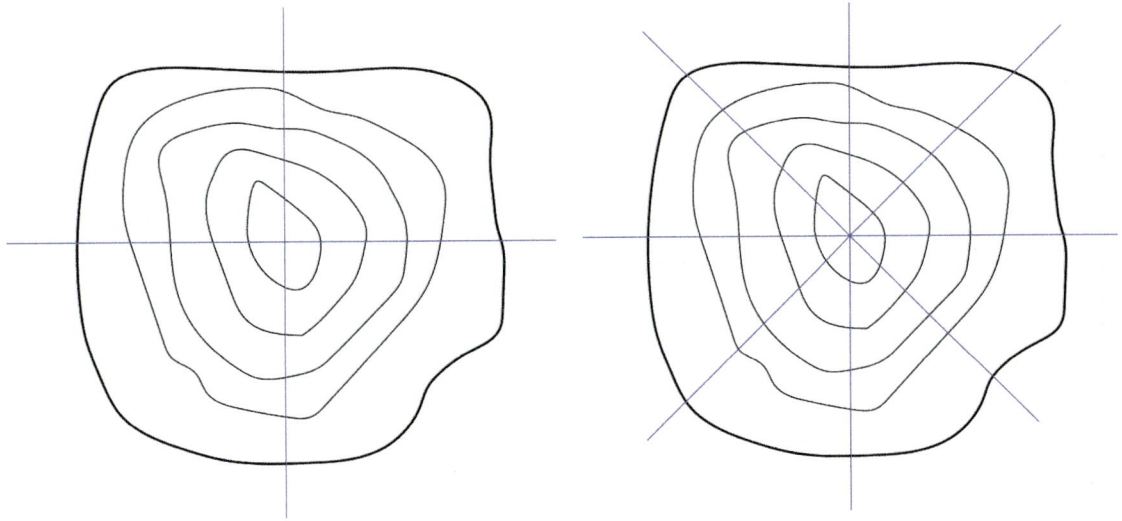

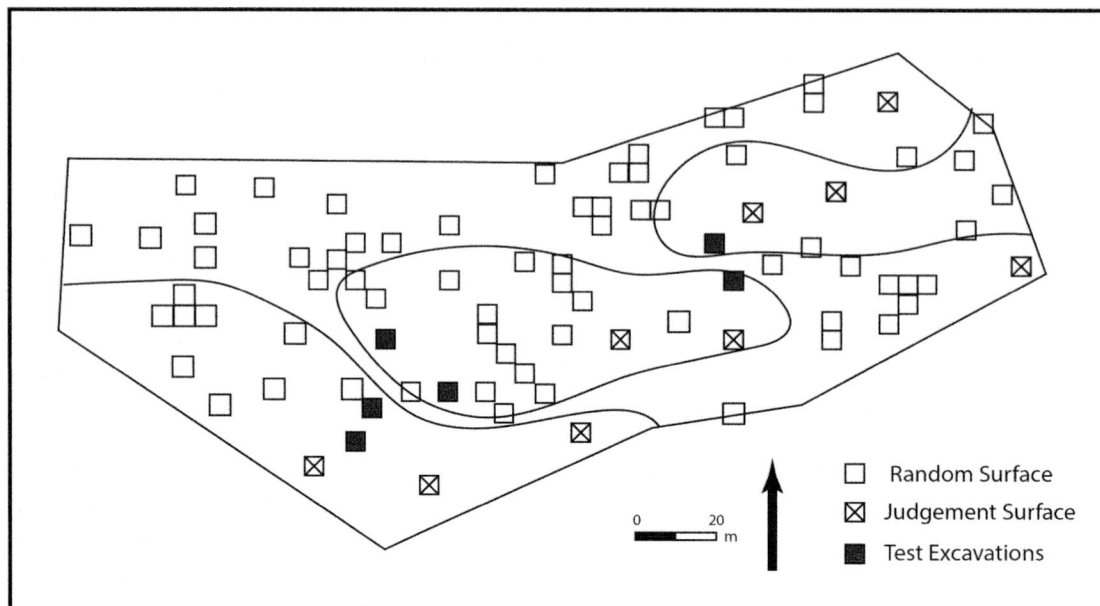

Figure 11.9 Collection of areas determined by random allocation, supplemented by areas selected by judgement and backed up by test excavations at the site of Çayönü in southeastern Turkey

method is that it may not take account of obvious topographical features and that the coverage may not be evenly distributed – in practice, though, this can be compensated for by additionally collecting from such features, regardless of the computer algorithm. This method has been used on prehistoric sites in America and also in surveys around villages in England where it has been effective at mapping settlement patterns over time.

In all these methods a decision needs to be made regarding what exactly to collect and how to record the results. In sites with intensive sherd scatters it is unlikely that you will want to collect all the sherds. It would, for example, be ridiculous to set out to collect all the surface ceramics at Nineveh or Babylon! There are two solutions to this problem. The first, already discussed above, is interval collection, that is not to collect material from the whole surface of a site but only from designated areas spaced out at set intervals. As mentioned, this was the approach taken at Qalatga Darband, where, in addition to furnishing material for dating, the collection allowed an analysis of the pattern of distribution of ceramics by weight and sherd, which gave us useable information on occupational density and settlement history.

The second solution to dealing with the problem of huge volumes of material is to only collect 'diagnostic' sherds – rims, handles, spouts, bases and any body sherds whose shape, fabric or decoration allows a determination of date and/or function. One drawback to this is that it does not allow patterns of occupational density to be discerned. Nevertheless, this is a very common protocol for collecting material, particularly from medium- and large-sized sites.

A third issue is the collection and recording of material other than ceramics. On the one hand this includes any chance small finds such as worked stones, figurines, tablet fragments, coins and so on that may be found. Obviously, finds such as this will be kept, but a decision needs to be made on how to record their location. There may very likely also be other materials such as baked bricks, roof tiles, *pithos* and tannur (bread oven) fragments, slag and so on. Here, two decisions need to be made. The first is whether to collect these materials, or just to make a note on their presence. The second is how to record them spatially. The approach you take will depend on which method of surface collection you are using, the volume of the material in question and the type of equipment available. At the very least, you will want to note the grid square or radial area where the material is found. A more refined approach would be to have a recording sheet for each collection area which includes a provision for a sketch plan so that the rough location of artefacts can be recorded as in the example below (a printable version can be found in the Appendices). Another is to record with GPS and take a photograph.

The most advanced procedure is to record the location of each piece with the surveying equipment. If time and resources allow, this is very effective, allowing the plotting of the position of every artefact and class of material found on the surface. A very good application of this approach was at Abu Duwari (ancient Maškan-Šapir), north of Nippur, where the mapping of surface materials enabled an extraordinarily detailed reconstruction of the layout of the Old Babylonian city, with plans showing the distribution of a wide range of artefacts – baked bricks, *pithos* fragments, whole pots, stone bowl fragments, baked clay plaques, models of chariots and boats, inscriptions, copper,

Figure 11.10
Surface
collection
at Qalatga
Darband

Surface survey record sheet

Site   Date

Grid Square   Supervisor

Sketch plan (indicate direction of north)

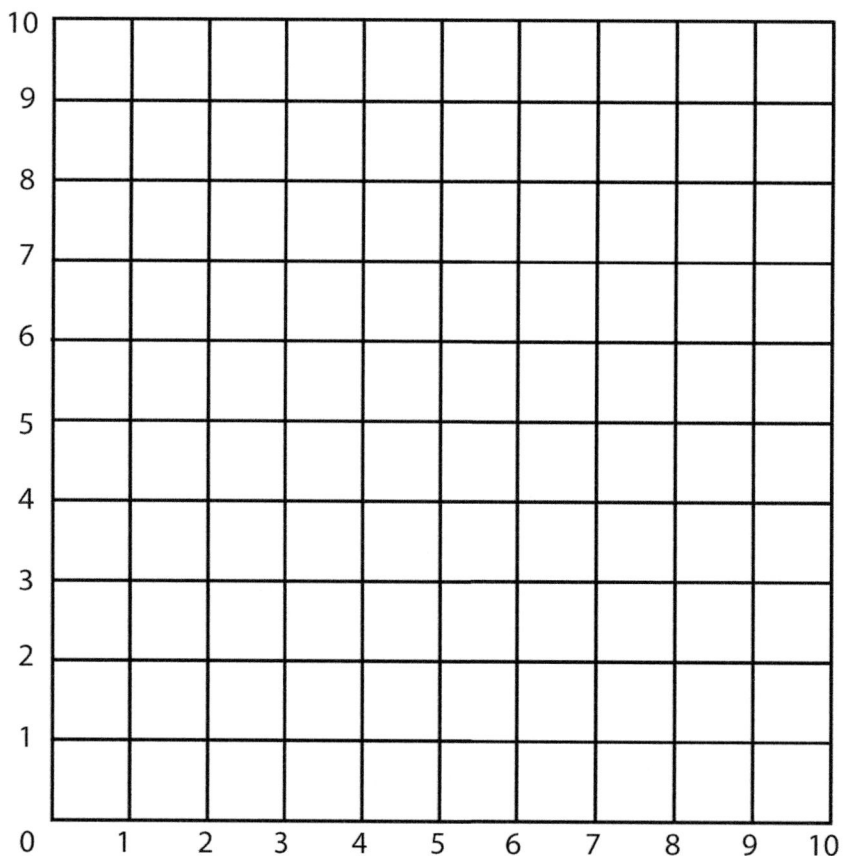

Notes

Figure 11.11 Example of form for recording surface collection of 10 x 10 m squares

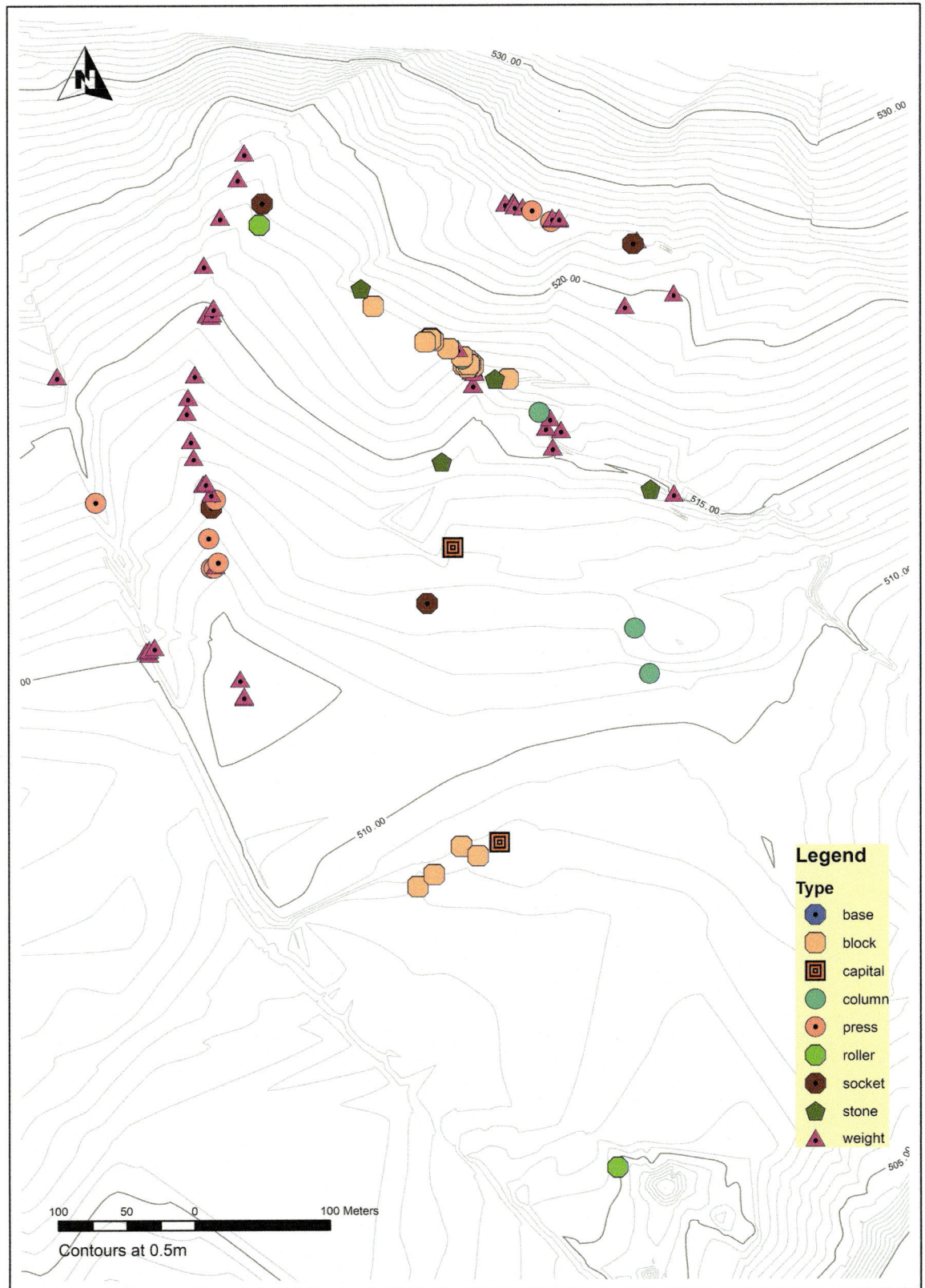

Surface Stone Survey

Figure 11.12
Carved
stone pieces
mapped in the
surface survey
at Qalatga
Darband

Legend

Type

- base
- block
- capital
- column
- press
- roller
- socket
- stone
- weight

100   50   0   100 Meters

Contours at 0.5m

slag, chipped stone, coins, glass, seals, grinders, weapons, jewellery, whetstones, loom weights and spindle whorls, as well as the distribution of objects from other periods. To give another example, the stone survey at Qalatga Darband plotted the position of column bases and capitals, ashlar blocks, bases and weights from olive presses, door sockets and roof rollers scattered across the surface of the site.

Periodisation maps

One advantage of using a system of collection which preserves spatial information is that it allows for the mapping of the extent of occupation at a site in different periods. There are some issues to consider here. One is the degree to which surface ceramics disintegrate, a phenomenon particularly prevalent in southern Iraq. Another is the degree to which ceramics from older layers work their way up to the surface from below. Nevertheless, such periodisation maps can give insight into settlement history.

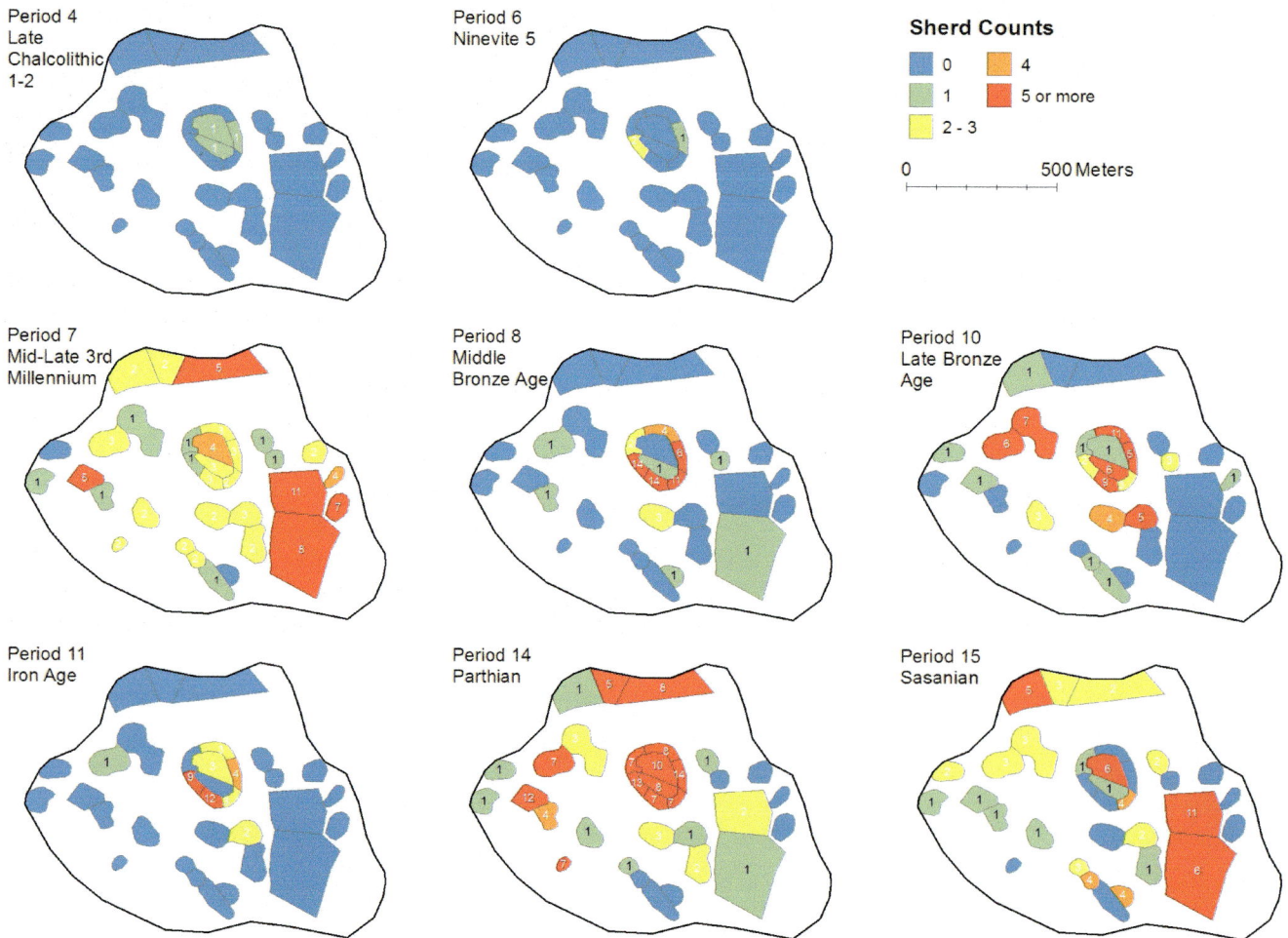

Figure 11.13 Maps showing occupational distributions at the site of Tell Baqrta in the Erbil plain (courtesy of Prof. Jason Ur)

Figure 11.14
Recording
the surface
collection from
a random 1 x 1
m square

Finally, a word needs to be said about the processing and storage of surface collection materials. Whether you are conducting an intensive survey of one site or less intensive collections in the framework of a regional survey, you will be amassing huge quantities of material. It is very important that you factor in right from the beginning, before actually starting on the field collection, how you will process and store this material. You need to make sure you have adequate resources to clean, classify, draw and photograph the recovered material. You will need to have a protocol with regard to what you do with the processed materials – you will certainly need to keep a representative sample of the surface collection, but do you keep everything? Where will you discard materials not being kept? Whatever your solution, you need to have the resources to package the kept materials in a neat and orderly fashion and to have a facility for long-term storage where the material can be accessed not just by your own team but by any other interested parties.

Chapter 12

Excavation Methodology

In the preceding sections we have discussed approaches to researching the archaeological landscape prior to, and indeed independent of, any excavation. We now turn to the methodology of excavation and the many stages and methods involved, from laying out a trench to the final report.

Laying out a trench

Laying out trenches by hand

Trenches can be laid out with a total station or multi station, but often it is easier and faster to lay out trenches by hand. This lets you adjust the size and position of the trench according to what you see on the ground.

Figure 12.1
Laying out a
baseline

Trenches are almost always rectangular or square. Making straight sides is easy, but making sure that the corners are right-angles (90°) is more difficult. The best method is to use simple trigonometry. According to Pythagoras's theorem, the square of the two sides of a rectangle is equal to the square of the 'hypotenuse' (the line going diagonally across).

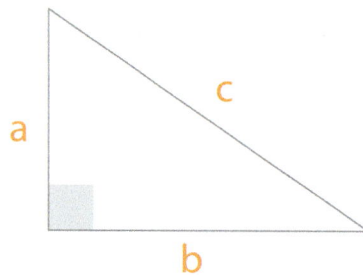

$$a^2 + b^2 = c^2$$

Using this formula, you can lay out a trench of any size with long measuring tapes.

The simplest application of this is to make a **3–4–5 triangle**: a trench with one 3-m long side and one 4 m long side will have a hypotenuse of 5m:

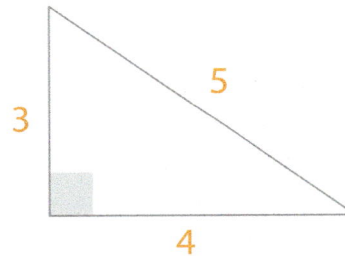

$$3^2 + 4^2 = 5^2$$

Having laid out a 3 x 4 m trench in this way, you can easily adjust the size to the size you want for your trench by extending (or shortening) the sides as appropriate.

Common trench sizes

You can always work out the distance across the corners of any trench using the formula above, but it can save time to remember the diagonal value for some common trench sizes, in particular 5 x 5 m and 10 x 10 m trenches.

5 m x 5 m trenches measure **7.07 m** across the corners

10 m x 10 m trenches measure **14.14 m** across the corners

Lastly, you can of course do the actual calculation for any rectangle size you want. If we want a trench that is 5 m long and 3 m wide, the distance between the opposite corners is found like this:

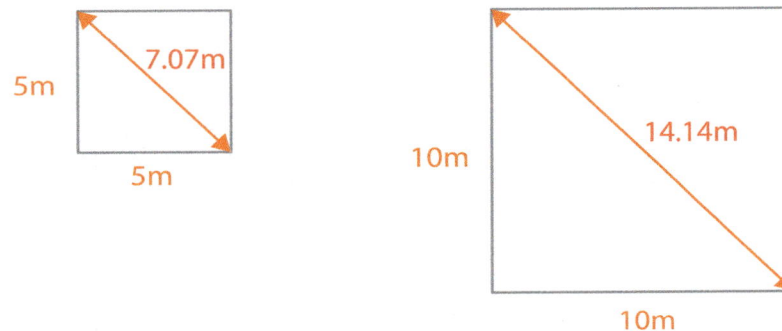

$$x2 = 52 + 32 = 25 + 9 = 34$$

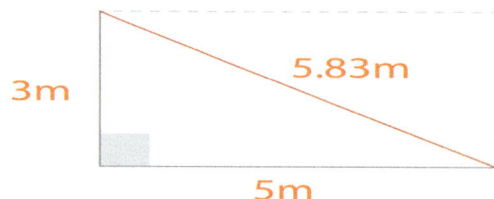

$$x = \sqrt{34} = 5.83$$

Now we can lay out our trench by making right-angled triangles with our measuring tapes. It is best to start with the shortest side of the trench, so first put a stake in the ground where you want the first corner of the trench to be. Then use a measuring tape to place the second corner 3 m from the first stake. Now we have one side of the trench.

To place the third corner, we need to use our calculation. The third peg must be 5 m from one stake and 5.83 m from the other stake. Use two long tapes and attach one to each stake at zero. Find 5 m on the first tape and 5.83 m on the second and cross them at these points. Find the spot where both tapes are straight and taut – this is the third corner, so mark it with a stake.

To find the last corner, simply swap the tapes so that the first is at 5.83m and the second is at 5m. Then move to the new position where they are both straight and taut. Put a stake at this point, then check how accurate you have been by measuring between the third and fourth stakes. If you have got it right, the stakes will be 3 m apart and your trench is laid out. If the distance is wrong

Figure 12.2
Establishing
the corner of a
square

by a few centimetres (5 cm or less) make a small adjustment. If it is wrong by more, you should start again as you might have made a mistake.

One tape method

Sometimes you only have one long measuring tape to lay out a trench, but this is not a problem. We can use one tape to make two sides of the triangle.

Set out the first side of your trench just like before, so the short side is measured in. Then attach the end of the tape to one of the stakes at zero. Run out the tape until it is the length you want your trench side and get a colleague to hold the tape at this point. Now run out the tape so that you add the diagonal value to the length of the trench side you are measuring in. Hold the tape at this point against the other stake you already placed, making a triangle. When the tape is straight and taut your colleague can put a stake at the corner of the triangle they are holding.

If we were measuring in the 5 m x 3 m trench in the example above, the end of the tape would need to be at 10.83 m (5 m + 5.83 m) so it would look like this:

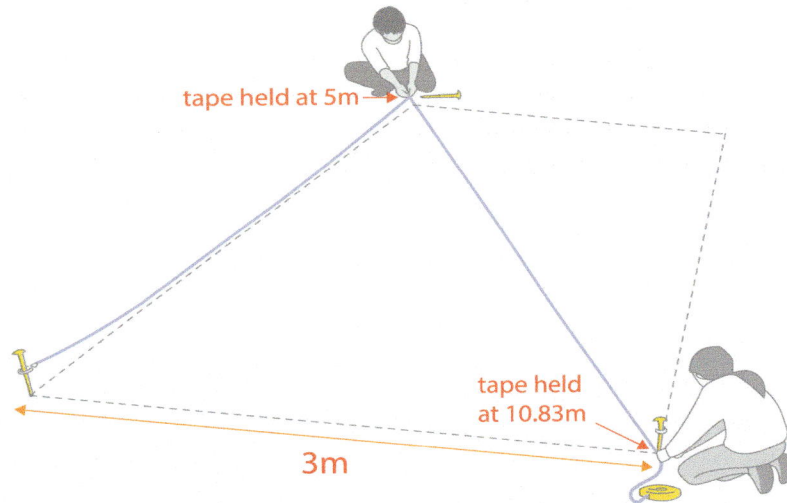

tape held at 5m

tape held
at 10.83m

3m

The second corner is easy to find. Keep both ends of the tape in place and now hold the tape at the value of the diagonal (5.83 m), instead of the value of the trench side. Make the tape straight and taut again and mark this point as the fourth corner. This method sounds more complicated, but it is very simple once you have done it a few times. The disadvantage of the one tape method is that you need two people unless you tie one end of the tape to your stake with a secure knot, which often damages the tape. If you are on your own the two tape method is easier.

Laying out on a slope

Sometimes you need to lay out trenches on ground which is not flat, such as on the slopes of a tell. If you laid out your trenches with the measuring tapes lying on the ground, looked at in plan your trenches would not be the right size because the tapes were not horizontal but on an angle. You can compensate for this using a plumb bob.

First lay out the two stakes forming the **up-slope** side of the trench. Set up the tapes (or single tape) as usual, but instead of holding them on the ground, hold them at the same height as the up-slope stakes so that the tapes are horizontal when taut (you can ensure the tape is horizontal by using a line level on a string). To mark the next stake, suspend a plumb bob from the corner of the tapes and place the stake where the plumb bob contacts the ground.

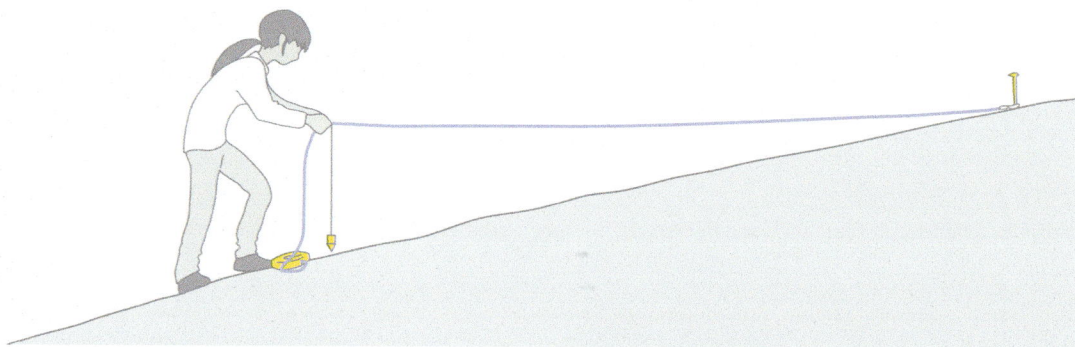

General trench operations

When excavating it is important to keep the excavation tidy. Try not to generate large piles of earth, but rather to dig and remove the earth in small batches, sieving as appropriate (see below). Keep the area clean and tidy, both the excavation itself and the area around the trench.

The excavation proceeds by following the stratigraphic method. This is central to the practice of modern archaeology. In order to record, interpret and use stratigraphy, every separate, identifiable element – whether a layer, a wall, the fill of a pit, a tannur – is recorded as a different context and given its own context number. When starting a new context, a new bucket or bag needs to be assigned for the ceramics from the context and,

Figure 12.3
To help keep your area neat and tidy do not allow large amounts of spoil to build up before transferring to buckets and wheelbarrows

Figure 12.4
Always keep the
trench clean

in all likelihood, bags for bones very soon thereafter. It is important to label these immediately – it is too easy for bags and buckets to get confused, material to get mixed and for them to arrive in the dig house not having been labelled at all.

Sieving

All primary contexts should be fully sieved. In addition to systematic sampling for recovering artefact and ecofact densities, there are times when it is appropriate for a deposit to be dry sieved for better artefact recovery. For example, when an unbaked clay sealing has been discovered, the deposit should be sieved in case other sealings are present. Or, when a newly excavated object has a new break, the missing piece may be recovered by sieving. It is important to record the mesh size (e.g. 5 mm or 1 cm), how many buckets were sieved, and the volume of earth in each bucket. The easiest way is to make sure only one sieve size is used, and that all buckets have the same size and are filled to the same (pre-measured) level.

Figure 12.5
Sieving a
primary context

Excavation workflow

For the day-to-day process of excavation, your work flow will probably look something like this:

EXCAVATION PROCESS – QD, Area E and F

★ ★ ★ ★ ★ ★ ★ ★
★

Finding objects alone does not allow us to understand why something happened. Excavation is by nature a destructive action: once you take any thing out of its place you can never put it back. Remember, once something is excavated it is gone forever. We have to document every single step. Always think of the future archaeologists. How can I explain for them what we did in Area E?

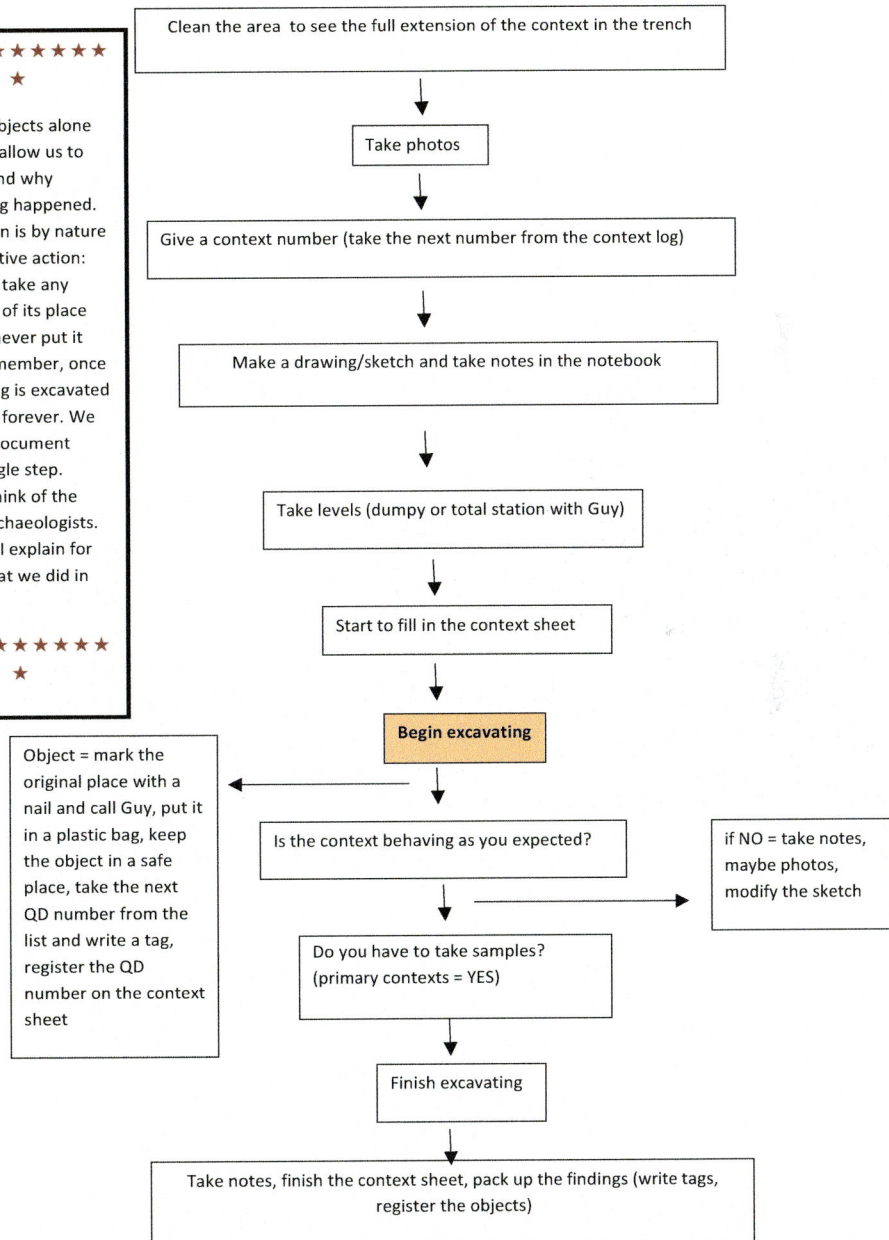

★ ★ ★ ★ ★ ★ ★ ★
★

Clean the area to see the full extension of the context in the trench

Take photos

Give a context number (take the next number from the context log)

Make a drawing/sketch and take notes in the notebook

Take levels (dumpy or total station with Guy)

Start to fill in the context sheet

Begin excavating

Object = mark the original place with a nail and call Guy, put it in a plastic bag, keep the object in a safe place, take the next QD number from the list and write a tag, register the QD number on the context sheet

Is the context behaving as you expected?

if NO = take notes, maybe photos, modify the sketch

Do you have to take samples? (primary contexts = YES)

Finish excavating

Take notes, finish the context sheet, pack up the findings (write tags, register the objects)

Chapter 13

Context Recording

Every site will have its own system for recording contexts, and probably no two systems are exactly the same. In all cases though, the aim is to have a system which records the essential information and is simple and easy to use. In the examples below we utilise the system at the British Museum excavation at the site of Qalatga Darband. In this system, all contexts are given a three-digit number. There is a single series of context numbers for each area – in Area A, for example, A-001, A-002, A-003 and so on. Supervisors allocate context numbers as required and maintain a list of these in their notebook, together with the essential information of the context (type, composition, size, stratigraphic relation, etc). On-site this information is recorded on the printed context forms; once back at the dig house the information must then be entered into the database.

Figure 13.1 Recording on-site

Surface finds

Surface finds from the vicinity of an excavation area are given the context number –000; e.g. a surface find from near Area A will be given the context number A-000; the field number can be assigned by the supervisor in the normal way.

When a surface find does not come from the vicinity of an excavation area, or if its exact provenance is unknown (but believed to be from the site), the context is recorded as Z-000; in such cases the Registrar/Databaser can assign a field number.

Context sheets

The information on each context is recorded on a context sheet (a printable version can be found in the Appendix). Here we use as an example the sheet used at Qalatga Darband.

Context number

This is the sequential number assigned by the supervisor; it should take the form of a letter designating the Area followed by a three-digit number, e.g. A-007.

Site

The name of the site, either written out in full or, more usually, a two letter abbreviation (in capital letters), e.g. QD for Qalatga Darband, UA for Usu Aska etc.

Area

Normally just a single capital letter for the Area in question, e.g. A.

Trench

Sometimes areas are divided into multiple trenches, which will be numbered 1, 2, 3, etc; this field can be left blank if it does not apply.

Start date

The date on which excavation of the context commenced.

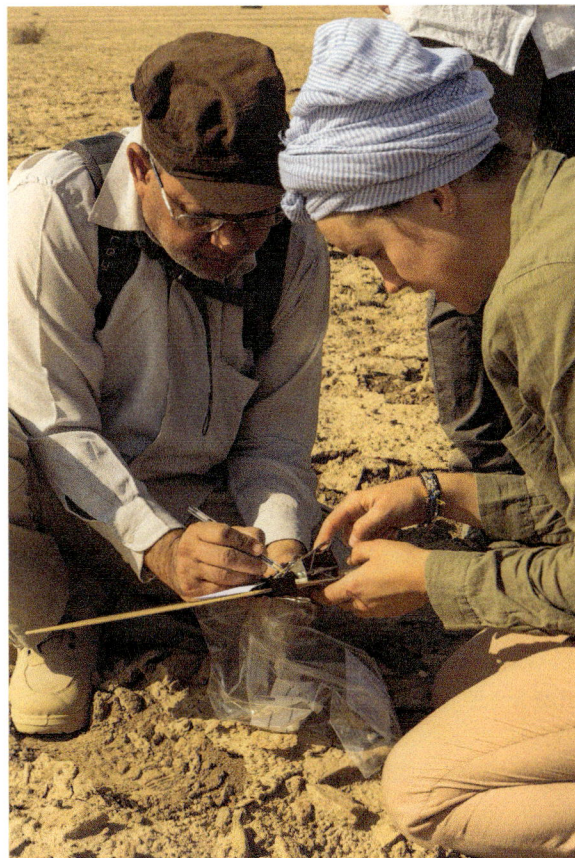

▶ Figure 13.2
Filling out a
context sheet

Supervisor

The supervisor, or supervisors, in charge during the period of excavation; normally written as initials, e.g. JM or JM/BD.

Context type

A general categorisation, in the database the options to choose from are Cut, Deposit, Fill, Structure, Skeleton.

Primary/Secondary/Tertiary

For the purpose of post-excavation processing, excavation units are classified as primary, secondary and tertiary contexts:

primary contexts are the in situ remains of human activity: these include walls, floors, pits, dumps, hearths, graves, drains and so on;

secondary contexts are deposits which are ancient but which may have not been created intentionally, for example room fill and building collapse;

tertiary contexts are top soil, plough zone and slope wash; while these have (almost) no intrinsic stratigraphic value, the material they yield is nevertheless important.

It is acknowledged that different excavators may have different views on classifications, nevertheless labelling material in this way helps in determining the importance it can be given in interpretation; this is particularly true with ceramics and environmental datasets. Tick the corresponding box if you are confident which category is appropriate, however, this is not always clear at the time of excavation, in which case the field can be left blank.

Clear/Merging/Mixed

Indicate whether the context is clearly distinguished from the context(s) above it, whether this distinction is not very clear, or whether more than one context was mixed together in excavation.

Date (archaeological period)

If you know the general period to which the feature dates – e.g. Ottoman, Assyrian, Ubaid – write this here.

Phase

If phases have been allocated, write this in here.

Figure 13.3
Example of a
context sheet
– the reverse
of the form
is a blank
page which
can be used
for drawing
sketches

Context no. رقم الوحده الاثريه	Site الموقع Area المنطقة Trench الحفرية	Supervisor المشرف Start date تاريخ بداية التنقيب

Context type نوع الوحده الاثريه	○ Primary رئيسية ○Tertiary ثالثية ○Clear واضحة ○ Merging مدمجة ○ Secondary ثانوية ○ Mixed مختلطة

Date (period) التأريخ (الفترة)	Phase السويّة	Room no. رقم الغرفة

Description الوصف

Measurements القياسات			
	length الطول	height/depth الارتفاع /العمق	width العرض
max. الحد الأقصى			
min. الحد الأدنى			

Elevations الارتفاعات	
max. الحد الأقصى	
min. الحد الأدنى	

Stratigraphic Relationships العلاقات الطبقية

Above فوق	Cuts تقطع	Fills تملأ	Abuts تتاخم	Part of جزء من	Equals مساوية لـ
Below تحت	Cut by مقطوع بـ	Filled by مملوئة بـ	Bonds with مرتبطة بـ	Consists of تتكون من	Associated with ذو علاقة بـ

Finds اكتشافات

Sieved? منخلة? ○   %

Find or Sample Nos.
رقم المعثر/العينة

Pottery	فخار ○	1.	6.
Bone	عظم ○	2.	7.
Glass	زجاج ○	3.	8.
Metal	معدن ○	4.	9.
Slag	خبث معدني ○	5.	10.
Lithics	صوان ○		

Additional records أرقام إضافية

Plan nos. أرقام المخطط	
Section nos. أرقام المقطع	
Photo nos. أرقام الصور	
Notebook p. رقم صفحه المدونة	

Room number

If you are digging a building with rooms which have been given numbers, enter the number here.

Description

This is the place to give a full description of the context. The information recorded will vary depending on whether the context is a deposit, part of a structure, or anything else.

Deposits: note the key features such as colour, composition, compaction, inclusions

composition: describe the composition of the soil, e.g. clay, clayey silt, sand, sandy silt, ash etc

compaction: this refers to how hard the matrix is – good terms to use are: very hard, hard, neither loose nor hard, loose, very loose

inclusions: describe inclusions in the matrix – typical examples might be grit, calcite, pebbles

Structures: note the material of which the structure is made; in the case of mudbrick and mortar, note the colour and any inclusions; where walls join note whether they are bonded or just abut.

Figure 13.4
Recording a
wall under
excavation

Measurements

This should be self-explanatory, but make sure you specify the unit of measurement (cm or m).

Elevations

You should give at least the maximum and minimum elevations (height above sea level) for each feature; it will often be desirable to give many more than that. Use the dumpy level or total station to do this.

Stratigraphic relationships

This is very important – note every context which the context in question is directly above or below, whether it cuts or is cut by any other feature, whether it fills or is filled by any other feature.

Bonds with applies to walls

Consists of can be used when one overall feature has separately numbered components

Equals is used when the same context has been given more than one number

Finds (bulk finds)

For bulk finds – pottery, bone, glass, slag and lithics (chipped stone) – simply tick if they are present

Find/Sample numbers

For individual finds, write the find number and a short description, e.g. 'QD-2134 iron knife', and the same applies for samples; the system for allocating finds and samples numbers is described below

Sieved

Tick if a deposit has been sieved and write in the numbers of buckets

Representations

This refers to photographs, plans and sections – write in the numbers accordingly; the systems for labelling photographs and for numbering plans and sections are described below.

Figure 13.5
Recording the
progress of
excavations

Notebook

Each supervisor needs to keep a notebook. The Chertwell type, with graph paper on one side and a lined page on the other, is ideal. In their notebooks, supervisors need to maintain a daily log outlining and summarising the day's proceedings in their excavation areas. All information relating to the interpretation of remains in a trench should be recorded here – new contexts assigned, with ample notes on material, measurements and stratigraphy; small finds recovered and the numbers assigned to them, lists of environmental samples with sketches of where they were taken from, and so on. The daily entries should explain the basis for the excavator's understanding of the contexts in the trench, including a discussion of any uncertainties in interpretation, and how this understanding evolved during excavation. Very frequently, when writing final reports the director will look at the daily logs for the testimony they give on the thoughts recorded at the time.

▶ Figure 13.6
Recording in a
site notebook

Sketch plans

Excavators must keep a sketch plan of each trench. Sketch plans can be done at whichever scale the supervisor chooses, 1:10 and 1:20 are probably the most common. These sketch plans should be clearly labelled, including context numbers, scale, date and north arrow. Sketch plans serve to illustrate the descriptions of work and consist of a sketch showing the location and horizontal relationship of all individual contexts, features, in situ objects, etc. within the trench. Although in principle sketch plans do not have to be drawn on a daily basis, they are necessary any time significant changes occur within the trench or any time new contexts are assigned. It is very useful if all contexts appear in at least one daily sketch plan.

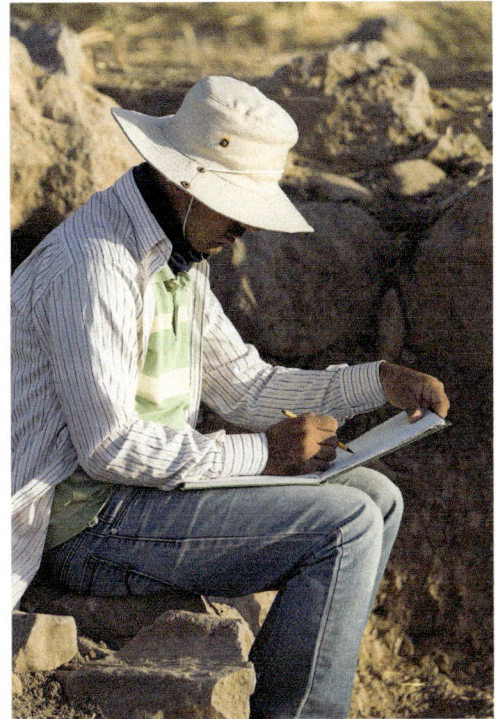

▶ Figure 13.6
Recording in a
site notebook

Figure 13.7
Discussing
contexts

Matrices

In simple terms, a stratigraphic matrix puts contexts into chronological order, with the earliest at the bottom and the latest at the top. This forms a sort of flow-chart describing the formation of the site. The most important thing to remember with a matrix is that it describes the chronological (stratigraphic) relationship between contexts NOT the physical relationships.

What this means is that it is irrelevant in a matrix whether contexts are physically adjacent to each other – they may be physically next to each other in the ground, yet far apart in the matrix. Similarly, the relative depth of the deposits does not determine their position in the matrix – a deposit may lie lower than another deposit and yet be higher in the matrix.

What matters is the order in which events occurred

Here is a simple example:

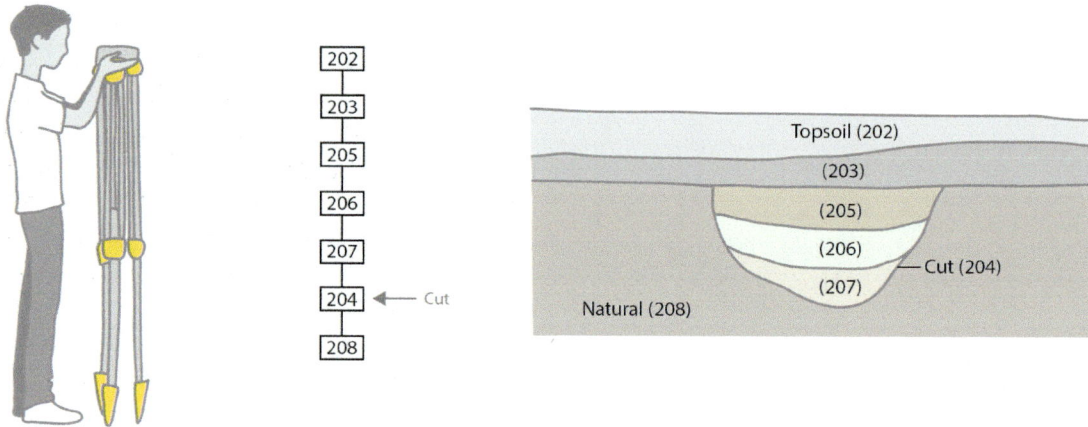

Now let us look at a more complicated example, involving two walls belonging to the same structure. The walls divide the deposits into three unconnected sequences, which are later all covered by three higher deposits.

Note how the walls lie close to the bottom of the matrix, even though they reach quite high in the section diagram. Also note that although in the physical diagram the walls are in contact with a very large number of other contexts, in the matrix each wall is directly above just one context (its foundation cut) and directly below just one other context (the fill of its foundation cut). If you think about the sequence of events, you will see why the walls are in this position in the matrix. Starting with the natural deposit, the builders then dig the trenches for their wall foundations. Then they build the walls. Then they fill the gaps between the wall and the sides of the cut. This gives us the sequence natural – foundation cuts – walls – foundation fill accumulate (whether

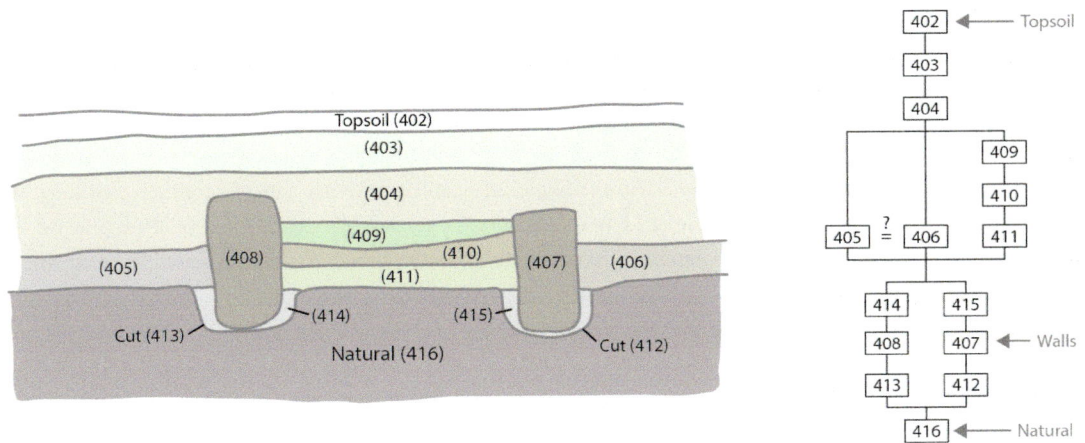

Figure 13.8 Recording details of a plan

deliberately or accidentally). After this, different deposits accumulate. Finally, after the building falls out of use, the walls and both the inside and outside deposits get covered with a destruction deposit, followed by a subsoil and topsoil. Matrices can be complicated, especially when the archaeology is rich in structures and cut features. However, if you start at the bottom with the earliest deposit and ask yourself at each step 'what happened next?' concentrating only on one step at a time, you can build an accurate matrix.

Chapter 14

Finds

With the possible exception of large stone pieces, all materials from the excavation are kept and sent to the dig house for registering and processing. As with context numbers, there is no one fixed way for doing this and every site will have its own system for labelling finds. Once again, the aim is to have a system which records the essential information and is simple and easy to use. In the examples below we utilise the system at the site of Qalatga Darband.

Bulk finds

Bulk finds – ceramics, bone, chipped stone, shell, roof tiles, and slag (vitrified clay from ceramic production, as well as slag from metal production) – are labelled by ticking the appropriate box on the tag and writing in the context number, date and supervisor's initials. Individual numbering of sherds will be done by the ceramicist.

Ceramic vessels

Whole pots, and vessels of which a significant profile is extant, as well as concentrations of potsherds which clearly represent the in situ remains of a smashed vessel, are bagged separately and given their own separate find number.

Figure 14.1 Example of tag (obverse and reverse)

Fragile sherds

In addition to this, any sherds which are particularly delicate and fragile (e.g. Palace Ware, or a sherd with glazed decoration or fugitive paint) should be placed in its own a bag (or small plastic box) and conveyed directly to the Registrar.

Bulk finds with finds numbers

Generally, bulk finds do not need a finds number, as the context number is sufficient. There can however be exceptions, where materials collected in bulk do also need a finds field number: good examples would be bulk finds of iron nails, bronze pins and large numbers of glass fragments. In these cases you can put all the nails/pins/glass from a context in one bag and give it a field number.

Context	Site

type of context

☐ primary ☐ secondary ☐ tertiary

Field No.

☐ sample ☐ artefact

Bulk Finds

☐ pottery ☐ shell
☐ bones ☐ slag
☐ lithics ☐ glass

Date **Initials**

---

recorded in database? Y

requires conservation? Y N
☐ conserved _____

requires photography? Y N
☐ record shot _____
☐ publication shot _____

requires drawing? Y N
☐ drawn _____

ceramics
☐ processed _____

☐ discard ☐ store
☐ export ☐ Museum

Figure 14.2
Writing a tag

Small finds

For all other, individual finds (which are not bulk finds), and for environmental samples, a single running system of find numbers is used. Each area is allocated a block of numbers at the commencement of work. The registrar will keep a list of the block allocations. In their notebooks supervisors keep a running list of numbers as they are assigned. When registering finds (and samples), and when referring to them in text, write the number with three digits and a hyphen, i.e. in the format QD-012. The find locations should be both marked onto a sketch plan and eventually, if appropriate, drawn on a final plan; it may also be decided to plot the position in with the multi station. In the case of small finds found in batches while washing pottery, the ceramicist will ask the relevant supervisor to supply a find number.

Initial packing of finds

Bulk finds will generally be put in plastic bags while other finds may be put in a plastic box or a bag as appropriate.

Important

When putting the tag for a sample in the bag, ensure that it is put in the right way up and with the front face showing through the clear side of the bag (i.e. the side without white stripes).

Also, note that bags or boxes containing unbaked clay artefacts, bones, soil samples and other organic material should not be closed. This is to avoid the build-up of moisture, which can lead to objects of unbaked clay disintegrating and to degradation of organic materials. Refer to the section on conservation below.

Processing of materials coming in from the field

When supervisors return from the field they should distribute the excavated materials as follows:

Ceramics should be delivered directly to the ceramicist's area.

All other finds should be put in the boxes individually marked for large small finds (principally ground stone, such as grinders and bowl fragments), delicate small finds (coins and metals, clay figurines, beads), chipped stone, glass, shell, bone and slag.

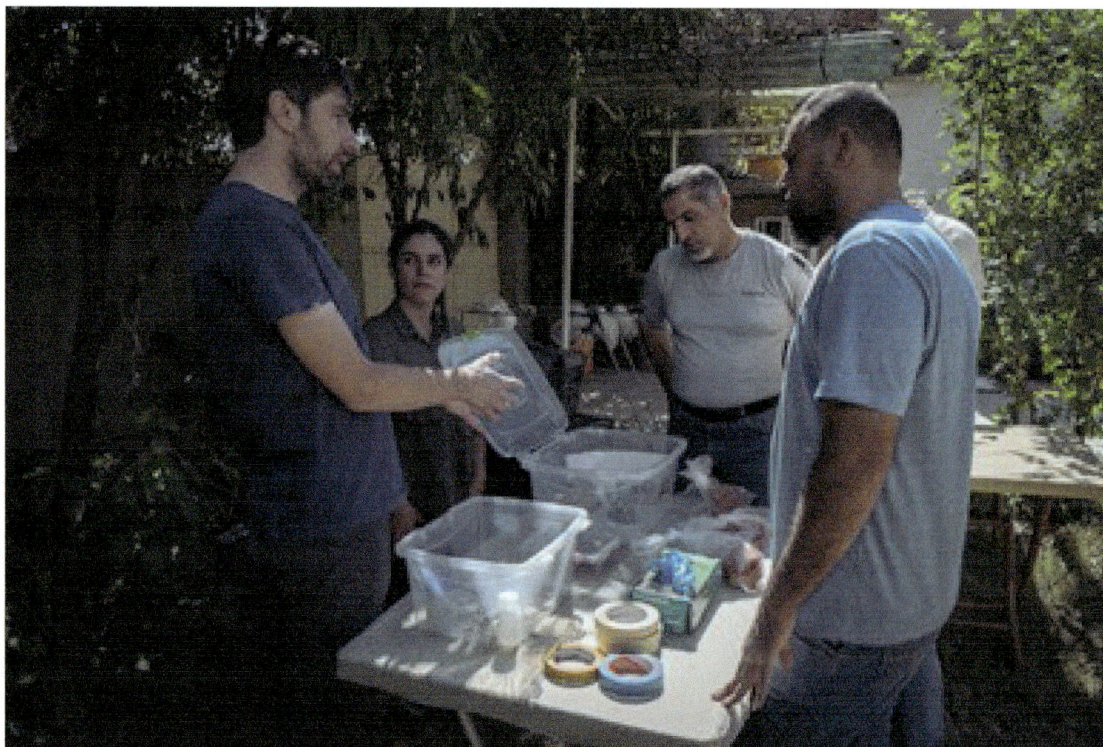

Figure 14.3
Discussing how
to pack finds

Chapter 15

Burials

Human burials should be excavated with care and always treated with respect. Burials come in many forms with lots of variations in burial method and grave goods. Most burials will have at least a grave cut, a grave fill, and skeletal remains, each of which will need a separate context number. A grave may contain several distinct fills, coffin remains, wrapping remains, grave goods and more than one dead person. All of these will need additional context numbers and separate recording.

Excavating burials

Try to define the grave cut as high up as possible. The level from which the grave has been cut is your best clue to its age and its relationship to the other features and phases present. This will also allow you to remove the grave fills as secure contexts. The grave fills should be sieved to make sure no small finds or small bones are missed.

Figure 15.1
Excavating a
burial

Human bone does not survive very well once it is exposed, especially in direct sunlight. The bone will quickly dry, crack and fall to pieces. To avoid this you should expose, clean and record the skeleton all in one operation and not leave it exposed any longer than is necessary. As you uncover the bones try to keep them shaded. If you have to leave parts of the skeleton exposed overnight, cover the grave with boards, sheets or sacking.

Figure 15.2 Sieve the grave fill as you excavate it

It is often difficult to expose bones without moving them, but you should do your best to keep the bones in place so you can plan them in their original positions. This will show what position the body was buried in, which can be important for assessing the date and cultural identity of the burial. Bones are soft; when you excavate them try not to mark or scratch them with tools. You can use wooden or plastic tools which are less likely to damage them than metal ones.

Figure 15.3 An Assyrian burial at Usu Aska

Planning burials

It is best to plan the skeleton in the trench, usually on drawing film at a scale of 1:10, as this allows you to look at the bones from different angles and see their exact extent and relationships. A planning frame is usually the best way of planning a skeleton if the frame can be placed just over the level of the bones. Otherwise you should off-set plan from a baseline set along the long axis of the burial. Remember to take levels. You should take at least three; on the skull, pelvis and feet.

If you are not confident with planning or if you are short of time, it might be easier to plan a burial using photo-rectification or photogrammetry, which are explained in the planning section of this manual. Be aware that planning skeletons from photographs can be difficult and less accurate because bones are small objects which cast a lot of shadow and are often in deep shade inside the grave cut. If you can, it is best to plan while you are in the trench.

Collection of environmental samples from graves

Phytolith samples

If the grave is well preserved, samples for phytoliths (remains of minerals formed inside plants) should be taken. Take about a teaspoon of earth (fine-grained particles with no stones) from the abdominal area and from any area where you see phytoliths, and also from inside any associated ceramics that are complete. The sample should be placed in a small appropriately labelled zip-lock bag. Ensure that the tools used for collection are clean and sterile (you can sterilise a steel blade with a hot light). It may be that at a later stage the researcher requests access to teeth from the grave as phytoliths can also be extracted from the tooth calculus.

Parasitology samples

If the grave is well preserved, samples for parasitology should also be taken. Take a tablespoon of earth (fine-grained particles with no stones) from the area of the head, the pelvic area and the feet. The sample should be placed in a small zip-lock bag, labelled appropriately bag. Ensure that the tools used for collection are clean.

Removal of the burial

When you remove the skeleton, it helps the bone specialist if you collect the right and left elements separately. So for instance, the right arm should go in one bag and the left arm in another bag, with each clearly labelled as right and left. The same should be done for the hands, legs and feet. It also helps if the left and right ribs are separated. Pack everything carefully, with particular attention to not damaging the ends of the bones, which are the most informative parts for study.

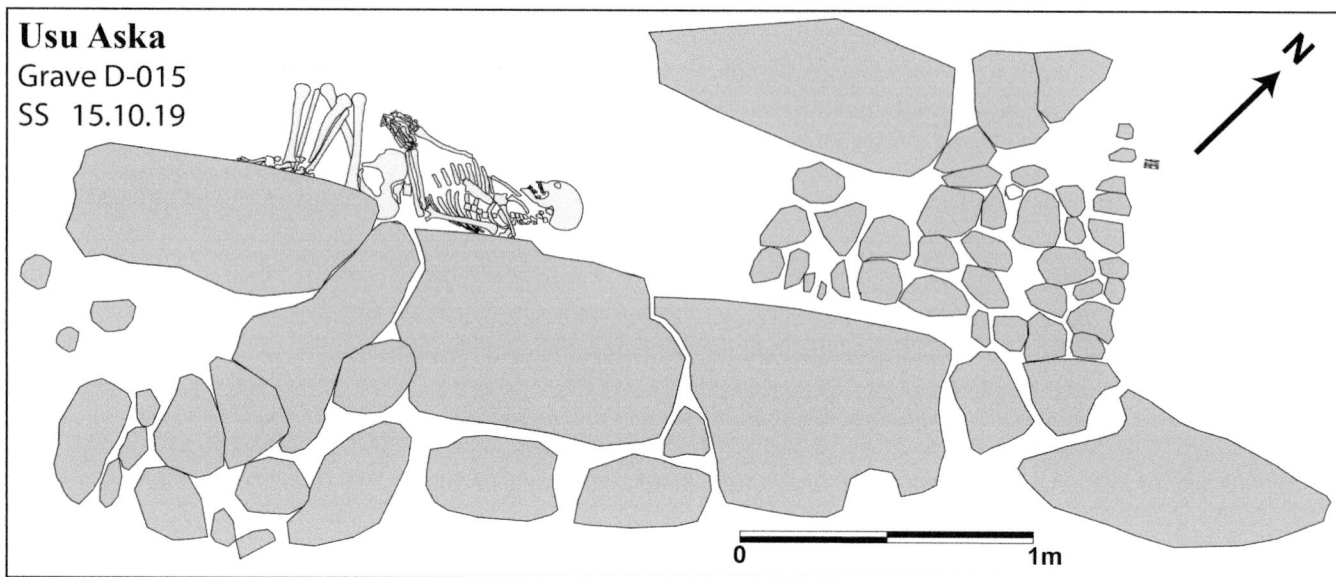

Usu Aska
Grave D-015
SS   15.10.19

0   1m

Figure 15.4
Plan of the
Assyrian burial
at Usu Aska
illustrated
above

Burial record sheet

There are many things to record in a burial, so it is essential to use a burial record sheet. Here we give the example used at Qalatga Darband. The sheet has two sides. On the front you record the general details and stratigraphic relations of the grave. On the reverse you record details of the preserved human remains. You will find printable version of this sheet in the Appendix.

Notes on completing the burial sheet

Front of the sheet (burial)

This is essentially the same as a context sheet. Record all aspects of the burial. Give a detailed description, including grave cut; overall state of preservation; whether the grave was disturbed or undisturbed; whether the remains were in coffin, urn, pot or double pot, etc.; grave goods; etc.

Back of the sheet (skeleton)

You should try to complete the skeleton sheet when the burial is exposed and you can see everything clearly, but this will not always be possible. In addition to filling out the sections on the sheet, ensure you note any further important information. Things to consider are:

Disturbed/Undisturbed: Is the skeleton in its original position or has the burial been disturbed by later activity, such as the grave being robbed or being cut through by a later structure?

**Figure 15.5
Front side of the
burial sheet**

Burial sheet

Context Number	Site Area Trench	Start Date Supervisor

Description and comments

disturbed/undisturbed (robbing / natural processes / other later activities)

evidence of matting or textiles

Measurements

mm / cm / m	Length	Width	Depth
Maximum:			
Minimum:			

Elevation

Maximum:	
Minimum:	

Stratigraphic Relationships:

Above	Cuts	Fills	Part Of	Equals
Below	Cut By	Filled By	Consists Of	Associated With

Finds:

				Find or Sample No			
Pottery ○	Sieved? ○	% Sieved:	Mesh Size:	1.		6.	
Bone ○	Finds Comments:			2.		7.	
Glass ○				3.		8.	
Metal ○				4.		9.	
Slag ○				5.		10.	
Lithics ○							

Representations:

Plan No:	
Section No:	
Photo No:	

Burial context no. ....   Skeleton find no. ....

Skeleton processed on .... by ....

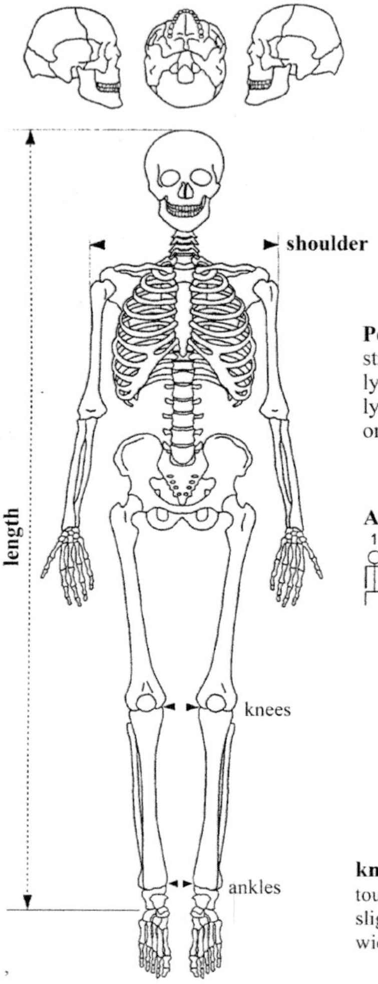

Preservation of bones
- well preserved
- partially decomposed
- badly decomposed

shoulder

Position
stretched out
lying face up
lying face down
on left / right side

Skull
frontal
facing left
facing right
supported

Mouth
open
closed

Arms
1 2 3 4 5 6 7 8 9 10 11 12 13 14

left over right ☐   right over left ☐

knees

Hands   right left
palm up
palm down
resting on edge

Legs   right left
straight
flexed
fetal

ankles

knees
touching each other
slightly apart
wide apart

feet   right left
out to each side
pointing forwards
turned to the left
turned to the right

length

Sex   **Age**

Height   **Other comments**

Key to indicating bones
in situ   shade fully
dislodged   hatch
missing   leave blank

Figure 15.6
Reverse of
burial sheet

Attitude of the body: Describe the general way the body lies in the grave. Is the body lying in an **extended** or **flexed** position?

Head: Which way up does the skull lie? In which direction does the face point? Is the mandible articulated?

Arms and hands: Describe the right and left arms separately. Is the arm straight or flexed? Does it lie against the body or extend away from it? Does it lie under the body or on top of the body? Where does the hand lie? Is the hand lying flat, or is it clenched in a fist?

Legs and feet: Describe the right and left legs separately. Are they straight or flexed at the hips, knees or ankles? Do the legs cross each other? If they do, which leg crosses on top?

Torso: Is the torso laid straight or does the spine curve forward or back? Is the torso twisted to one side or the other?

Extent of in situ bone degeneration: How well preserved was the skeleton in the ground? Describe the condition of the bones before you try to remove them. Are the bones whole, or full

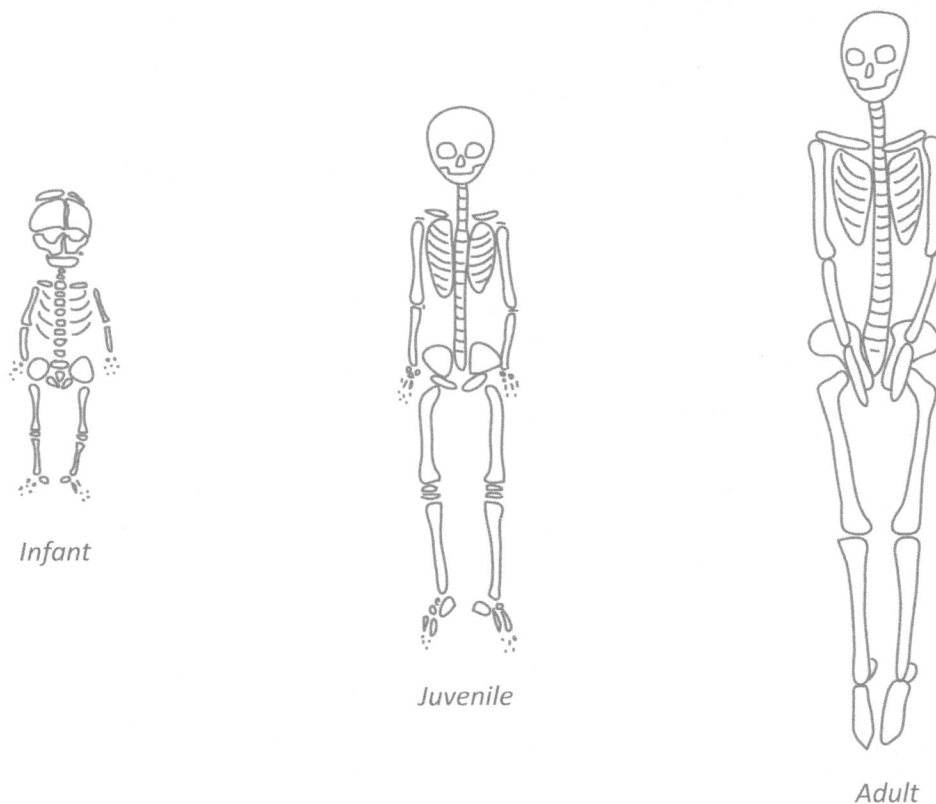

Infant

Juvenile

Adult

Figure 15.7
Infant, juvenile
and adult
skeletons

of cracks? Are some or all of the bones fragmented? Have the bones degraded to powder, or even just stains in the deposit?

State of the bones after lifting: What are the bones like after you have removed them from the grave? Are they still whole? Did they break into big pieces or into tiny fragments? Did they turn to powder?

Age of skeleton: If you are not a specialist in bones, you do not need to try to estimate the exact age at which the person died, but you can make a general interpretation. If it is clearly a baby or very small child you could say it is an **infant**, if it is definitely older than a baby but not an adult you can call it a **juvenile**, and if the bones are fully fused you can call it an **adult**.

Evidence of matting or textile: Is there any evidence of wrapping or matting around the body? This might be remains of the matting or textile itself or staining or phytoliths around the body or on the bones from its decay. Sometimes the pattern of the matting or textile is preserved where it has been pressed against a surface or a metal object.

Interpretation: Sum up what you think about the burial; what it contains and its relationship to the rest of the archaeology. For example: *'Juvenile burial in a supine extended position with traces of textile wrappings. Postdates the phase 2 floors, which the grave is cut through.'*

Measurements: Usually you will only need to record the maximum length and width. Where the skull is intact, the maximum depth will usually be the size of the skull, but where the burial has been heavily compacted the depth will be much less. Maximum elevation is the highest point of the highest bone. Minimum elevation is the lowest point of the lowest bone, which you will have to measure after the skeleton has been removed.

Stratigraphic relationships: Fill this in just as for any context. In a simple burial the skeleton will usually be above the grave cut context and below the grave fill context.

Finds: Here you should record any finds recovered from the grave. You can also note here how much of the grave fill was sieved.

Representations: You should enter the plan, section and photograph numbers here so they can be easily located.

Skeleton image: On the diagram, use a pencil to shade the parts of the skeleton you recovered from the grave. Leave any bones which were lost, missing or completely disintegrated unshaded on the diagram. It is helpful to note on the diagram whether the missing bones were not preserved, not present, or were accidentally removed with a shovel, etc.

Figure 15.8
Discussing a
burial before
planning

Chapter 16

The Dumpy Level

A dumpy level is the easiest thing to use for finding the vertical level of deposits and features. Dumpy levels are cheap, light to carry and quick to set up compared to total stations or multi stations, but they can only measure relative heights, not horizontal position. Dumpy levels are perfect for when you need to add levels to drawn plans and sections.

Setting up the level

Take the level legs and release all the legs so they can extend. Pull the top plate of the legs up to the level of your face, with the feet resting on the ground, then lock the legs at this length. This should ensure that the level will be at about the right height for you when you have set it up. But remember, not everyone may be as tall as you.

Figure 16.1 Preparing for taking levels with a dumpy level

Figure 16.2
The parts of a
dumpy level

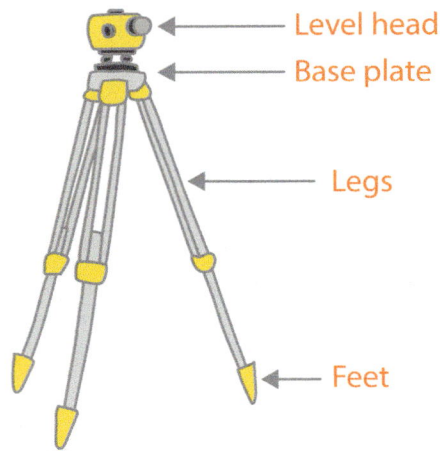

Level head
Base plate
Legs
Feet

Spread the legs so that they make a stable base and so that the top plate, where you are going to place the level head, is roughly flat. Now stamp each foot into the ground firmly. This is important because if the feet are not stamped in the machine can easily become un-levelled when it is knocked or leant on while you are using it.

Place the head of the level at the centre of the top plate and screw it in firmly. Then use the three adjustment wheels to centre the bubble in the spirit level. Before you start this, it is good to check that none of the adjustment wheels are close to the limit of their movement. It is best to return all three wheels to a middle position before you start trying to centre the bubble.

Figure 16.3
Setting up a
dumpy level:
extend the legs
– make a wide
base – make
the top roughly
level – stamp
the feet down
– screw on
the level head
– adjust the
wheels to centre
the bubble

Figure 16.4
Using the
screws to centre
the bubble on a
dumpy level

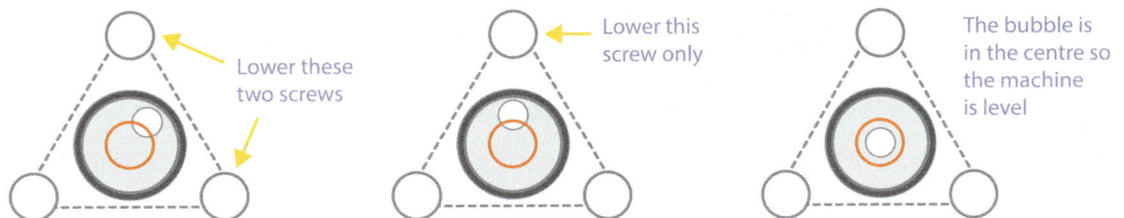

Lower these
two screws

Lower this
screw only

The bubble is
in the centre so
the machine
is level

Once you have set the level up be careful not to push it, kick it or lean on it too heavily. If you do, check the bubble is still in the centre of the circle before you take any more levels. If it starts to rain, it is important to cover the level head as soon as possible; if water gets into the level, condensation can mist the lenses and make it difficult or impossible to use.

Taking spot heights with the dumpy

Every time you are going to take levels, first check that the bubble in the spirit level is still in the centre of the circle. Even if you set it up a short time ago, someone might have knocked into it or tripped over it and made it un-levelled.

Focusing

If you look through the level sight, you should see a thin black horizontal line and a thin black vertical line, crossing at the centre, dividing the view into quarters. These are called the crosshairs. **If you cannot see the crosshairs**, you need to rotate the end of the eye piece a little to one side or the other – not everyone's eyes are the same and yours might have a slightly different focal length to

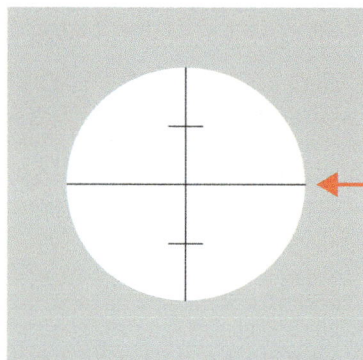

Take all levels from this line

Figure 16.5
Make sure to read the level from the central line cross-hair

Figure 16.6
Focusing the level

Figure 16.7
Adjusting the
focus on the
cross-hairs and
on the staff

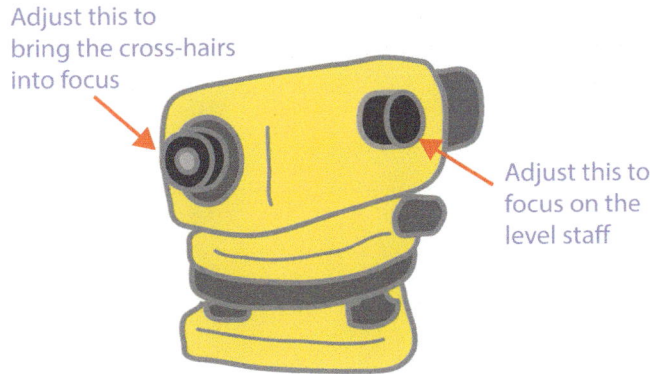

Adjust this to
bring the cross-hairs
into focus

Adjust this to
focus on the
level staff

the last person who used the level. With most dumpy levels, there will be additional shorter lines crossing the central vertical line above and below the main central horizontal line. When you take levels, it is very important to **only read from the main horizontal line** which goes across the whole view finder and to ignore the shorter horizontal stadia lines above and below.

To read the level on the staff you will need to bring the staff into focus in the viewfinder so that you can clearly see both the staff and the cross-hairs. You can point the level head roughly at the staff using the small sight on top of the level head. Look through the main view finder. **If the view is blurry**, turn the large knob on the side of the dumpy level until the level staff comes into focus.

The level staff

The measuring staff for the level is extendable. Extend as many stages as you need for the depth you want to measure, but make sure you extend the staff from the bottom upwards, leaving the upper stages un-extended if you do not need them. Make sure that each stage extends fully and clicks into place; if any stage up to the height you are measuring is not fully extended all your measurements will be wrong.

Most dumpy staffs will have measurements marked on both sides. The back side has every centimetre individually numbered just like a measuring tape, which makes it easy to use when there is only a short distance between the dumpy level and the staff. However, over longer distances, the numbers become too small to see.

▶ Figure 16.8
The marking on
the staff

In most circumstances, the front side of the level scale will be used as this can be seen up to 50m away from the dumpy level. This side

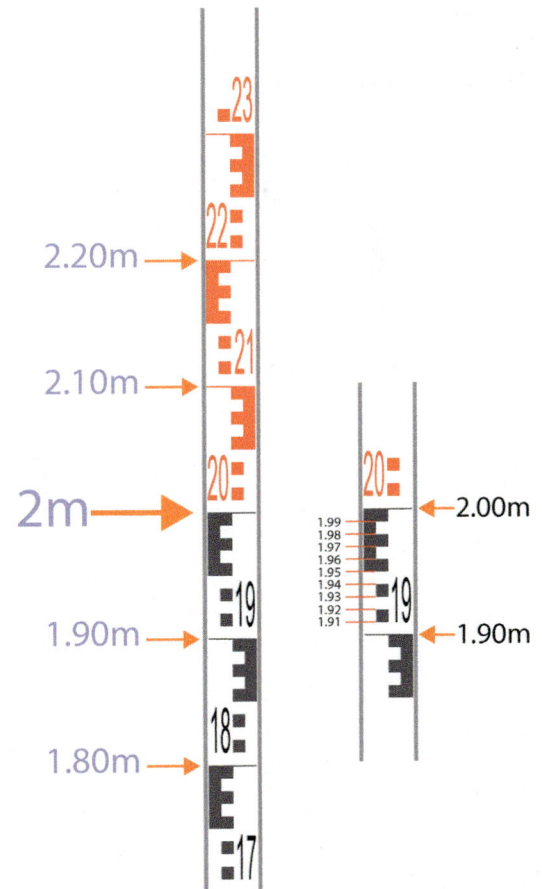

is marked with a pattern of lines and blocks and much fewer, larger numbers, which change between black and red every metre. A horizontal line is marked every 10 cm and a number sits just above each line. These numbers refer to the number of 10 cm intervals the horizontal line is above the ground, so for example, the number 19 would mean that the horizontal line it sits above is 1.90 m above the ground.

The 10 cms between each horizontal line is marked off with alternating white and coloured

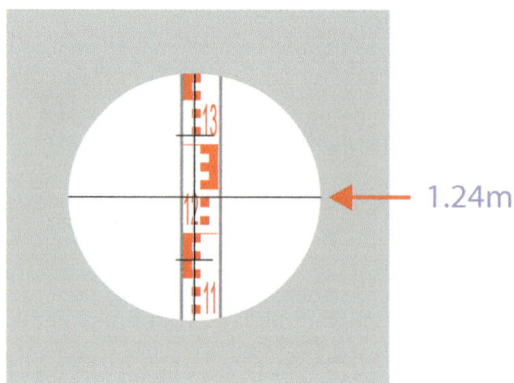

Figure 16.9 Reading the level on the staff

1.24m

1 cm blocks. In the first 5cm, the coloured blocks are isolated against a white background, but the upper 5 cm are linked with a bar of colour. This helps you to count the centimetre blocks more easily.

Reading the level

Place the base of the staff on the thing you want to measure and make sure the person holding the staff is holding it roughly vertically; you can check this against the vertical line of the cross-hairs. Focus on the staff and look for where the main horizontal line of the cross-hairs runs across the staff. Now look down to find the nearest horizontal line on the staff with a number. This number tells you how many 10 cm intervals to the ground. Now count the number of 1 cm blocks and spaces between the horizontal line and cross-hairs and add this to the height of the horizontal line on the staff. For example, if you count four 1cm blocks up from the '12' line, the level reading is 124 cm, or 1.24 m.

If the cross-hair line lies between two blocks, round up or down to the nearest cm.

Backsights, foresights and bench marks

Bench marks and temporary bench marks

Level readings are used to find the height of objects and deposits by comparing them to a fixed point of a known height which is re-measured every time levels are taken. This fixed point is called a bench mark (BM) or datum. Its height is found through a range of survey techniques and is usually expressed in metres above sea level (ASL). For bench marks, the point chosen is usually something solid and permanent which will not move or change, such as part of a structure or the top of a rocky outcrop. This is particularly important if you will be coming back to a site over several years. A survey stake can also be used but will ideally be hammered a long way into the ground and cemented in. Even then, you should record the positon, and cover the stake with sand or rocks when you are finished work for the season, in order that you can find it again in the future.

If the nearest permanent bench mark is inconveniently far from where you are excavating, a temporary bench mark (TBM) can be set up. This is a less permanent spot chosen close to the trench, such as a large rock or a stake in the ground, the height of which is found by comparing it to the permanent bench mark.

If there is no available known bench mark when you start excavating you can still take levels. Just establish a temporary bench mark and make sure to take a backsight on it every time you take levels. The calculations can be done later when you or the surveyor has found the height of your TBM.

Backsights and foresights

The **backsight** is a level reading taken with the staff placed on the bench mark. It is essential to take a backsight every time you use the dumpy level or all your readings will be useless. It is best to take the backsight at the start, before you take levels on the things you are measuring. If you do it at the beginning, if someone knocks over the dumpy level while you are using it you can still use the readings you have made up to that point. Also, it is easy to forget to take the backsight if you leave it until the end.

Foresights are the readings you take by placing the base of the staff on the features you want to find the heights of. The foresight readings tell you the height of the dumpy level above the target features.

When you set up the dumpy level, pick the most convenient spot for what you want to do; it does not have to be the same place every time. Choose somewhere roughly flat where you can see both the bench mark and all the things you want to measure, but not too close to any of them. Be careful not to put it where it will be in the way or where it might get knocked over.

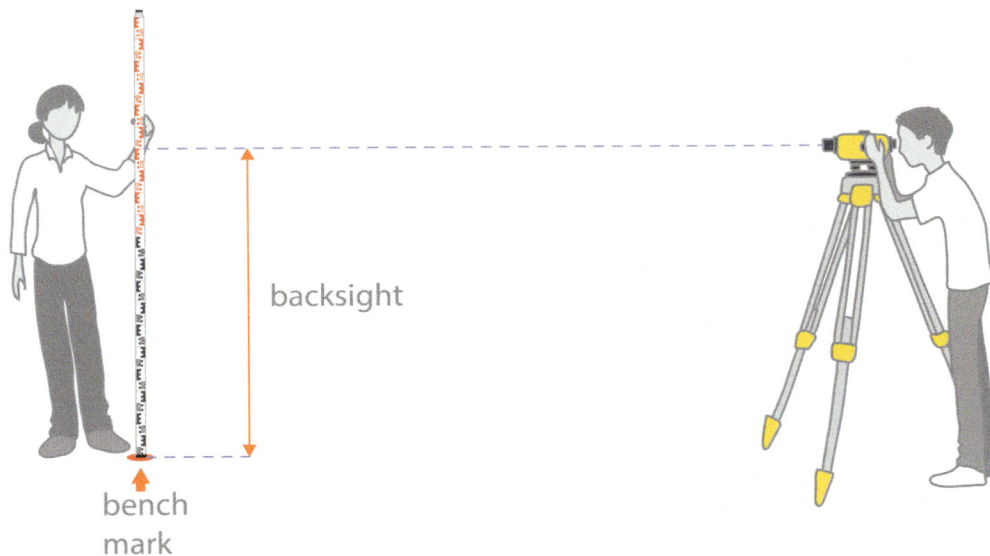

backsight

bench
mark

Figure 16.10
The backsight
reading tells
you how high
the dumpy level
is above the
bench mark

Calculating your reduced levels

Instrument height

The reduced level is the height of the object you are measuring in metres above sea level. The backsight reading tells you how high the dumpy level is above the bench mark. You know the height of the bench mark, so you can work out the height of the level head, the **instrument height**. Simply add the backsight (BS) to the bench mark (BM) height.

Instrument height = bench mark + backsight

IH = BM + BS

If you know the instrument height (IH), and the foresight (FS) is the height of the level head above the thing you are measuring, you can find the height of the target object (the reduced level) by subtracting the foresight from the instrument height.

Height of target object = Instrument height (IH) – Foresight (FS)

Reduced level = IH – FS

We can combine these two steps into a single calculation to give:

Reduced level of target object = bench mark + backsight – foresight

Reduced level of target object = BM + BS – FS

Example calculation

Let us say you are working on a site and you want to take some levels on a wall you have found. The surveyor has set up a temporary bench mark on a big rock close to your trench with a level of 156.82 m above mean sea level.

TBM = 156.82 m

You set up the dumpy level and take the backsight by asking your colleague to hold the staff on the big rock which is your temporary bench mark. You take the reading, which is 1.25m.

BS = 1.25 m

Now you need to take the foresights on the wall. First take your plan and mark the spots on the wall where you want to take levels. You decide to take two readings on the top of the wall and two at the bottom of the wall so you will know how tall it is. On your plan you label these points 1, 2, 3 and 4. Then you take readings on each point with the dumpy level and record the foresights:

$$1 = 1.86$$
$$2 = 1.89$$
$$3 = 2.47$$
$$4 = 2.51$$

Now you can calculate your reduced levels. First calculate the instrument height, which is the bench mark plus the backsight:

Instrument height = 156.82 + 1.25 = 158.07

To find the reduced levels we just need to take each foresight away from the instrument height:

$$1 = 158.07 - 1.86 = 156.21 \text{ m}$$
$$2 = 158.07 - 1.89 = 156.18 \text{ m}$$
$$3 = 158.07 - 2.47 = 155.60 \text{ m}$$
$$4 = 158.07 - 2.51 = 155.56 \text{ m}$$

The maximum height of the wall is the highest level minus the lowest, so $156.21 - 155.56 = 0.65$

So the wall is 65 cm high.

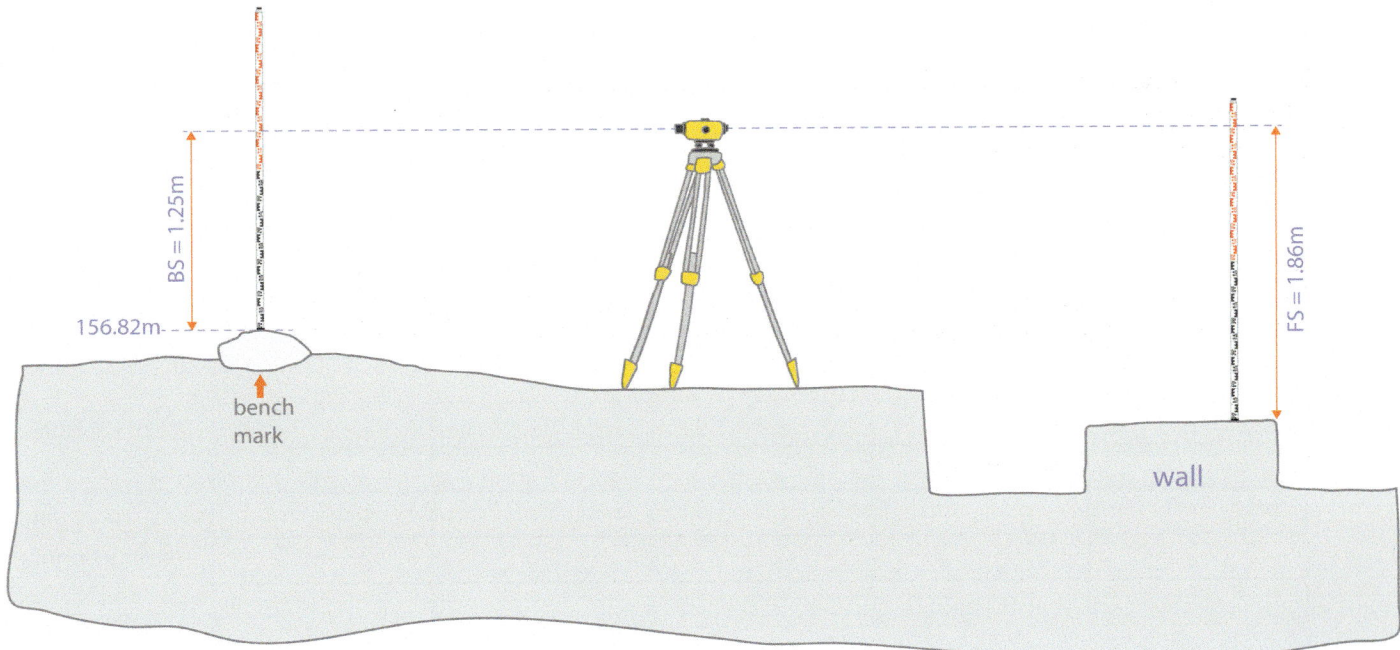

Figure 16.11
Taking the backsight and foresight

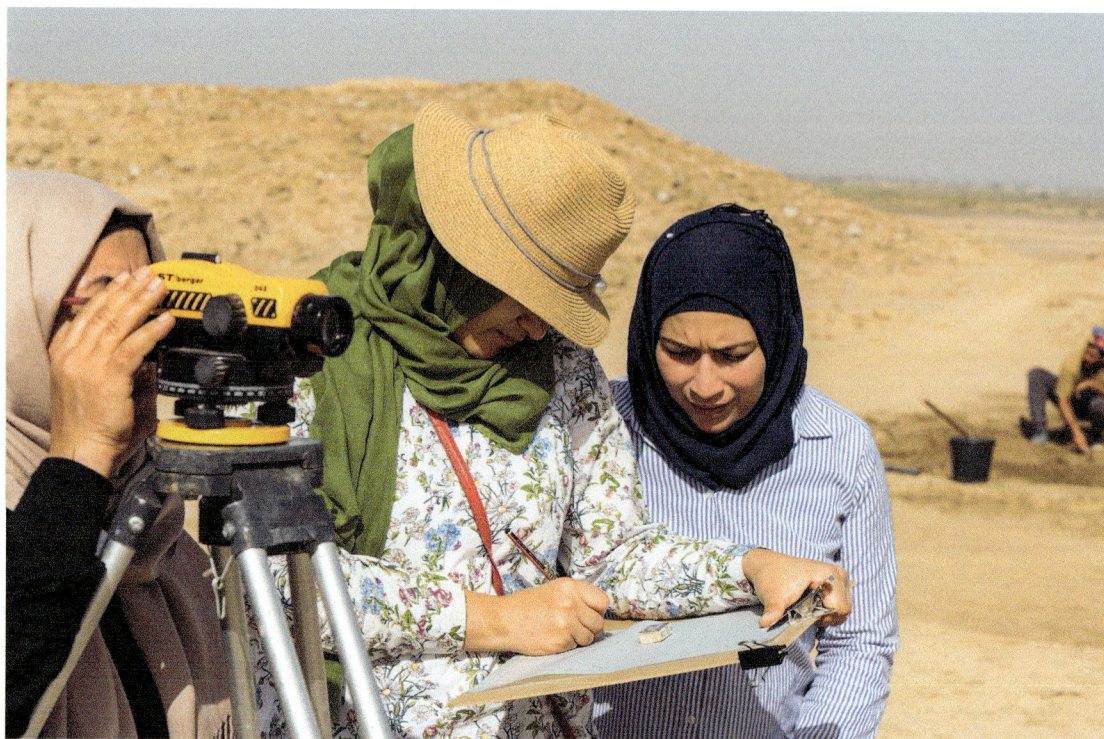

Figure 16.12
Recording levels
on site

If you need to take a lot of levels, you can use a level recording sheet formatted like this (a complete sheet to print out can be found in the Appendix):

Levels recording sheet

Site   **Trench**   **Date**   **Supervisor**

	TBM =		Plan no.	
Level no.	**Backsight**	**Instrument height**	**Foresight**	**Reduced level**

16.13 Typical format of a sheet for recording the taking and calculation of levels

Chapter 17

Environmental Protocols

The recovery of environmental datasets – the 'ecofactual record' – is an essential part of modern excavation practice, yielding information on the presence and exploitation of animal and plant resources, and what these can tell us about the environment, climate, diet, economy, social hierarchies and many other aspects of ancient societies.

The principal categories are as follows:

Animal and fish bones

Study of animal and fish bones can give information on species present, diet, butchering methods, environment, economic strategy and social differentiation; animal bones may also be used for radiocarbon dating.

Figure 17.1 Collecting samples from a gridded surface

Shells

Study of shells can give information on environment, diet, trade, use in jewellery and decoration (e.g. of statues, inlays on furniture) and ritual; shells may also be artefacts in their own right, for example used as containers for cosmetics/pigments.

Charcoal and wood

Study of charcoal and wood can give information on the use of fire, types of trees present, environment, exploitation strategy. Charcoal samples are also useful for radiocarbon dating (but beware of long-lived trees) and for dendrochronology (but only on some trees – note that in some tropical areas trees grow all year round so do not have annual growth rings, so cannot be used for dendrochronology).

Seeds, fruits and nuts

Study of seeds, fruits and nuts can give information on species present, agriculture, environment, diet, economic strategy, social differentiation; being very short-lived, these are excellent for radiocarbon dating; funerary offerings.

Pollen

Study of pollen can give information on the environment, possibly use of flowers, changing vegetation through time; be careful though, because pollen can be transported long distances by wind/water, so pollen on site may not reflect the immediate environs of the site.

Animal hairs and plant fibres

Study of animal hairs and plant fibres can give information on the exploitation of plants and animals in the local environment, evidence for use in textiles (flax), matting, basketry, ropes and string (hemp, goat hair), tents, can be used for radiocarbon dating.

Human bones

Study of human remains can give information on age, gender, disease, occupation, injuries, social differentiation, geographic origin, genetic characteristics and burial practices. It may also be possible to use the remains for radiocarbon dating.

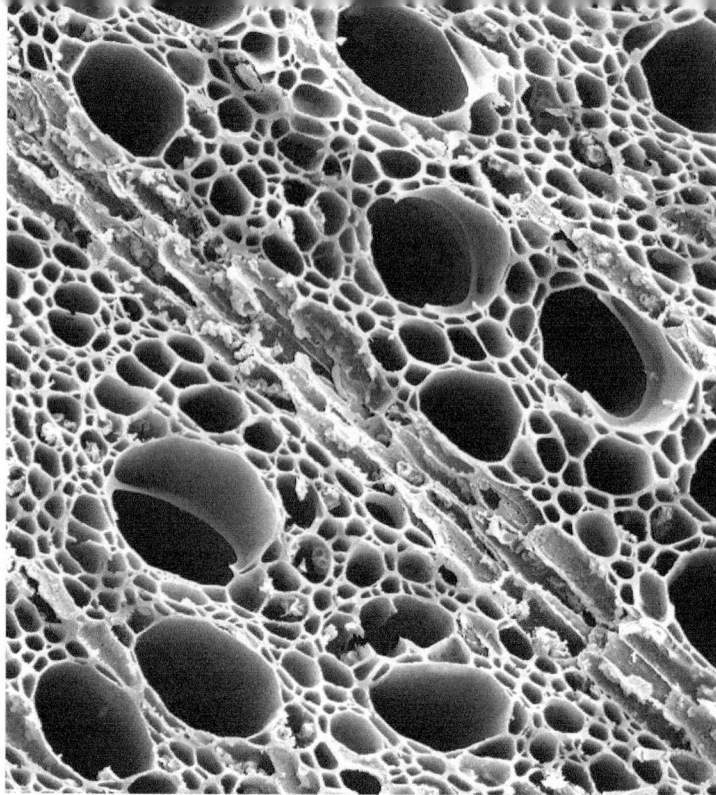

Figure 17.2 A sample of charcoal – in this case hawthorn – as seen under a scanning electron microscope (courtesy Dr Caroline Cartwright)

Soils and sediments

Study of soils and sediments can give information on local geology, site formation, climate, presence of animals, use of rooms and surfaces; use as raw materials, e.g. clay for pottery, mudbrick, plaster floors and walls, etc.

Residues on ceramics

Study of residues on ceramics can give information on the contents of vessels, which may in turn give information on the exploitation of animal (milk, yoghurt), vegetable (oil, wine, date syrup) and mineral (bitumen, pigments) resources. Due to environmental conditions, these residues do not survive well in normal conditions in the Middle East (unlike the case in northern or western Europe), but consideration should be given to taking residue samples from very well sealed contexts such as burials or destruction levels.

In order to recover all of this information, it is important to have a protocol for the recovery of ecofactual data. While in some cases (e.g. many animal bones, shells, potsherds with residues, large

Figure 17.3
Sherd from an olive oil storage jar selected for residue analysis

pieces of charcoal) samples might be recovered by hand (avoiding actual contact if necessary), a very large amount of data is recovered by dry sieving and flotation. So an established procedure for carrying this out needs to be worked out prior to the start of excavation.

Sampling and Flotation

Soil sampling

A key part of the environmental protocol is taking soil samples for flotation. As with any other sample, it is important that the context is meaningful: there is no point in taking soil samples from tertiary contexts like topsoil, and in general it is also not meaningful to take samples from secondary contexts, with the important exception of burnt destruction debris, as ashy soils are excellent for the preservation of charred seed remains. However, all primary contexts should be sampled. In the case of most primary contexts – other than surfaces – that is pits, layers, fills, ovens, hearths, drains, latrines, etc, a single sample of 5 litres of soil should be taken (on some projects the standard is 15 litres). In the case of floors and outdoor surfaces, the area should be divided into a grid of either 50 cm or 1 m squares (depending on the size of the area), and a 2 litre sample taken from every other square by scraping over the whole surface of the square. The excavator should take note of which grid squares the samples come from and label each sample carefully. Each sample must be given a unique sample number, which again must be entered in the supervisor's notebook and drawing on a sketch plan. The sample should be double-bagged,

Figure 17.4
A floor gridded
for soil
sampling

with the soil put in one large bag and that bag put inside a second larger bag, as otherwise they can easily tear or burst. Two labels should be written: put one in a small bag of its own and put this in with the soil; put the second between the two large bags. To repeat, the notes must include a sketch showing where the sample was taken from.

With regard to materials (small finds and ceramics) in the samples, policies vary as to whether to extract these or retain them in the sample. Protocols will generally dictate that small fragments of potsherd are retained in the sample. In the case of larger pieces – particularly if they are part of a vessel which could be reconstructed – opinions differ: some directors may expect all ceramics to be kept in the sample, others not. It is also important to note that there are some small finds that may be damaged by flotation (for example, metals, glass and ivory) and some artefacts (unbaked clay, for example sealings and fragments of cuneiform tablets) that can be destroyed by flotation. If in doubt, please consult the director. Of course, any small finds, as well as significant ceramics (not small fragments), that are removed from the earth being sampled should be labelled separately, and it is important to make a record of this. Also, any rocks and stones should be excluded from the sample: this is primarily to avoid damage to the flotation machine. Initially the bags should be left open and out in the sun to avoid moisture build-up and potential mould; once dried out the bags should be securely tied. The remaining part of the floor should of course be sieved as excavated. The outcome of the flotation process consists of the 'light fraction', elements which float, most importantly, the archaeobotanical material; and the 'heavy fraction', elements which sink such as debris, fragments and micro-artefacts of stone, clay, metal, bone, shell, slag etc.

Animal bones

All animal bones are collected and labelled with their context; in order to avoid moisture building up in the sample, **the bags should not be closed**. Bones should be excavated carefully using wooden tools and soft brushes. It is very important that clusters of bones are given their own number and photographed and drawn in situ before lifting.

Carbon samples

Samples of burnt wood, seeds, phytoliths or other organic material suitable for radiocarbon dating should be collected from all primary

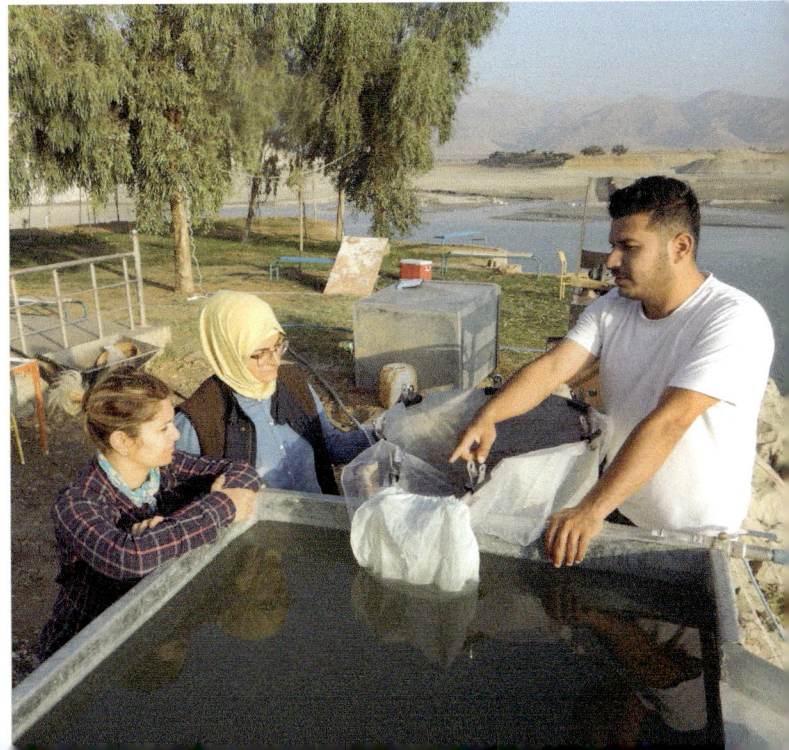

► Figure 17.5
Flotation on site

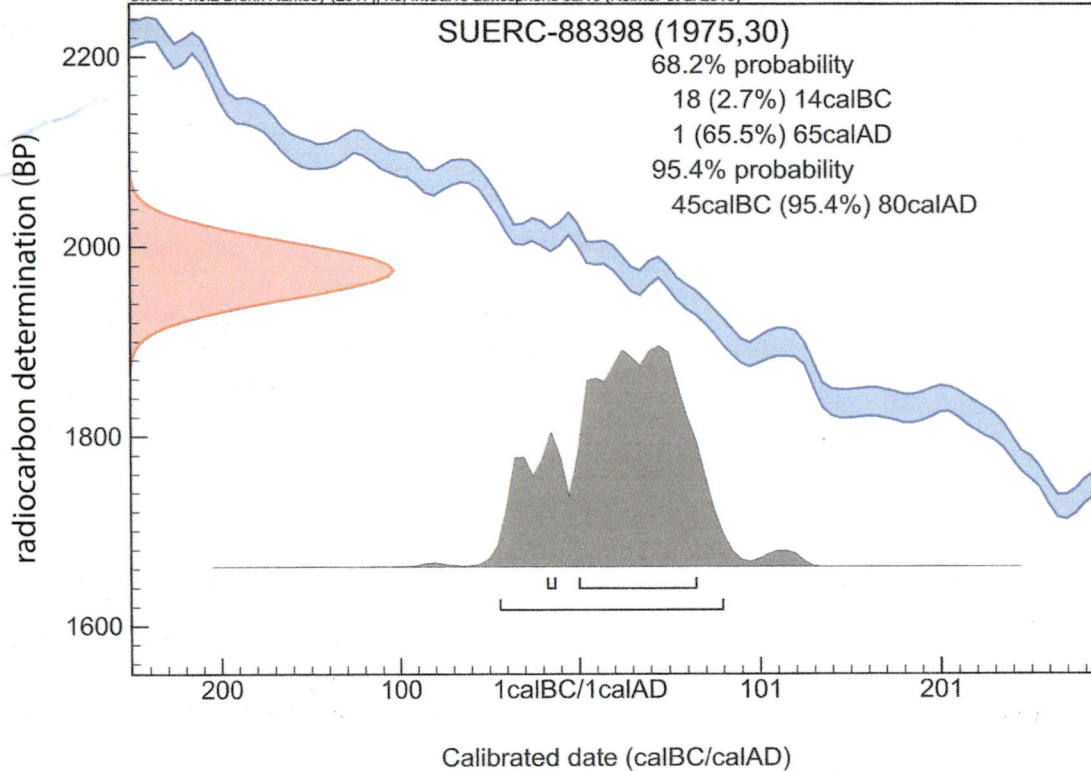

OxCal v4.3.2 Bronk Ramsey (2017); r:5; IntCal13 atmospheric curve (Reimer et al 2013)

SUERC-88398 (1975,30)
68.2% probability
18 (2.7%) 14calBC
1 (65.5%) 65calAD
95.4% probability
45calBC (95.4%) 80calAD

Figure 17.6
A radiocarbon
plot

Figure 17.6 A radiocarbon plot

contexts. Do not collect radiocarbon samples from secondary or tertiary contexts. For AMS dating a sample of 5 g is sufficient. When collecting the samples, the burnt material should be carefully excavated and lifted using a trowel or other metal implement, taking care not to touch the sample with your hands. Samples should be wrapped gently in aluminium foil and then placed inside a plastic zip-lock bag. A tag should be placed inside the bag recording the find number, sample type (e.g. radiocarbon sample) and context number; this bag should then be double-bagged inside another zip-lock bag. The validity of charcoal samples for dating will be destroyed by cigarette smoke: **DO NOT SMOKE IN THE EXCAVATION AREA.**

Phytolith samples

Most contexts from which it is desirable to take soil samples are also suitable for the retrieval of phytolith samples. Typical contexts would therefore be surfaces of all types (unless they have been rigorously cleaned), including outside areas, streets and alleys, pits, middens, hearths, kilns and any ashy deposit. Take a sample of about a teaspoon of earth (fine-grained particles with no stones) and put it in a small zip-lock bag, appropriately labelled. With interior occupation surfaces and floors, one or two samples should be taken from each floor (or suprafloor). In all cases, if there are ashy parts of the deposits concentrate the sampling strategy on these. Phytolith samples can also be taken from graves (see the section on burials elsewhere in this manual).

Parasitology samples

For the collection of parasitology samples from graves, see the chapter on burials above.

Chapter 18

Drawing Plans and Sections

All archaeological contexts need a plan of some kind. This can range from a carefully drawn scaled plan, to a digitised photogrammetry image, or even just a quick sketch plan with a few levels. There are a very large number of ways to produce a plan, both digital and non-digital. You should choose the method which best suits what you are planning, the equipment you have, and the time available. Often how you plan is simply a question of personal preference.

Plans, sections, elevations and profiles

It is important to understand the differences between plans, sections, elevations and profiles.

Plans show archaeological contexts viewed from directly above, showing their horizontal extent.

Sections show features and deposits which have been cut through vertically, such as at the sides of a trench.

Elevations show the vertical faces of an up-standing structure or feature, such as a wall face.

Figure 18.1
Drawing a
section at
Qalatga
Darband

Figure 18.2
Using a
planning frame

Profiles are a single line showing the change in surface height across a structure, feature or building. Profiles are often drawn to illustrate the shape of a pit cut or a change in level across rooms.

Traditional drawing of plans

Despite advances in laser scanning and photogrammetry, the best way to plan is still by hand, whether you do this with a pencil and drawing film, or with a digital tablet and stylus. The main advantage of this is that you do all the drawing in the trench where you can see what you are drawing with true colour, depth and texture. If there is anything that is not clear, you can take a brush or a trowel and resolve the problem before you draw. This is not possible when drawing a plan from digital images.

However, there are disadvantages to drawing plans by hand, mainly that it takes a lot of practice before you can plan quickly and accurately. Even for an experienced planner, it will often be quicker to plan from digital images, even if some accuracy is sacrificed.

If you are using pencil and drawing film (often called permatrace), the usual set up is a planning board with graph paper taped to it. Drawing film is then taped over this so that the graph paper is visible through it. Drawing film is better than tracing paper as it does not warp, is stronger and can be used in rain. Remember that you will need a hard pencil, because if you use an HB or softer on drawing film the lines will be very thick and smudge easily. 6H pencils are generally thought to be best. You cannot use a pen on drawing film.

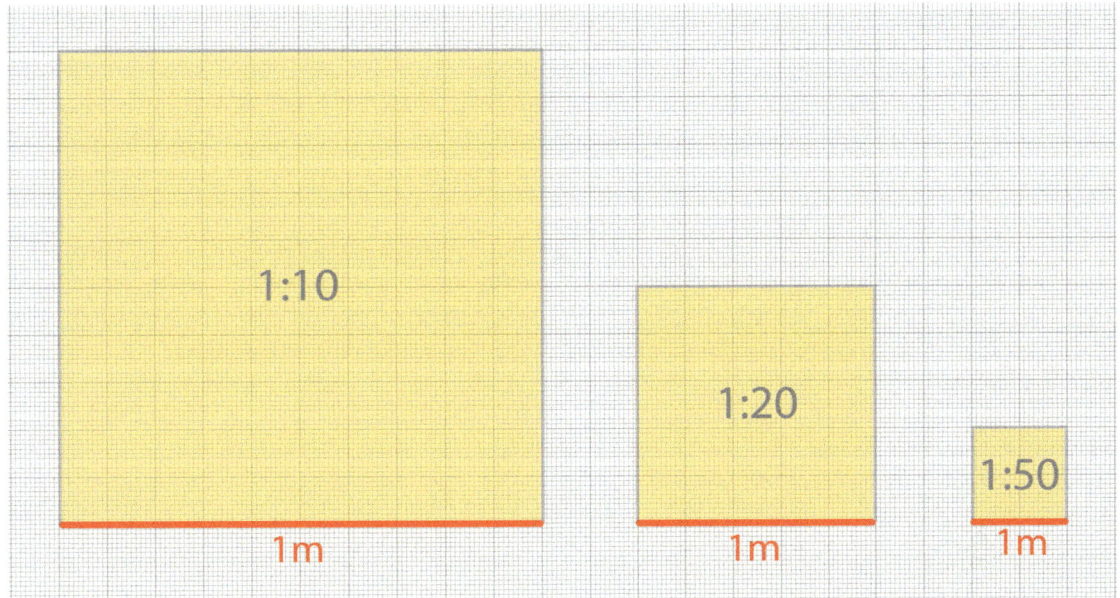

Figure 18.3
Drawings of a
1 m square at
different scales

Scale

Choosing the right scale is very important as it determines how much detail you can include. The most common scales for drawing plans are 1:10, 1:20, and 1:50; which one you choose depends on the size of what you are drawing and how much detail you need to show.

To draw at scale you need to convert the measurements of the features you are planning in the trench into centimetres on the paper. Drawing plans at 1:10, 10 cm in the trench is 1 cm on the paper. At 1:20, 20 cm in the trench is 1 cm on the paper, and at 1:50, 50 cm in the trench is 1cm on the paper.

Plans are usually drawn at 1:20

For features where you want to show a lot of detail, like burials, you should plan at 1:10.

For large plans which **do not** need much detail, like surface plans, 1:50 is a good scale.

Sections, elevations and profiles are usually drawn at 1:10

If the section, elevation or profile is very long, more than 6 or 7 m, you might consider doing it at 1:20. Sometimes profiles are drawn across large areas to show large scale level changes; these can be drawn at 1:50.

Plans

There are lots of ways of drawing plans. Here we cover the most usual.

Off-set planning

Off-set planning is probably the most common method and involves measuring everything relative to a baseline. The first thing to do is set up the baseline, which is usually a long measuring tape stretched between two points, running across or beside the things you want to plan. There are two ways of doing this; you could measure your baseline relative to known points, such as the trench corners, or you could survey your baseline in using a total station or multi station. If you measure from known points you do not need to set up the multi station or retrieve the information later but you will have to carefully measure in your points relative to known points, which can be tricky as known points are usually outside the trench at surface level. If you use the multi station you can place your baseline wherever you like and just shoot the points in with the machine.

Next, mark the baseline on your plan, placing it along one of the grid lines on the graph paper. It is helpful to mark off every metre along this line as a guide. Now take a hand tape (some people prefer a folding ruler), place the zero-end on the point you want to measure and hold the hand tape so that it crosses the baseline tape at a right-angle. Where the tapes cross will tell you how far along the baseline, and how far away from the baseline the object is; converting these distances to your scale, you can draw the point on your plan.

When you have marked the key points of a feature, look at what you are planning and use the points as a guide to draw it. Try to get the shapes right; if you simply join the points you have measured with straight lines your plan will be ugly and inaccurate.

As well as the things you are planning, you will need to plan the limits of excavation and any fixed points, such as the trench corners or other survey points.

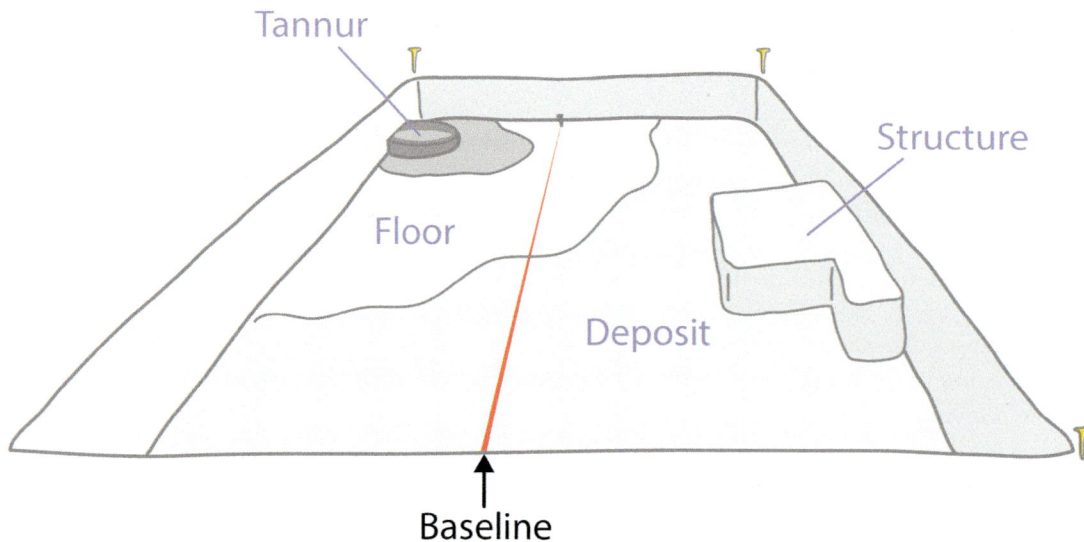

Figure 18.4
Example trench
with a baseline
tape

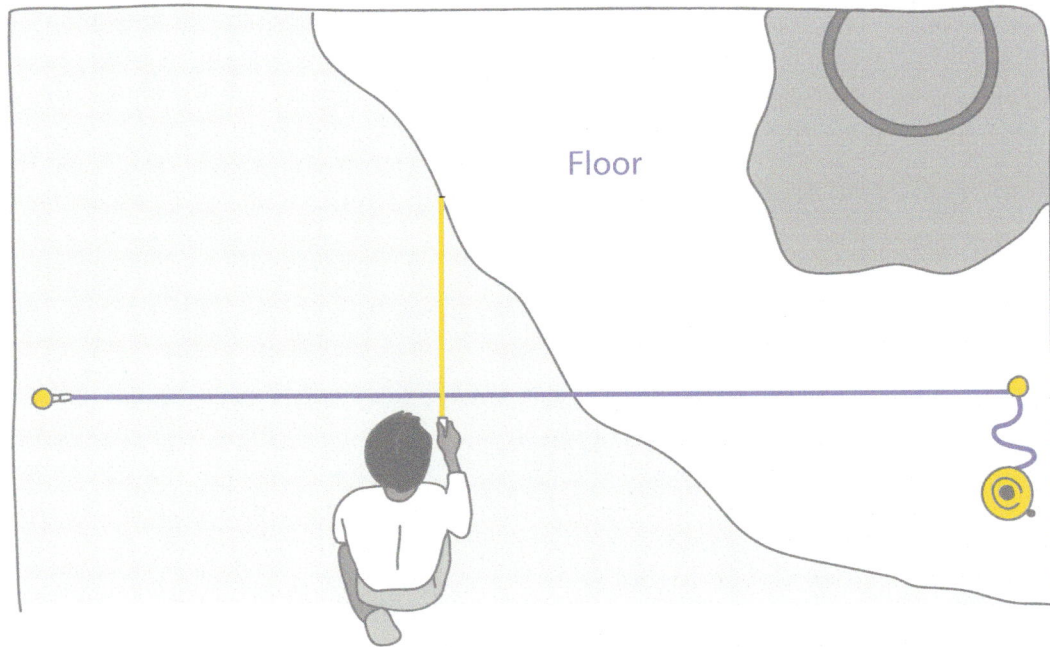

Figure 18.5 Off-set planning viewed from above

Floor

Using a planning frame

A planning frame is a rigid square frame, usually 1 m x 1m across the **inside** edges, strung with strings at regular intervals to make a grid. If the strings are placed every 10 cm, so that the frame is divided into 100 small squares, it is called a 1:10 frame because if you draw so that each square of the planning frame corresponds to 1 cm^2 on the graph paper, the plan will be at a scale of 1:10. Similarly, if the frame is strung every 20 cm, so that it is divided into 25 squares, it is called a 1:20 frame; if each of these squares is drawn so that it corresponds to 1 cm^2 on the graph paper the plan will be at 1:20.

▶ Figure 18.6 Crossing the tapes at a right angle: in this example, at 129 cm along the base line, the point is 70 cm away from the baseline

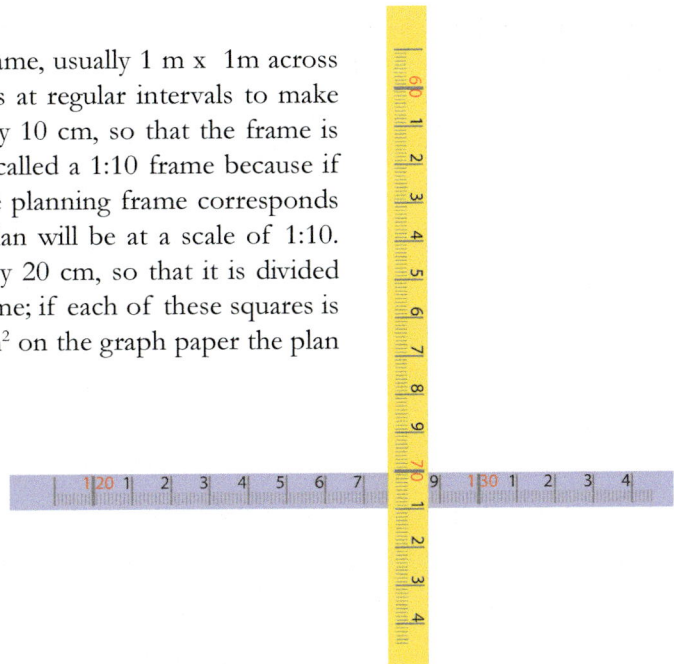

To use a planning frame it is best to establish a baseline across or next to the things you want to plan, just as you would when you draw an off-set plan. Then place the planning frame so that one side, or one of the strings, runs exactly

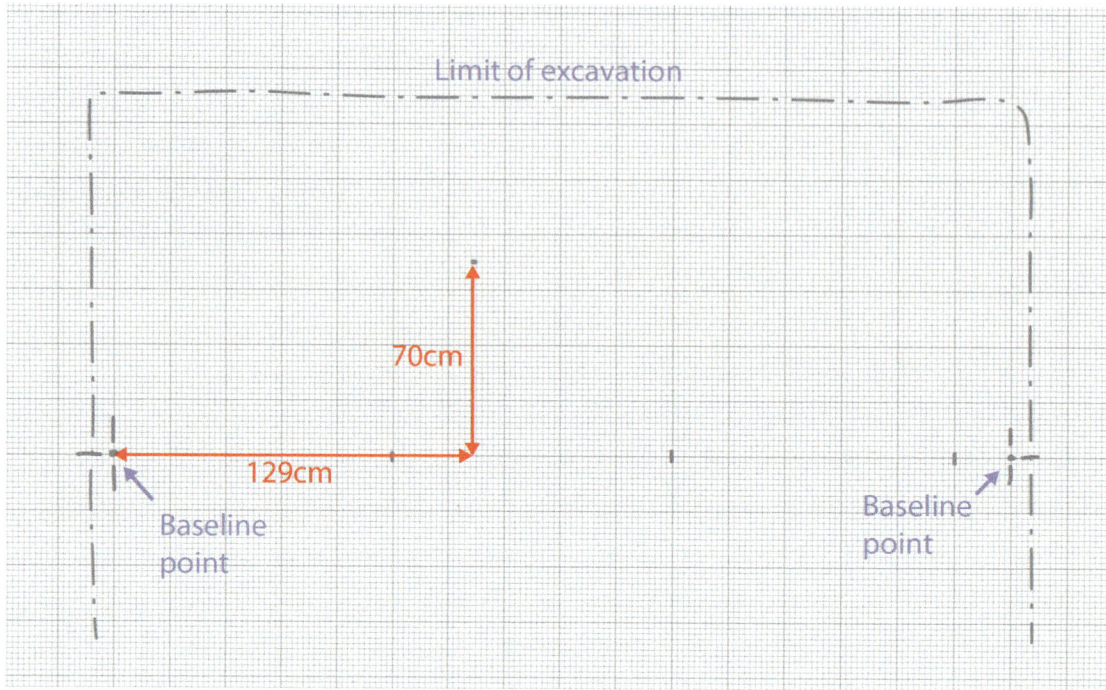

Figure 18.7
Measure the
point onto your
1:20 plan like
this

along the baseline tape, and the corners of the frame's squares lie at the tape's 10 or 20 cm interval marks. This effectively lines the frame up with the squares on the graph paper. Now mark the corners of the planning frame onto your plan.

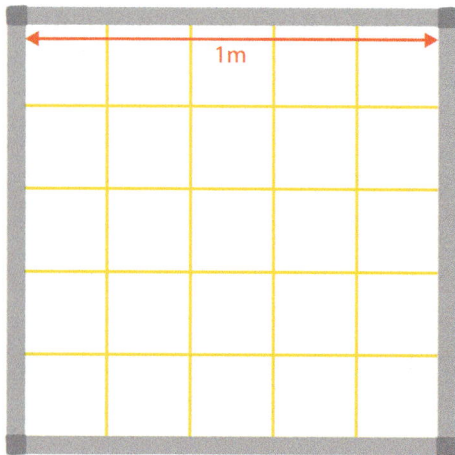

1:20 frame

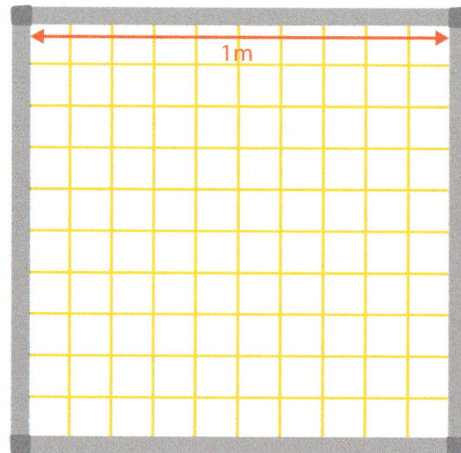

1:10 frame

Figure 18.8
Planning
frames

Figure 18.9
Planning with a
planning frame,
viewed from
above

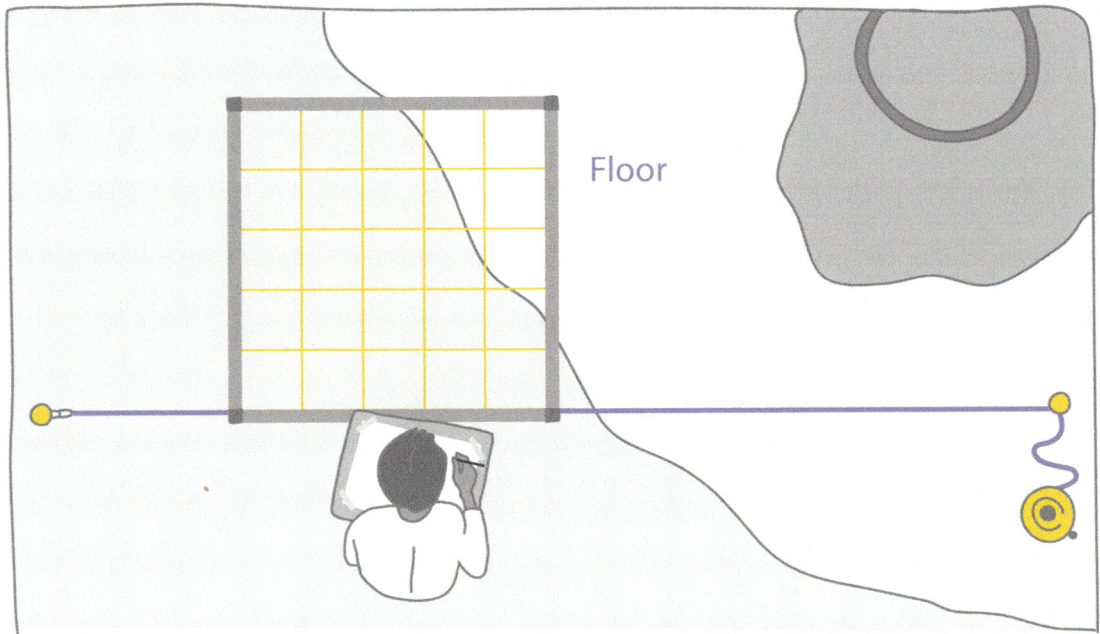

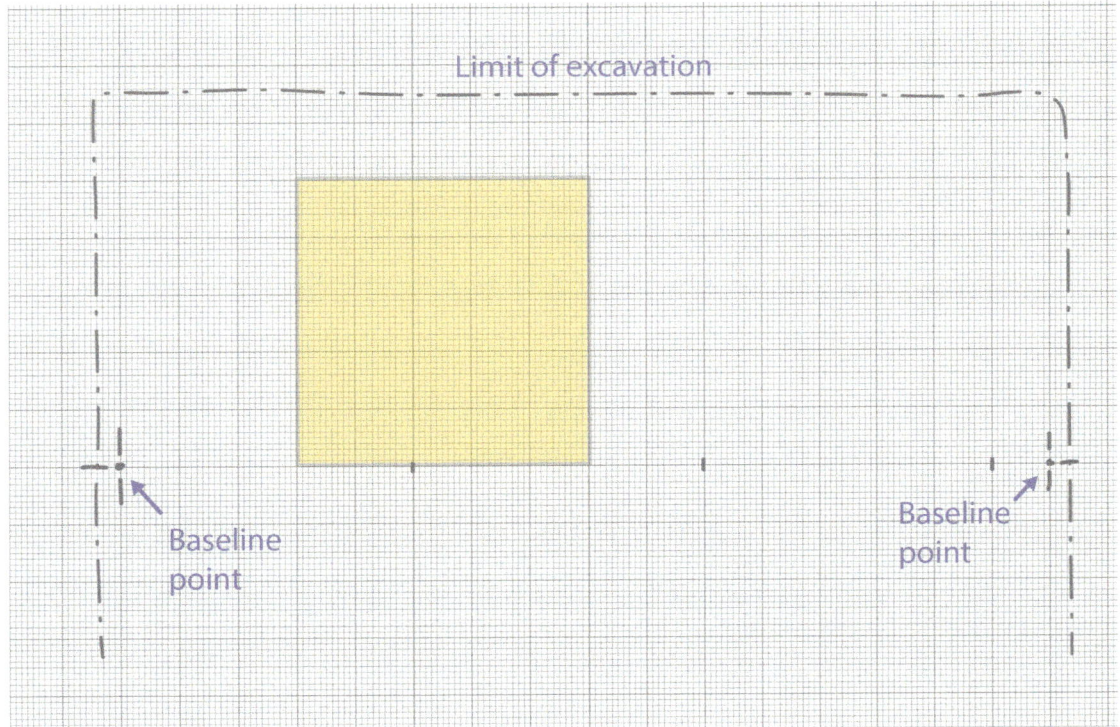

Floor

Limit of excavation

Baseline
point

Baseline
point

Figure 18.10
Planning frame
marked on the
1:20 plan

Now each square of the planning frame corresponds to a 1 cm square on your plan. Simply draw what you can see in each square of the frame in each square on your plan. When you have completed the frame, just shift it down the baseline tape to draw the next metre square and so on. With practice, drawing with a planning frame can be very fast. Unlike with off-set planning, once the frame is positioned there is no need to measure anything; you can just look and draw. Planning frames are particularly good for drawing more complicated structures and contexts such as brickwork, stone scatters or paving. Planning frames are not so good for planning things which are not very flat; the frame needs to lie fairly flat to be accurate. You can compensate to some extent by propping the corners of the planning frame up, or sometimes by using a plumb bob, but if the archaeology is really not on one level it is better to use off-set planning.

Sections and elevations

Drawing sections is very similar to drawing plans but transferred into the vertical plane. The main difference is that **the baseline must be made horizontal** so that all of the deposits and features are shown at their correct relative levels.

Setting up a section line

You can set up a baseline string which is roughly level using a line-level; a small spirit level which can be suspended from a taut string. First take a large nail and hammer it into one end of the section about half way up its height. Tie a string to the nail and run the string out to the other end of the section. Tie a second nail to the string at this length. Now attach the line-level to the string next to the second nail, make the string really taut and move the nail up and down until the bubble of the line level is in the centre. Knock the nail into the section at this height, but not too firmly; you may need to adjust it.

The string should now be roughly horizontal, but you need to make sure it is really level. Check the height of the two nails using the dumpy level or the multi station. If there is more that 2 or 3 cm difference between the two nails, adjust the height of the second nail to compensate. **You must record the level of the two nails on your section.**

Drawing a section or elevation

First you need to run a measuring tape along the section line. You can attach the tape to the two levelled nails, but you must be careful not to let the tape sag; the tape is much heavier than the

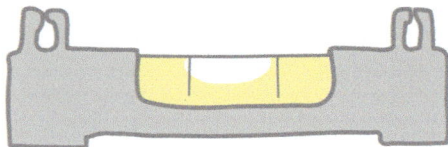

string and harder to secure tightly to the nails. Instead it is best to use two more nails to run the tape just below the levelled string, but if you do this you must remember to **measure from the level of the string** and not from the tape.

◀ Figure 18.11
A line-level

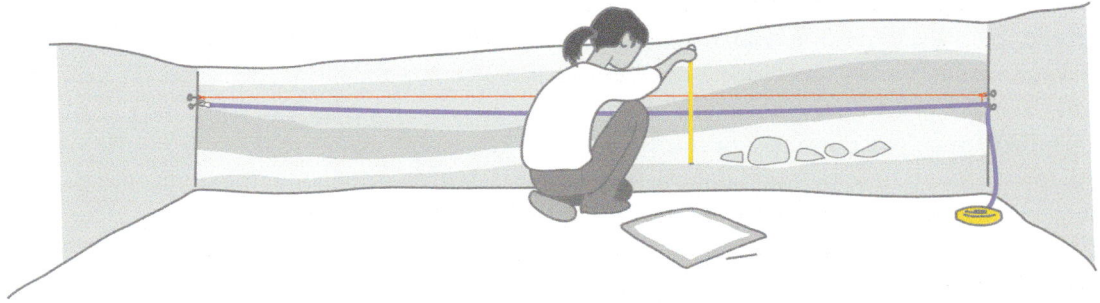

Figure 18.12
Planning a
section from a
baseline (red
string), with the
tape below

Just as when you draw an off-set plan, mark the two levelled nails on your drawing film. Remember the usual scale for a section or elevation is 1:10. Now you can measure and draw the deposits and features by using a hand tape to measure up and down from the section line string at different points along the section line tape. As with an off-set plan, measure in the key points of the features you are drawing and then use these as a guide to draw each feature as you see it. If you simply join the points with straight lines your section will be ugly and inaccurate.

Profiles

Drawing a profile is slightly different to a section or an elevation. This is because the levelled baseline must be above everything you need to draw. In some cases where the feature you are

Figure 18.13
Remember to
plan from the
string, not the
tape: here, the
point being
measured is 48
cm below the
baseline at 132
cm along the
baseline

recording is sunken, such as pits or grave cuts, you can simply hammer a stake at each end of the profile you want to draw and adjust the height at which the string is tied to each stake to level it. If your profile is across upstanding features you may need to use a long metal rod at one or both ends to get a string level higher than all the things you are drawing. Once you have established a levelled string line, drawing a profile is very easy; you simply measure down from the string to the top of the archaeology as you move along the baseline tape, then join the points to produce a single line which follows the top level of the features and deposits.

Conventions

Archaeological drawings use a series of conventions to represent the various things you are drawing. There is no fully standardised system used by all projects of all nationalities, but there are a few basic conventions which are very common and very useful.

Limit of excavation – this is usually the edge of the trench. If one or more edges of your trench is a wall or other feature you should show this as a solid line labelled with the context number. The limit of excavation line is also used to mark the edge of soundings; smaller exploratory cuts you might excavate within the trench. Limit of excavation is shown using long dashes separated by a dot:

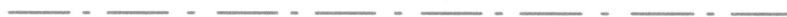

—— · —— · —— · —— · —— · —— · —— · ——

Edge of context – the edge of a clearly defined context should be shown as a solid line:

————————————————————

Truncation – this marks the edge of a context where it has been cut away by a later feature. Truncated edges are shown as short dashes, each separated by two dots:

—— ·· —— ·· —— ·· —— ·· —— ·· —— ·· ——

Edge uncertain – this is a context edge which is diffuse or unclear. An uncertain edge can be shown with a line of short dashes:

— — — — — — — — — — — — ·

Slopes – slopes are shown using hachures. The length of the hachure line shows the length of the slope. In general, the steeper the slope the closer the hachures should be. Vertical edges are shown using just the base of hachures, but these do not have to be spaced very close together:

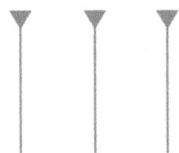

Slope

Shorter, steeper slope

Vertical edge

Other things you need to include

As well as your drawing, you need to make sure your plan includes the following information:

A north arrow – make sure you have indicated north somewhere on your plan.

A plan/section number – without a number it will be hard for people to find the right drawing later.

Scale – make sure you say which scale you have drawn at.

Date – This can help to relate the drawing to notes and photographs.

Your initials – By including you initials, if there are any problems or questions about the drawing people will know who to ask about it.

Levels – Most plans will show where on the features levels have been taken. If the levels are recorded elsewhere you should note on the plan where they can be found.

Labels – All contexts should be labelled with their context number. In addition you should add extra explanatory labels to anything which you feel is not clear and obvious from the drawing.

Numbering plans and sections

It is essential to have a methodical system for numbering plans and sections. Once again, every site will have its own system. In the examples below we utilise the system at the British Museum excavation at the site of Qalatga Darband. Plans and sections are all labelled in a single sequence for each area in the format A-1-P, A-2-S, etc., where 'A' is the area, '1' is the number in the running sequence, and 'P' or 'S' denote whether the drawing is a plan or a section. This number should be recorded on the context sheet and marked clearly on the plan itself. All contexts appearing in the plans and sections should be labelled and elevations marked in. By the end of the season, whether in the writing up period or before, all final plans and sections need to be digitised.

Planning with photogrammetry

Photogrammetry is used more and more in archaeological planning as software has made it increasingly easy. Photogrammetry is very good for planning things with clear, well defined edges and has particular advantages for intricate, detailed features which take a long time to draw in the trench, such as stone walls or sherd scatters. Photogrammetry is particularly useful when there are lots of stones or stone walls.

However, photogrammetry is not very good if the contexts you need to plan are diffuse or are not very distinct from their neighbouring deposits in terms of colour or level. In these cases it is better to do all your drawing in the trench, where you can see colour and texture variation up-close and further investigate if necessary.

The deposits and features you want to plan should be well defined and cleaned before the photographs for photogrammetry are taken. The photographs should be taken all in one go or the different shadows will make the edges of the contexts unclear. Once you have built the photogrammetry model and produced the rectified images you need, digitise them using Adobe Illustrator. Remember to adjust the size of the images to the right scale before you start digitising them.

Conventions for digitised plans

Each project needs to have its own style guide for the digitsation of plans. The following applies to the system in use for the digitisation of plans at Qalatga Darband. The basic formats, including a plan with colour swatch, line styles, scale and north arrow, are available in the Illustrator file 'StyleExample.ai'.

Colour Swatches – when you start your plan, import the swatch library from the example plan provided. Each swatch is labelled with the material it shades.

Layers:

Top: Scale and arrow
        Labels
        Levels and survey pts
        Outlines (including hachures)
        Shading
Bottom: Scan

Scale and north arrow should be the ones on the example plan. The scale may require re-sizing if the plan is not 1:100. The scale bar is made up of two sub-groups: if you want a 2-m scale instead of 4-m (for a small plan), make the lower group 'scale extension' invisible.

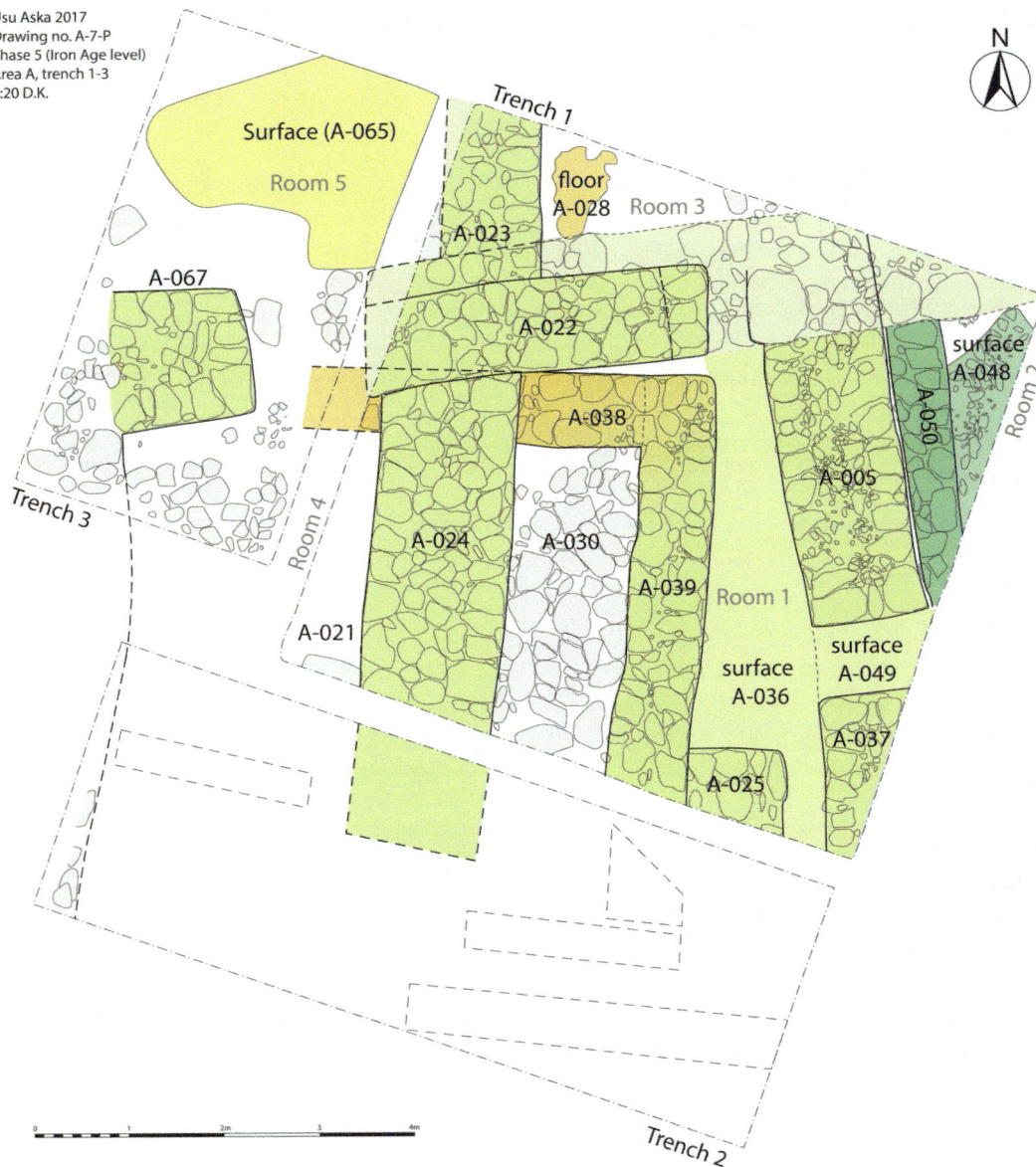

Figure 18.14 A
digitised plan

Usu Aska 2017
Drawing no. A-7-P
Phase 5 (Iron Age level)
Area A, trench 1-3
1:20 D.K.

Trench 1

Surface (A-065)
Room 5

floor
A-028

Room 3

A-023

A-067

A-022

surface
A-048

Room 2

A-050

A-038

A-005

Trench 3

Room 4

A-024

A-030

A-039

Room 1

A-021

surface
A-036

surface
A-049

A-037

A-025

Trench 2

0   1   2m   3   4m

Labels should use Illustrator's default font Myriad Pro. General labels should be 12 pt with context numbers in round brackets. If you need to connect the label to the object use a plain straight line 0.75 pt. Information about the plan should be added to the top left corner of the plan in 24 pt and include the information shown on the example plan.

Levels and survey points: Use the symbols given on the example plan: the red cross for survey points and the 'pi' symbol for levels. Both should be labelled as on the example plan in Myriad Pro 10 pt.

Pencil thicknesses

Architectural feature outlines (walls, etc.) – pencil tool, freehand – 2 pt

Bricks or stones within a feature/wall – pencil tool, freehand – 0.75 pt

Fragment scatters (pot, bone, stone) – pencil tool, freehand – 0.75 pt

All other outlines (context limits, emplacements, tannurs, etc.) – pencil tool – 1 pt

(If the object is of a very small size or very detailed, a smaller line width can be used at your discretion).

Uncertain edge dashed line – pencil tool – 1 pt weight – 6 pt dash/6 pt gap – rounded line ends

Edge of excavation dashed line – pencil tool (freehand, not straightline tool) – 1 pt weight – 15 pt dash/6 pt gap/1 pt dash/6 pt gap – rounded line ends

Figure 18.15
Planning wall
foundations
with planning
frames

Hachures (slope indication marks) – use the little triangles from the example plan and add a straight line of the appropriate length (0.75 pt, rounded ends) running from the body of the triangle.

Shading should be done as a separate layer for future convenience. Select the outline of the object or feature, copy and paste it, transfer it into the shading layer, remove the outline stroke and fill it using the appropriate swatch from the example plan. Line up the shading with the original outline. Make sure the shading layer is below the outlines layer.

Chapter 19

Registration

Archaeological registration is the process of recording the information available about finds at the time of discovery. It is essential to the documenting of the excavation activities and outcomes and essential that it is done as thoroughly as possible. By recording the information available at the time of excavation, the registration process keeps track of how, where and when the finds were excavated, as well as details of subsequent processing in the dig house and elsewhere. Registration thus serves both as a record-keeping activity during the season and as a preparatory step for post-excavation work and specialised study of the material. Registration applies to all classes of finds, objects and samples of all kinds. The registration process for ceramics normally has its own specific protocol and is usually carried out by ceramicists.

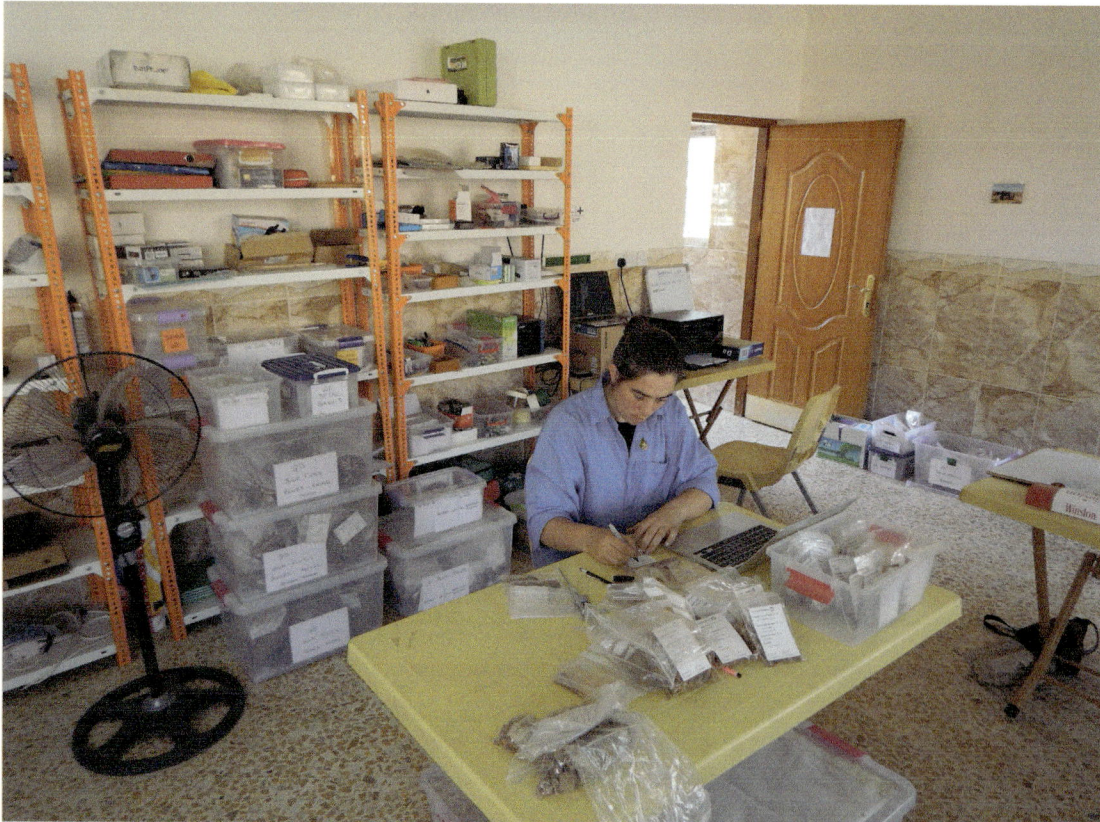

Figure 19.1
Registering
material
coming in from
the field

The main steps of archaeological registration are to:

– record finds as they are excavated

– allocate each find a unique identification number

– keep a register of all the finds by area and excavation context

– keep track of their processing by specialists in the dig house

The main objectives of archaeological registration are:

– to keep track of the relationship between each find and its archaeological context

– to prepare for the accession of finds in museum registers

– to prepare for the post-excavation study of the finds

Registration thus interfaces with all aspects of documentation in the field. In practice, the registrar is responsible for keeping track of all activities relating to finds from the moment of their arrival in the dig house. This aspect of archaeological registration can be divided into three main activities: the numbering and labelling of finds, the cataloguing of finds, and the packing and storing of finds.

Journey of an archaeological find: from excavation to storage

Excavation

The registration process begins as soon as a find is excavated in the field. As part of the process, archaeologists document the discovery, giving it a field number, noting the context and recording its location and state at the time of discovery, with photography and in plans (often sketch plans) as appropriate. Finds are then brought back to the dig house and handed over to the registrar.

Registration

In the dig house, the registrar takes over after the field director has validated all finds for registration (this step is necessary as there are inevitably occasions when items sent in from the field turn out to be natural objects). Each find is labelled, described, measured, categorised and recorded in the database. Registered finds are then sorted according to excavation area, type (object or sample), and material (e.g. organic, metal, stone, baked and unbaked clay).

Processing

Registered finds then go through a set sequence of processing, comprising at a minimum conservation, photography and illustration. The conservator will determine whether the find needs to be treated prior to being handled by other specialists. Following any such treatment the find can then be passed to the photographer and illustrator and other specialists as required. During this step, the registrar keeps track of the location of each find. After processing by the specialist, finds are returned to the registrar for final checks and packing.

Updating the registration

Once the finds have been processed they go through the final registration step. Records are updated if new information has become available – for example if an object could not be described accurately during the initial registration because it needed cleaning and/or conservation. The registrar keeps track of the find as it goes through each step of processing, assisting the specialists in the use of the database as needed.

Figure 19.2
Measuring
a find for
registration

Packing

Registered finds are packed and stored by site and excavation area, type (object or sample), material (organic, metal, stone) and registration number. It is best practice for the registrar and conservator to work together at this stage to ensure optimal storage conditions. Finds will then be handed over to the authorities at the end of the season along with the finds catalogue prepared by the registrar.

Cataloguing finds

Cataloguing finds is one of the core elements of archaeological registration. The registrar is the first person to examine and describe a find in detail. The results of the registrar's observations affect the next steps that the finds will go through. For example, the registrar may flag up finds requiring immediate conservation treatment, identify the presence of an inscription, or highlight particular features that need to be photographed and/or illustrated.

Essential information

The initial step of cataloguing consists in recording three essential pieces of information: identification, typology, and material.

Identification

The identification of a find must include its unique field number, the archaeological context it came from, the date it was excavated, and the initials of the supervisor. This basic information is the find's ID card. Identification numbers must be unique: one find – one number. The numbering system should apply to all finds and be consistent across the project. It should therefore be worked out in advance of the commencement of the excavations. There is no one standard numbering system: there are different approaches and it is up to the director to decide what he/she feels works best for the project. Whichever system is used should then be systematically and consistently applied throughout to avoid creating duplicate numbers or any other cause of confusion. One possible system is to allocate each excavation area a letter code (between one and three letters). For example, if an excavation area is designated Area A, the finds coming from the area can be numbered in running sequence, A1234, A1235, A1236, and so on. This system is best adapted to large projects with different areas being excavated simultaneously.

Typology

Object typology is an essential component of the information to be recorded during cataloguing as it facilitates further processing by enabling searching and retrieving finds by type. For example, all examples of a category (such as coins, figurines, seals, etc.) may be retrieved for specialist study. Typology cataloguing should aim at consistency to ensure that finds can be retrieved easily and efficiently. It is therefore recommended to choose from a list of object types prepared in advance. The list should be integrated into the database and should be left flexible to allow for the possibility of additions as the excavation progresses (any addition to the list should be agreed between the field director and the registrar). The list should include the main object types expected to be found, e.g. 'arrowhead', 'bead', 'coin', 'ring', 'statue', etc. What is included in the object type list depends on the nature and scope of each archaeological project. In any case, the list should aim at classifying objects using terms which are general enough to cover broad categories but informative enough to enable the sorting of finds. For example, 'fragment' is not specific enough and should not be included in the list. Conversely 'truncated bead' is too specific and 'bead' should be used instead. The list should also include an 'unspecified' entry for the rare cases when the object type cannot be identified.

Measurements

Recording the measurements of an object is an essential part of the cataloguing process. It is normal to measure both dimensions and weight, and the measurement unit should be systematically recorded. To ensure consistency, it is best practice to choose a default unit of measurement, e.g. centimetres for dimensions and grams for weight. The tools for taking measurements include callipers, a measuring tape for larger objects, and a precision scale. In general terms, dimensions include length, width/thickness, height and/or diameter. For vessels and some other artefacts it may be that the capacity (volume of contents) should also be measured. The dimensions to be recorded should be adapted to each object according to its type and shape.

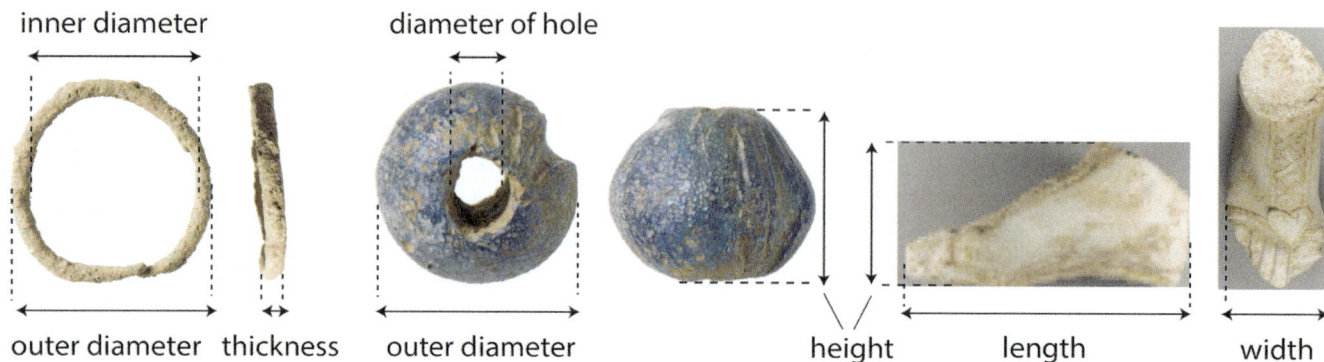

inner diameter

diameter of hole

outer diameter   thickness   outer diameter   height   length   width

Figure 19.3
Dimensions to
measure on
small finds

Material

Material type is a piece of information important at multiple levels. The material a find is made of influences the decisions made with regard to conservation, handling for photography and illustration, and packing and storage whilst in the dig house and afterwards in museums or storerooms. Material type also informs on the particular sensitivity of a find to environmental conditions and handling. For example, an object made of ivory is particularly sensitive to hygrometry (moisture) and should be stored and monitored accordingly. Finally, classifying objects in the database by material type will facilitate specialist study focusing on different materials.

There are two levels of cataloguing for materials. The main type identifies the general nature of the material, e.g. 'faunal', 'metal', 'stone', 'vitria'. The sub-type identifies the material further, e.g. 'ivory', 'iron', 'alabaster', 'glass'. Note that the main type should be systematically recorded, whereas it may not be possible to identify the sub-type before conservation and/or laboratory analysis. Just as with typology, it is important that cataloguing the material is done consistently to allow for reliable searchability and retrievability in the database. It is therefore once again recommended that a list of material types should be prepared ahead of the excavation season.

Description

Another important part of the cataloguing process is describing the find. The description should be objective and restricted to observable information only. The registrar should aim at clearly describing visible features such as shape, colouration, motifs, etc. Specialised typologies – e.g. for shapes of beads, seals and weights, or different types of figurines or tablets – may be of help to describe objects consistently.

The description should also refrain from making assumptions. Having said that, the registrar is in the privileged position of spending time with each and every find, and the experience gained through this close familiarity may help in adding interpretations to the description.

Bead Shape Table: Typical Bead Shapes Throughout the World

The name for each bead shape is from Classification and Nomenclature of Beads and Pendants by Horace C. Beck, which remains the classic bead shape reference guide. The shapes depicted on this chart are those most commonly found in stone and glass.

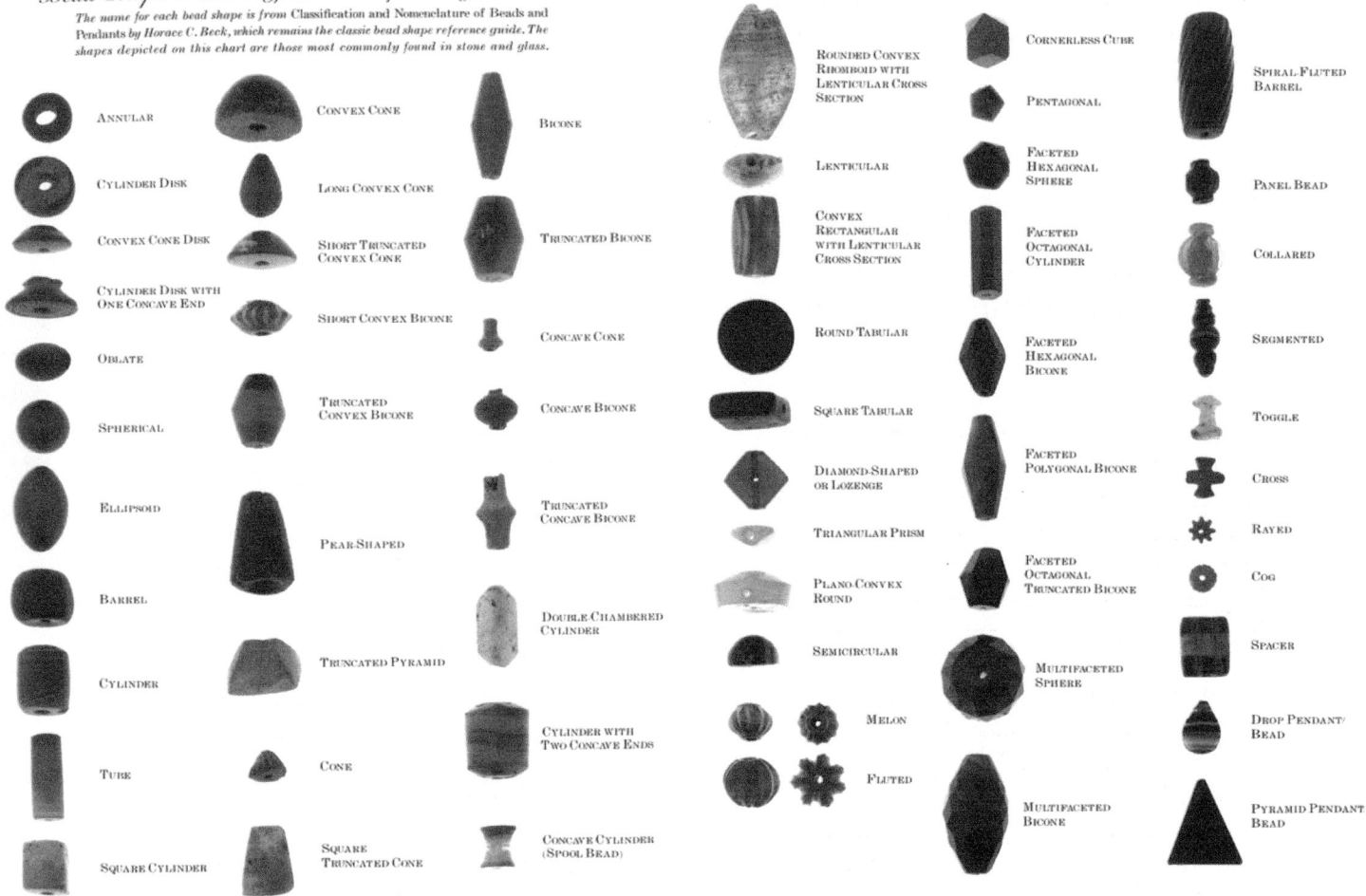

ANNULAR

CYLINDER DISK

CONVEX CONE DISK

CYLINDER DISK WITH ONE CONCAVE END

OBLATE

SPHERICAL

ELLIPSOID

BARREL

CYLINDER

TUBE

SQUARE CYLINDER

CONVEX CONE

LONG CONVEX CONE

SHORT TRUNCATED CONVEX CONE

SHORT CONVEX BICONE

TRUNCATED CONVEX BICONE

PEAR-SHAPED

TRUNCATED PYRAMID

CONE

SQUARE TRUNCATED CONE

BICONE

TRUNCATED BICONE

CONCAVE CONE

CONCAVE BICONE

TRUNCATED CONCAVE BICONE

DOUBLE CHAMBERED CYLINDER

CYLINDER WITH TWO CONCAVE ENDS

CONCAVE CYLINDER (SPOOL BEAD)

ROUNDED CONVEX RHOMBOID WITH LENTICULAR CROSS SECTION

LENTICULAR

CONVEX RECTANGULAR WITH LENTICULAR CROSS SECTION

ROUND TABULAR

SQUARE TABULAR

DIAMOND-SHAPED OR LOZENGE

TRIANGULAR PRISM

PLANO-CONVEX ROUND

SEMICIRCULAR

MELON

FLUTED

CORNERLESS CUBE

PENTAGONAL

FACETED HEXAGONAL SPHERE

FACETED OCTAGONAL CYLINDER

FACETED HEXAGONAL BICONE

FACETED POLYGONAL BICONE

FACETED OCTAGONAL TRUNCATED BICONE

MULTIFACETED SPHERE

MULTIFACETED BICONE

SPIRAL FLUTED BARREL

PANEL BEAD

COLLARED

SEGMENTED

TOGGLE

CROSS

RAYED

COG

SPACER

DROP PENDANT/ BEAD

PYRAMID PENDANT BEAD

Figure 19.4 Example of a bead shape typology (from Dubin, The History of Beads)

It should be kept in mind that the description provided by the registrar is the first step of many in the study of a find. Further specialist studies will follow and refine this first description.

Cataloguing Samples

The cataloguing process for samples follows the same principles as for objects, although with some differences. Samples cataloguing should record the same three pieces of information essential for any find – identifying information, type of sample, and material – but it is not (generally) necessary to describe samples.

Identifying information

The identification of a sample must include its unique field number, the archaeological context it came from, the date it was sampled and the initials of the supervisor. Samples can be numbered in the same sequence as objects, e.g. A-1234.

	Two joining fragments of an iron object with three holes preserved: colander (?)
	Silver coin of Orodes II. Obverse: head of the king facing left, bearded and with hair cut to the top of the neck, wearing a tasseled headband, dressed in a garment with a collared neck. Reverse: inscription in Greek giving the titles "Arsaces, the king of kings, beneficent, the just, the manifest, friend of the Greeks"
	Right foot of a stone statue, broken at the ankle, wearing a laced-up sandal decorated with a heart in the lower part. The surface of the sole is carved with hatches throughout. The big toe is missing. Traces of polychromy: light yellow (sandal), bright ochre/yellow (inner side of the sole, shoelaces, near the big toe), red (side of the sole at the heel), blue (inner side of the shoelace, under the inner sole

Figure 19.5 Examples of descriptions for catalogue

Type of sample

Samples are destined to be analysed in due course. The method(s) to be applied will depend on the type of sample and this information should therefore be consistently recorded. To ensure consistency, a typology of sample types should be prepared in advance and include the types most relevant to the excavation project, e.g. 'archaeobotanical', 'C14/carbon', 'soil', 'phytolith'.

Material

Recording the material type for a sample follows the same principles as those outlined above for objects. It differs, however, in that only the main material type is recorded. In practice, the material is often (but not always) implicit in the type of sample.

Final packing and inventory

Once you have finalised which objects will be packed together in larger storage boxes, give a number to each box and make an inventory of its contents. The entries should contain the same basic information as appears on the tag – site name, season and/or year, context number, small find number, description, initials of the site supervisor – and it may be that a Registration number (assigned by the representative of the State Board) and a Museum number (assigned by the museum receiving the finds) also need to be added. Place a printed copy of the appropriate list in each box, and ensure that the authorities have copies of the complete inventory in both printed and electronic format.

Figure 19.6
Registering
pottery

Chapter 20

Conservation

Any excavated small find needs to be checked by the conservator once registered by the registrar. The conservation treatment investigates and helps to preserve the evidence inherent in excavated physical remains of the past, as well as the object itself. Objects not properly conserved in a timely manner can deteriorate at a very rapid rate and will then become useless for any future analysis or display.

There are three kinds of conservation:

Preventative conservation: Conservative methods directed to remove or reduce causes of degradation, and consisting in indirect and optional interventions on the object's environment. Any agent that can cause degradation of an object should be reduced to a minimum. This can be

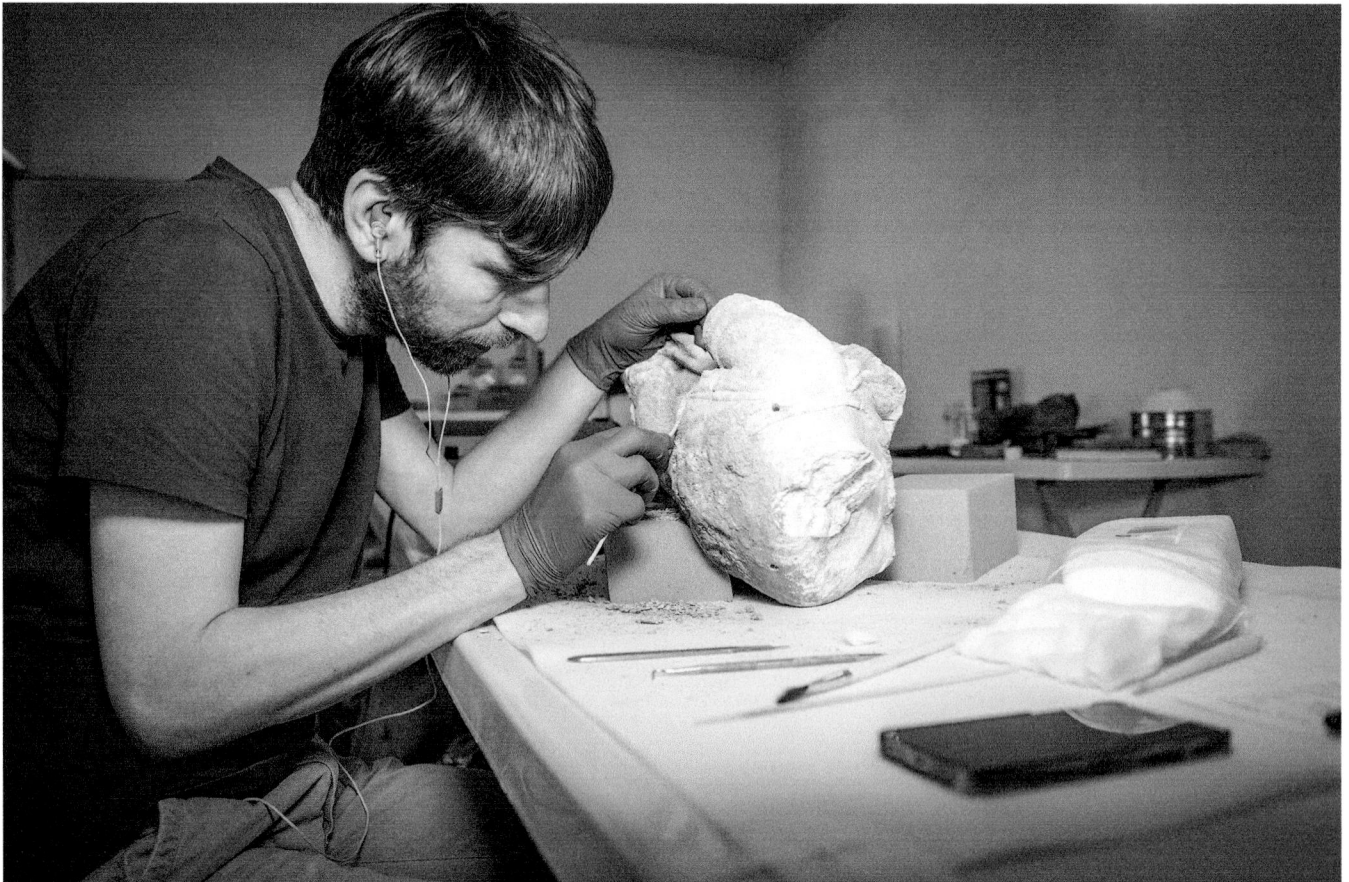

Figure 20.1 Working on conservation of a Hellenistic statue from Qalatga Darband

done by covering the object when freshly excavated, securely packing the object for transport or (temporary) storage, and handling the object as little as possible.

Curative conservation: Action undertaken to remove the effects of degradation, and stabilise the object. These conservation treatments are carried out by the conservator and take place in the conservation studio in the dig house.

Restoration: An optional intervention on the material of the object with the aim to improve the reading. This can be the reconstruction of broken objects (ceramics, metals, glass, stone, or other). A full restoration is time-consuming and almost never done on-site. When a full restoration is needed later it must be done in a conservation studio.

For most objects, the only conservation treatment they will get is when they are freshly excavated, before they find their way to a storeroom or museum display. Treatments carried out on-site (or in the conservation studio in the dig house) are most often first-aid treatments to stabilise the object and reduce any further degradation of the material. Treatments to an object should, if possible, be done in a controlled environment in the conservation studio in the dig house. Only when an object is too fragile to lift or to be transported to the dig house without causing further damage should a treatment be carried out in the field. More elaborate restoration treatments are only done when it helps to read the object.

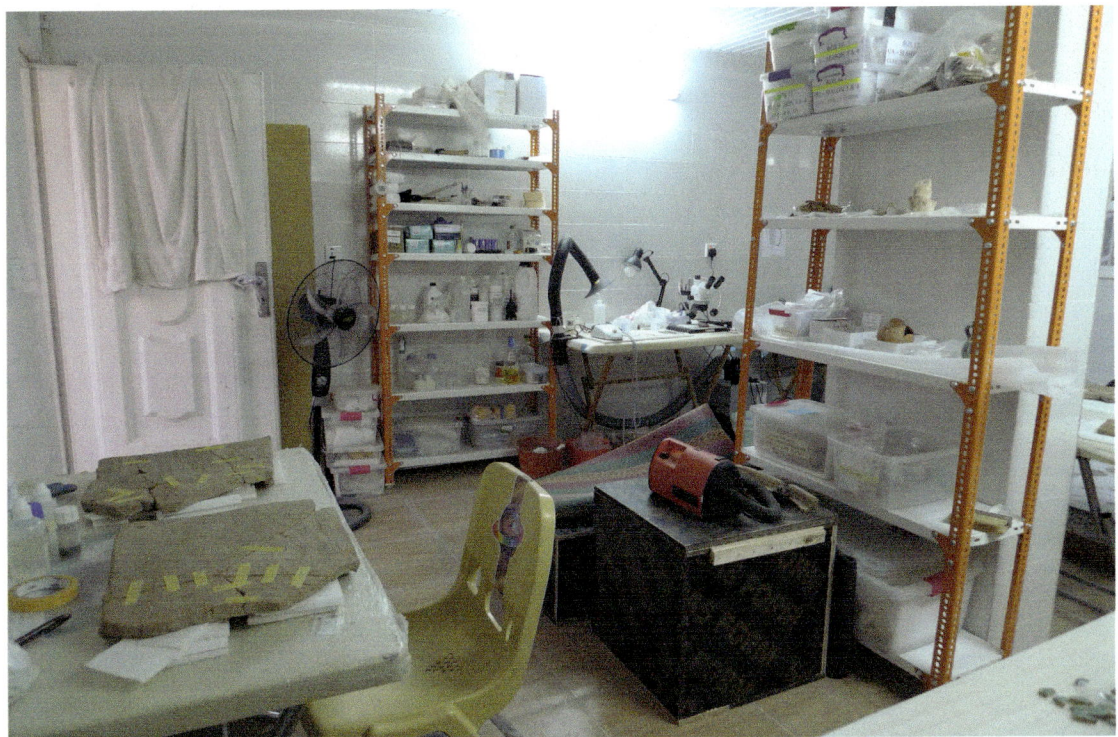

Figure 20.2
A conservation
field laboratory

Carrying out any of the conservation treatments should always be done with the ethics of conservation in mind. These include (a) that any interventive treatment should only be carried out within the professional competence of the conservator, (b) that a full record, including photographs and/or drawings, should be made for any interventive treatment, and (c) that any treatment should be confined to the minimum necessary to achieve a given conservation or analytical aim. Both the short- and long-term effects of any techniques or materials used should be understood as far as they are known, and all techniques, materials, and equipment used should be recorded in the conservation documentation. Any treatment applied to an object must be reversible and any chemical materials must only be used if necessary.

Although objects may look the same, they very rarely are. The condition of an object is affected by the way it was produced, the materials employed, the way it has been used during its life, the burial conditions, and the conditions when excavated. This means that every object has to be assessed separately.

Degradation of objects

The environmental conditions of any object buried in soil are different to the environmental conditions in which it was made and used. The soil conditions in which an object is buried can vary, but there are a number of factors that affect the condition of a buried object:

the absence of light

– water: materials can either dissolve in water or be broken down by substances dissolved in water

– gasses: the availability of oxygen in the soil is one of the most important factors in the degradation of materials; the acidity of the soil is related to the presence of oxygen

– salts: salts can cause corrosion on most metals, as well as tension in porous materials; salts dissolved in water can penetrate a porous material, and when this water evaporates the salts stay behind and crystallise, causing tension in the material

– temperature: most soils have a stable temperature; degradation processes accelerate with higher temperatures

– mechanical damage: the weight of the soil can deform or break an object

– micro-organisms: micro-organisms can break down or damage an object

The combination of physical, chemical and biological factors will affect the buried object and can change its characteristics. The deterioration may begin immediately upon excavation, or after a long time, but either way a process of deterioration will set in if the object does not find a state of equilibrium in its new environment. Sometimes this will lead to the object's total degradation,

Figure 20.3 Copper-bronze vessel after mechanical cleaning and before chemical conservation

or it will change in colour, weight, or material.

Whenever an object is excavated the conditions can change again rapidly, starting further degradation of the material. Some materials are more sensitive to these changes than others, but some form of deterioration will take place with all of them. There are many different agents that can cause degradation. In most instances there are combinations of different agents affecting the material together. Most commonly, these are the result of changes in conditions in light, temperature, relative humidity and air.

To reduce degradation of freshly excavated objects, it is important to minimise the changes in environmental conditions during excavation, recording, transport and storage. It is important to be aware of the environmental conditions in which the object was buried and the changes that it may already have undergone. When burial conditions are known to the excavator and the conservator they can better anticipate the treatments needed to safeguard the objects.

Handling of freshly excavated objects

Objects should be inspected carefully, and any cracks, breaks, flaking and powdering surfaces identified before touching or lifting. Always hold the objects gently. When objects are wrapped or packed, gently remove the packaging to remove the object. Do not try to grasp the object only by the visible part. Never handle by fragile parts, e.g. the neck or handle of a vessel, or the head of a figurine.

On-site materials

Gloves

Gloves protect objects from acids, heat, fingerprints, sweat and grease marks. Wear gloves whenever possible. For a short video explaining the benefits, take a look at:

https://www.youtube.com/watch?v=VAzLunt6Lr0

Disposable nitrile gloves come in different sizes and grades. Make sure you wear the right size – too small will probably rip, too big and you will loose delicacy and sensitivity.

Figure 20.4
Inscribed cone
in the process
of excavation

Trays and containers

Whenever possible objects should be carried in appropriate containers which allow for initial examination without the need to touch them. A range of trays and containers should be available on-site to minimise handling and to provide better protection for the objects. Tupperware containers, clear plastic boxes and polyethylene bags are all good for conservation purposes.

Padding

Padding materials such as acid free tissues and various type of inert foams (plastazote, ethafoam, jiffy foam) are essential on-site to support objects during handling, carrying and packaging.

When placing objects into their trays and boxes, make sure that they are not tightly squeezed into the container, and not in contact with other objects (which will result in surface abrasion).

N.B. do not use pens, pencils or any sort of excavation tools to physically examine an object – this may mark or damage the object.

Labelling

Make sure that all relevant information – site name, season and/or year, context number, small find number, description, initials of the site supervisor – are properly recorded on the tag using a **permanent spirit-based marker pen** and that the tag can be seen and read inside the bag or container **without the need to open it**.

Ceramic artefacts

Most ceramic artefacts can safely be transported to the dig house for further analyses. Low-fired ceramics, or ceramics affected by soluble or insoluble salts from the surrounding soil, are more susceptible to crumbling or flaking and may therefore need extra attention. If the vessel is complete, it is best to lift it with the contents preserved because remnants of the original contents may still survive. If the artefact is complete, but fragile, additional support may be needed prior to lifting. Depending on the fragility, shape and size of the vessel, the object can be block-lifted with the surrounding soil still supporting the vessel, or the object can be supported with plaster-impregnated bandages. Make sure to always use a barrier layer (aluminium foil) in between the object and the plaster-impregnated bandages. If the artefact is fragmented or extremely fragile, ask the conservator to come out to the site.

Artefacts made of metal

If the artefact is intact, after carefully freeing it from any surrounding soil, gently lift it with an underlying support and put it in a rigid container, resting in sand or something similar. The artefact then needs to dry out slowly. DO NOT seal the container with a lid that will seal the moisture in: this can lead to further corrosion of the artefact; a perforated lid is ideal. If the artefact is fragmented or extremely fragile, ask the conservator to come out to the site.

Figure 20.5
Excavating
a smashed
storage jar

Artefacts made of unbaked clay, including sealings and cuneiform tablets

If the artefact is intact, after carefully freeing it from any surrounding soil, gently lift it with an underlying support and put it in a rigid container, resting in sand or something similar. The artefact then needs to dry out slowly. Keep the object out of direct sunlight. DO NOT seal the container with a lid that will seal the moisture in: this can lead to the artefact disintegrating; a perforated lid is ideal. If the artefact is fragmented, ask the conservator to come out to the site.

Artefacts made of ivory or bone

Artefacts made of ivory or bone should be carefully lifted and put in a rigid container, resting in sand or something similar. The artefact then needs to dry out slowly. Keep the object out of direct sunlight. DO NOT seal the container with a lid that will seal the moisture in: this can lead to mould or the artefact disintegrating; a perforated lid is ideal. If the artefact is fragmented or extremely fragile, ask the conservator to come out to the site.

Lifting of small finds

Once exposed in the soil, if a material is too weak to be handled or too fragile to support its own weight, then some form of stabilisation is required prior to a specialised lifting process. Fragile finds may require additional support before they can be retrieved from the soil. Lifting involves removing the finds from their surrounding soil matrix with the use of various support materials

Figure 20.6
Discussing
how to lift
a smashed
ceramic vessel

and techniques, which can then be carefully removed in the laboratory. It is essential to assess the condition of the find and the surrounding soil first before planning the lifting process, i.e. deciding on the method to use, the necessary equipment, labour requirements, and assessing possible damage to the surrounding contexts. It is also important to be prepared for unexpected situations arising. Finds and their excavation contexts must be recorded photographically and with notes and drawings before lifting – this includes information on context and stratigraphy, and noting any association with other finds. Note that some lifting processes can be time-consuming and extremely disruptive to the site.

Pre-lifting preparation

Where the find is fragmentary and the association of pieces to one another is important, the pieces can be secured in position during the lifting process by 'Facing up'. This involves attaching a layer of inert material (nylon gossamer, Japanese tissue, polyester papers, muslin, canvas) to the exposed face of the object so that all the individual pieces are stuck to it, enabling the find to be moved and lifted while keeping all the pieces in place. This technique can also be used to ensure that loose or detachable parts of a find are not lost during the lifting process. If there are loose fragments already detached from the object, they must be packed and labelled separately and kept with the object. It is essential that any facing materials and adhesives used can be completely removed without damaging (or staining) the object once the lifting process has taken place. Once the surface of the object is stabilised then it can be wrapped, covered and supported using materials such as cling film, aluminium foil, fabric gauze and plastered bandage or acid free paper.

Bandage technique

This technique can be used for the objects which can be excavated to stand proud of the surrounding deposit. It is important to assess the condition of the object first and determine all the weak points and any damage present. The objects must be exposed carefully, strengthening it as you go along by binding the progressively exposed section with gauze or plaster bandaging. It is crucial to use a barrier layer between the bandage and the object to prevent any marks from the bandage transferring onto the surface of the object. Use acid free tissues or small sand bags to support the undercuts and unsupported areas. If there is any soil inside the object, this must be left intact, both because it may it contain important archaeological information and because it supports the object. Once the object is secured, then the surrounding soil can be excavated with care, and the soil below the object cut through with a metal sheet or a tool such as a blade or rod in order to free it. The object can then be lifted, placed on a tray or board, and supported as need be to keep it stable during transportation to the dig house.

Figure 20.7
Block-lifting
a section of
painted wall
plaster

Block lifting

This technique, which is used for larger, fragile finds and assemblages of finds, involves supporting the object within its associated soil matrix so that the object and any accompanying evidence can be removed *en bloc* and excavated and investigated under more controlled conditions. This requires the following materials:

– gauze or plaster/polyurethane bandage

– cling film, aluminium foil

– padding material (acid free tissues, small sand bags, fabric, etc.)

– wooden box

– metal rods

– metal sheet

– wooden or metal boards for transportation

Excavate around the object to create a soil pedestal and pad the object, ensuring that there are no gaps or unsupported areas, and that the object will not be crushed when the soil block is

► Figure
20.8 Cleaning
an inscribed
Sumerian cone

lifted. Cover the object with cling film to serve as a barrier layer. Place the custom made box around the pedestal. Secure the lid over the box, cut through the soil underneath and lift the box, placing onto a wooden board. Make sure the whole box is fully secured before transporting. If no box is needed, then apply rigid support around the soil matrix to prevent movement or collapse using fabric gauze or plaster bandage (or failing this, cling film or aluminium foil).

Cleaning of small finds

Many freshly excavated objects have dirt attached to the surface. There can be three different categories of dirt:

Soiling is any solid particulate matter sitting on or bonded to the surface of an object.

Staining is when liquid matter is carried into a porous material by capillary action. This normally results in a darkening or discolouration of the object's surface.

Corrosion is when the surface's original composition is altered by chemical processes.

In most cases, dirt on an object is a combination of two, or sometimes all three, of these. The method of cleaning is selected according to the type of dirt and the type of object. There are four different methods of cleaning:

Mechanical cleaning is when foreign matter or corrosion is physically removed from the object's surface. This is done by using external force applied by hand or with the help of a machine. Most often, mechanical cleaning can be done with the help of simple tools such as brushes, a dry cloth or a scalpel. It is useful to always have a wide variety of tools available on-site. These can include brushes in a number of shapes and sizes, including toothbrushes and fine artist brushes, dental tools and scalpels with a mixed collection of blades. Always make sure the tools used are appropriate for the dirt you want to remove and will not damage the object itself.

Wet cleaning is when a liquid (wetting agent) is used to dislodge soiling from the surface of an object. The liquid is commonly applied to the object's surface with a cotton swab. The dirt is then absorbed by capillary action into the swab. The type of liquid used is selected depending on

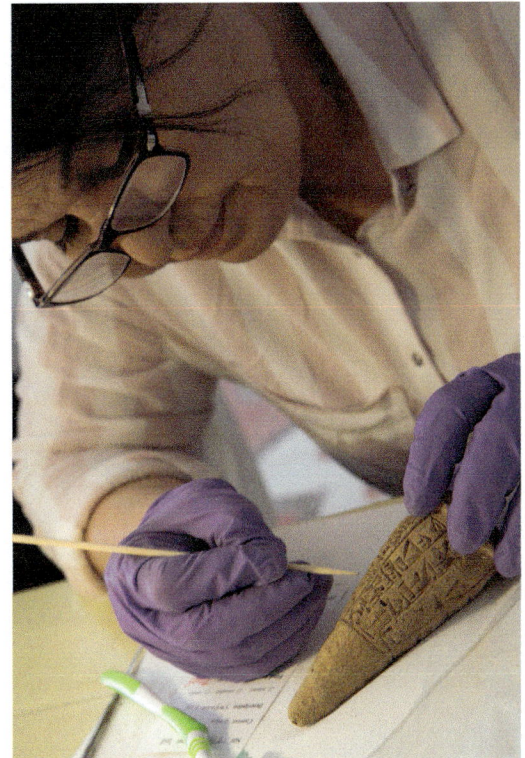

the nature of the material to be dissolved. Solvents such as water, acetone, or ethanol are most commonly used. Sometimes a soap or detergent is added to the liquid to increase the attractive forces between the particulate matter and the liquid.

Chemical cleaning is when a chemical reaction between the liquid and the particulate matter on the surface of an object is used to remove the soiling. This can, for example, be done by changing the pH of water, or with the use of a chelating (binding) agent (such as EDTA).

Chemical or electrochemical modification is when corrosion products on an object's surface can be chemically transformed to clean and stabilise the object. However, this is hardly ever done on-site.

Most of the tools used in the cleaning of objects are easily available. When working with solvents, make sure to use brushes with natural hair and cotton swabs made of wood and cotton. Any tools made of plastics may dissolve in the solvents used.

Packing and storage

Conservation treatments can slow down, or sometimes stop, the degradation of objects. Whenever objects are inadequately stored, however, the degradation process can continue. It is therefore important to have objects packed and stored properly so that the degradation of these objects can be reduced to a minimum. When objects are packed during and after excavation, both for

Figure 20.9
Cleaning small
finds

temporary storage in the dig house as well as for long-term storage in a storeroom, this should be done in a manner appropriate to the needs of the objects. Remember the following points:

– artefacts should be clean and stable before being packed for permanent storage

– object numbers must be clearly visible on the bag or box containing the artefact

– fragile or important artefacts should be packed separately in sealed plastic boxes

– only use proper museum-quality materials such as inert foam and acid free tissues

– never use cotton wool, newspapers or paper towels

– jiffy foam and bubble wrap should not be used in direct contact with artefacts in long-term storage

– do not fold textiles and paper

Factors that can influence the degradation or loss of objects during storage are:

Dislocation – objects should always be labelled or numbered so that any object and its context can be identified at all times. Objects should have a label attached, and boxes, bags and any other methods of packing and storing of objects should have an accompanying list giving the contents. Labels should ideally be made of inert waterproof materials and written with a waterproof and light-stable ink.

Unsuitable environment – unstable environmental conditions can (re)start degradation processes on a large number of materials. It is therefore essential to have the environmental conditions as stable as possible. This can be done in the storeroom itself, but also in the packing of objects. Different materials need different environmental conditions, so it is best to pack objects by material type. For most materials it is best to have them stored at a room temperature of around 18°C. Relative humidity (RH) should be around 50–55% for most materials. When the relative humidity is higher it can cause moulding. A low relative humidity can cause cracking of the material. The exception to this are metal objects, which should be stored with a low relative humidity (30% or less). To achieve this, metal objects should be stored in airtight containers with a supply of silica gel added to the container to keep the humidity low. The silica gel should never be in direct contact with the object. When metal objects are packed in smaller bags or containers within the larger container containing the silica gel, the smaller bags or containers should be perforated in order for the silica gel to reduce the relative humidity. Containers with silica gel should be monitored to assure the relative humidity is still correct. A relative humidity strip can be placed on the inside of a container to easily see the condition of the silica gel inside without having to open the container. All other materials should be packed in containers that are not airtight to ensure that no microclimates are formed. Wood, leather, bone, horn, antler, ivory and textile artefacts should be padded or supported within their bags or boxes, or on trays and drawers, with acid free card or acid free paper. The relative humidity for organic objects should be in the range of 45–60%RH. Fragile or friable sherds (whether ceramic or glass) should be packed in acid free tissue paper inside bags or boxes. Ceramics and stone with salt damage should be stored in 35–45% RH with no or minimal fluctuations. Large stone objects should be stored on shelves or pallets to keep them off the floor to avoid damage from water arising from rain water, floods or leaks.

Unsuitable packing materials or techniques – it is important to use only inert and acid free archival materials for the packing and storage of objects. Other materials can directly affect the material of the object and cause degradation, or they can disintegrate over time. This can lead to the unstable support of an object or dislocation of objects. It is best to keep objects in strong, chemically stable, and closed (but, except for metals, not airtight) containers to protect them from dirt or dust and mechanical damage. The packaging should be easy to handle and to open whenever needed for monitoring the objects' condition, or for further study or analysis.

Incorrect handling – objects should always be well supported, both when packed or when handled. Most excavated objects are fragile and should be handled as little as possible. It is therefore important that objects can be studied or looked at with a minimal amount of handling. When packed for storage it should be easy to lift an object by lifting its support. Fragile parts should be indicated, secured and protected if possible.

Pests – collections should be kept in storerooms free of pests. Pests such as insects and rodents can cause damage to the objects and should be kept away from the storerooms.

Some important tips

Indelicate, hasty or careless excavation practices may cause irreparable damage to finds.

Handling with bare hands can leave staining or impressions.

Handling fragile objects firmly or packing them tightly or inappropriately may cause damage.

Make sure you collect all flakes and broken pieces and pack them carefully together with the object so they do not get lost.

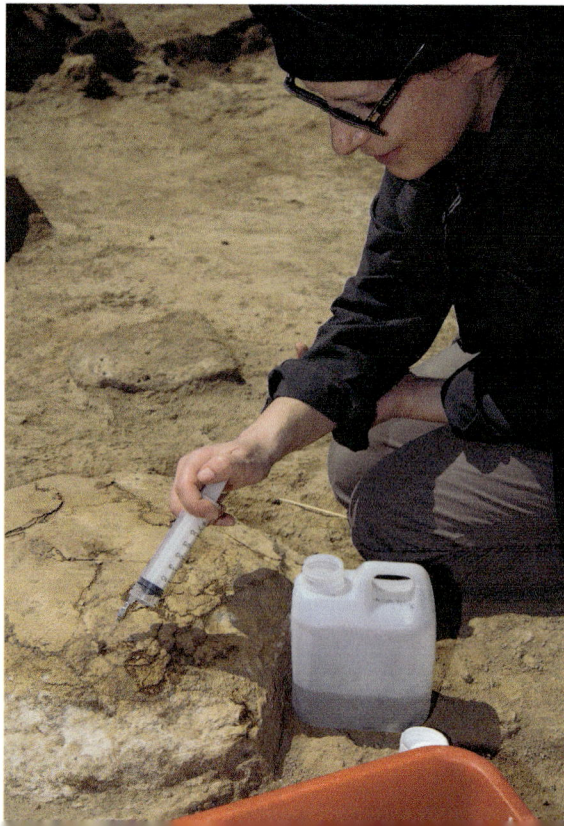

Figure 20.10 Conserving a door socket in situ

Take care not to touch powdery surfaces, for example painted artefacts or glazed ceramics, as this will both smear and remove the original surface.

Only open bags and boxes containing artefacts when necessary, and make sure that you do not lose or drop any piece or fragment, and that there are no spores, mould or insects in the environment.

Chapter 21

Small Finds Illustration

This section covers the basic principles for small finds illustration, practical methods, and inking and digitisation for publication.

Basic principles

Why draw finds?

A picture conveys information about an object better than words.

Archaeological drawings form the primary on-site visual record and the visual archive, along with photography.

While a good photograph provides a clear image, there are aspects of an object it cannot show: this is where a series of drawn views and sections is more informative. A good illustration shows accurately and to scale the technological evidence implicit in the artefact, its structure, shape and decorative elements. A 'cut through' section demonstrates its construction, method of manufacture and constituent parts. Details which are difficult to see can be clarified in additional drawings. Non-important features, such as corrosion or modern breaks, can be de-emphasised or left out.

Figure 21.1
Illustrating
small finds

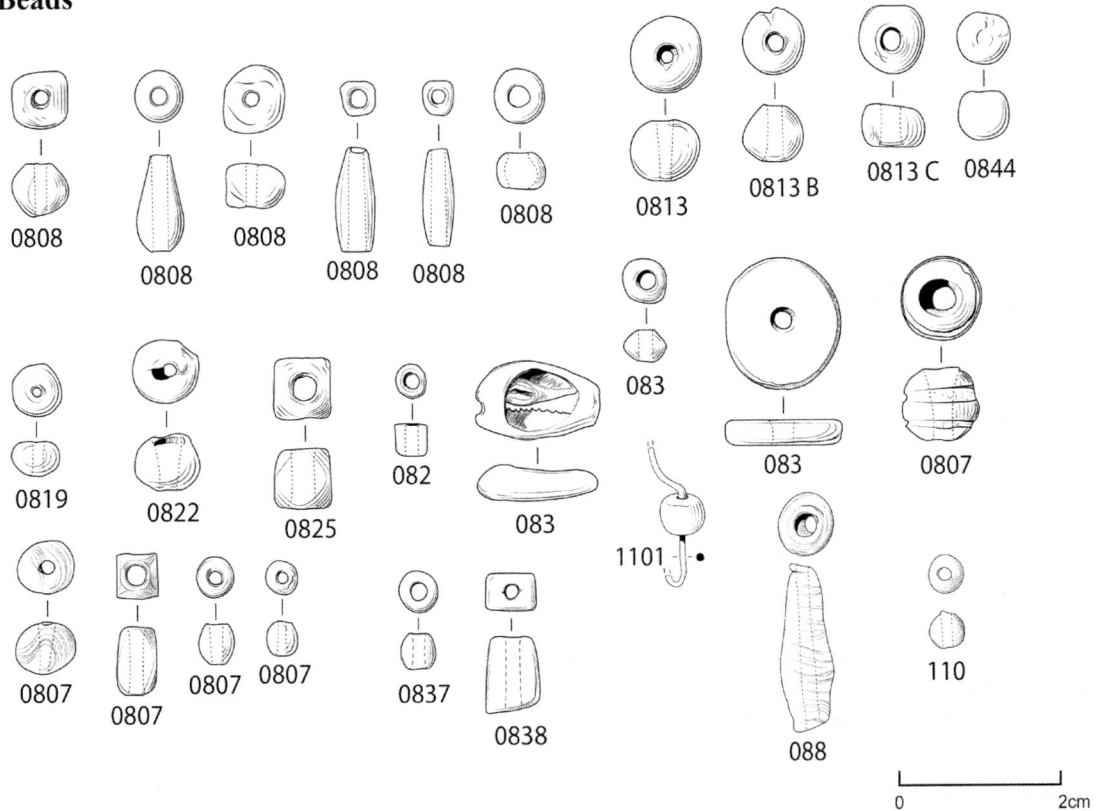

QD Area E
Beads

Figure 21.2
Good use
of standard
conventions

* In archaeological illustration a set of best-practice standard conventions is used to convey information. This means a good illustration enables any archaeologist viewing it to immediately understand the object, without needing to see the object itself. This is a necessary factor where objects often go straight into storage, or can be broken, destroyed or lost.

* For archiving and comparative study. Finds drawn using the standard conventions enable comparison between similar types of finds across excavations, and aid the creation of visual typologies used in research. For example, in the sheet of drawings above (Fig. 21.2) the beads are all drawn at the same scale and with the same layout, enabling easy comparison.

Black and white illustrations are often clearer and cheaper to reproduce than photographs. Although digital technology is increasingly enabling effective sharing of images for research, clarity of printed material remains a major consideration.

What makes a good archaeological illustration?

A drawing of an archaeological find functions as a two-dimensional replacement of the original three-dimensional object so it has to be:

Measurable – all drawings are drawn at a specific scale, for example 1:1 (100%) or 1:2 (50%), so that measurements can be taken directly from the drawing in the absence of the object.

Accurate – it should convey correct dimensions, shape and detail, with enough views and sections to give all essential information.

Drawn with standard archaeological conventions – using the correct conventions regarding scale, views, sections, layout and shading style across all drawings enables the drawn objects to be compared to one another.

Easy to understand – use of a clear style and logical layout incorporates an understanding of the object's component parts.

Drawings should be produced in *consultation* with the archaeologist or small finds specialist who may have specific requirements with respect to the style and content of the drawing. A quality drawing enables the object depicted to be *fully understood from the drawing alone*. As an illustrator you will have your own style, but you should remember that you are producing a technical drawing, so it is important to keep all these aspects in mind. In short, a good drawing is a clearly understandable, accurate, technical representation of the object, and not an artistic rendering.

Figure 21.3
Making a pencil
drawing of a
small find

▶ Figure
21.4 Drawing
an inscribed
Sumerian brick

Drawing equipment

A basic illustration kit includes:

– drawing board covered with 1 mm/1 cm gridded paper

– bright directional desk lamp or good natural light

– tracing paper or matt coated plastic 'drafting film'

– acetate sheets, clear plastic film for tracing detail from the object

– adhesive tape for securing papers to board

– assorted foam blocks or similar to support object whilst drawing (modelling clay may be used with non-delicate objects)

– pencils, assorted 4H, 2H, H, 2B, etc

– soft eraser

– pencil sharpener

– ruler

– set squares for ensuring vertical alignment when outlining

– dividers for measuring dimensions and detail

– callipers for measuring dimensions and detail

– profile gauge for transferring profiles from object to paper

– fine marker pens for tracing on acetate

– ink pens for inking final drawings

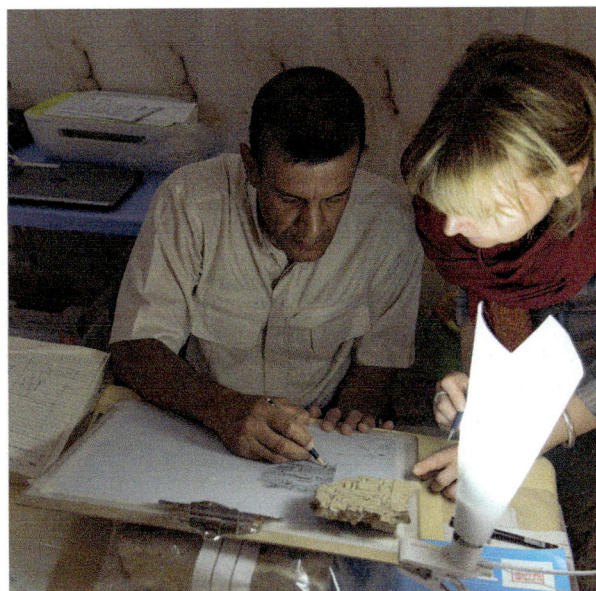

▶ Figure 21.4 Drawing an inscribed Sumerian brick

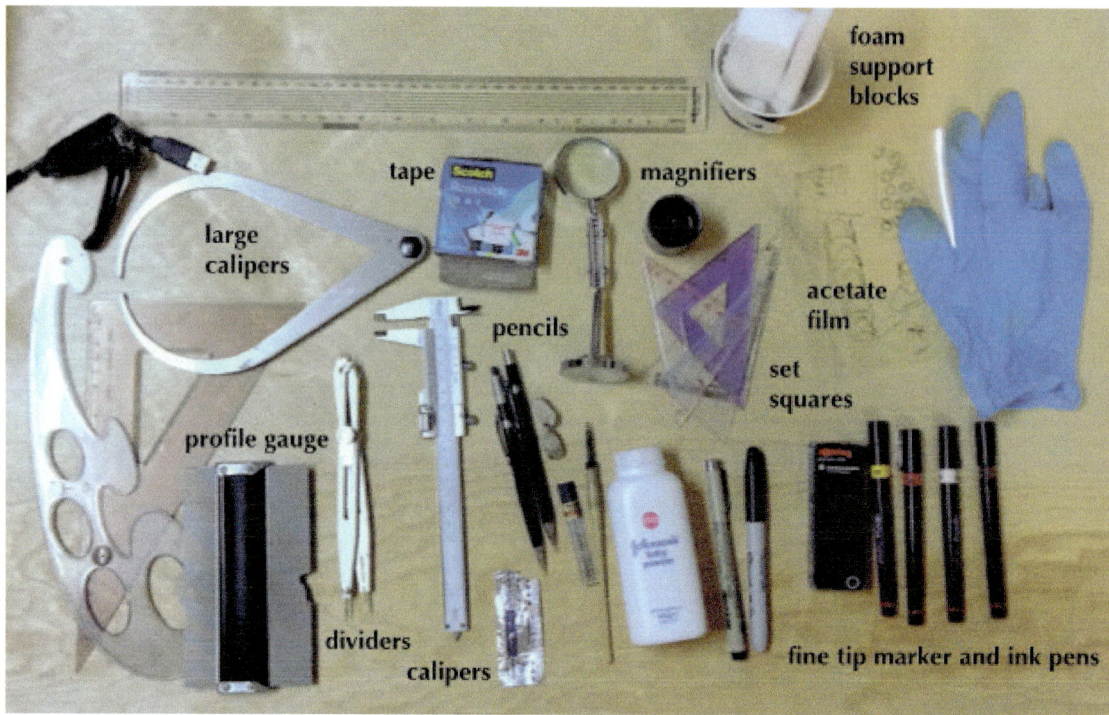

Figure 21.5 Illustration equipment

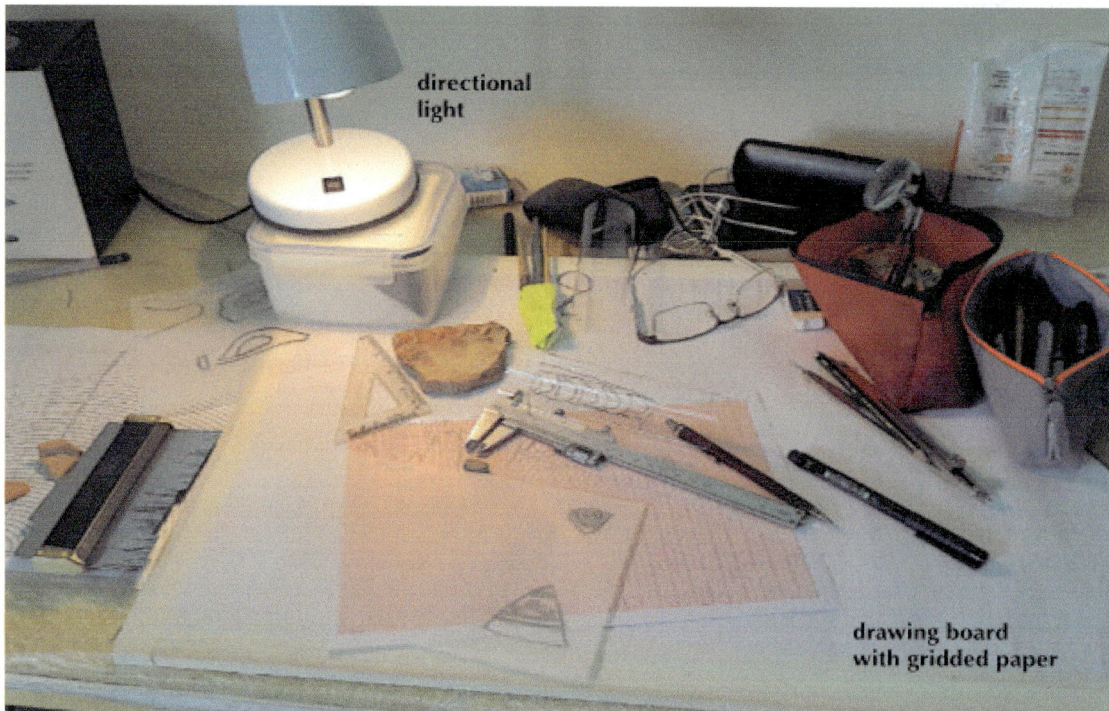

Figure 21.6 Drawing table setup

Drawing Conventions

Scale

Before starting you need to decide on the scale at which the object will be drawn, and also the scale at which it will be published, as it is usual to reduce the size of the drawing for publication (a common reduction is 50%). There are standard scales for drawing common objects (see Fig. 21.7) however these are guidelines and you may find a different scale more suitable. The size and complexity of the object itself will determine your choice.

Figure 21.7
Standard
illustration
scales

Many objects are likely to be suitable for drawing at their original size, where the measurements on paper reflect the actual measurements on the object; e.g. an object 10 cm long is shown as 10 cm long on the drawing. This scale is written as 1:1 or 100%.

Suggested sizes for drawing archaeological artefacts
Drawings are always printed at a reduced scale

Silver
Draw 1:1 or 1:2
Reproduce 1:2 or 1:4

Pottery
Draw 1:1 or 1:2
Reproduce 1:2 or 1:4

Copper alloy
Draw 2:1
Reproduce 1:1

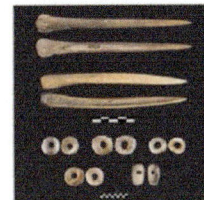

Terracotta
Draw 1:1 or 2:1
Reproduce 1:2 or 1:1

Gold
Draw 2:1 or 4:1
Reproduce 1:1 or 2:1

Iron
Draw 1:1 or 1:2
Reproduce
1:2 or 1:4

Wood
Draw 1:1, 1:2 or 1:4
Reproduce 1:2, 1:4 or 1:8

Stone
Draw 1:1 or 1:2
Reproduce
1:2 or1:4

Bone
Draw 1:1 or 2:1
Reproduce 1:2 or 1:1

Glass beads
Draw 2:1
Reproduce 1:1

A very small object, such as a bead, may be drawn at twice its size which enables drawn detail to be shown more clearly. Here the measurements on paper are twice those on the actual object, e.g. a 1 cm object is drawn at 2 cm, written as 2:1 or 200%.

A very large object, such as stonework, may need to be drawn at half its original size, or even smaller, e.g. a 50 cm stone object may be drawn at 25 cm (written as 1:2 or 50%), or even less.

Scalebar

Always include a scalebar with your drawing. Do not make your scalebar too visually prominent as you want your object drawings to be the focus on your sheet. A plain ruled line of suitable length, marked in cm or mm, provides a simple and unobtrusive scale.

Figure 21.8 Examples of scale bars

Which views should you draw?

Look at the object carefully and identify the front, back and sides, plus the top and bottom, so that you can orientate it correctly on your drawing sheet.

Some objects with multiple faces of interest, such as a bone die, will require each side, plus the top and bottom to be drawn, as each side is of importance. For objects with a complex structure, it will be necessary to draw a number of cross-sections as well as the main views to demonstrate this complexity. Other objects may only require a single view of the main face, plus a cross-section, e.g. a terracotta plaque with a plain back.

Use your common sense to decide how many drawings are necessary; the key is to draw as many views and cross-sections as are needed to represent the object fully.

Layout

Regarding arrangement of the drawings on your sheet, archaeological illustration uses a practice called 'orthographic projection', where each drawn face is placed alongside adjacent faces to reflect their true positions on the actual object.

To see how this works, hold the object upright in your hand, main face uppermost. Roll the main face over slowly to the *left* by 90 degrees at a time and you see that as you rotate the object each adjacent face appears, starting at the front, then the left side of the object, then the back, then the right side. The drawings of the object are placed similarly on the page adjacent to one another.

This is easiest to explain with a figure:

The ophidian figurine has each view (front – left – back – right) placed alongside each other as if the object is rolling to the left, and reflecting the *actual positions of the adjacent faces on the object*. The

Figure 21.9 Figurine with multiple faces – multiple views needed. As in this example, you may need to draw up to six views plus sections to completely represent the object if all sides are different

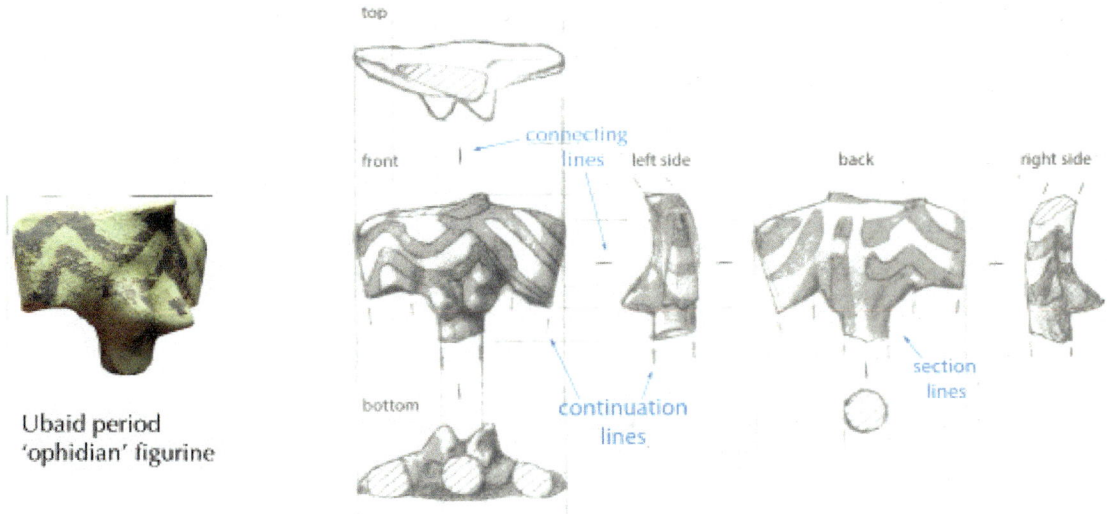

Ubaid period 'ophidian' figurine

top and bottom views are placed above and below the front view, rotating the front view towards you to see the top view and away from you to see the bottom view.

Correctly align the features which appear on adjacent views by drawing faint pencil guide lines.

This terracotta plaque, which only requires a single view, has sections placed alongside:

Short **connecting** lines between drawings link one view to the next, indicating they are adjacent faces (cf. Fig. 21.9)

Short broken **continuation** lines (Figs. 21.9.10) following an object's outline indicate where an object is truncated, e.g. the arms on the ophidian figurine.

Shorter **section** lines on either side of the object or part of the object indicate where a 'cut through' for a cross-section has been made (Fig. 11).

Hellenistic period terracotta plaque

▶ Figure 21.10 Object with detail on one face only – draw main view and section. Decide if more than one section is needed to show the object fully

Light and shading

Light is always shown as if shining on the object at an angle of 45 degrees from the top left of the page. Natural daylight is fine if no other light is available, but a bright directional light, such as that from an angled desk lamp, is best. Shading is added to indicate the relief on the surface of the object, and help define its form.

Why does archaeological illustration have this convention on top left directional light?

The advantage of this convention is that any researcher or archaeologist who is familiar with archaeological drawings will immediately be able to understand an object's shape *from the drawing alone*, without having to see the original object or read its description. Fig. 21.13 demonstrates this. As the light is always from the top left, it is immediately obvious that the object on the left is ball-shaped, whilst that on the right is bowl-shaped.

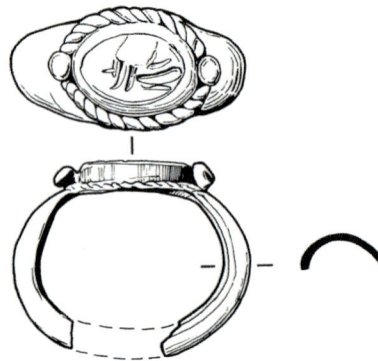

Figure 21.11 Broken continuation lines showing how a missing part of an artefact is to be understood

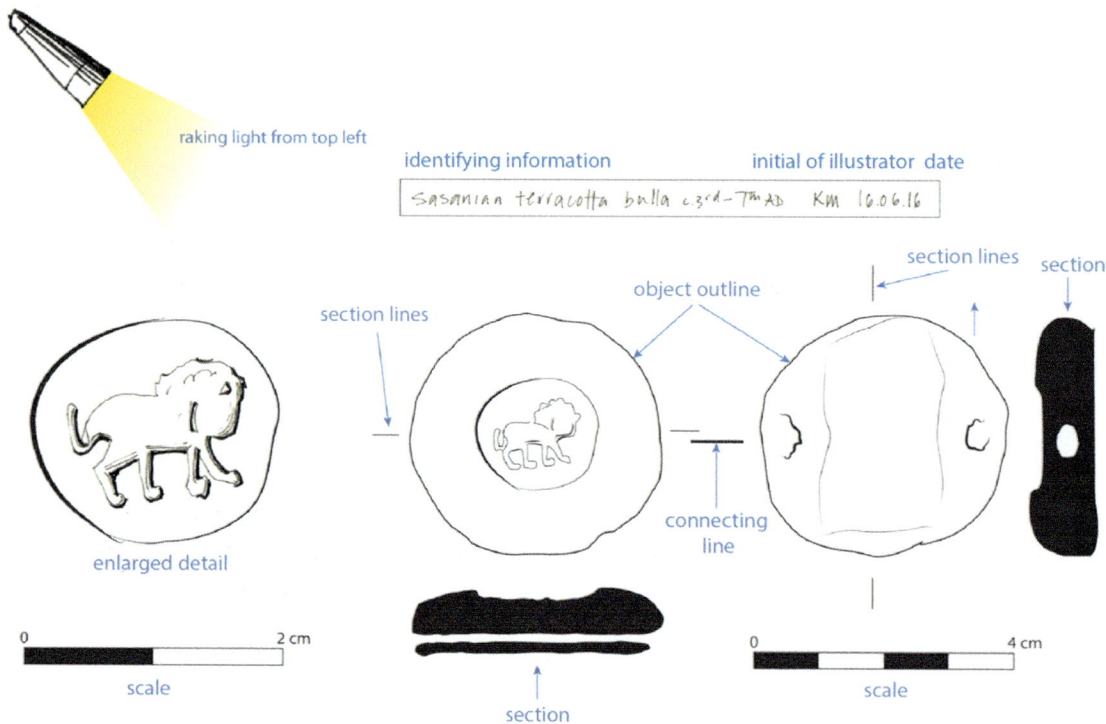

raking light from top left

identifying information   initial of illustrator date

Sasanian terracotta bulla c.3rd–7th AD   KM 16.06.16

section lines   section

object outline

section lines

enlarged detail

object outline

connecting line

0   2 cm

scale

section

0   4 cm

scale

Figure 21.12 Drawing showing correct use of conventions – note a more detailed drawing of the main decoration is shown on the left, with an additional scalebar to indicate that this is an enlargement

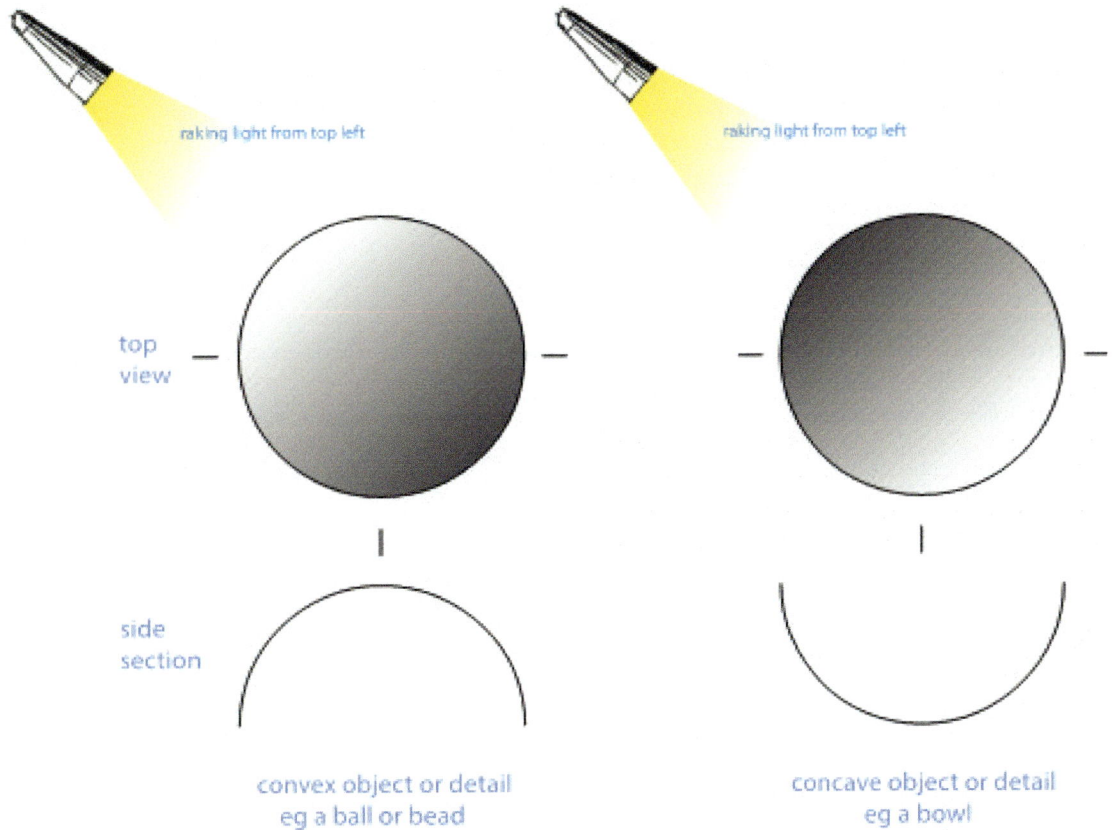

Figure 21.13 Directional light as an indicator of form

raking light from top left

raking light from top left

top view

side section

convex object or detail
eg a ball or bead

concave object or detail
eg a bowl

N.B. the shadow of the object on the table surface is never drawn. All shading should lie within the object's outline – you are drawing the object not the table!

Some exceptions on shading:

– drawings of flints are never shaded in pencil but simply have lines indicating the facets

– very corroded or encrusted objects, where the original object shape can only be seen in x-ray, should be drawn from the x-ray in outline only; spending time drawing surface corrosion or encrustations is wasted as it does not help understand the original object

– common objects being drawn for a typology or archival purposes may need accurate outline and section drawings only

Sections

A *section (cross-section)* is an imaginary 'slice' made through an object, to indicate the object's profile at that point.

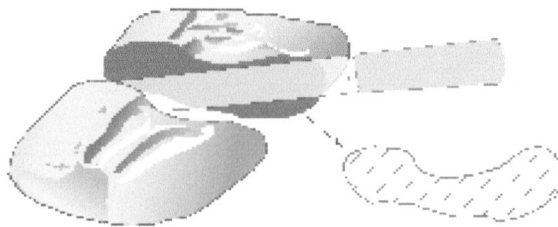

Figure 21.14
A section is a 'slice' through the object

Sections help indicate the shape of an object, along with the drawn views.

Sections do not have to be drawn across the full dimensions of an object – a section across only part of the object may be needed to help understand its shape at that point.

Short *section lines* indicate the position at which the section was 'cut' through the object, and the drawn section is generally placed alongside the object at this point.

A profile gauge is helpful in section drawing but it is important to use one along with accurate measuring instruments such as callipers, as a profile gauge is less precise.

Sections should be blacked in or, if this appears too 'heavy', can be left in outline only, or hatched. The hatching must be at an angle of 45 degrees, and applied neatly and with a ruler.

Illustration in practice – step-by-step

Assemble your drawing equipment, including board, paper, tools and a directional light source.

Carefully examine the object under the light, identifying details and features which need to be shown. You need to decide:

- which, and how many, views are needed to fully represent the object?
- are sections needed to show structure? If so, how many?
- are there any details or decoration which need to be shown?
- can you see the method of manufacture – does the drawing need to show this?
- is it made of more than one material? How can you show this?
- what scale should it be drawn at?

The colour of the object is not shown in the object drawing. If colour is relevant is can be shown in a photograph, or described. Exceptions to this are when specific elements are coloured differently by intent, such as painted decoration or when parts are made of a different material.

Tape a piece of tracing paper to your drawing board. The number of views/sections which need drawing will dictate where to place your drawings on the paper.

Start by drawing the outline

Place the find on your board and support it so that it does not move whilst being drawn, this can be done with small wedges of foam, paper or plasticine. If the object is fragile, be careful not to support it with any sticky material which could damage the surface.

You may find it helpful to draw faint horizontal guide lines at the top and bottom of the object, and a line on either side, thereby placing the object in a drawn box with the same exact dimensions as the object. This will help maintain accuracy when drawing the outline.

If your object is fairly two-dimensional (i.e. more or less flat) you can trace the outline directly using the object itself. Mark dots around the outline of the object then connect the dots. To obtain an accurate outline it is important that the points marked on your paper lie vertically below the corresponding points on the object, so place the tip of the pencil *exactly* beneath the edge of your object (Fig. 21.15).

With a more three-dimensional object it is necessary to use a set square which can be held vertically against the edge of the object. Mark points on your paper then connect these carefully by eye using the object as a reference. Check the drawing's dimensions against the object to make sure your drawing is accurate. Take time at this stage, as accuracy here is extremely important.

Once you have the outline, place the object close by so that it can be referred to whilst measuring the detail. A pair of dividers or callipers should be used for measuring internal detail. As with the outline, place measured dots within your outline to build up a framework of key points, then join these with lines to create a 'wire-frame' of the internal detail. Keep checking your drawing with the object to see if it looks correct.

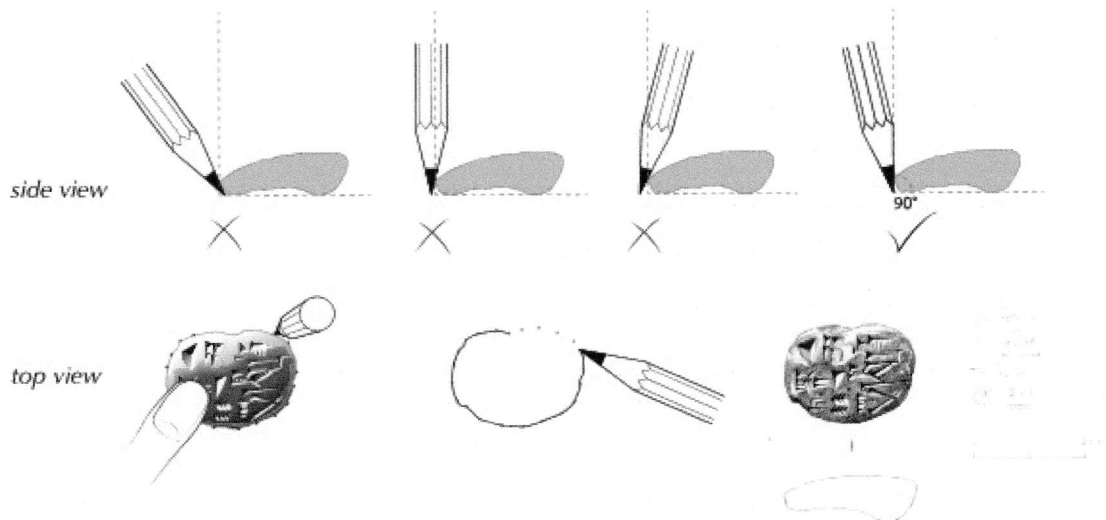

Figure 21.15 Outline method 1. Suitable for two-dimensional objects

side view

top view

Figure 21.16 Outline method 2. Suitable for three-dimensional objects

Figure 21.17 To accurately add the outline and internal detail for large three-dimensional objects, use callipers or dividers with a set square to measure the offsets

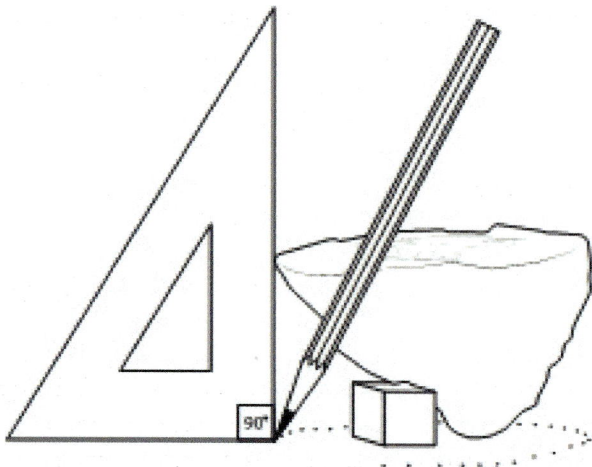

internal detail - measure from edge using dividers or calipers

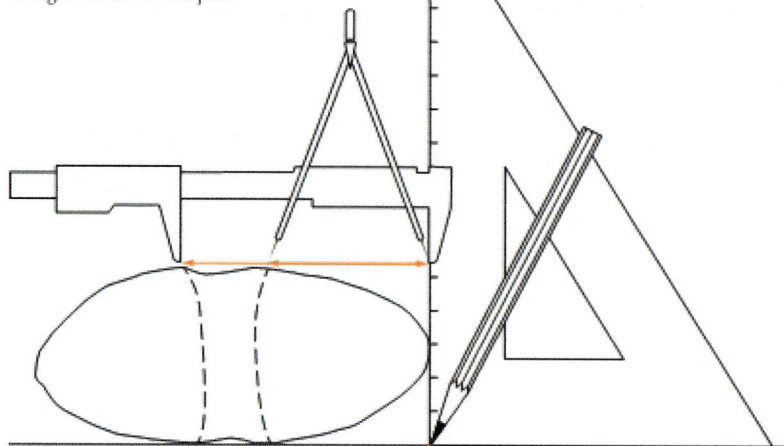

outline - mark points using a set square

If the object is fairly flat, a simple way of transferring detail is to trace the detail onto a sheet of clear acetate or plastic laid over the object, using a fine pen which writes on plastic. Tape the acetate to ensure it does not move. Copy the detail from the acetate to your drawing by sliding the acetate under your drawing sheet and aligning the tracing with your drawn outline.

N.B. you MUST check your drawn measurements at this stage to make sure all inner measurements are correct. It is easy to make poor tracings and transfer incorrect information.

Once the outline and key points of the detail are added, complete the details and shading by eye, continually referring back to the object.

Remember the light direction is always from the top left. Look at the object with the light shining on it and add shade to your drawing only where there are areas of darkness on the object. This means that relief on the surface of the object facing *away* from the light will need more pencil shading.

To achieve best effect when shading, the lightest areas (those angled towards the light) should be left white. A soft pencil easily allows you to add subtle grades of shadow.

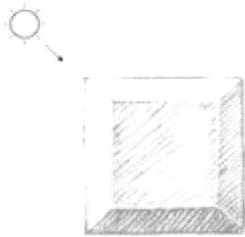

Figure 21.18
Pencil shading

Keep in mind that too much shading can obscure surface detail and that the darkest areas are almost never shaded completely black.

Continue to draw all necessary views of the object then add sections.

Drawing a section

Decide where you need to draw a section. You may need just one section across the main body of a simple object (Fig. 21.19), or several to show different structural elements.

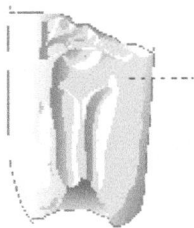

Figure 21.19

Measure the width and depth of the object at this point.

◀ Figure 21.20

Draw a box with the same dimensions within which the shape of the section will be drawn.

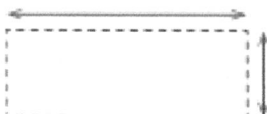

◀ Figure 21.21

Use a set square/ruler to create a box around the object.

Use dividers or callipers to measure 'offsets' from the edges of this imaginary box and plot these measurements inside the box you have drawn.

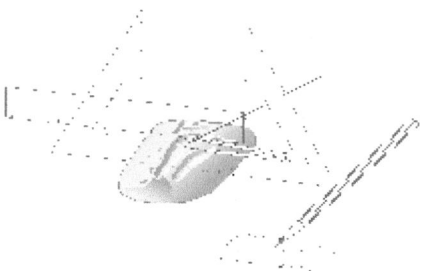

◀ Figure 21.22

A profile gauge or 'toothcomb' can help greatly when finding section profiles but as this is a less precise tool the width, depth and rough outline of the section should first be plotted as above.

Finishing the drawing. Black-in or hatch the section. Remember to add small 'section lines' to show where the section cuts the object.

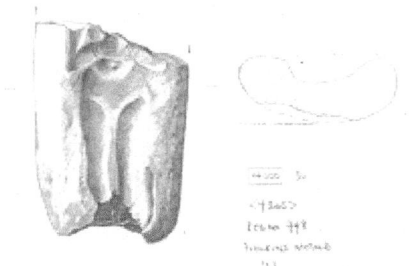

◀ Figure 21.23

Figure 21.24
Drawing a
Parthian juglet

Final completion

Look at the drawing and make any final corrections. At this stage it is usual for the finds specialist to have a look at the drawing to check for accuracy and that everything is drawn that needs to be.

Check that there is a scalebar and that the drawing is clearly labelled with its unique identifying details such as the site code, registration and/or catalogue number and perhaps drawing number. Add your initials and date.

Preparing a drawing for publication

A folio of pencil drawings forms an invaluable visual archive record of the carefully studied objects. However, scanned or photocopied reproductions of pencil lines can appear faded and imprecise. To produce a high definition, black and white image that is easily reproducible for hard copy and screen, the pencil drawing needs to be prepared for publication by replacing the faint pencil lines with black lines.

Inking and Digitisation

There are two ways to do this, either by inking or digitising the drawing. It is possible to use either the inking or the digital method for both small finds and pot drawings, but it is advisable to use the inking method for small finds drawings and the digital method for pot drawings. This is because small finds often possess surface texture or decorative detail that need to be shown clearly and these characteristics are easier to reproduce with pen lines. As described in the following section, pencil drawings of pottery are technical, schematic and diagrammatic and therefore the digital approach is more suitable. Different illustrators will have their own preferences and different projects will have their own protocols.

Inking

Inking is the traditional way of preparing the pencil drawing for publication. Since the 1960s illustrators have used a standardised set of drawing conventions that are universally accepted by archaeologists and specialists and so objects can be compared to each other because clear consistent publication-quality drawings make such comparisons possible.

The aim of the process of inking drawings is to end up with a two-dimensional representation of the object that displays all the important characteristics of that object through careful shading.

Figure 21.25
Inking a small
find

Many illustrators still feel that pen and ink drawing produce the most sensitive and nuanced result, which is why, despite the availability of graphics software, this is still a widely used technique. Also, and importantly, it can take the same or less time to ink an object drawing by hand than doing so digitally.

There are two basic requirements for the inking process:

– a smooth paper that ensures smooth black pen lines

– a set of pens that hold permanent, archival black ink and have a range of pen nib thicknesses

Be mindful of the final publication scale before inking. At publication stage it is usual to reduce the inked drawing in size, usually by 50%, as this makes the drawing 'crisper' by tightening the lines together so the eye sees tone rather than a series of lines. An object inked at too small a scale may not allow for this reduction.

Paper

It is advisable to trace over the pencil lines onto a fresh sheet of paper, this way you keep the original pencil drawing intact. This is also preferable because it leaves the pencil drawing intact for the archive and allows you to use your drawing to trace from again should you make any mistakes! The paper you trace onto therefore needs to be transparent.

Tracing paper does not have a smooth enough surface to take technical pen lines as the ink tends to spread into the paper. It is best to use a matt coated plastic film (drafting film) of the type which is often used on-site for plan drawings. If this film is unavailable then use the best quality, heaviest tracing paper you can find.

Pens

Before starting the inking process, it is important to decide on the most appropriate pen thicknesses for different areas of the drawing. It is important to use consistent pen thickness in each drawing, so pens that have numbered nib sizes are best. Technical pens such as Rotring Rapidographs and Isographs have been the industry standard for many years, however they are expensive and high maintenance and so only economical when a large amount of drawing is to be produced. High-quality fibre-tip fine

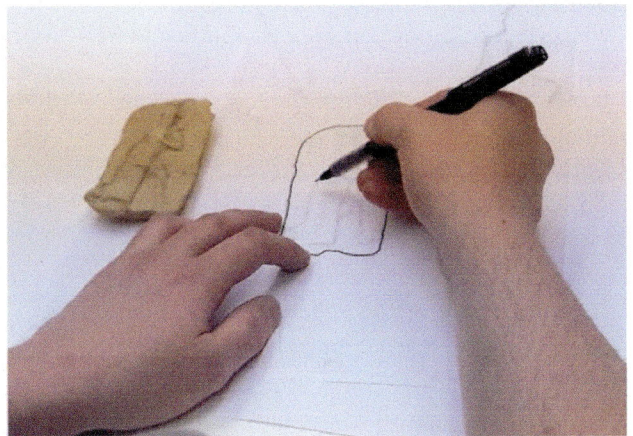

▶ Figure 21.26 Inking in an illustration with a pen

liner pens can be used instead. Rotring Tikki Graphic pens, Pigma Micron fine liner or Uni-PIN Drawing Pens are examples of suitable brands available today.

The outline of the object is drawn with a thicker pen line than the internal detail. A 0.35 mm or 0.5 mm nib is usual depending on the size of the drawing and scale of reduction. For the internal detail fine nibs should be used so that the lines do not appear too bold – 0.1 mm, 0.13 mm or 0.18 mm.

Figure 21.27 Examples of pens suitable for the inking process

Shading techniques

The inking of the internal detail is done by carefully replicating the depth of shade in the pencil drawing underneath. The shadows drawn in pencil using a shading technique are simply enhanced at the inking stage and so the density of ink on paper should follow the pencil drawing. Shading should not obscure the object's details but rather highlight elements such as decoration, texture, shape and relief.

Shading in ink is usually added using either of two standard techniques:

stippling – placing small dots closer together or further apart to achieve the desired level of shading.

linear shading – placing lines of various thicknesses closer together for darker areas and further apart for lighter ones. Lines may be either vertical or horizontal, but generally not angled. Do not use cross-hatched lines when inking as this can appear untidy.

Areas highlighted by the directional light should be left unshaded and areas in heavy shadow should have the densest shading. Both techniques should reflect the appearance of the surface of the object. The figure above shows how simple variations in the pen shading technique can reflect a smooth or uneven surface. It is helpful to have the object to refer to at this stage, or a high-resolution photograph if the object is not available.

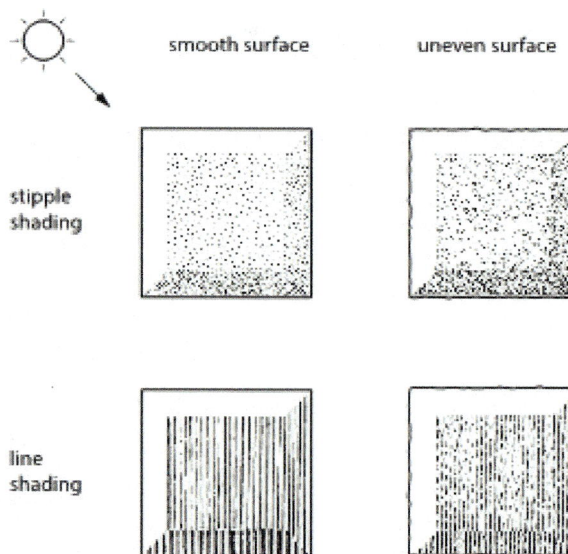

Figure 21.28 Ink shading techniques

It is a good idea to test whether your shading looks right by photocopying your ink drawing at a reduced scale, you can then remove areas that look too heavy with a razor blade or add ink where the shadow needs to be darkened.

Remember to ink the scale bar added at the pencil drawing stage. This ensures an accurate scale is maintained when copied or seen on screen.

Digitising the ink drawing for publication

The ink drawing then needs to be scanned. This will allow the drawings to be inserted into reports and publications as well as ensure that a backup copy is kept in case the physical drawing is lost or damaged. It is usual to scan the drawing as a black and white (bitmap) image at a high resolution (600 dpi minimum). It is best to scan the drawing at 100% scale for the archive, a copy of the file can then be reduced to the scale to be used in the publication in Adobe Photoshop.

It is very important to take care when scanning as a bad scan can make a good drawing into a bad drawing. If the resolution is not high enough the lines will 'pixilate' and the line quality of the original ink drawing will be lost. Image file sizes can be reduced by turning the black and white (bitmap) file into a greyscale image and saved as a 600 dpi jpeg. The type of file you choose will depend on the project protocol and how you intend to use the image in print or digital media.

Learning archaeological illustration is a continual process. For inspiration, keep looking at good examples of drawings in quality publications and online resources ... and keep practising!

Figure 21.29
Illustrating
small finds

Figure 21.30 Preparing for an illustration

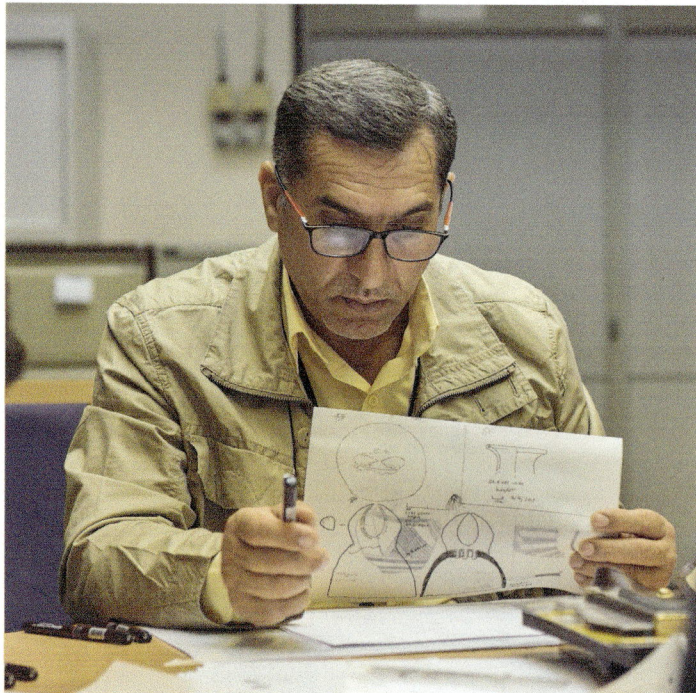

Figure 21.31 Checking an illustration

Chapter 22

Ceramic Illustration

Pottery drawing functions to record and convey information about ceramic finds such as their shape, size, thickness of walls, decoration and method of manufacture. Pottery drawings are fundamental during the whole process of study, from the initial research into parallels to the publication of the final analysis. The graphic work on pottery consists of two phases. Firstly the objects are drawn with a pencil on paper. Then the drawings are digitised on a computer using software such as Adobe Illustrator for data storage, study and publication.

Ceramic drawing is a technical process following established conventions that have to be applied with consistency. The usual practice is not to draw all the pottery finds from the excavation, but only complete pots and the so-called 'diagnostic' sherds – rims, handles, spouts, decorated body sherds and bases (Fig. 22.2) – which can often point to the full form of the original vessel.

Figure 22.1
Illustrators
ready to start
work

Equipment for drawing

– good lighting

– flat surface (table, board)

– millimetre squared paper

– smooth tracing paper or transparent drafting film (such as permatrace or mylar)

– hard (2H-6H) pencils which give precise strokes and do not smudge like soft (B) pencils

– mechanical pencils (0.5 mm and 2 mm)

– rulers (10 cm and 30 cm, at least one angled)

– set squares (45°/45° and 60°/30°)

– metal (toothcomb) profile gauge

– callipers

– pair of compasses

– rim diameter chart

– erasers, pencil sharpener, scissors

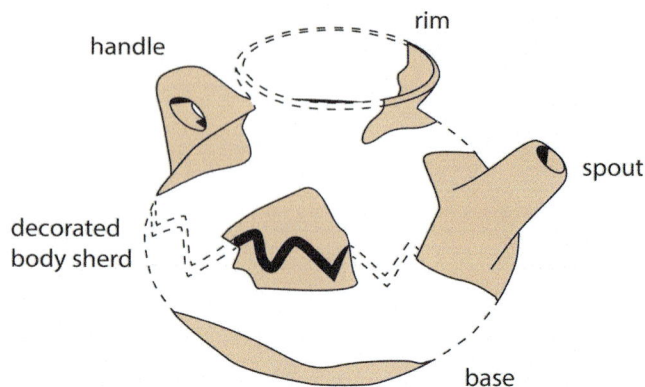

Figure 22.2
Diagnostic finds

General rules

The three-dimensional ceramic object is represented on a two-dimensional surface (the paper) through a system of orthographic projections which includes sections, elevations and plans. The **section** is the representation of the internal structure of the pottery piece as if it has been cut through vertically. The section shows the thickness of the pot wall and of any other parts such as handles, spouts, feet and lugs. The **elevation** is the view of the piece from the front. The **plan** is a view drawn either from above, to show, for example, decoration on the top of the rim or inside a plate; or from below, to show decoration on the outer side of a base. As a general rule, the left-hand side of a pottery drawing shows the section and any internal details of the piece, while the right-hand side shows the front view with external details such as decoration (Fig. 22.3).

Preparing to draw ceramics

Tape a sheet of transparent paper or film over a sheet of millimetre squared paper.

Then look at the pottery and study it carefully (Fig. 22.4). Consider its:

Shape: What is it? A complete vessel? A fragment of rim? Of the body? A base? A handle? What is its orientation? Was it a closed or open pot? Is there any trace of a lost element such as a handle?

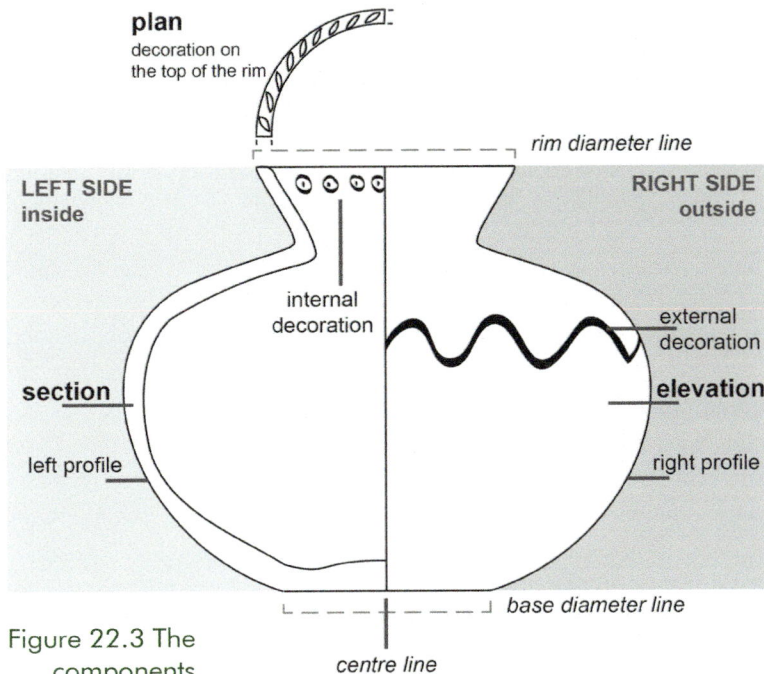

plan
decoration on
the top of the rim

rim diameter line

LEFT SIDE
inside

RIGHT SIDE
outside

internal
decoration

external
decoration

section

elevation

left profile

right profile

base diameter line

centre line

Figure 22.3 The
components
of a pottery
drawing

Size: How much of the original object is preserved? How big is it? Is there enough space to draw it on the paper?

Surface treatment and decoration: Is there any decoration? Is it a continuous decoration or a single element?

Method of manufacture: For example, are there indications that it is wheel-thrown or coil made?

Once this is done, you should plan the arrangement of the drawing on the paper. If the sherd is plain and the original pot was symmetrical in shape, you can draw just the left-hand profile together with the section of the sherd and the radius and centre lines. The right-hand profile can be traced to complete the drawing later on, during the digitisation phase. If the sherd is decorated, you will need space for elevation and/or plan views.

You need to choose the **scale** of the drawing most suited to the piece. The scale will most often be 1:1, but large pots are drawn at 1:2 or an even larger scale if necessary. It is very important to make a note of the scale on the drawing. As the transparent film has no dimensional references, you may, if you like, draw a scale bar on the sheet.

It is important to maintain an inventory of the plates/sheets that have been drawn. Each plate/sheet must be given a number and the name of the site, season, context number and sherd number all recorded, as well as the date and the name of the illustrator.

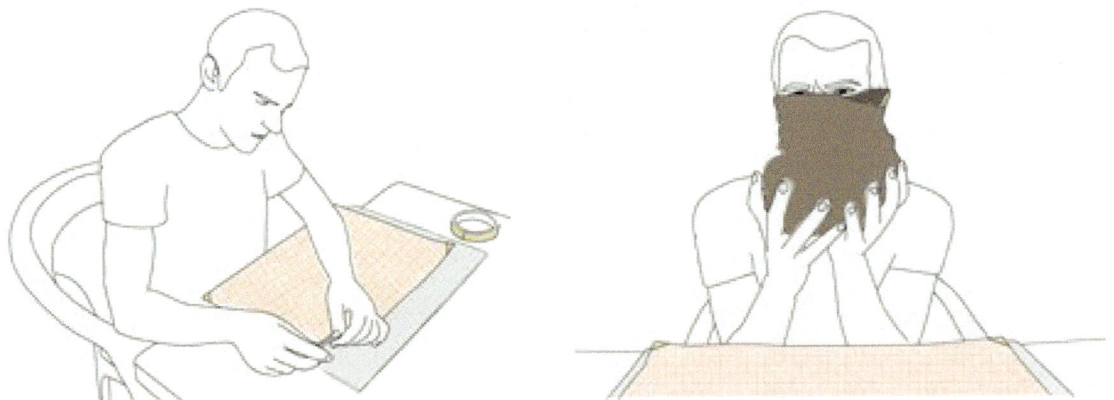

Figure 22.4
Preparation
for drawing
and initial
observation
and study of
ceramics

Open shapes   **Closed shapes**

Figure 22.5 Some examples of open and closed-shaped vessels

Orientation of the sherd

Pottery forms are divided into **open and closed shapes** (Fig. 22.5).

The sherd must be drawn according to its correct orientation, which means as it was situated in the original complete vessel. To understand the angle of a rim, hold the sherd in front of you and tilt it slowly back and forth until the rim appears as a straight line. To check the orientation, place the rim upside-down on the board/table and tilt it slowly back and forth until you do not see any light between the sherd and the paper (Fig. 22.6). In the case of a base fragment, do the same operation, but without turning the piece upside down. In the case of a body sherd, if it has wheel-thrown marks, these appear horizontal when the piece is properly oriented. If it is not possible to identify the original orientation, the sherd has to be drawn in a particular way, which will be discussed below.

Measuring the diameter

Hold the rim upside down in its correct orientation. Trace around the rim with the pencil held perpendicularly onto a piece of transparent paper (Fig. 22.7a). Take the diameter chart and match the rim curve you have traced with the circle which best fits, and make a note of the diameter (Fig. 22.7b). You can also hold the rim upside down, in its correct orientation (angle), on the diameter chart and move it until you find the curve it matches with. The diameters of bases can be measured in the same way.

You can also measure the diameter of the body, as long as the body sherd is big enough and regular. Press the profile gauge horizontally against the correctly oriented sherd (Fig. 22.8a), then compare the curve against the diameter chart until you find the curve that fits best with the profile (Fig. 22.8b). Note that you need to be aware of which part in the profile of the original lost pot this diameter belongs

Figure 22.6 To find the correct angle of the rim, no light must be seen between the sherd and the paper

Figure 22.7
Measuring the
diameter of a
rim

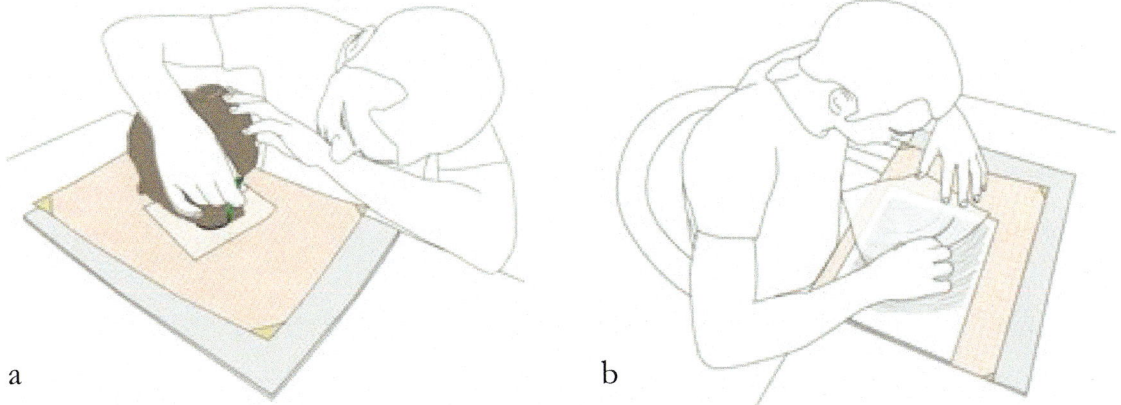

Figure 22.7
Measuring the
diameter of a
rim

a

b

to. Remember to always write down the diameter measurement, ideally close to the point where you have measured it (for example, in the inner or outer side of the top of the rim, or by the wall at a particular height, see Fig. 22.25). If the fragment is too small and it is not possible to measure the diameter, write a question mark next to the diameter symbol: Ø?

Drawing a rim

Place the rim upside-down on the drawing board and tilt it slowly back and forth until you find its correct orientation (angle). As mentioned above, find the angle at which no light can be seen between the sherd and the paper. Hold a set square against the upper edge of the rim held in this position (Fig. 22.10) and mark the point at the base of the square (A), the corresponding point where the rim touches the paper (B), and make a note of the height of the sherd (H). If you have to deal with a closed-shaped pot, it is easier to measure the external side of the section. If you have to deal with an open-shaped pot, it is easier to measure the internal side of the section. Record these points A, B and H on your paper, upside-down.

Using the profile gauge take the profile of the sherd along the line of these points (Fig. 22.11a). Place the profile gauge flat on the paper at the edge of the board/table (Fig. 22.11b) – do not hold

a

b

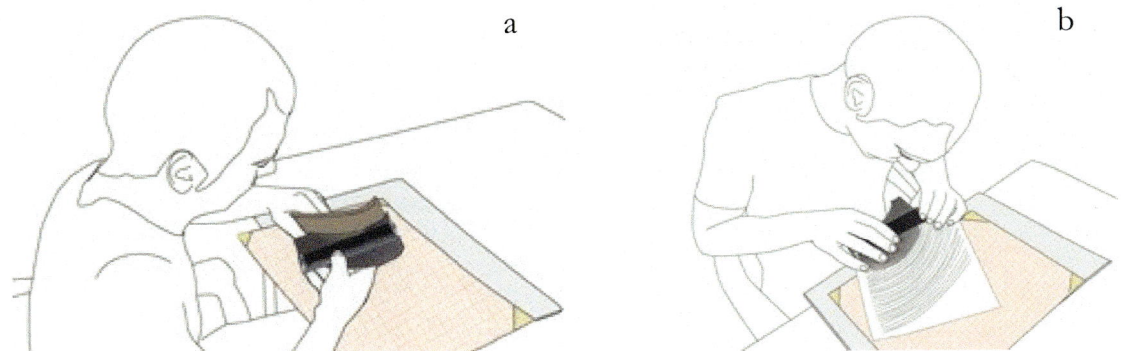

Figure 22.8
Measuring the
diameter of a
body sherd

Figure 22.9
Using a circle
gauge

it at an angle. Move the paper until you match the profile taken with the profile gauge with points B and H, then draw the outline. Note that at this stage the outline will be jagged as the teeth of the profile gauge cannot fully reproduce the exact curve of the actual profile.

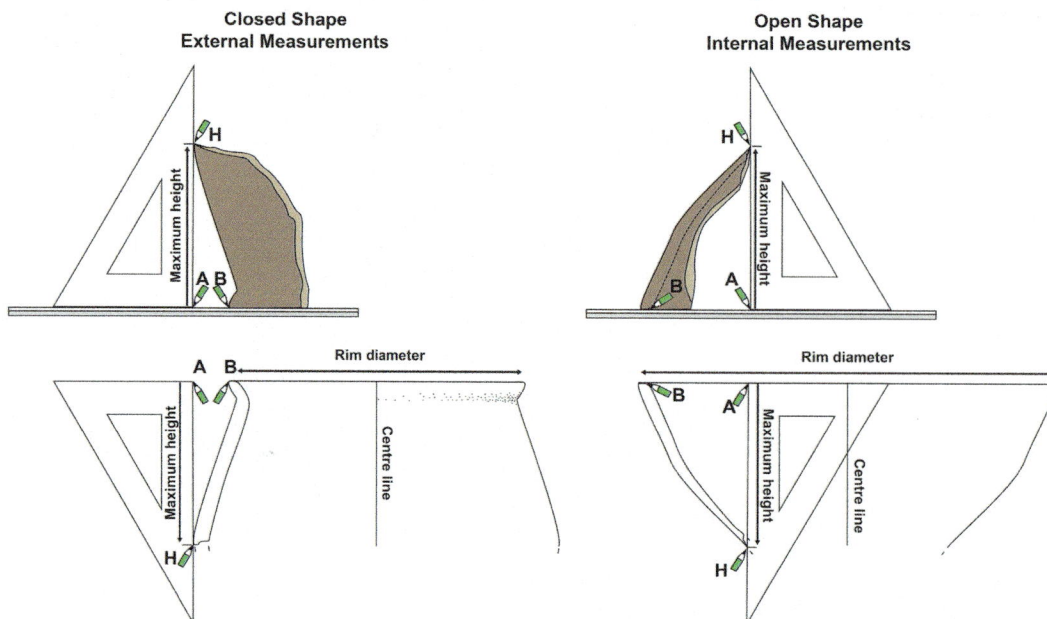

Figure 22.10
Rim drawing:
points to record

Figure 22.11
Tracing the
profile with the
profile gauge

a

b

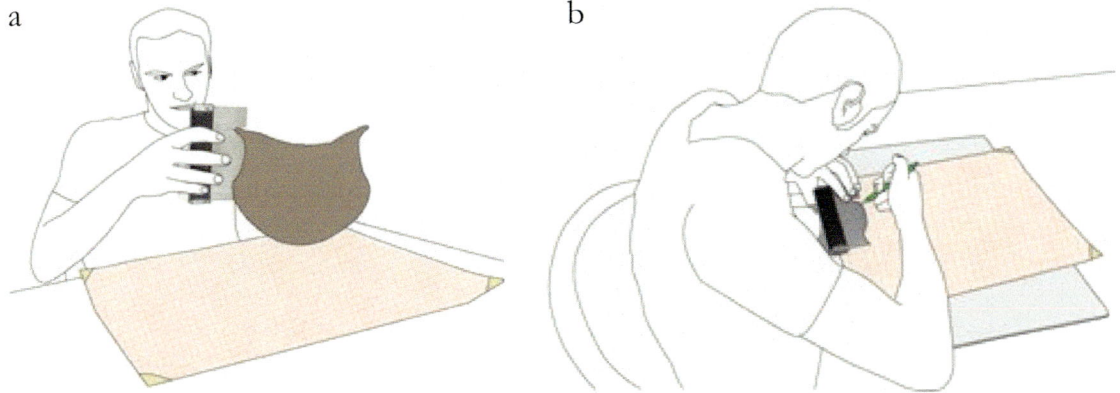

Often you will need to repeat this operation to get the complete profile of the sherd. In that case, obtain the missing profile using the profile gauge once again, taking care to include a part of the profile that has already been traced, and superimpose the remaining part of the profile on the part already drawn. You can also take additional points of reference along the profile, recording their height and their distance from the vertical edge of the set square (Fig. 22.13). Once these points are plotted upside-down on your drawing, you can match them with the profile taken with the profile gauge.

Figure 22.12
Using a profile
gauge

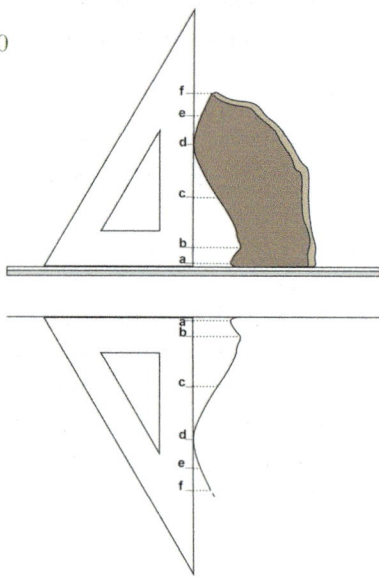

◀ Figure 22.13
Drawing the
profile, taking
several points
of reference

After you have drawn the external (or internal) profile of the section at the correct orientation (angle), complete the illustration of the section, i.e. drawing the other side of the wall of the sherd. To do this, measure the thickness of the sherd at the most significant places with callipers (Fig. 22.14) and mark these on the paper. Take the profile of the opposite side with the profile gauge and draw it.

Complete the lower part of the section, closing it with an irregular (not straight) **fracture line** to indicate it is broken at this point. Draw two short parallel lines (**continuation lines**) below the fracture to indicate the probable continuation of the original vessel body. Draw a straight, horizontal **diameter line** of the appropriate length (Fig. 22.15). Holding an angled ruler against it, draw a vertical line at a right angle from its mid point to make the **centre line**. As already noted, as a general rule, the inner side of the sherd should be represented on the left of the centre line, and the external appearance on the right (Fig. 22.3).

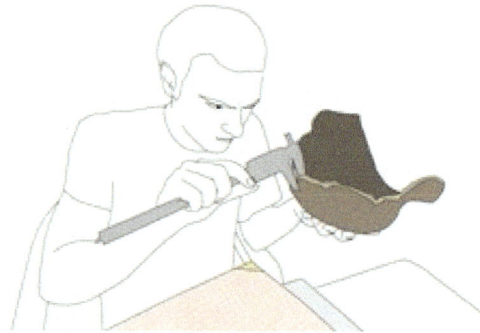

Figure 22.14
Measuring
sherd thickness
with callipers

Figure 22.15
Drawing the
diameter and
centre line

If the sherd is not decorated, you only need to draw its section, the radius line and the centre line. The drawing can be completed during the digitisation phase, when the diameter line and the correct profile of the fragment are drawn out in full. If you have to represent the right profile of the sherd, trace the left profile of the section, the radius line and part of the centre line (to keep the correct orientation of the sherd) on a piece of transparent paper. Reflect this vertically. Place the paper with the copied left profile under the transparent sheet, positioning it correctly at the end of the diameter line on the right-hand side, and trace over the profile. Remove the inside parts of the profile that are not visible in an external front view (Fig. 22.16).

Figure 22.16
Any parts of the
profile that are
not visible from
the outside are
not shown in
the external
view on the
right-hand side
of the drawing

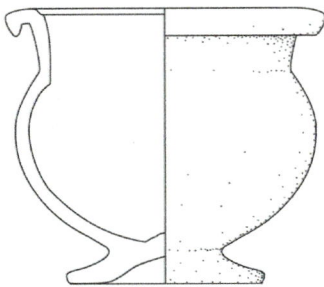

The external elevation only needs to be actually drawn if there is decoration. To represent the elevation of the sherd, hold the fragment parallel to the paper and incline it according to the orientation represented in the section (Fig. 22.17). Check that the top of the rim matches with the diameter line using an angled ruler. Holding the pencil perpendicularly to the paper, trace around the outline of the sherd.

The length of the elevation and that of the section must be the same. The elevation of the outer side of the sherd must touch the centre line in the drawing. Any breaks or fracture lines should be drawn. If the sherd is bigger than one quarter of the original complete vessel, the excess part of the elevation is ideally drawn behind the front view, around the right profile. To record the dimension of the rim, you can draw a pie-chart, a small circle divided in four parts, and record the portion of the preserved rim, starting from the quarter at the bottom on the right (Fig. 22.18).

▼ Figure 22.17
Sherd held
in its correct
orientation
for drawing in
elevation

► Figure
22.18 Pie-
chart recording
the proportion
of the rim
preserved

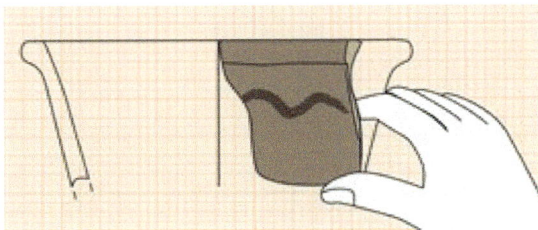

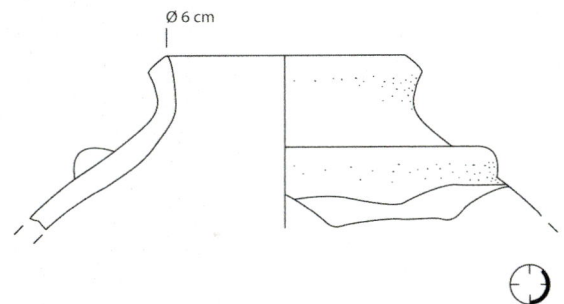

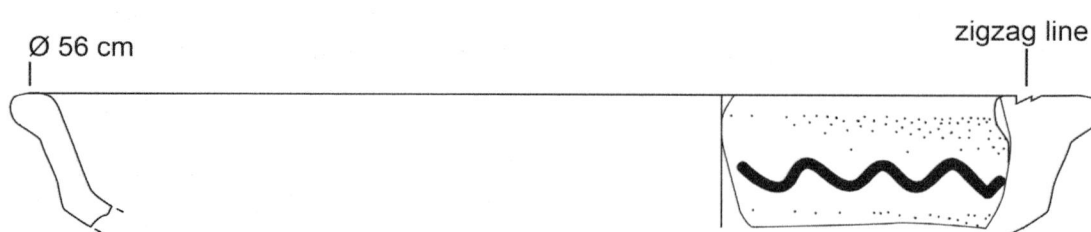

Figure 22.19 Zigzag symbol indicating reduced diameter line

In the case of an externally decorated sherd with a diameter too wide to draw in full, the diameter line on the right-hand side of the centre line can be drawn shorter, indicating this abbreviation with a zigzag line (Fig. 22.19).

With continuous relief **appliqué decoration**, the section of the decorative element is separated from the section of the sherd wall (Figs. 22.18, 22.21c, 22.21g, 22.22c, 22.22g). A single/isolated appliqué decoration is drawn separated from the section of the sherd wall and shaded to indicate a lateral view (Figs. 22.21d, 22.21h, 22.22d, 22.22h). **Incised decoration** or **deep impressions** should be indicated in the section (Figs. 22.20, 21b). Remember that ceramic illustrations are always shaded, when depicted in elevation, as if lit from the top left at a 45° angle. In the case of decoration on a steeply angled body sherd that cannot be clearly shown in the elevation, draw a view from above, over the section. If the decoration covers a large part of the body, the plan view can be represented above the diameter line.

Decoration on the top of a rim should be depicted in the drawing of the section on the left-hand side, above the diameter line, as a plan view. In the case of continuous decoration, you can represent just a part of the top of the rim (Fig. 22.3); however, with irregular decoration the complete top of the rim should be drawn. If the diameter of the sherd is known, the view from above the rim is depicted above the radius/diameter line and its ends are marked by continuation lines (Fig. 22.20a). If the diameter is not known, the plan view of the sherd is depicted obliquely to one side, connected to the section by a short line (Fig 22.20b).

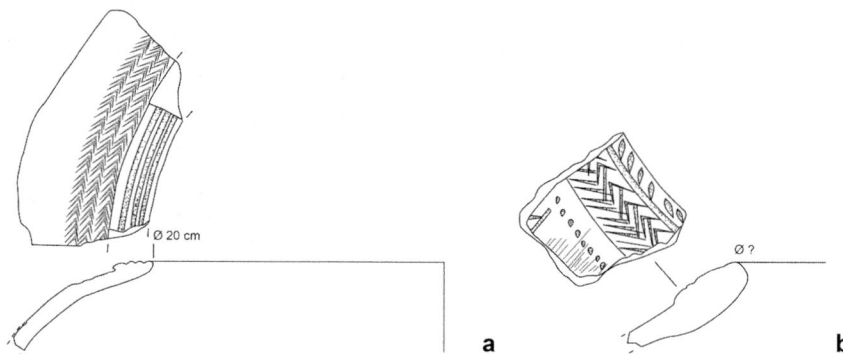

a   b

Figure 22.20 View from above for representation of the decoration on a steeply inclined body sherd

The representation of the elevation of decorated sherds depends on both whether their diameter is known or unknown and on the position of the decoration on the inner or outer surface.

Representation of the front view of a decorated rim with known diameter

In the case of external continuous painted or incised decoration, a portion of the decoration can be schematically depicted in a rectangle to the left of the section (Fig. 22.21a). The drawing can be completed during digitisation, completing the diameter line and the right profile and any decoration on the right of the centre line. Isolated or irregular painted decoration (Fig. 22.21b) as well as continuous (Fig. 22.21c) and isolated decoration in relief (Fig. 22.21d) should all be drawn as part of the elevation on the right-hand side. The elevation of a decorated inner side should be represented between the section and the centre line (Fig. 22.21e-h).

Representation of the front view of a decorated rim with unknown diameter

In the case of a **sherd with unknown diameter, decorated externally**, draw the section of the sherd with a short construction (diameter) line. Then on the right, draw the elevation of the outer side with two lines level with the top of the rim. In the case of a **sherd with unknown diameter, decorated internally**, draw the section of the sherd with a short construction (diameter) line, then, on the right-hand side, draw the elevation of the internal side, and finally, to the right of this, draw the elevation of the external side, even if without decoration; the three parts of the drawing are connected by lines at the top. Remember when drawing a sherd with a decorated inner side to always also draw the elevation of the outer side, even if it is plain, to avoid any misunderstanding.

Drawing complete pots

Place the pot upside down on the paper. Hold a set square against its outermost point (H). Mark the points at the base of the set square (A) and the corresponding point where the base touches the paper (B). Plot the point H onto your drawing (transferring the height measurement, keeping in mind if there is blank space before the 0 in the ruler). Take the shape of the vessel with the profile gauge. Match the profile on the gauge with the points B and H and trace it. Take the profile of any missing part with the profile gauge, including a portion of the profile already traced. Then overlap the two portions of the profile and complete the drawing. Use callipers to measure the thickness of the wall at the most meaningful points. Then use the profile gauge to take the profile of the inner side of the section and draw it. When the inner side cannot be reached with the callipers and the profile gauge, try to represent the profile as accurately as possible with a dashed line (Fig. 22.23). Measure the diameter of the rim and the diameter of the base and draw the diameter line, the centre line and the base line. Reflect the left profile over to the right-hand side. Draw any features inside the pot on the side left of the centre line, and any external features on the right-hand side.

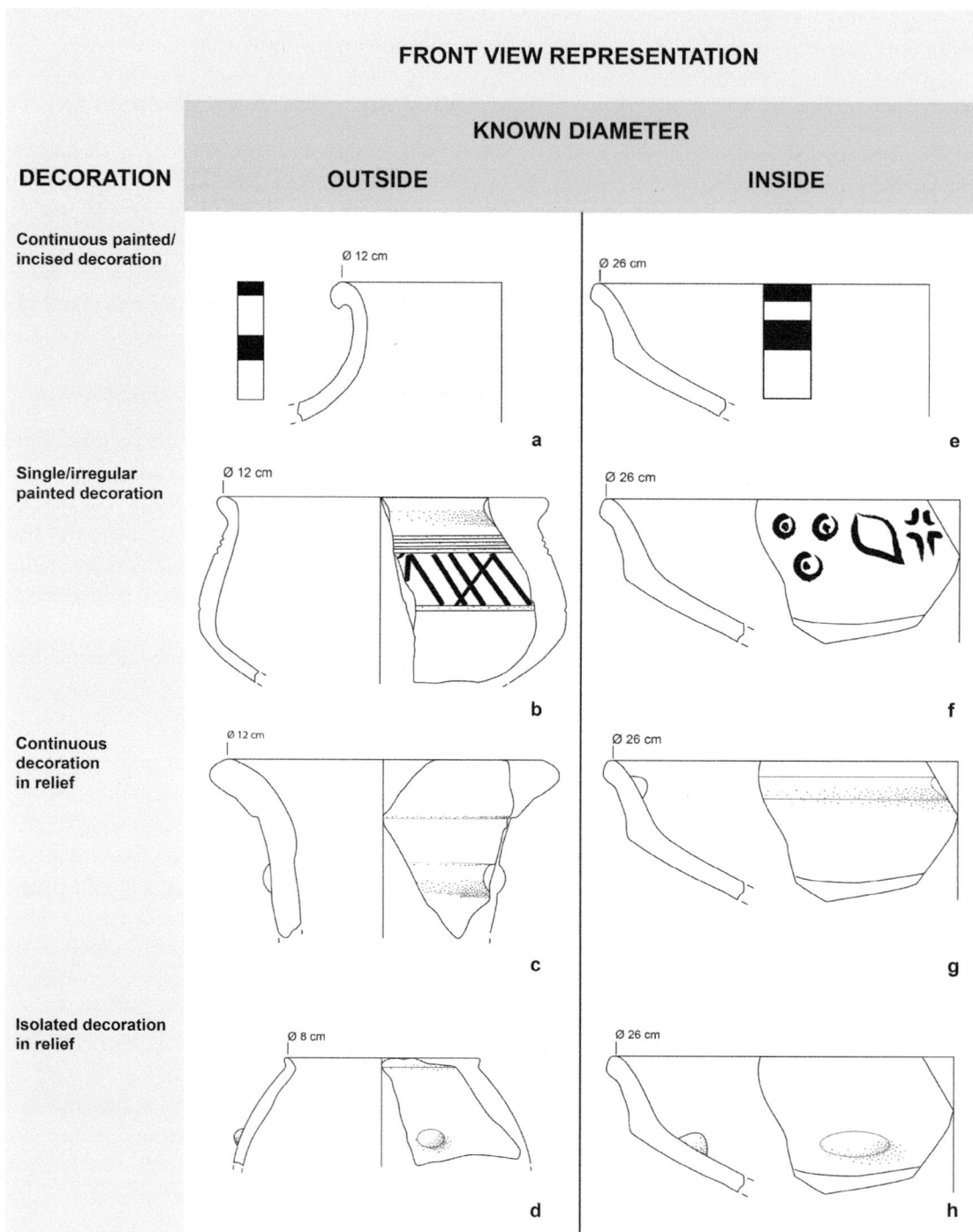

Figure 22.21
Front views
of externally
and internally
decorated rims
with known
diameter

Figure 22.22
How to draw
the front views
of externally
and internally
decorated rims
with unknown
diameter

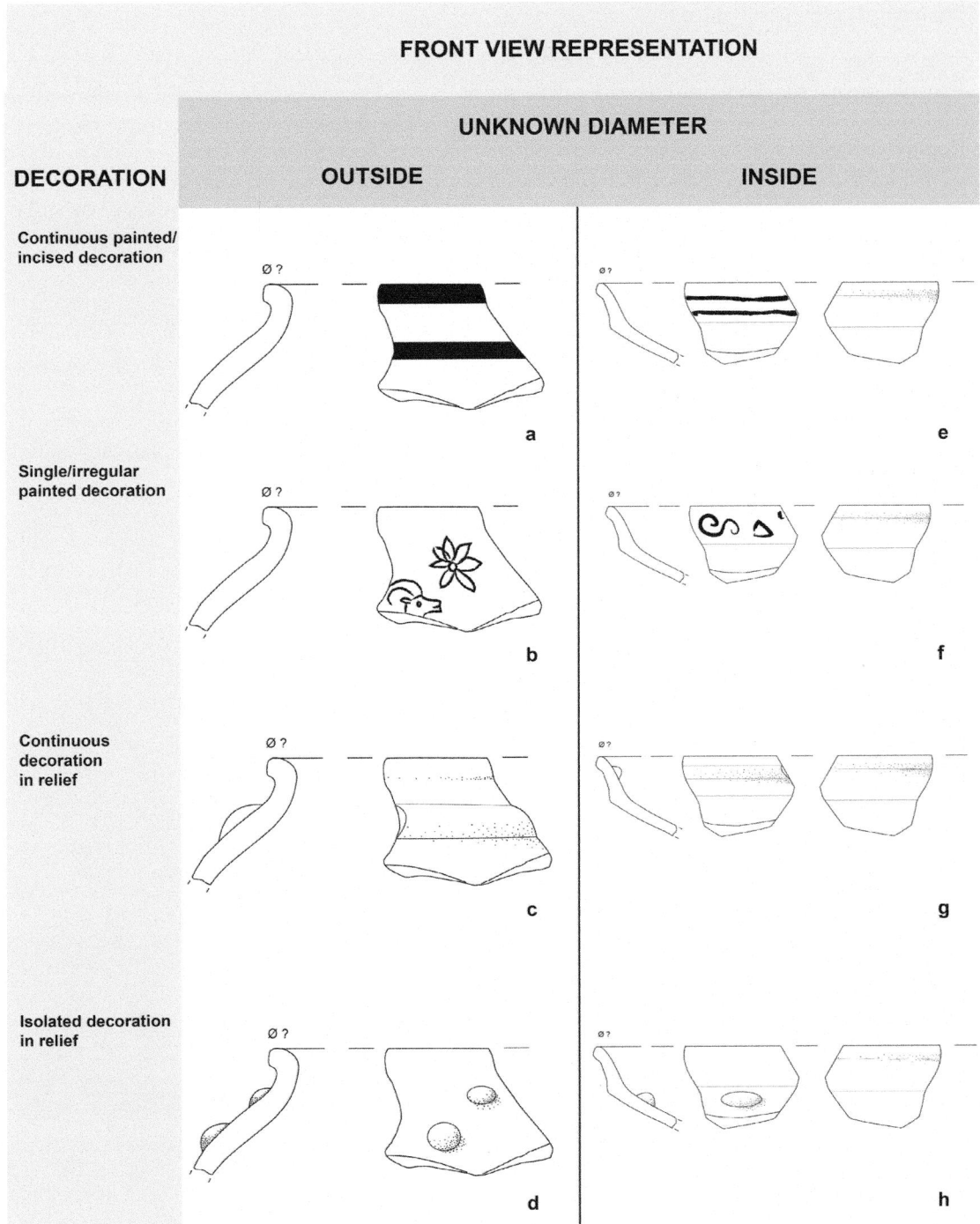

FRONT VIEW REPRESENTATION

UNKNOWN DIAMETER

DECORATION

OUTSIDE

INSIDE

Continuous painted/
incised decoration

Single/irregular
painted decoration

Continuous
decoration
in relief

Isolated decoration
in relief

Drawing bases and plates

Place the base on the sheet. Take the measurements of the maximum height (H), its projection onto the paper (A) and the correspondent point at the base (B) (Fig. 22.23). If the base is undecorated, draw its section, with line and centre line. The diameter line and right profile can be completed during the digitisation.

If the **outer side of the base is decorated and the diameter is known**, a plan view should be drawn below the section in a quarter circle (Fig. 22.24a); in the case of complex decoration, draw the complete plan/view from below.

If the **inner side of the base is decorated and the diameter is known**, a plan view should be drawn above the section in a quarter circle (Fig. 22.24b); in the case of complex decoration, draw the complete view from above (Fig. 22.24c).

If the **inner side of the base is decorated and the diameter is unknown**, a plan view should be drawn diagonally above the section and connected by a line (Fig. 22.24d).

In the case of decoration on the outer side of the base and on the body of the pot, a representation of the whole decoration can be depicted inside a circle or portion of a circle below the section/ diameter line (Fig. 22.24e).

Figure 22.23
Points to record when drawing complete pots

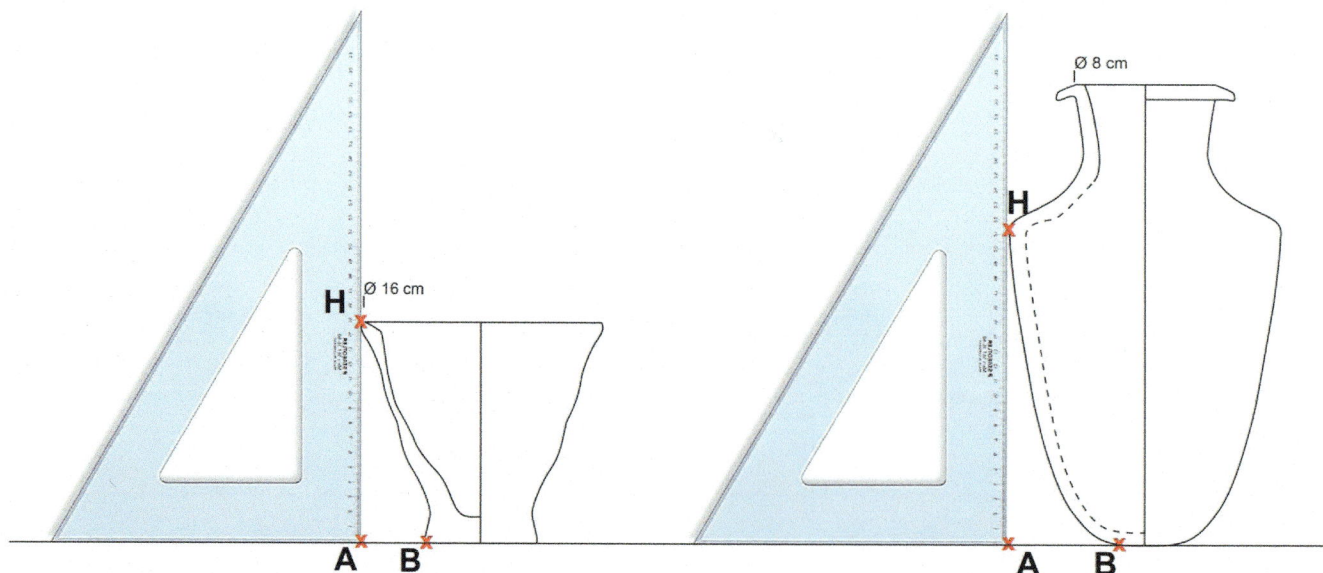

Figure 22.24
Drawings of
decorated
bases

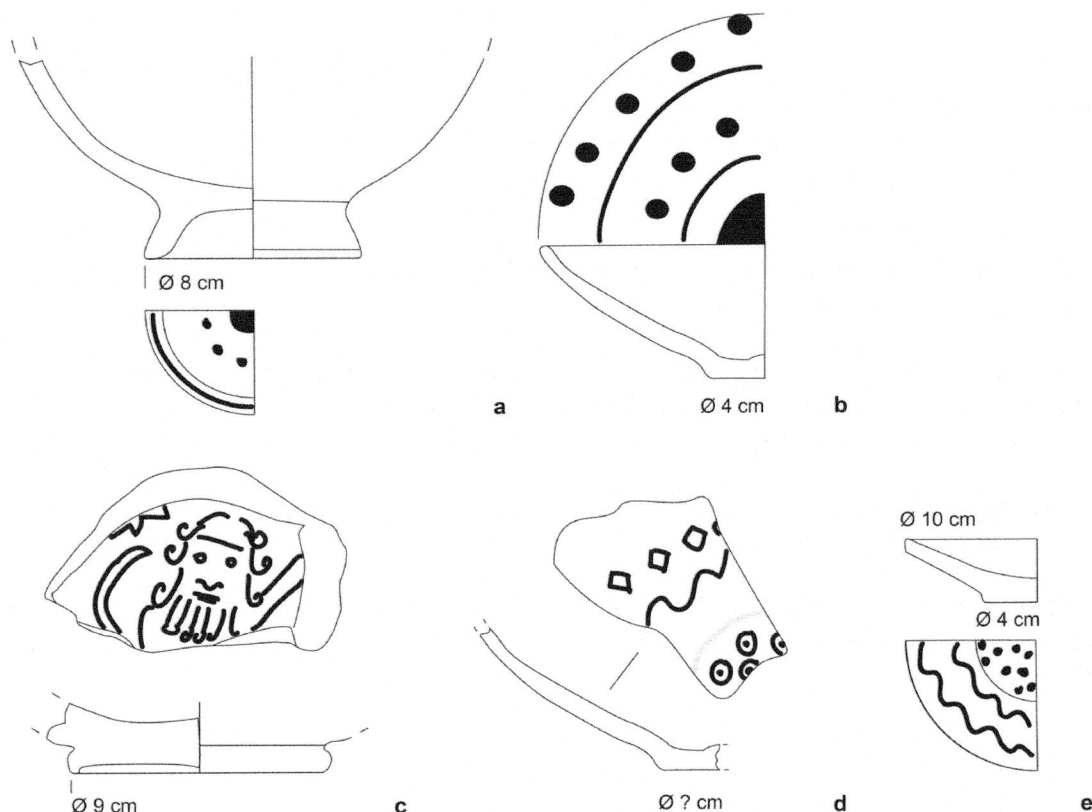

Drawing decorated body sherds

Body sherds are usually only drawn if they are decorated. If possible, the sherd should be drawn, both in section and elevation, oriented at the angle it had in the original vessel; the height of the two representations must be the same. When the orientation of the sherd is known, follow the same rules for drawing rims. Thus, when the orientation and the diameter of the sherd are known, the elevation of the inner side (if decorated) should be drawn to the left of the centre line, while the elevation of the outer side should be drawn to the right (Fig. 22.25a). The diameter measurement should be indicated close to the section, in the exact position where you have taken it.

When the orientation is known, but the diameter is not known, the elevation of the outer side is represented to the right of the section with a short horizontal line in between (Fig 22.25b), while the elevation of the inner side is represented between the section and the elevation of the outer side of the sherd, depicted in this case even if without decoration, separated by short lines (Fig. 22.25c).

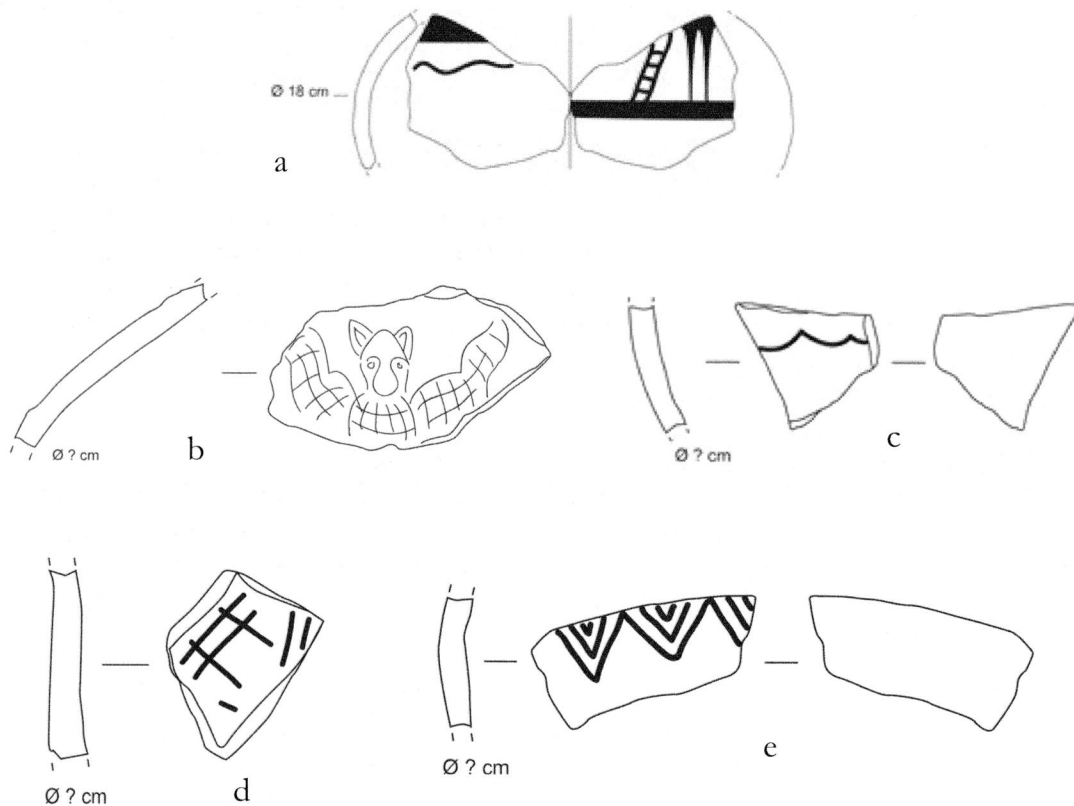

Figure 22.25 Drawing body sherds: (a) sherd of known diameter, decorated inside and outside, oriented correctly; (b) sherd of unknown diameter, decorated outside, oriented correctly; (c) sherd of unknown diameter, decorated inside, oriented correctly; (d) externally decorated sherd, arbitrary orientation; (e) internally decorated sherd, arbitrary orientation

When the orientation of the sherd is unknown, follow the same rules for the representation of rims with unknown diameter. The elevation is represented to the right of the section, with a short horizontal line in between (Fig. 22.25d). The elevation of the decorated inner side is represented between the section and the elevation of the outer side, even if the latter is not decorated (Fig. 22.25e).

If you have a highly decorated sherd with a flat curvature, and you have access to a photocopier you may want to protect the photocopier glass with a transparent film and then make a black and white copy of the sherd: you can then trace the copy and finish by measuring the important details. This is particularly useful if you have lots of stamped pottery.

Drawing handles and spouts

In the case of handles attached to a rim or the body wall with known diameter, a lateral shaded view of the handle should be drawn attached to the section of the sherd in its correct orientation. Trace the profile of the handle with the profile gauge and measure it with the callipers. Take the horizontal section of the handle with the callipers and the profile gauge and draw the cross-section with the outer profile uppermost. Mark the points where you have taken the horizontal section with two short lines next to the lateral view of the handle. If the handle is decorated, draw its elevation on the left of the lateral view (Fig. 22.26a). If the handle is not attached to a body wall, draw both the horizontal section and the elevation to the left of the lateral view (Fig. 22.26b). If the handle is attached to a body wall of unknown diameter, the elevation must be drawn on the right of the lateral view and horizontal section (Fig. 22.26c). In the case of a complete vessel, if the pot has only one handle, draw the lateral view of the handle attached to the right profile, with its elevation on the right. If the vessel has two handles, draw one handle on the right to show the exterior profile and one handle on the left, in section, to show how the handles were fitted to the body. Pots with more than two handles are drawn with one handle on the left and the others placed as close as possible to their real position. You can, if necessary, add a schematised view from above, or even a plan to show the location of the handles.

Similarly, with spouts, if the diameter of the sherd is known, the section of the spout is drawn attached to the section of the body wall, while its elevation is depicted to the left of the section. On the other hand, if the diameter of the sherd is unknown, the elevation (or drawing) of the spout is represented to the right of the section (Fig. 22.27). If the spout is not attached to a wall, draw it in section together with an elevation or lateral view.

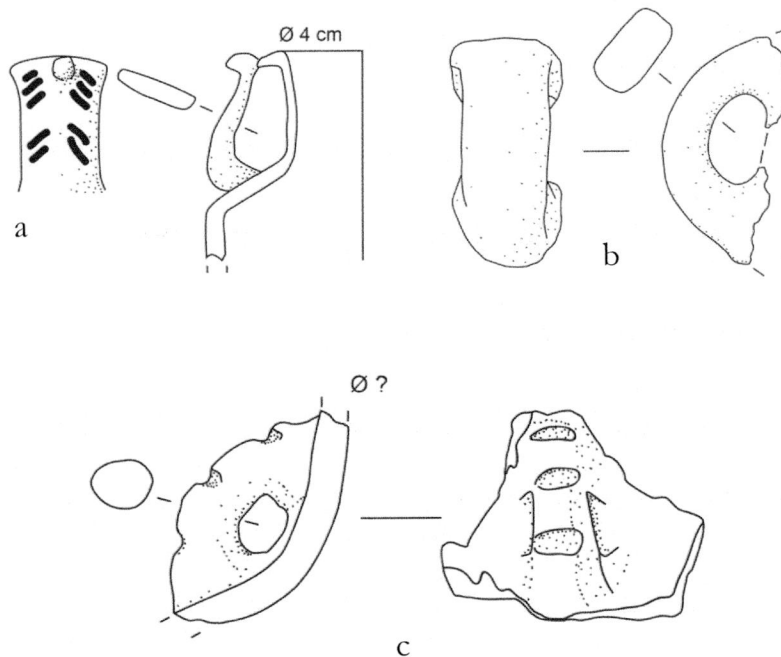

Figure 22.26
Drawing
handles

Another element that often has to be recorded is a spouted lip made by an outward protrusion of the rim. Draw the lip attached to the section of the rim, using the profile gauge to take the section through the centre of the lip in profile (Fig. 22.28). If necessary, add a view from above.

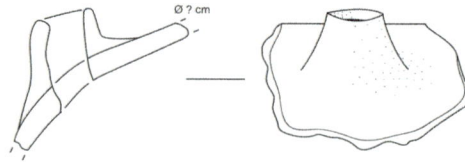

Figure 22.27 Drawing a spout of a sherd with unknown diameter

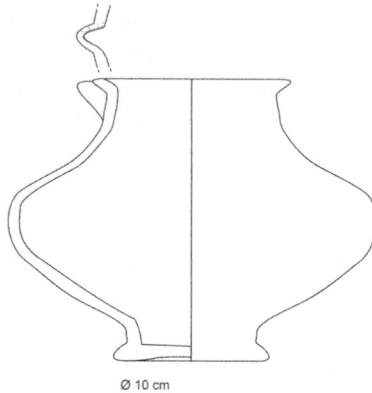

◀ Figure 22.28 Drawing a lip

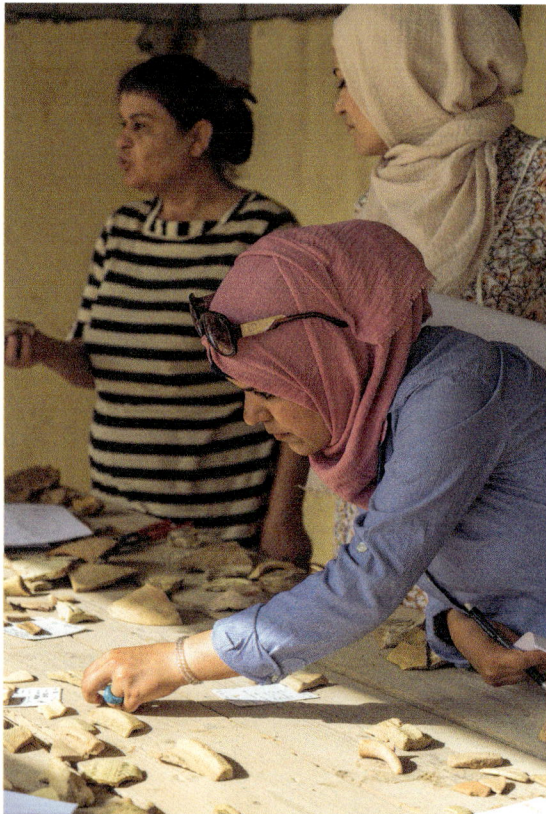

◀ Figure 22.29 Examining ceramics

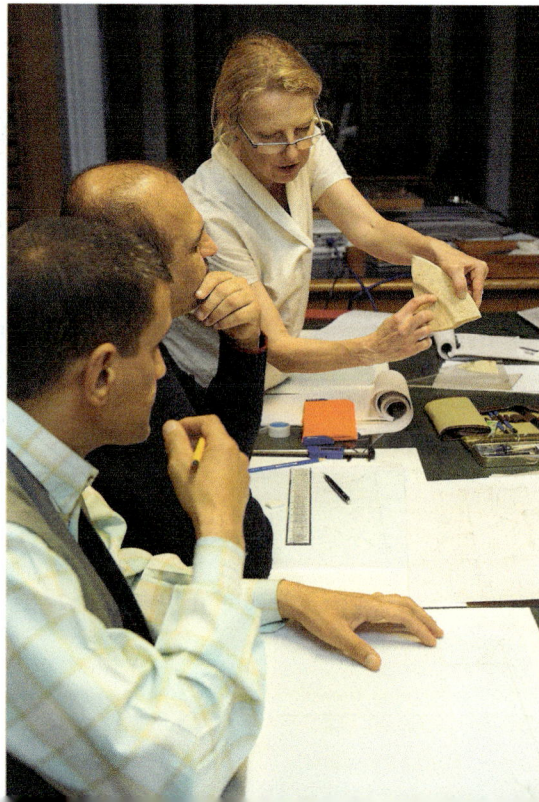

▼ Figure 22.30 Ceramic illustration lesson

Chapter 23

Photography

The photographic record is a crucial part of the site recording. Huge numbers of photographs are very rapidly generated. It is vital to start out correctly, with the correct settings established on the camera and a clear understanding of the aims of the photographic protocol, the technical procedure and the system for labelling and archiving images. It is important to have a record of every feature. But there is a difference between record photographs and photographs for publication. Record photographs may be more informal and can be taken with any camera. Publication photographs need to be well composed, the area completely cleaned, taken in optimal lighting conditions and using a professional camera.

It is important to ensure that the metadata (date and time settings) is set correctly; this should be checked once a week.

It is also essential to have a clear and logical system for labelling photographic images. Every site will have its own system. In the following we refer to the system we used at Qalatga Darband.

Figure 23.1
Checking
camera settings

List of Photographs

Supervisors should keep a log of photographs in an Excel file listing key data with the following columns: (a) running number for the sequence of photographs; (b) the photograph title (e.g. QD_A-001_1-JM). jpg, (c) date; (d) the contexts/find numbers of the features photographed; (e) short general description.

Preparing an area for photography

It is very important to prepare a site properly for photography. The very first thing is to be aware of how the natural light changes in the course of the day and when the best time will be for the area or feature in question. Often this is early in the morning before the sun casts direct light on the trench; conversely, you may want limited shadow to highlight features.

There are then a number of things you need to do to prepare for the photography itself:

– Check whether the trench needs smartening up – make sure the sections are straight, trim any protruding roots etc.

– Thoroughly clean the excavation by brushing (if dry) or trowelling (if wet) as appropriate, making sure not to leave shoe marks, which are very distracting in the published image.

Figure 23.2
Photography on site

Figure 23.3
Early morning
photography

Make sure that all tools and equipment are removed from the photograph; it is also often desirable to remove string lines – if you leave the nails in place the lines can always be easily restrung after the photography is complete

Position the scale, making sure it is parallel to either a major feature or the trench edge; you may want to use two scales, one positioned horizontally and one vertically

Add a north arrow (use a compass or the angle of sun to determine north)

Make sure there are no shadows being cast by the photographer or anyone else

If the trench is in shadow, but sunlight is breaking through, use shades to block it out

Labelling photographs

Site photographs

A board with letters is available but it is not essential to use this as the corresponding data – site, area, context and date – is included in the description of the photograph in the Excel file.

Record photographs

Individual features (contexts)

Photographs should be taken of individual features as appropriate: on discovery, in the course of excavation, and once fully excavated. At Qalatga Darband these are labelled in the format **QD_A-**

Figure 23.4 Photograph of steps of Hellenistic tiles at Qalatga Darband, made for the general record – while clear, note that the light is not ideal (as would be aimed for with a publication photograph)

001_1_JM.jpg, where '**QD**' is the site code, '**A-001**' is the context number, '**1**' is the sequence number and '**JM**' is the initials of the supervisor/photographer.

Individual features (objects in situ)

Photographs of objects in situ are labelled both with the context number and the find number, e.g. **QD_A-001_QD-1234_1_JM.jpg.**

Rooms

When an overall photograph of a room is being taken, the room number can be inserted in the following manner, e.g. **QD_A_Room1_A-001_1_JM.jpg.**

Sections

Photograph of sections can be labelled in the format **QD_A_south-section_1_JM.jpg, QD_A_ Room6-south-section _1_JM.jpg**, etc.

General photographs

In addition to the other photographs taken in the course of the morning's work, photographs should be taken of each excavation area whenever digging has progressed to the extent that there is a significant change and that such a photograph is meaningful. At Qalatga Darband these are labelled in the format **QD_A_GR_2018.10.31_JM.jpg** where **GR** stands for General Record

Notes

Note that the date is in the format YEAR.MONTH.DAY

It is very important that photographs are downloaded and labelled after work in the field each day and not put off to a later time.

Once downloaded, images need to be removed from the camera.

Keep the number of photographs down. If you have taken a number of identical pictures, select the ONE you want to keep.

Record photographs should be saved as jpegs (5 MB is the minimum required).

Final (publication) photographs

Individual features (contexts)

Final photographs are labelled at Qalatga Darband in the format **QD_A-123_1_JM_P** where A-123 is the context number, 'JM' is the initials of the supervisor/photographer, '1' is the sequence number and 'P' stands for Publication.

Individual features (objects)

Photographs of objects in situ should be labelled both with the context number and the find number, e.g. **QD_A-001_QD-1234_1_JM_P**

General photographs

General photographs of site areas should be labelled in the format **QD-A_GR_1_2018.10.31_JM_P**

Final photographs should be saved as Raw Files.

Figure 23.5 A final publication photograph from excavations in the Assyrian fort at Usu Aska

Small Finds photographs

Preparing an object for photography

First of all, in coordination with the conservator, make sure the object is clean and in a fit condition to be handled. Check whether gloves need to be worn. With very fragile or large artefacts, it may be that the conservator needs to be present to move and position the object as required. Plan your shots: consider how a set of images will best record all necessary views of the artefact, both as record shots and images suitable for publication, including any angles which may be necessary to bring out specific details. Choose the right lens among the ones available and frame the picture allowing just some space around it. As a rule of thumb, the more images the better – remember that there will not always be an opportunity to re-photograph the object at a later date. For the same reason, when in the studio shoot RAW rather JPEG. Try to keep background and lighting as consistent as possible. It is usually best to use one light source at an angle that emphasises diagnostic features. Shadows can be lightened with reflectors.

Figure 23.6.
Object
photography
– a Cone from
Tello

There may be special requirements – for example, cuneiform tablets need to be photographed with the light coming from the upper left hand corner with respect to the writing, and any writing that goes round the sides or over the top or bottom edges needs to be photographed specifically with the light coming from the upper left hand corner with respect to the writing at that location. The light source can be daylight or artificial, but not mixed. It can be large or small, diffuse or specular to suit the object. A white background is normally used for record images. For publication a coloured or graded background can emphasise the object – but should not compete with it. You may want to experiment with more than one approach until you find the best combination for the artefact or group of artefacts. When working with black, white, use 18% gray (pure gray) non reflective materials whenever possible. Start by taking an image of the finds tag. Do not forget to put in the scale, making sure that it is parallel with and at the same height as the surface on which the object is resting. And also do not forget to use a colour chart to calibrate your pictures when processing. They can be removed later when preparing the images for publication, where the information is within the text or caption.

Individual objects

Photographs of small finds should be labelled in the format **QD-1234_1**, where '**QD-1234**' is the object number and '**1**' is the sequence number.

Groups of multiple artefacts

Photographs of a small group of multiple artefacts (up to 5) can be labelled in the format **QD-1234_QD-1258_QD-1315_1**

Figure 23.7
Checking an
image using the
indirect viewing
screen

Photographs of larger groups
of multiple artefacts should
be labelled in a format such as
QD-potdisks_group1_1.jpg
– the photographer will need
to maintain a list of which
artefacts are included in each
group.

Publication photographs

Publication photographs of
small finds should be labelled
in the format **QD-1234_1_P**

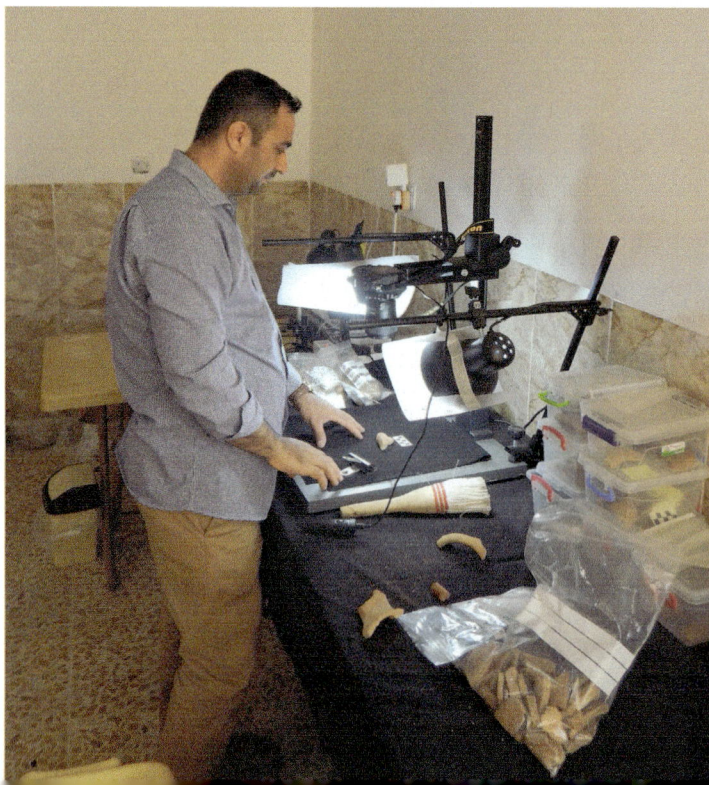

Figure 23.8
At work in the
photographic
studio

Chapter 24

Photogrammetry

Photogrammetry is the science and technology of creating reliable information about physical objects and the environment through the process of recording, measuring and interpreting photographic images – in short, making digital 3D models from photographs. The principle of photogrammetry was realised very soon after the invention of photography itself – the use of photographs to create topographic maps was first proposed by the French surveyor Dominique Arago in 1840. The actual term photogrammetry was coined by the Prussian architect Albrecht Meydenbauer in 1867. There are many products derived from photogrammetry, including 3D digital models and extraction of three-dimensional measurements from original two-dimensional source data. Photogrammetric analysis may be applied to one photograph, or many by using high-speed photography and remote sensing. Close-range photogrammetry refers to the collection and processing of photographic images from a shorter distance than traditional aerial or satellite photogrammetry.

The core principle of photogrammetry is to obtain geometric information such as the position, size and shape of any object from images previously obtained. To achieve this, points on the object need to appear on two or more images taken from different angles. Whereas until recently acquiring and processing images for photogrammetry required a considerable investment in hardware, software, expertise and time, the advent of cheap digital cameras capable of capturing high-quality imagery, together with advances in the processing capability of personal computers, means that photogrammetric models can now be undertaken by anyone with these resources.

Of course, it is still necessary to capture the photographs, organise them, and process the model following a defined procedure. In this section we offer a guide to the basic process of

Figure 24.1 Assyrian winged bull recorded in (a) a drawing from the nineteenth century, (b) a twentieth century photograph and (c) a modern photogrammetric image

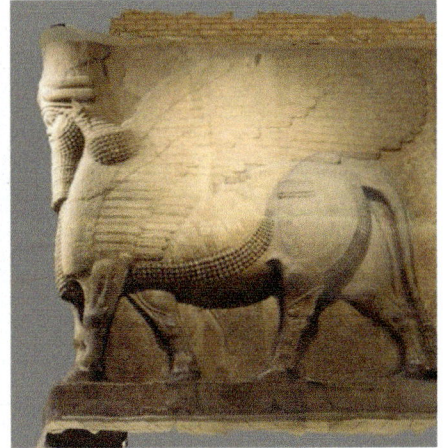

a   b   c

photogrammetry, from the capture of images through to the creation of models, followed by some resources to help users advance their knowledge and understanding. While there are many different forms of hardware and software available today for photogrammetric work, this guide will focus on the use of Agisoft Metashape (formerly called Photoscan), which is easy to use, intuitive, and affordable.

Capture of images

Before any photogrammetric processing can take place, the first step is the capture of the basic photographic images. This must be done following a clear method in order for the next step to work. If this initial image capture is not done properly the results will fail and a model cannot be processed.

In short, the image capture should be conducted systemically using the following core rules:

– a series of photographs needs to be taken with an overlap of 60% across photographs

– at the corners or end point of the object, more photographs need to be taken, with up to 80% overlap

– all photographs need to be taken at the same distance from the object

– all photographs need to use the same camera settings (focal length, aperture and exposure)

Once you have taken a sequence of photographs, it is very important to check this carefully to ensure you have a full and adequate set of images.

Geometric, camera and procedural rules

The basic rules are summarised in the table below.

There are three sets of three rules – nine in total. The first column relates to the Geometric Rules, the second to Camera Rules, and the third to Procedural Rules. These are discussed below. While this may at first seem confusing, practice will soon make them familiar.

The 3 x 3 rules for the documentation of monuments		
Geometry rules	Camera rules	Procedural rules
1.1 Control	2.1 Properties	3.1 Record
1.2 Cover	2.2 Calibration	3.2 Log
1.3 Stereo	2.3 Exposure	3.3 Save

Figure 24.2 Rules for conducting photogrammetry

Figure 24.3
Sketch for
with control
measurements
for
photogrammetry

1 Geometric Rules

1.1 Control

This relates to taking basic measurements of the subject from points or targets that can be seen. This includes identifiable points such as corners, windows and other features which can be placed into the software to scale the model. While a model can be processed without measurements in the software, it will not have the correct real-world dimensions.

The image above illustrates the minimum of control on a sketch of the site with a horizontal and vertical measurement, both of which are to corners of the building visible in the photograph.

Figure 24.4
Preliminary
attempts at
capturing
images for
photogrammetry

1.2 Cover

This refers to the 60% overlap of images. While the images may seem nearly the same, they are actually taken from slightly different positions and angles, allowing the software to calculate distances.

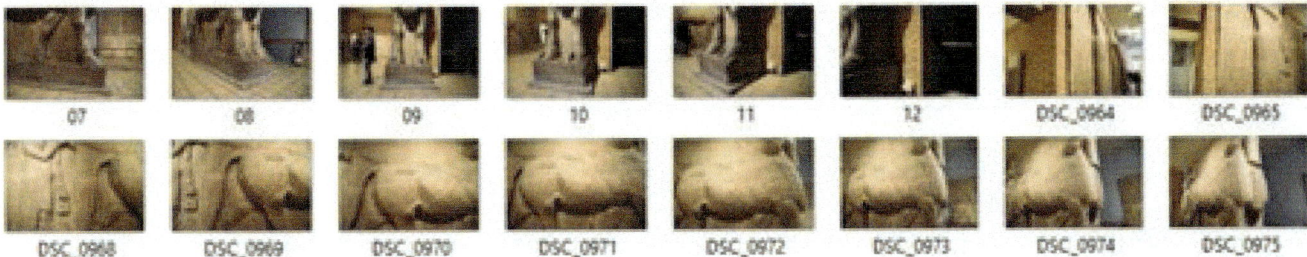

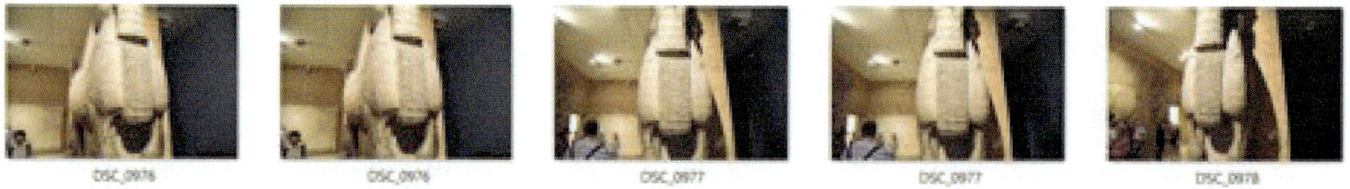

In the example above the images in the series 07–12, a first attempt to take a series for photogrammetry, represent an extremely poor overlap. With the second set of images DSC_0968 – DSC_0975 the coverage is better but there is still room for improvement: there is a large jump between DSC_0972 and DSC_0973, and the distances change between DSC_0968 and DSC_0972. Even so this sequence was adequate for the software to process and create a model.

The third attempt DSC_0976 – DSC_0978 has given a good series of images. The photographer is the same distance from the object, there is 60% overlap, the focus is on infinity, and the same camera geometry (i.e. zoom and focal length) is utilised. The images have been captured in an organised and methodical manner, scanning from left-to-right horizontally in layers, then repeating above and below, also overlapping by 60%.

Figure 24.5 A successful sequence of images

1.3 Stereo

This relates to the fact that the same section of an object can be photographed from slightly different viewpoints. The resulting images may look very similar, but this approach can work very well, particularly when a corner of a building or object is being recorded, as demonstrated in the image below.

Figure 24.6 Although these two images may at first glance seem exactly the same, they are in fact slightly different – a stereo pair

With this rule the distance between stereo images (Dc) should be 1/5 of the distance to the object (Do). So, if the distance to the object is 5 m, the distance between the two images recorded should be 1 m.

2 Camera rules

The second set of rules relates to the camera used to capture images.

2.1 Properties

This relates to the properties of the camera used. For the photogrammetric software to function properly and create the best digital 3D models, the internal geometry of the camera (zoom and focal length) must be kept constant. This means NO zooming in and out. Determine the best distance from the subject and set the zoom. Make a record of this in case the setting is accidently changed. For best results, the auto-focus should be disabled and the focus done manually. Focus should be set at infinity (though with more advanced cameras this is less of a concern). It is essential that all images are captured using the same camera settings (focal length, aperture and exposure). To achieve this in the various lighting conditions that will exist around the object, several tests must be conducted from various angles and points of view.

2.2 Calibration

This rule is about the adjustments of the camera. Use the best camera possible set to the highest resolution. This cannot be stressed enough. A normal angle lens (between 24 mm and 50 mm) is better than a wide angle (10mm) or telephoto lens. It is best to use a digital single-lens reflex (DSLR) camera. However, if this is not available, the camera on a mobile telephone is better than no photographic record at all. The photogrammetric processing from the camera on a mobile can produce mixed results depending on the make and model. Of course, the same capture rules, including 60% overlap, still apply. If colour is important, use a colour chart such as the IFRAO chart and capture the images in a non-compressed format such as TIFF or RAW.

An IFRAO colour chart not only calibrates the camera for colour but also provides a scale. These are available for free – see, e.g., http://www.cesmap.it/ifrao/scale.html and the references at the end of this section.

Rule for stereo pairs

*The distance between cameras shoud be
one fifth of the distance to the object*

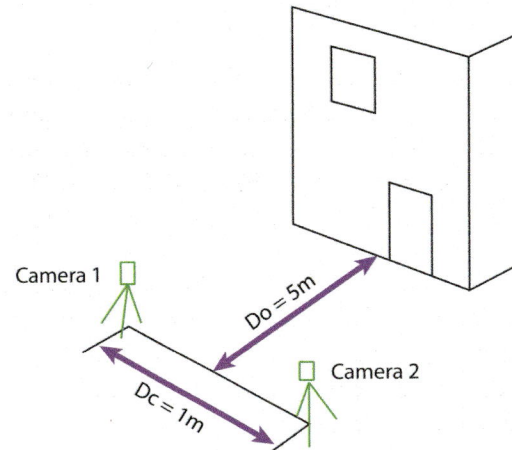

Camera 1

Do = 5m

Dc = 1m

Camera 2

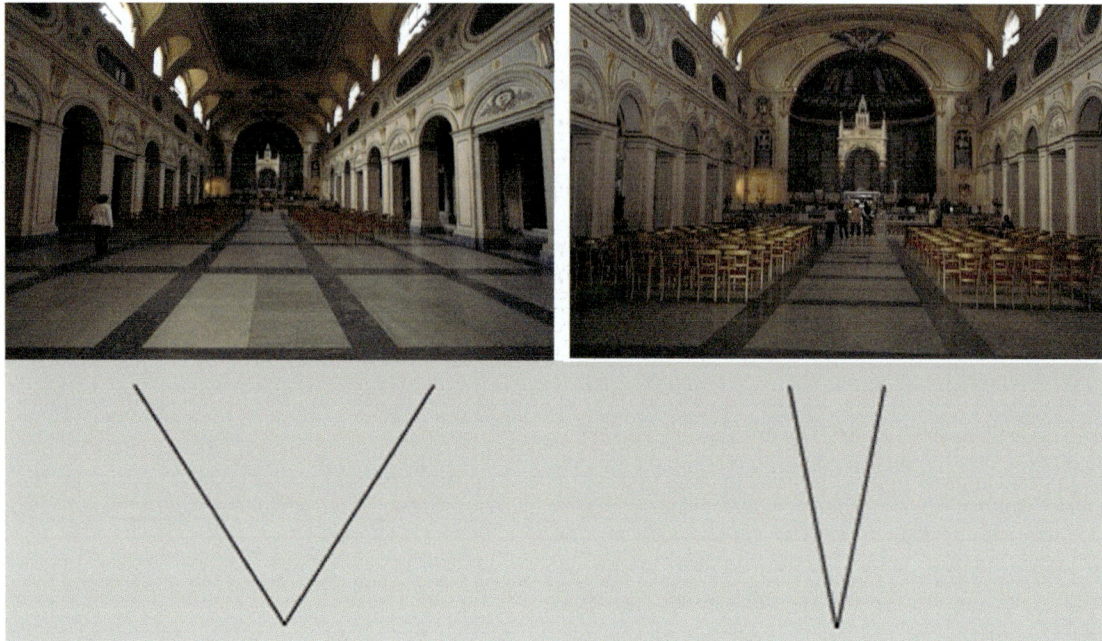

Figure 24.8 The image on the left was captured with a wide angle 10 mm lens and the image on the right was captured with a 50 mm lens. The image on the right is better for photogrammetric processing

2.3 Exposure

The exposure should be captured in the camera's manual mode and should be the same for all images captured. Often this is difficult due to ambient lighting conditions, so you need to plan to be on-site at a time with suitable lighting conditions. In dark places with little ambient light, such as interiors and recesses, where it is difficult to get an adequate exposure, use a tripod.

Figure 24.9 An IFRAO colour chart

3 Procedure rules

The last set of rules relates to the procedures for finishing the recording of the site.

3.1 Record

It must be remembered that even with good photographs and measurements you still need a sketch plan with a north arrow, the location and direction of where the photographs were taken (ideally with the individual image numbers), the location of the stereo pairs, the location of measurement control points, distances, and so on. You may wish to create several plans to record individual spaces or details. These sketches are important. It is often the case that the person

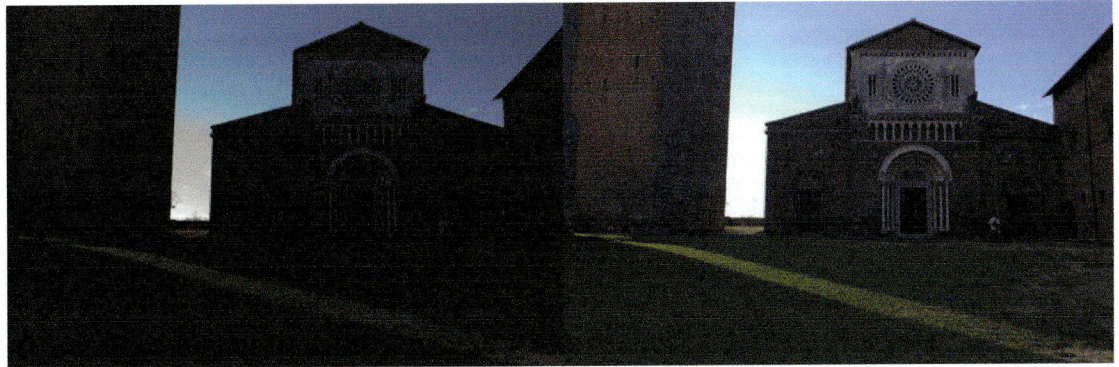

Figure 24.10 Exposure matters – very little information is captured in the image on the left, and while more is captured in the image on the right, both images are of poor quality due to the time of day (late in the afternoon): you need to plan to be on-site at the time when natural lighting is at its best for recording the object in question

recording the dimensions and photographing the site is not the person who will be processing the photogrammetric model. Such sketches will ensure that there is good communication and a record of what was recorded.

A good sketch can illustrate elements impossible to photograph. The measurements, exact locations of photographs and notes can all be recorded on the sketch. This should be done in the field when you are still at the object or site.

3.2 Log

This means having a standard recording form to ensure consistency between different objects or sites. The log should have entries for the name of the object or sites, address or coordinates, owner, date and person or people involved. It must also contain a brief description of the site,

Figure 24.11 The series of images above again illustrates how finding and using the correct exposure is important. The image to the left is underexposed, and not enough light has entered the camera; the image on the right is overexposed, with too much light entering the camera. The image in the centre has achieved a good balance between these two extremes

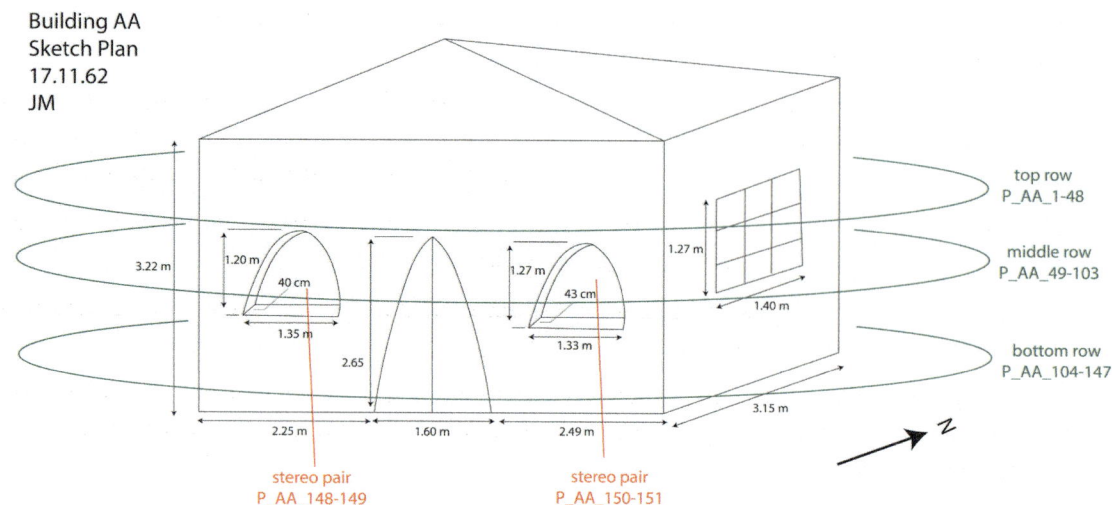

Building AA
Sketch Plan
17.11.62
JM

top row
P_AA_1-48

middle row
P_AA_49-103

bottom row
P_AA_104-147

3.22 m

1.20 m

40 cm

1.35 m

2.65

2.25 m

1.60 m

2.49 m

1.27 m

1.27 m

43 cm

1.33 m

1.27 m

1.40 m

3.15 m

z

stereo pair
P_AA_148-149

stereo pair
P_AA_150-151

Figure 24.12
Sketch plan
with building
measurements
and the
numbering of
photographs
taken for
photogrammetry

object and history, and short notes concerning the condition, any damage observed, and threats and safety measures. It is also important that the form includes the camera used, with a description of the model, lens(es) and the fixed position of the focus and resolution used. While these camera details are recorded in the metadata of each digital image, this information can be deleted from the file. Finally, there should be space to record conversations, interviews and any other relevant information.

3.3 Save

This last rule relates to double-checking the data recorded on-site. The person or team must do a final check of all the rules and images. Reviewing the images while on-site saves a return trip if any images have not been captured or are of poor quality – and it may also be that a return to the site is impossible. It is in any case easier to do this on-site while the object and the procedure you followed are fresh in your memory. If possible, the digital data should be duplicated by saving to a laptop or portable hard drive to ensure that there is a backup.

Creating 3D models

After the photographs are captured, the next step is to create the 3D digital model. While the following process relates to Agisoft Metashape (formerly called Photoscan), the process is similar with other software. There are links to written and video tutorials in the references at the end of this section.

A few notes of caution before you begin:

You MUST use a mouse. The trackpad on a laptop is not sufficiently accurate and can create difficulties. Make sure that if your mouse is wireless it has batteries and a good connection.

The left-hand button is for rotation, the right-hand button is for panning and the wheel – which is necessary – is for zoom.

You must do this processing while the laptop is plugged in. Do not operate on batteries as the processing time necessary for creating a model can sometimes take several hours – many models have failed due to the laptops shutting down before the process is complete.

Close all other programmes – you need all the computer's resources, memory and central processing unit. This includes closing the web browser.

Firstly, conduct test samples at low resolution before committing to larger models that may take a day or more to render.

Transfer your images to a project directory – and remember where you have placed them. You will need to ensure you are very organised – so decide where and how you will store the data before beginning processing.

Delete poor and out-of-focus images, repeat images and mistakes. Only use good images.

DO NOT edit images in a photo-editing software such as Photoshop – this will change the image and it will not work.

Step-by-step procedure

The following is a step-by-step guide to processing photogrammetric models in Agisoft Metashape. As with all software programmes, you may find there are slight differences between these images and how the programme appears on your own screen. If you have issues with the software installation, consult the manual. The programme must be licensed, if not you will receive a warning and you will need to enter the registration number or proceed in a demonstration mode. In the demonstration mode the steps can be followed but the model cannot be saved.

Step 1 – Opening the programme

Find the programme icon and double click to open the programme. If the programme icon is not visible search using the Windows search function or look in the Programme Files directory. You will see a blank screen typically divided into three parts with the upper pull-down menu and icons:

Commands may be entered by icons, the menu or by keyboard shortcuts. In this example the menu will be used as it is easier to remember. The grey central area is the main 3D viewing space and usually has a rotational ball to view the model. The lower white screen is where individual photographs load and the area to the right displays the model menu and accuracy results.

Step 2 – Uploading photographs

Click on the WORKFLOW Tab. This is the principal menu that you need to be using and all the steps are sequential. If the menu items are grey this indicates that you cannot move forward and must repeat the earlier steps. The programme starts by default in a new project.

Click on ADD PHOTOS:

Navigate to the directory where you placed your photographs and click OPEN:

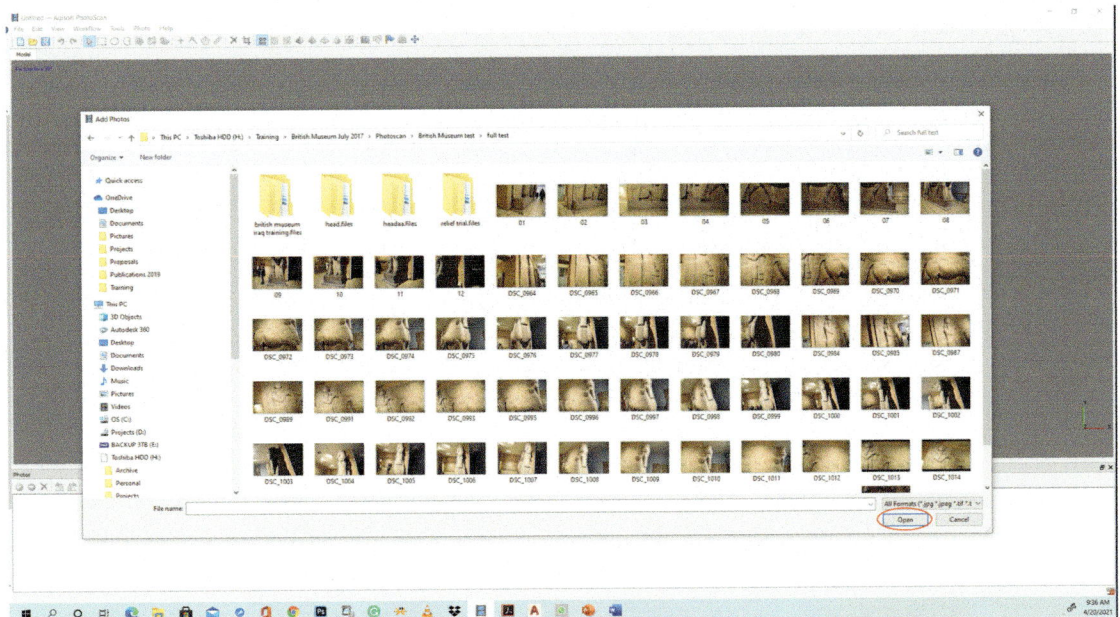

The photographic files are shown in the lower part of the screen. You can double-click on an image to enlarge it and a tab will be added to the top of the main screen with the image name (any number of images can be displayed this way) – to change back to the model view, just click the Model tab:

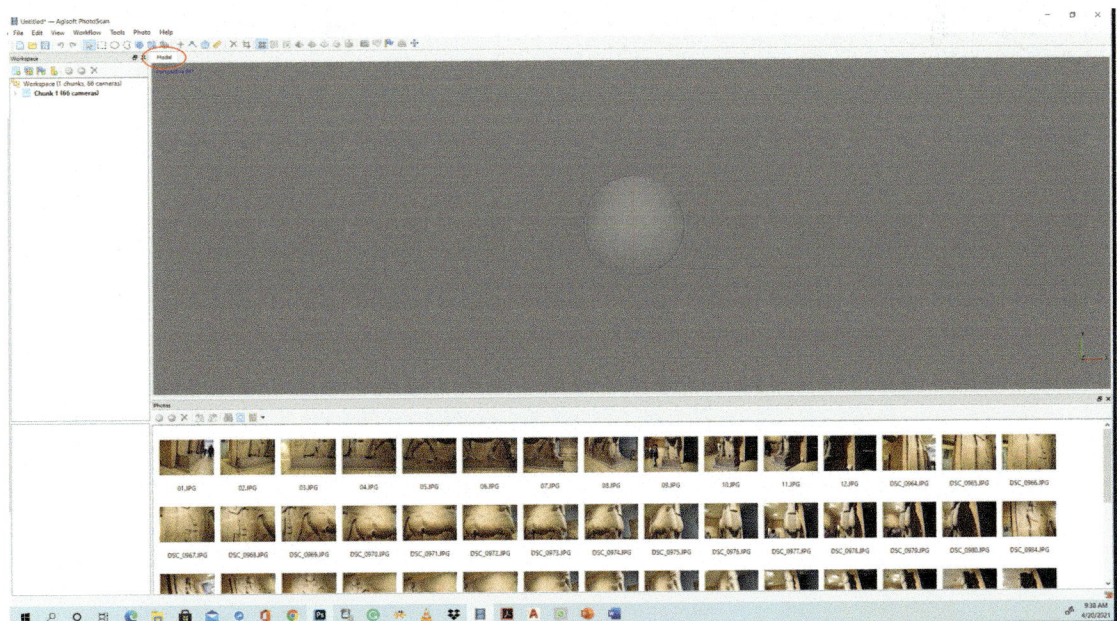

You are now ready to begin processing.

Step 3 – Aligning the photographs

Go to the Workflow directory and click on ALIGN PHOTOS:

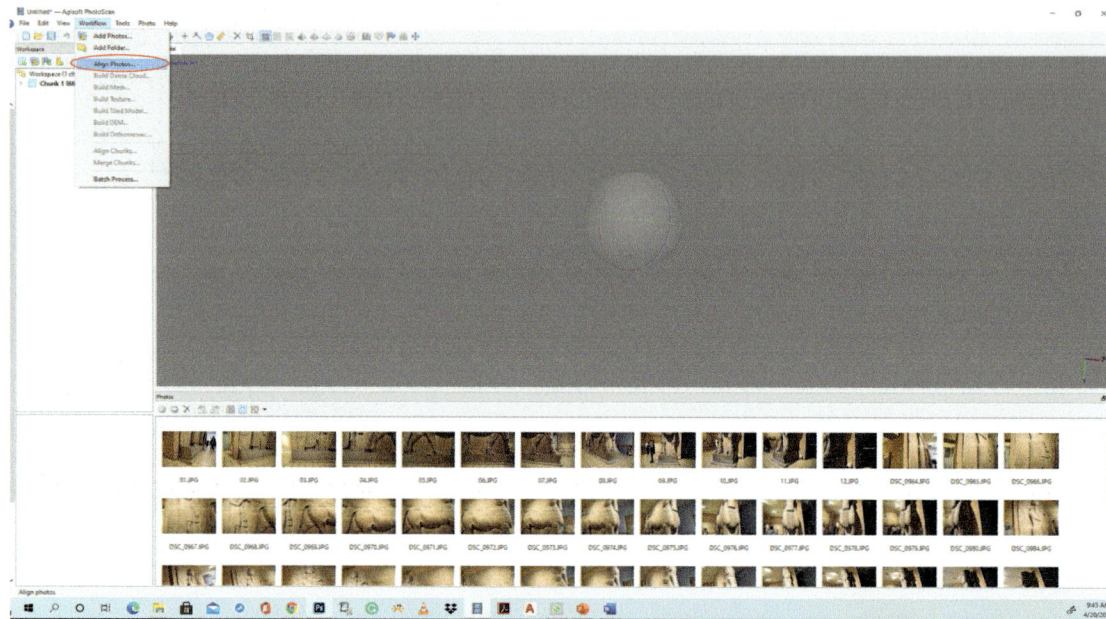

This will search for pixels or points common in all the photographs and align them in three-dimensional space. Next you need to choose the level of accuracy. A sub-dialog box or pop-up window will appear. This is to set the accuracy of the steps. On the first run, choose the LOW or LOWEST setting:

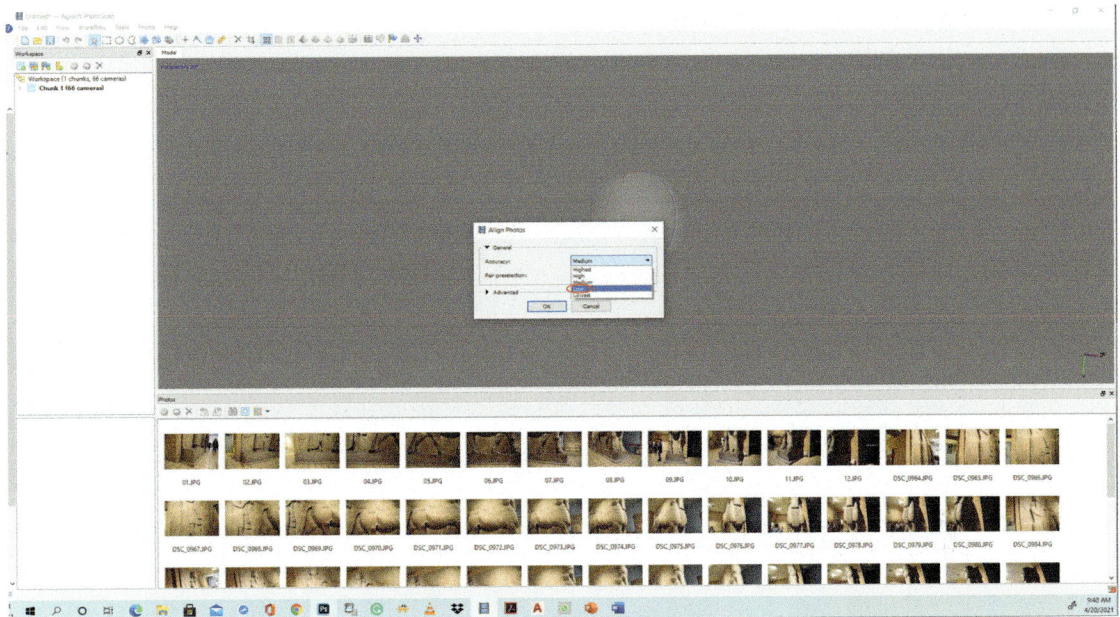

It is VERY IMPORTANT to make test models to determine if there is sufficient coverage before making a high resolution model. Click OK.

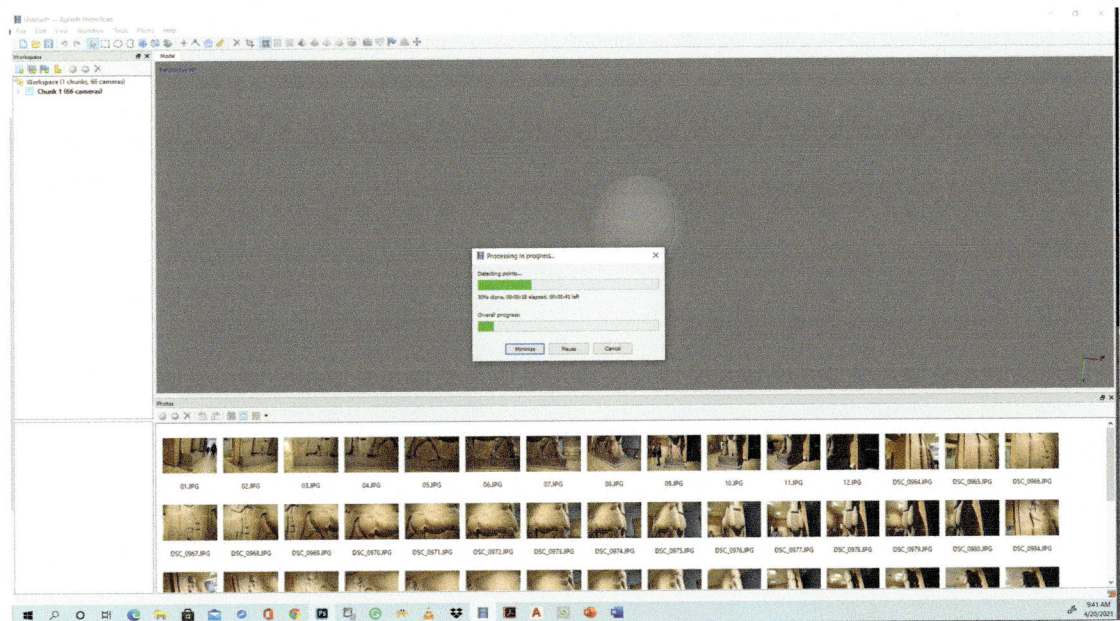

This photo-alignment may take anywhere from two minutes to two hours depending on the number of photographs, the computer, and the complexity of the subject. Wait patiently!

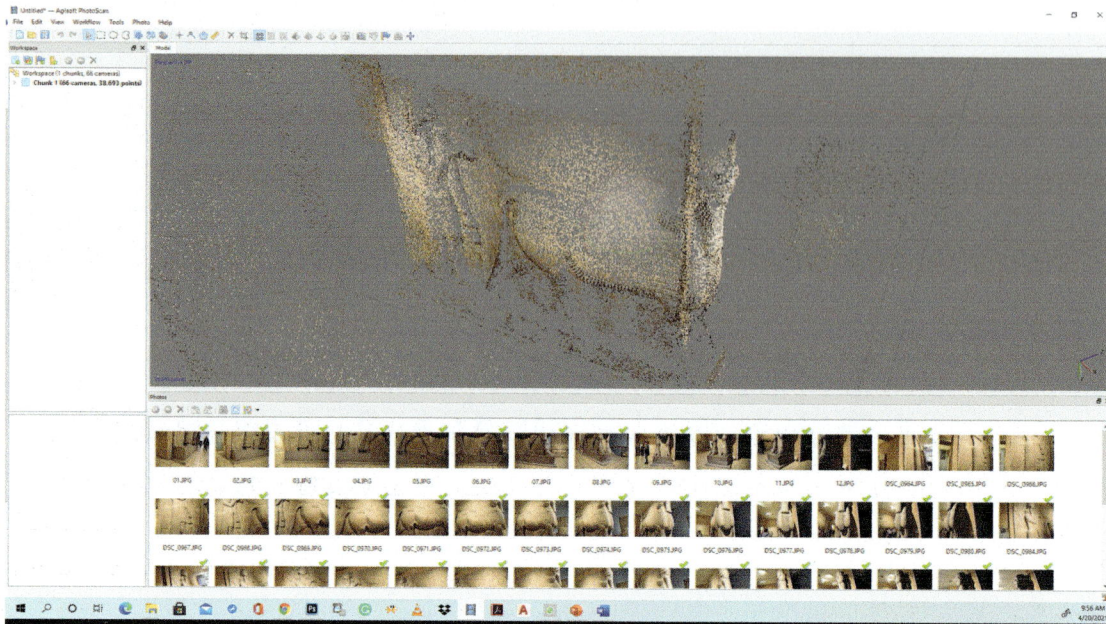

You will end up with something that looks like an array of dots. Save this to your working directory – it is important to save at each and every step. To do this go to File then Save in the pull-down menu.

Step 4 – Building the point cloud

Go to the Workflow directory and click on BUILD DENSE CLOUD:

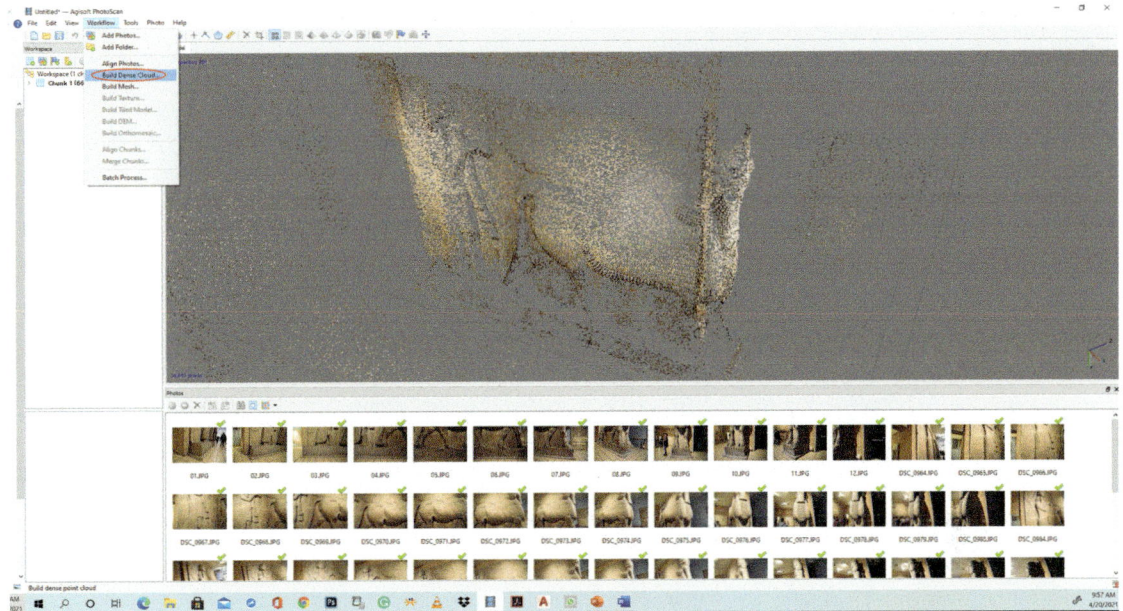

This will create a dense cloud of points. As in the Align Photos stage, a pop-up menu will appear to determine the number of points generated. Once again, for the first run select the LOW or LOWEST setting:

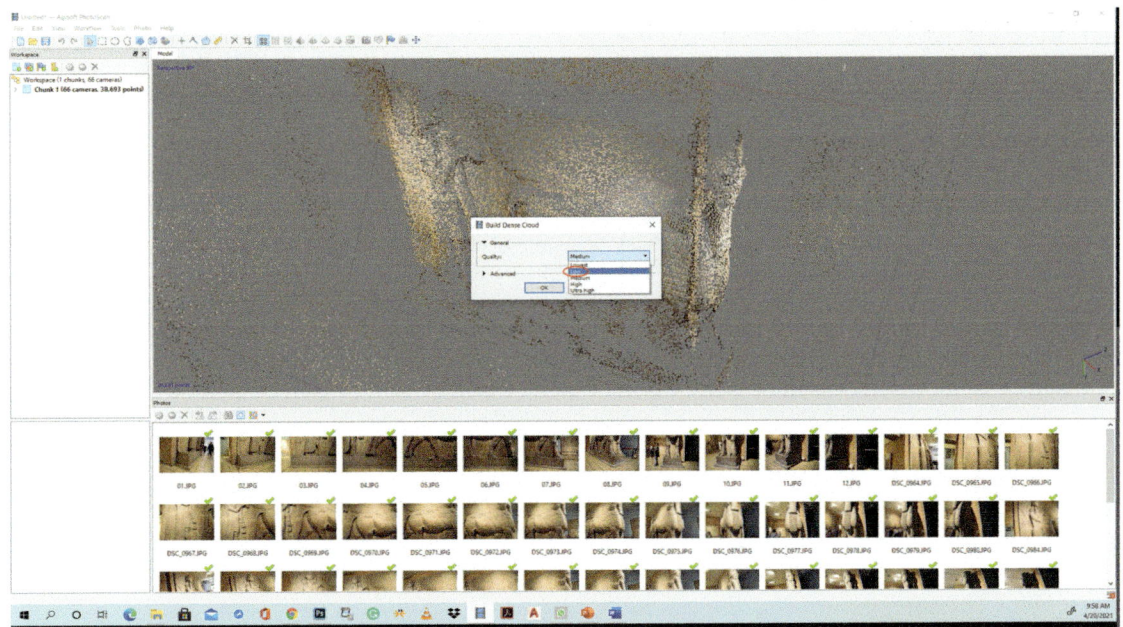

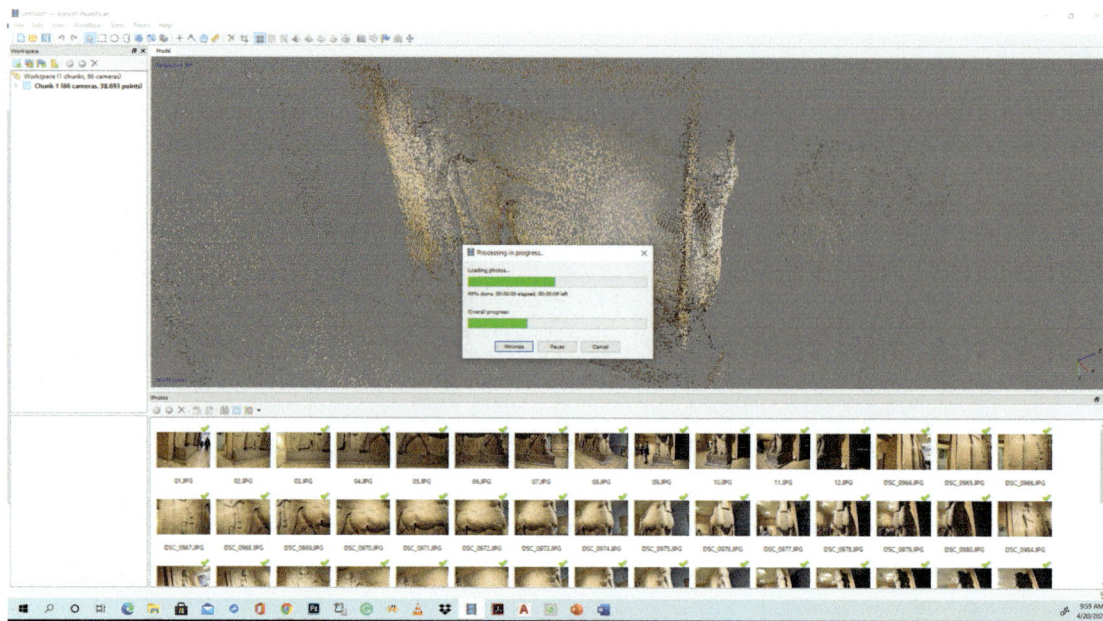

A low resolution model will be created first. Later, if all goes well, you can repeat the process generating higher resolution models – and note that if a higher resolution model is needed the ENTIRE process must start from Step 2.

As with the previous step, the computer requires time to process. Depending on the size, complexity and resolution of the model, this step can take anywhere from a few minutes to as much as a day! For very high-resolution models this step may take more than a day, so set it up to run overnight if you can.

N.B. ensure your computer has adequate ventilation as this process is very computationally intensive and the central processing unit of the computer can reach 100^0C.

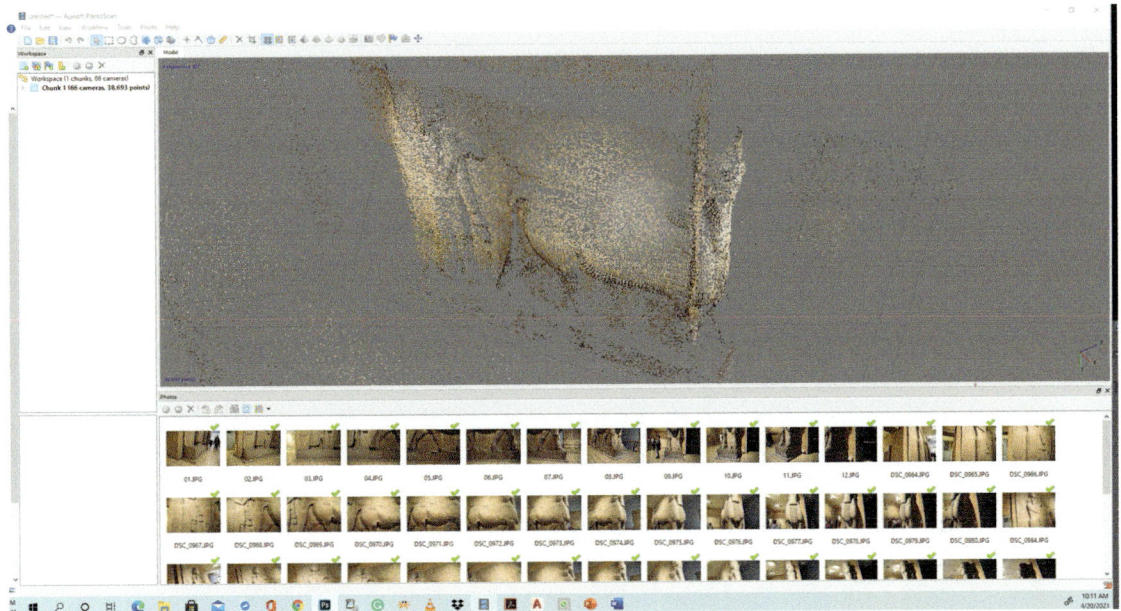

This step will generate a dense point cloud that you can rotate and look at. It will now begin to look like the object that was photographed. Save your project at this stage too.

Step 5 – Building a mesh

Go to the Workflow directory and click on BUILD MESH:

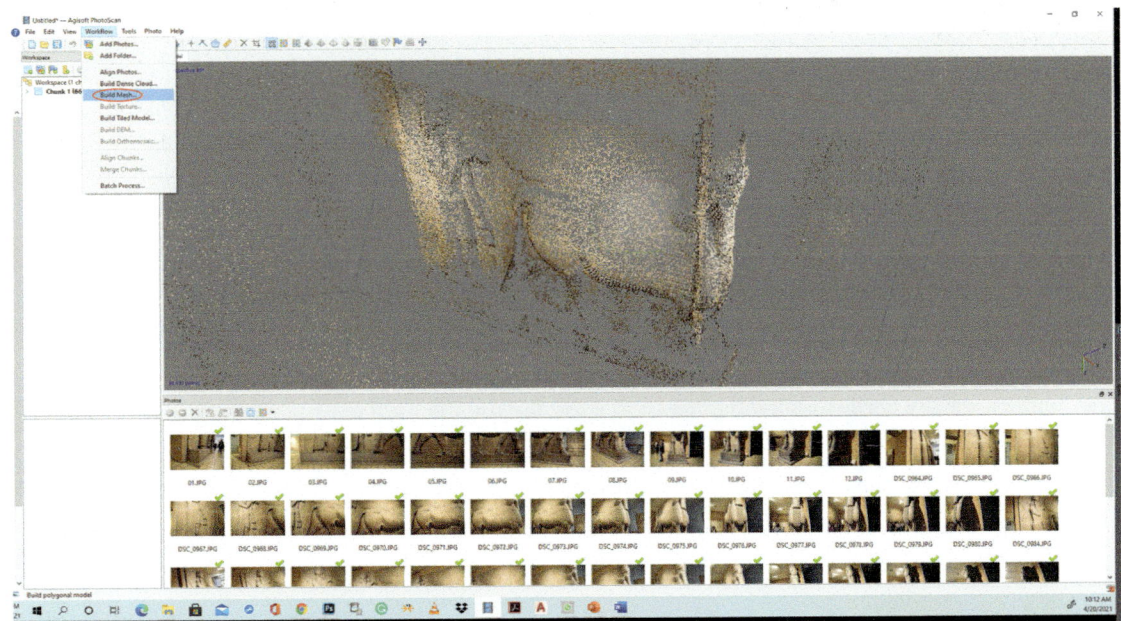

This will connect the various points with triangular polygons to create a 3D model. As with the other steps, a pop-up menu appears and, once again, in the first instance select the lowest setting:

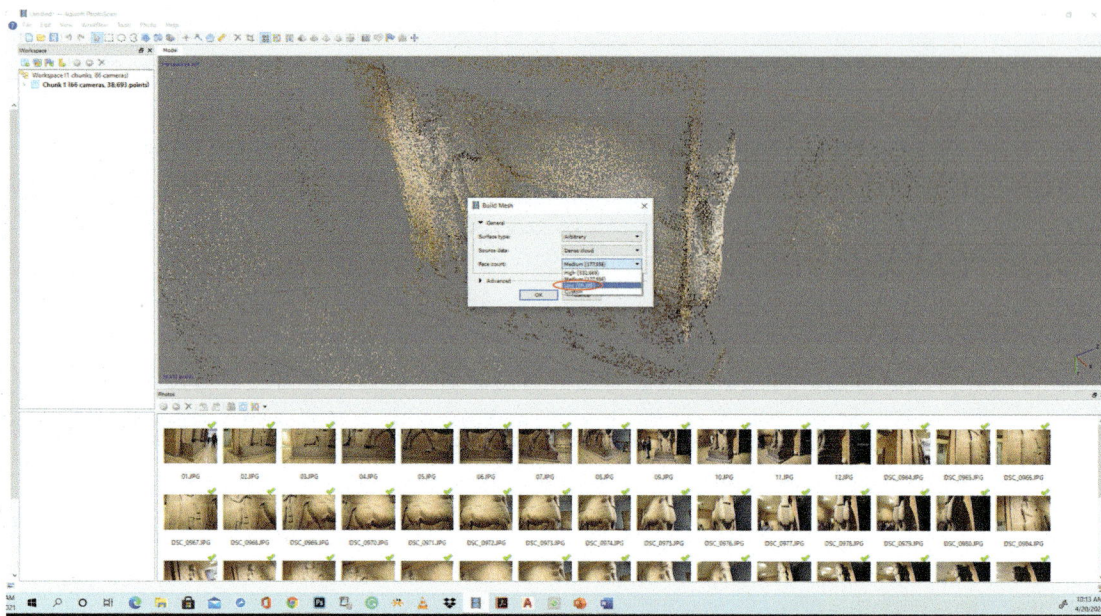

This also will take time to process. The result should now be beginning to look very much like the actual object.

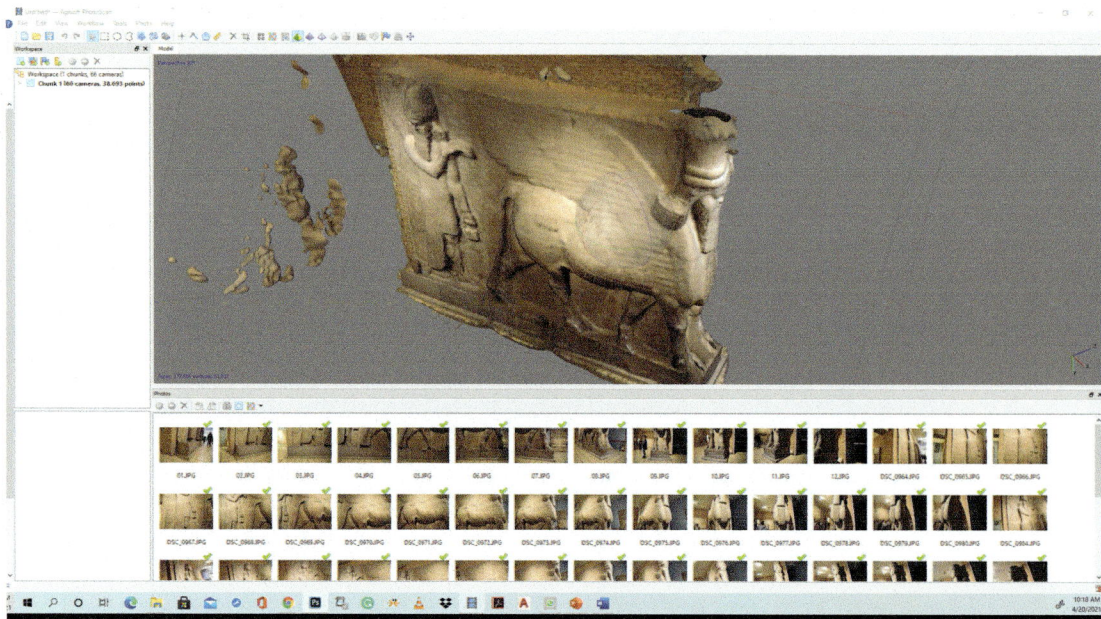

But the process is not yet finished. Once again, save the file at this stage.

Step 6 – Adding texture

Go to the Workflow directory and click on BUILD TEXTURE:

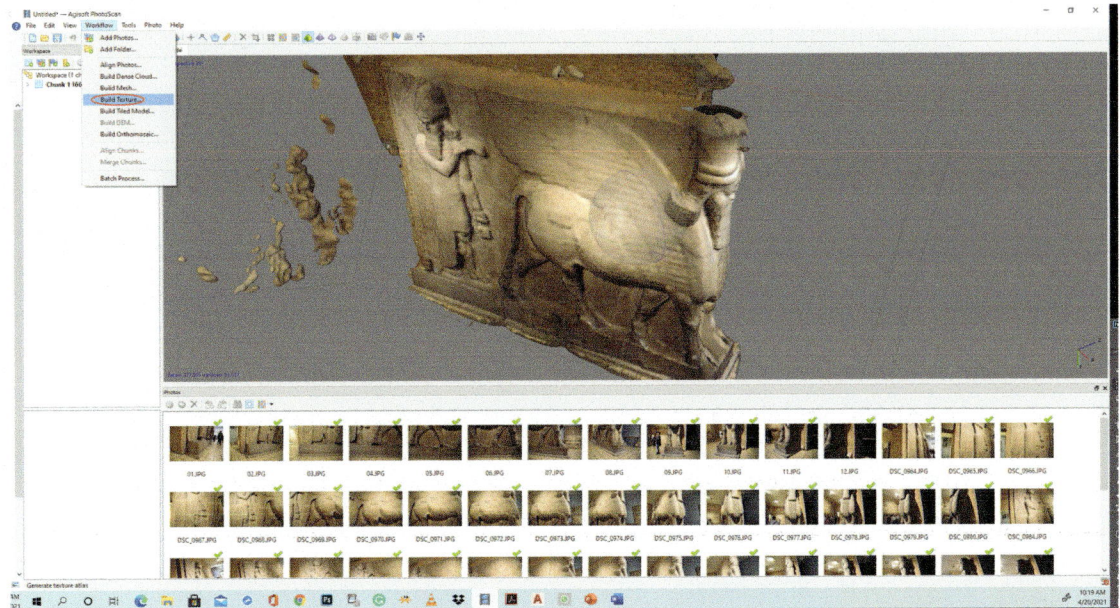

This will take all the source images, combine them, and then apply them to the polygons in the 3D model. This is the last major step.

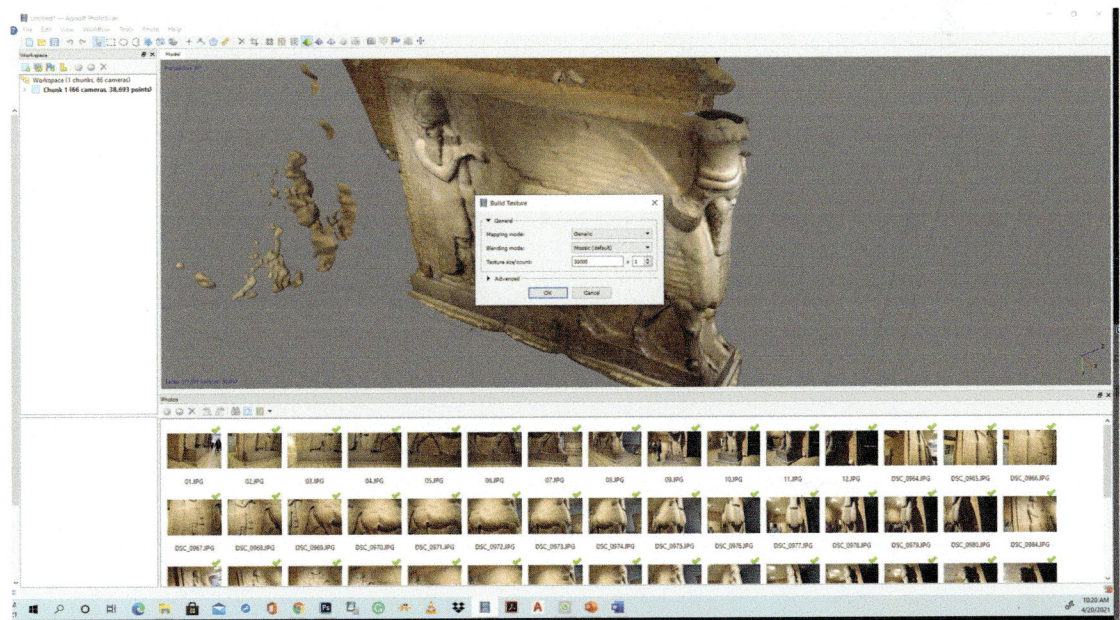

Like all the previous steps, there is a quality selection. As before, for the first model select the lowest, then press OK. Once again, the processing will take some time.

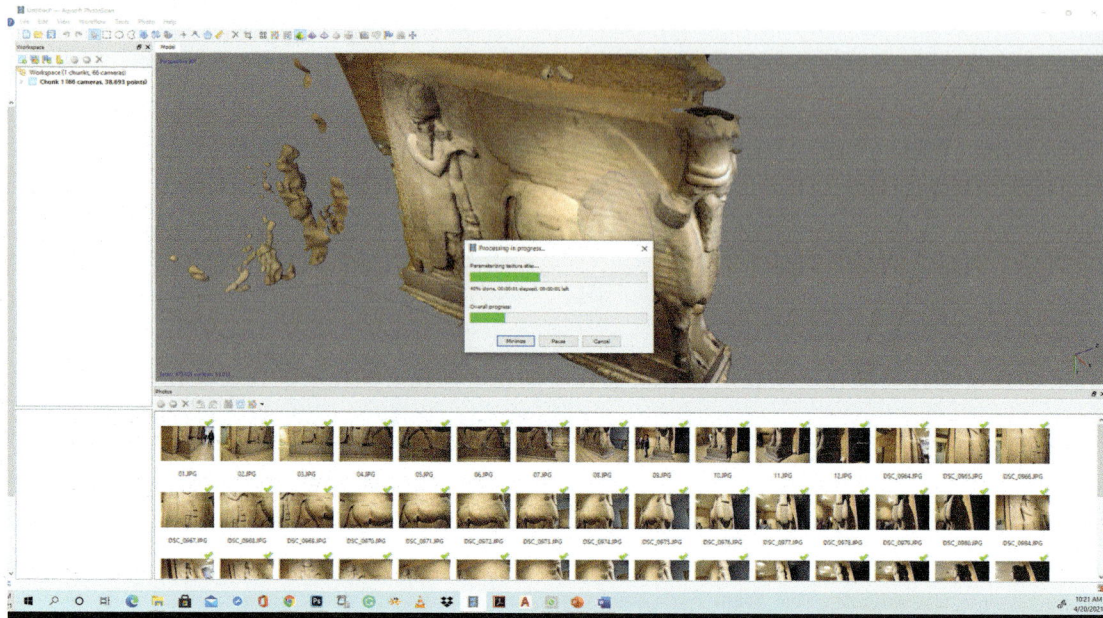

When the processing is completed the final output is a fully textured digital 3D model. Zoom, rotate, pan around the model to inspect it. As before, make sure you SAVE this!

Repairing 'holes'

In this example we have a very good model with many elements recorded. However, where there was inadequate overlap between images or no coverage there are 'holes' in the model. Look carefully at the image below – the dark grey blank areas are holes.

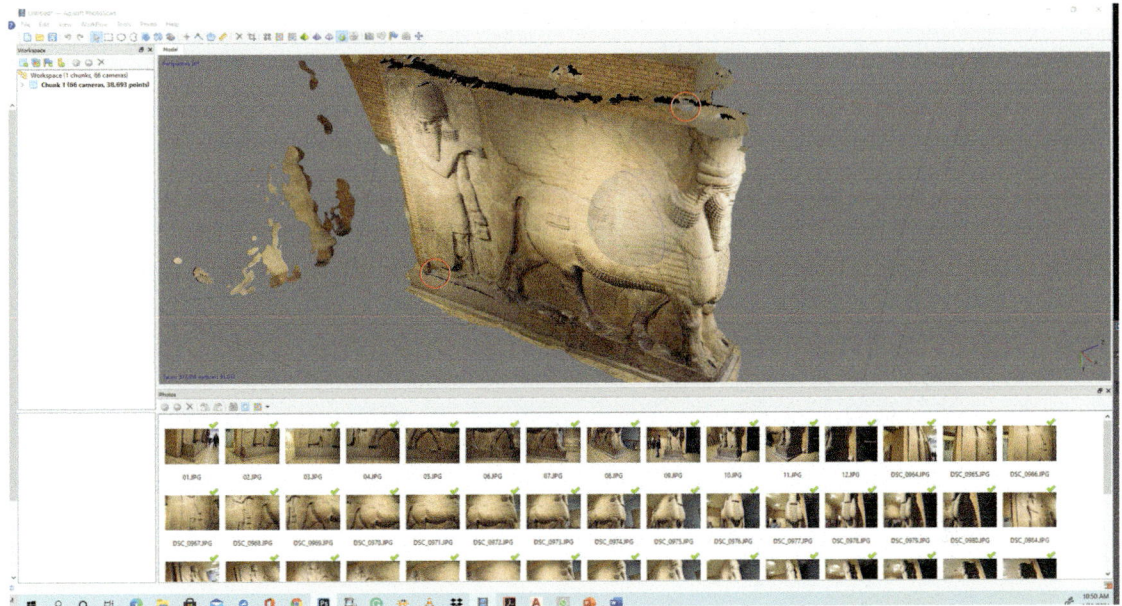

A close inspection will show where the photography capture was insufficient – there are actually several holes in this model:

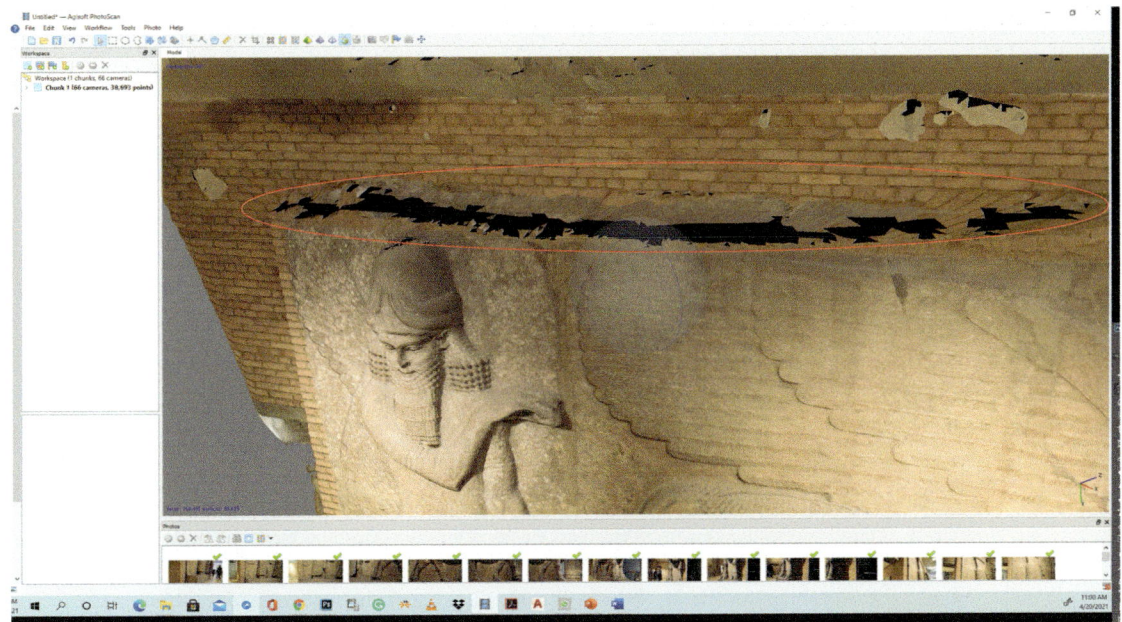

These could be 'patched' with additional software, but a better approach is to recapture with photographs and reprocess the model from Step 1. The positions of the cameras can be turned on by using the Show Cameras icon on the upper menu:

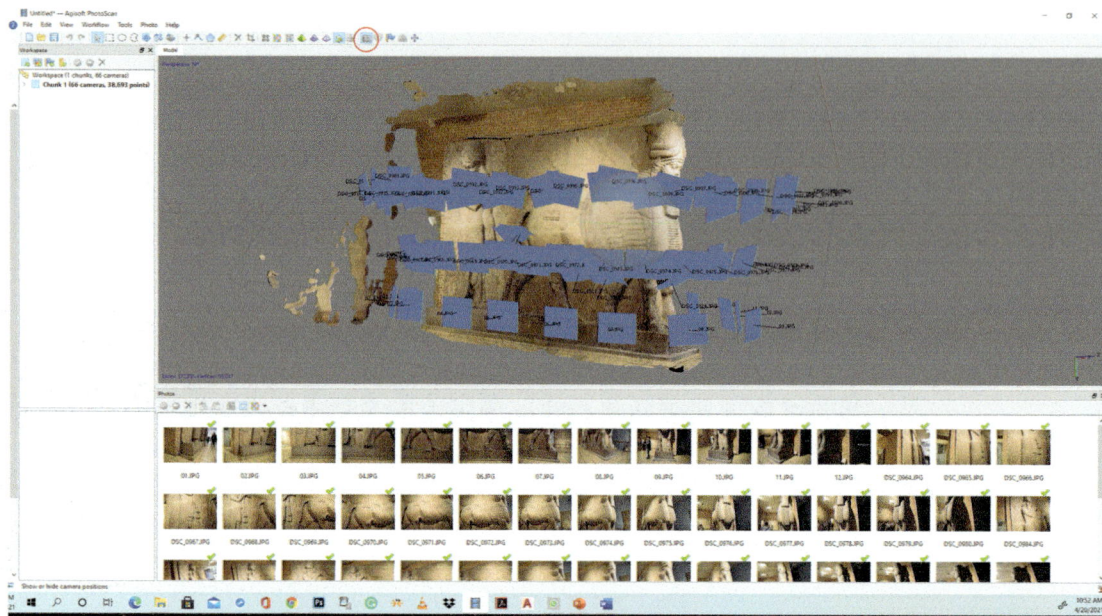

The cameras are shown as blue rectangles with their corresponding names. In the image above, the coverage and stereo pairs are well represented – the coverage is particularly good. This Show Cameras icon can be toggled off and on. Additionally, the icons to the left and right will show the model with and without texture, as a wireframe, or a simple model.

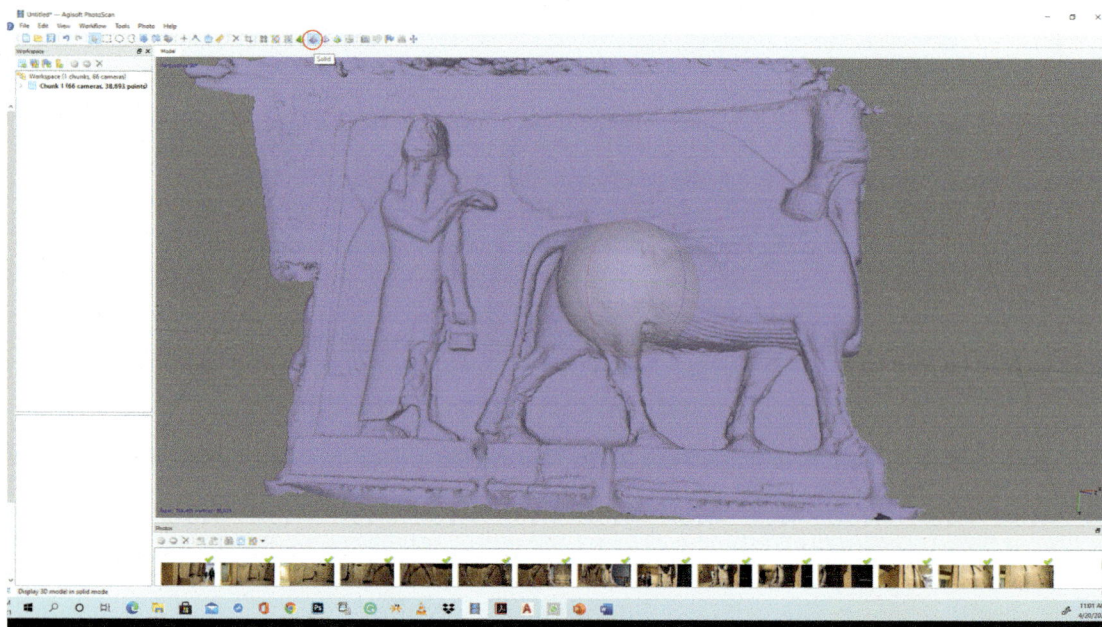

In this selection above, the model is shown without texture, which is useful for identifying holes and areas that did not process well. Experimentation is necessary to get to know the programme – take the time to explore all the options offered.

The model will also have extraneous elements that are not related to the subject:

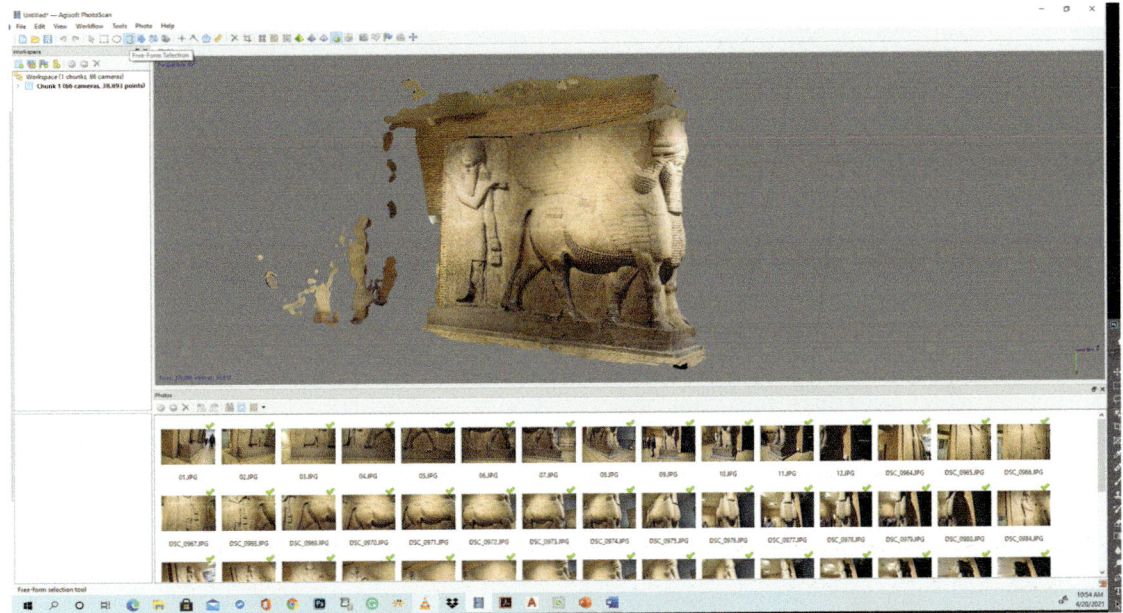

Switch from the arrow icon in the menu to the Free Form Selection icon to draw an irregular line around the objects which are extraneous. These extra elements can be deleted. They will appear as pink or grey. Go to the EDIT pull-down menu and click on DELETE:

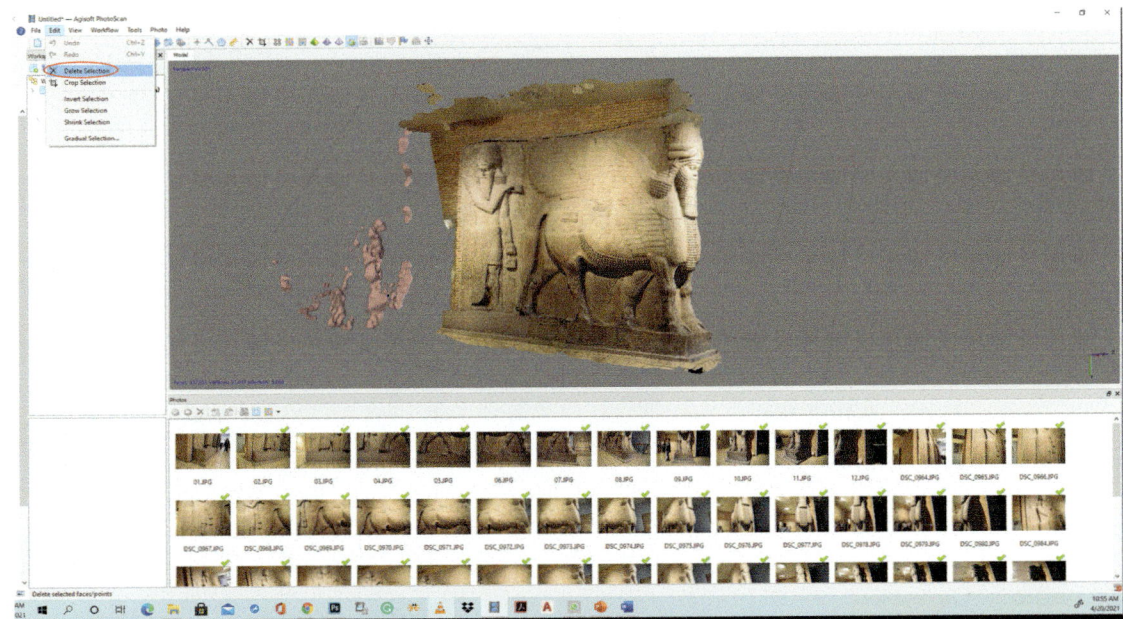

They will be deleted. You can undelete if you make a mistake.

You can also inspect the texture for areas which are out of focus or too dark. The expanded photo menu shows the images used with a green check:

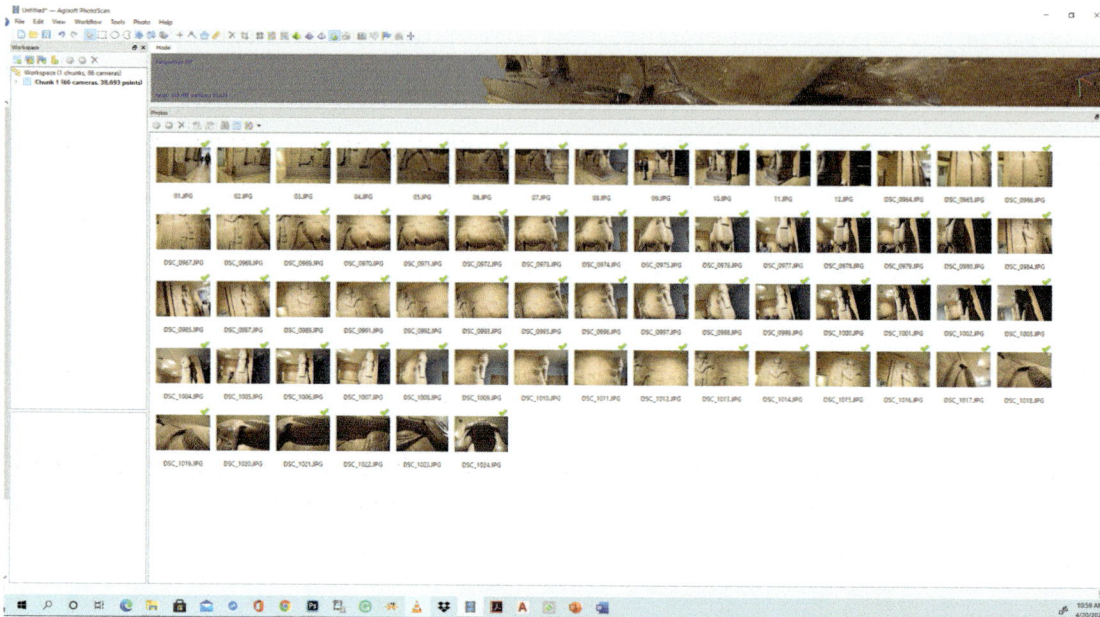

One or more of the original images may be dark or blurry (though they can still be used for the creation of the geometric model), so you can uncheck these at this stage and re-run the texture step to correct this – it is simply a matter of unchecking the relevant photograph(s) and returning to reprocess Step 6 and remake the texture.

Incidentally, note the lack of organisation in the capture sequence of the photography above.

Step 7 – Saving your final model

Do not forget to do this!

Figure 24.13 Carrying out photogrammetry of a small find

Step 8 – Exporting your model

You can export the model to other popular 3D formats such as 3D Studio or Wavefront by going to the File pull-down menu, clicking on EXPORT and following the options.

Conclusion

Three-dimensional models aid in understanding sites, buildings and objects. They extend our knowledge and ability to record and protect cultural heritage in case of loss or damage, help in making decisions, and can be shared to improve our understanding. Photogrammetric capture techniques and software allow us to study objects and sites as never before. The method described here is easy to follow and helps create a better record than simple two-dimensional photographs alone.

References

For those wishing to improve their knowledge there are numerous resources online. While not exhaustive, a few of these references are included below.

https://historicengland.org.uk/images-books/publications/photogrammetric-applications-for-cultural-heritage/heag066-photogrammetric-applications-cultural-heritage/

https://www.isprs.org/commission5/tutorial02/gruss/tut_gruss.pdf

http://www.cesmap.it/ifrao/scale.html

https://www.researchgate.net/publication/317059805_HISTORICAL_PHOTOGRAMMETRY_AND_TERRESTRIAL_LASER_SCANNING_FOR_THE_3D_VIRTUAL_RECONSTRUCTION_OF_DESTROYED_STRUCTURES_A_CASE_STUDY_IN_ITALY#:~:text=The%20historical%20photogrammetry%20offers%20the,to%20support%20their%20real%20anastylosis.

https://www.cipaheritagedocumentation.org/join/

https://www.icomos.org/en

https://www.agisoft.com/

https://www.agisoft.com/support/tutorials/beginner-level/

https://www.agisoft.com/pdf/PS_1.0.0%20-Tutorial%20(BL)%20-%203D-model.pdf

https://www.youtube.com/watch?v=NuJCRIkmn60

https://www.cipaheritagedocumentation.org/wp-content/uploads/2017/02/Waldh%C3%A4usl-Ogleby-3x3-rules-for-simple-photogrammetric-documentation-of-architecture.pdf

https://www.cipaheritagedocumentation.org/wp-content/uploads/2017/02/CIPA__3x3_rules__20131018.pdf https://www.researchgate.net/publication/325468503_3D_CULTURAL_HERITAGE_DOCUMENTATION_A_COMPARISON_BETWEEN_DIFFERENT_PHOTOGRAMMETRIC_SOFTWARE_AND_THEIR_PRODUCTS/fulltext/5b0ff6b20f7e9b8f5883f2ee/3D-CULTURAL-HERITAGE-DOCUMENTATION-A-COMPARISON-BETWEEN-DIFFERENT-PHOTOGRAMMETRIC-SOFTWARE-AND-THEIR-PRODUCTS.pdf

http://www.chnt.at/wp-content/uploads/Waas_Zell_2014.pdf

https://nautarch.tamu.edu/class/anth489/501/Analyticalmethods/Readings/Week14.pdf

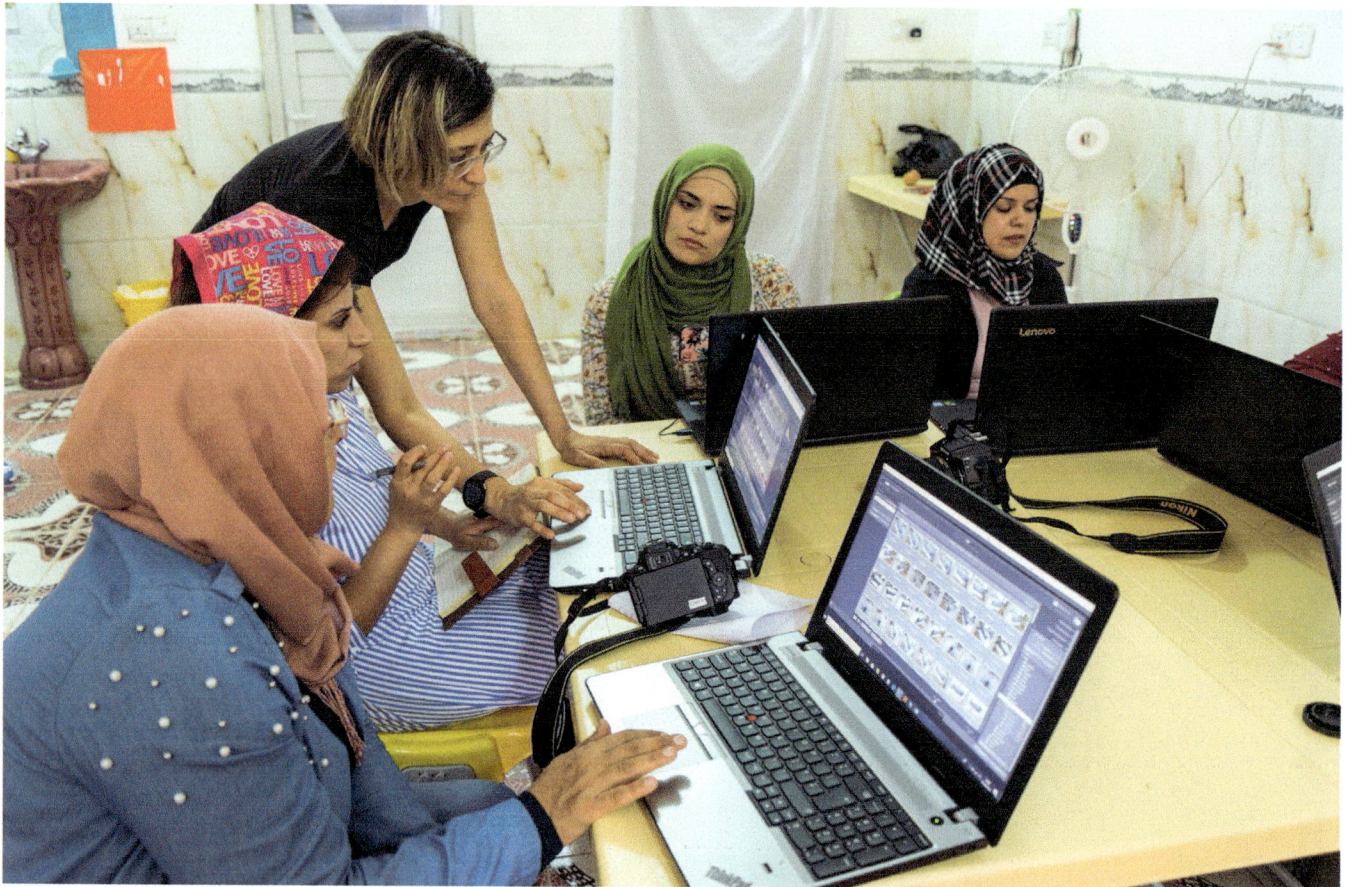

Figure 24.14 Processing images for photogrammetry

Chapter 25

Damaged and looted sites

Sadly, damage to archaeological sites is a worldwide phenomenon. The list of causes is very large and includes natural as well as man-made causes: earthquakes, landslides, volcanic activity, flooding, construction of roads and buildings, agricultural encroachment, the removal of soil for use as fertiliser, digging pits for refuse or for material for making bricks, use as burial grounds, canal digging, drilling wells, robbing stones, looting, even the deliberate targeting of heritage. This damage occurs in both war and peace-time. Sites damaged by these activities need urgent archaeological attention. Approaching this requires care. Information can still be retrieved from looted and damaged sites, even when the scale of destruction has been very large. It is important to stress that the procedures to follow in such cases are no different from the approaches and techniques employed at any other excavation. That said, there will be factors of safety to take into account, and there may be some urgency in addressing the situation.

Figure 25.1
The site of
Dura Europos
decimated by
looters' pits

With this in mind, conducting field work at a damaged or looted site is likely to comprise the following steps: (1) an assessment of safety and security; (2) survey and recording; (3) a report on the state of the site with recommendations for appropriate action; and (4) implementation of a programme for follow-up work. The exact approach, and how you schedule these tasks, will depend, among other things, on the resources available, the amount of time you can spend on the site, and whether or not you will be able to return for a second visit or a more protracted period.

Safety

Key safety matters need to be identified and addressed before any further work can take place.

Unexploded ordinance or IEDs

The very first step is to make sure that a site is safe in terms of potential unexploded devices left over from conflict. This needs to be undertaken by relevant military and/or civic authorities. Information from local residents will also be important.

Structural integrity

The next stage is to make sure that the site is safe in terms of structural integrity. Are there damaged buildings, tunnels in danger of collapse, dangerous protrusions of pipes and wires or overhanging masonry? Any such areas need to be fenced off pending being made secure.

Survey and recording

The survey and recording of a site can proceed according to the methods outlined elsewhere in this manual. The aim is to create a dossier giving as much information about the site as possible. This should typically include name, registration, location, details of the inspection, local contacts, description of the site, satellite imagery, drone imagery, topographic survey, maps, photographs and possibly a surface collection.

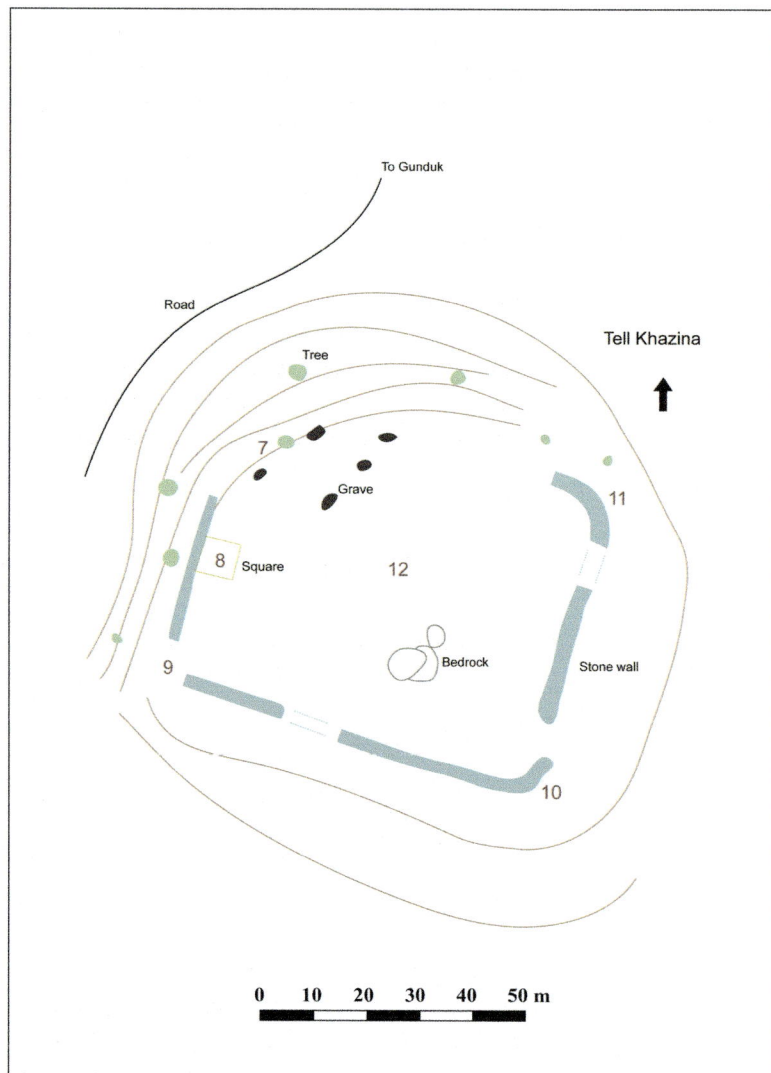

Figure 25.2
Sketch map made during a brief inspection of the site of Gird-i Khazina

Name

The name of the site, and its name in antiquity (if known).

Registration

The site's registration number in any surveys or government inventories where it may have been recorded.

Location

Geographic coordinates; distance and direction from major nearby landmarks such as towns, villages and watercourses, as well as local features such as wells, radio masts, farm buildings and other identifiable items in the landscape; directions on how to locate and access the site.

Details of the inspection

The date when the inspection took place and the names of the individuals who participated.

Local contacts

Names and mobile numbers of any locals who have an involvement with the site – the designated guard, if there is one, but also other individuals who may live nearby, be concerned for the preservation of the remains, or have other useful local knowledge.

Description

A general description of the site giving its size, shape, topography, standing structures, and type and extent of surface scatter; also, modern features crossing the site such as tracks, water courses, electricity cables, pipelines and fences. It is important to record any damage to the site, including how it was caused (if known), as well as any continuing threats.

Satellite imagery

Any available satellite images – in addition to being part of the portfolio, it is very helpful to have copies of these with you when actually on the site.

Drone imagery

You will want to get a good coverage of images by drone for the purposes of: (i) showing the site in its wider landscape or (urban) setting; (ii) a range of views of the site; and (iii) a series of adequately overlapping images to form the basis for the creation of (a) a Digital Elevation Model, (b) a 3D model and (c) an ortho-image. Another important function is that drones can be used to investigate and document sites, or parts of sites, that are too dangerous to approach for whatever reason.

Topographic survey

You will want a topographic plan of the site. The easiest way to do this is to map the site with a drone and use the images to create a Digital Elevation Model with photogrammetric software.

Sketch map

In addition to the topographic plan, or if it is not possible to produce one at the time, you may want to make a sketch map of the site. If you have a good satellite image, you can draw on this. Otherwise you can make a rough map of the site using tape measures, and even pacing. Such sketch maps can show all the features referred to in the description above, with annotations and measurements as appropriate. They can also show locational indications, such as directions and approximate distances to key landmarks, the locations of ceramic surface collection areas together with the find spots of any individual surface finds that you may collect, and any other comments or information that may be useful. The information on a sketch map can be related to features observable in overhead imagery and feed into the map created in a GIS.

Figure 25.3
Assessing
damage to
a standing
monument

Photographs

A good set of photographs of the site, giving multiple views and including close-ups of key features and any significant damage.

Surface collection

You may want to do a collection of surface material. If you only have a short time on the site you will not be able to do an intensive collection, but it may be helpful to carry out a limited collection with the option of conducting a more intensive operation at a later date.

Establishing the site boundaries

It is important to establish the boundaries of the site. This is not always straightforward. Natural topography should be a guide, as will certain aspects of the site morphology, but judging exactly where a mound ends is not necessarily easy, and even when there is a feature such as a fortification wall, you need to establish whether or not there are archaeological remains on the outside. Data from overhead imagery and the surface collection (particularly the fall-off in sherd density and the limits of the scatter) will feed into this. It may be that parts of the original site have disappeared completely. In all cases, a thorough exploration on the ground remains essential.

Report and assessment

Having completed the on-site survey and recording, the next stage is to compile a report putting all these pieces together to give a comprehensive overview of the nature, extent and condition of the site. This should include all the elements above, and indicate the periods of occupation and any previous work on the site. Two important components will be an accurate map created in a GIS and a list of recommendations for follow-up action.

Delineation map

A key element in protecting a site is producing a map delineating the site boundaries. As noted above, this may require some work. Once established, the limits of the site should be indicated on maps for distribution to the relevant authorities, for whom they will be an important tool in the struggle to protect sites from further damage. It may be that subsequent work refines your understanding of the site boundaries, in which case the map can be updated as required.

Action plan

Follow-up work that will need to be conducted at the site will fall into two categories: measures to ensure the safety and security of the site that need immediate action; and further exploration and documentation that are desirable but less pressing.

Immediate actions

Safety and stabilisation

Is there standing architecture that needs to be stabilised? Are there deep holes that present a danger to humans and animals, whether from archaeological trenches, military installations or looters' pits? If so, these need to be addressed urgently, and the areas fenced off securely until they are made safe.

Protection

Is the site in imminent danger of damage from looting, agricultural encroachment, robbing of materials, building works or any other illicit activity? If so, it will need to be fenced off and placed under a guard.

Conservation

Are there exposed remains at risk of destruction or degradation from the environment? If so, you will need to decide the best way of protecting these, whether by reburying, conservation or the construction of a shelter.

Further exploration

Further archaeological work may be recommended to more fully document and understand the remains. As numerous sections in this manual should make clear, there is a huge amount that can be learnt prior to any excavation, and indeed, excavation may not be necessary. In addition to the acquisition of overhead images, whether from satellites or drones, other non-intrusive approaches you may want to consider are photogrammetry, 3D scanning, geophysical prospection and a more intensive surface collection.

Photogrammetry

If there are standing remains it will be important to capture a series of photographs adequate to create a photogrammetric model.

3D scanning

Depending on the nature of the remains and the equipment available, you may also want to carry out

Figure 25.4 Map showing the delineation of archaeological remains at Qalatga Darband

DARBAND-i-RANIA 2018
ARCHAEOLOGICAL SENSITIVE AREA BOUNDARY
DATUM: UTM ZONE 38S - EGM2008
SCALE 1:7500 @A4
GUY HAZELL FOR
FILE: Darband-i-Rania 18.9 - Site Overview B
DATE DRAWN: 31/10/2018
DATE OF POINT ACQUISITION:

▶ Figure 25.5
The site of
the Lagash II
(Gudea) temple
in Girsu after
cleaning of
looters' pits

3D scanning of any standing remains. For fine detail, laser scanning can offer a very high level of accuracy (particularly over a distance) and also has the advantage that the results are immediately available.

Geophysics

You may want to commission a geophysical survey – in addition to helping to better understand the subsurface remains, this may help establish the limits of the site (and so feed into the site delineation map).

Surface collection

As stated, you may want to conduct a more intensive surface collection than was possible at the initial visit to the site. As discussed elsewhere in this manual, there are numerous options of how to carry out surface collections depending on the size and type of site, as well as on the resources available in terms of survey equipment and the time and personnel on-site. You will also want to factor in the resources available to fully process and store collected surface materials.

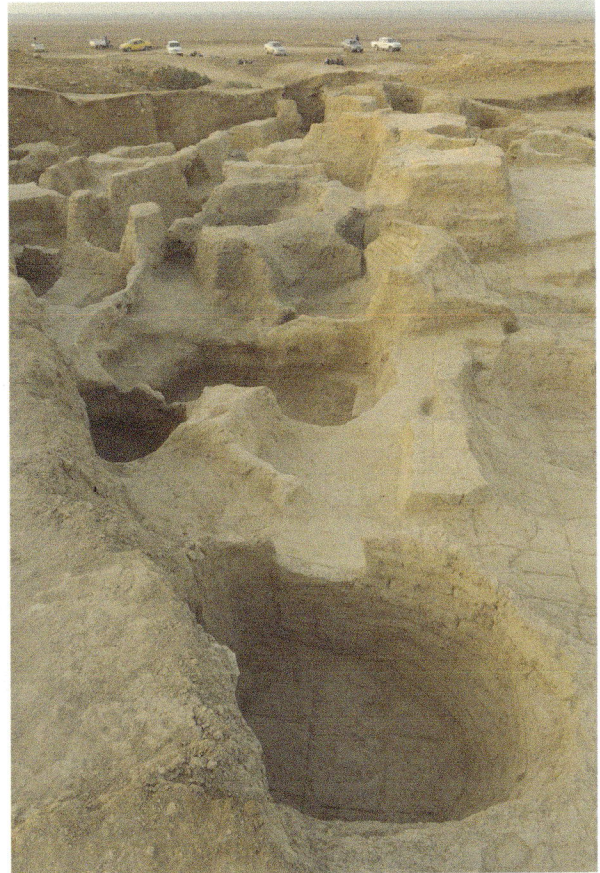

▶ Figure 25.5
The site of
the Lagash II
(Gudea) temple
in Girsu after
cleaning of
looters' pits

Excavation

There are a number of reasons why you may decide to carry out an excavation: to record parts of a site before they are further damaged or destroyed; to better understand individual features, perhaps newly come to light; to record an area that needs to be disturbed in order to undertake conservation, install fencing, or other work. Of course, the procedures for working at a damaged site are no different from working anywhere else – the same rules apply. The task is to clean the area, record what was there, and then excavate the archaeology stratigraphically, removing latest features first in the normal way. The task presented by a looted site is no different.

Looters' pits

It is worth saying something about looters' pits. The damage caused by looters' pits is distressing. Nevertheless, they now form part of the site and should be approached in a methodical archaeological manner to record the information that can still be retrieved.

Preliminary mapping

The first stage will be to create a plan showing the full extent of pitting on the site. At this first stage a sketch plan may be adequate, but a drone photograph is ideal. Each pit needs to be given a context number, which can be added to the photograph in Photoshop or Illustrator (or a similar programme), and a copy of this annotated photograph taken back out to the site for fieldwork.

Sieving the soil

The soil from each pit will almost certainly have been thrown around the edge of the pit. Some locational information is therefore preserved. Sieving the soil from looters' pits will allow you to recover artefacts missed by the looters with this approximate locational information. The soil needs to be given a separate context number from the pit itself. Having sieved the soil around the outside, the pit itself can then be cleaned, again sieving the material of course, and again allocating a separate context number.

Figure 25.6 Pits dug into the Neo-Assyrian palace at Ziyaret Tepe in antiquity. The task of defining and excavating these pits to expose intact underlying remains is the same as that faced by archaeologists working at sites looted in modern times

Recording

Once these cleaning and sieving operations are completed, the next stage is to record the pits in detail. This is done in exactly the same way as one would record a pit in any other excavation – measure its dimensions (including depth), take elevations, draw it on a plan, perhaps draw the section, and take at least one coordinate (at the centre). The easiest way to plan pits, particularly if there are a large number, will be using an ortho-photo entered into an illustrator programme. Take a set of photographs. Last but not least, you need to record the stratigraphic information visible in the side of the pit where it has cut through archaeological layers. The best way to do this may be to create one or more straight sections that can then be drawn and photographed in the normal way.

In due course, if resources allow, the sites of looters' pits can be turned into proper archaeological excavation areas – laying out a rectangular trench and proceeding as a normal excavation. This could be done over an extended area. In this respect, approaching an area damaged by multiple looters' pits is not greatly different from excavating an area that was pitted in antiquity.

Chapter 26

Site Management

The excavation is finished and the recording is complete – final photography, drawing of plans and sections, photogrammetry, context recording and the making of final notes on-site are all done. But the work is still not finished! Following the completion of digging there is still a lot to do, not just the writing up, the handling of samples and small finds and the myriad other tasks in the dig house – which will be intense – but also in terms of managing the site itself.

Site management

To close the excavations properly and leave the site in the best state possible there are numerous tasks which need to be carried out – backfilling trenches, the protection of exposed standing remains, restoration, erecting fencing and signage, engaging a guard.

Figure 26.1 Discussing site management strategy

Backfilling

Backfilling the trenches is necessary for multiple reasons: to protect the remains, discourage illicit excavations, restore the visual harmony of the site; in other cases, the site may lie in farmland and, if authorised, the area may need to be returned to agricultural use.

In earlier times it was common not to backfill at all, or to simply shovel the excavated earth from the spoil heap back into the trench, at most covering the excavated remains in plastic sheeting. All of these approaches are wrong.

— Simply not backfilling exposes the preserved archaeological remains to degradation from the environment and looting. It may also mean leaving deep excavations open and unguarded, an unacceptable danger to both animals and people.

— Backfilling with the excavated earth from the spoil heap with no intervening barrier obscures the interface between preserved ancient material, compromising the archaeological integrity of the site.

— Use of plastic sheeting can also not be recommended due to the fact that plastic traps moisture in the layers below, which can lead to serious degradation of both built fabric (particularly stone and wooden architecture) and artefacts.

The correct approach is to backfill the trench, but in a method which does not trap moisture in the ground and does not compromise the archaeological integrity of the site. Two solutions are possible.

Geotextiles

The best and modern approach is to lay down geotextiles over the excavated remains prior to backfilling. Geotextiles are synthetic permeable materials specifically designed to let water and air to pass through, thus avoiding the problem of water being trapped in the remains and allowing the site to breathe. If possible, it is good to put down a double layer rather than just a single layer of geotextiles over the remains. In addition to this, geotextiles can also be used to reinforce earth slopes to prevent erosion. The range of geotextiles manufactured in different quality, complexity and price is very large; for simple backfilling the cheaper types are perfectly adequate.

Sand/gravel

An alternative, which may be more practical in some circumstances (particularly if geotextiles are not available), is to lay down a barrier of neutral natural material such as sand or gravel, and to backfill above this with earth from the spoil heap.

Protection of exposed standing remains

In some cases it may be possible and desirable not to rebury the remains but to preserve them visible above ground for visitor viewing. There are multiple aspects to this process. The first is

protecting the remains from the environment. This may involve building a roof or shelter over the site, digging channels around the sides of the remains to lead away rain flows and drain off ground water, and other minor works to offer shielding from the elements. Of course, it is very important that any such work does not itself damage archaeological material. It should also be mentioned that roofing is often unsightly and can bring its own problems such as creating micro-environments which can destroy more than they protect as the wind can create vortexes and increase localised erosion.

Another method in protecting ancient remains is to carry out limited non-destructive restoration. Mudbrick walls, for example, can be replastered with mud plaster. Also, it is possible to fill gaps in a wall and to add courses on top of eroded wall lines by using mudbricks made to the same dimensions as the ancient ones – this will both protect the remains and make them more comprehensible to the public. In this case, it is important that the material added in restoration is differentiated from the original (ancient) masonry. It is also important to be aware that such measures can slow down but not completely prevent further deterioration.

It may be that more extensive restoration is needed. This may be for a number of reasons – it may be considered essential from a basic engineering point of view (for example, reinforcing a structure to prevent further collapse), for aesthetic considerations (i.e. to make the site more attractive), or to make the remains more comprehensible to visitors. There are many different views on whether, or how, or to what extent such restorations should be undertaken – but such partial restorations can be a solution which allows preservation of the existing remains to co-exist in tandem with making the site comprehensible and attractive. It is important that such work is undertaken by professionals who know the material and understand the archaeology in order that the reconstructions are both accurate and do not cause damage to the archaeology, whether the remains being restored or the surrounding deposits.

Reconstruction

The most extensive intervention is reconstruction. At the extreme end this can entail complete reconstruction of a building, but this is rarely contemplated today as it will almost certainly involve serious damage to the existing fabric as well as raising questions of authenticity and being hugely expensive.

Figure 26.4
Restoration
of the third
millennium
bridge at Tello

Fencing

Consideration should be given to erecting fencing. The aim might be to fence off the entire site, or sections which are particularly fragile, vulnerable to attracting looters, or dangerous (such as unstable masonry or deep excavations). Another reason to fence a site might be to deter damage from road building, house construction and agricultural encroachment. The type and extent of fencing will depend on the funds available, but large-scale projects should include a provision for the erection of fencing in the budget as a matter of course. However it is important to stress that fencing on its own is not a complete solution. Fencing can be stolen and circumvented, and therefore needs to be seen as one component of a package of measures – ideally including oversight by a guard and/or the local police – for protecting a site.

Guard

The engagement of a guard during the excavation season, when remains are exposed, is a legal (and moral) responsibility. For larger sites it may well be necessary to maintain a guard permanently through the year. Whether or not this is possible, all sites will benefit from the links established in the course of the project with the local community and the local police, who are best placed to keep an eye on the site and report any incursions.

Signage

In the case where visitors can be expected – which means not just major sites which are well known but any sites which are reasonably accessible – it is important to put up one or more signs explaining the site to both local inhabitants and tourists – as well as other archaeologists! Such signs should present the historical setting, the work that has taken place and the finds that were made, with an explanation of their importance and implications. It cannot do harm to explain that the remains are part of the country's priceless heritage and need to be protected.

A case-study: the Sumerian bridge at Girsu

At the Sumerian site of Girsu (Tello) a programme specifically dedicated to heritage management and site conservation was implemented in the context of the Iraq Scheme. The preliminary

Figure 26.5 The walls of Nineveh as reconstructed in the late twentieth century

Figure 26.6
Planning
conservation
work on the
bridge at Tello
(Girsu)

assessment of this unique monument of Mesopotamian engineering, left opened and exposed for the better part of a century, stressed the urgency of carrying out a comprehensive conservation programme. The bridge at Tello was discovered and excavated from 1929 to 1932. Described at the time as an 'enigmatic construction', it has been variously interpreted as a hypogeum, temple, dam, and water regulator. Recent studies using the 1930s old photographs as well as recently declassified space imagery from the 1960s, reinforced by new fieldwork, led to the confirmation that it was a bridge over an ancient watercourse. Built in the third millennium BC, it is, to date, the earliest-known bridge in the world. Since excavation, the bridge has remained open and exposed, with no identifiable conservation work to address long-term stability or issues of erosion, and no plans to manage the site, or engage with a local or wider audience.

Aims

The principal aims of the Bridge Project were:

— to offer the participants of the Iraq Scheme an additional and complementary training programme focusing on conservation of ancient monuments and heritage management

— to establish with them a conservation approach for damaged sites using the Bridge of Girsu as a case-study

— to develop in collaboration with SBAH and Iraqi delegates a management plan, including site panels and visitor centre, to engage with the local community and wider audience

Figure 26.7 Drainage channels installed to drain off water from the bridge at Tello

Practical training objectives

To achieve these aims, a number of training objectives were identified:

– Understanding the significance of the site

– Recording the site in its present-day condition

– Mapping the current state to understand the vulnerabilities of the site, including:

- a topographical plan to determine issues of water damage through ponding water, efflorescence and sub-florescence, and direct physical damage through water action

- a map plotting the deterioration of the site since the excavation in the 1930s

– Preparing conservation options to address vulnerabilities

– Testing conservation methodologies to address the condition and vulnerabilities of the site:

- Emergency repairs for the purposes of Health & Safety

- Emergency repairs for the purpose of site preservation (i.e. to address immediate issues of collapse)

- Works to understand and facilitate the removal of water and salt

- Works to understand and address basal wall erosion and collapse

– Carrying out archaeological investigations and inspections, including rescue excavations below and around the walls of the bridge prior to restoration, boreholes and other scientific analyses

– Implementing the comprehensive conservation plan for the bridge

Figure 26.8
Recording in
advance of
restoration
on the early
dynastic bridge
at Tello

– Preparing site panels, including visualisations, and the outline of the management plan with visitor centre

The short to mid-term aims of the project were to document, study and preserve the Girsu Bridge. The long-term aim is to develop a co-created, sustainable conservation and heritage management strategy for the wider Tello/Girsu cultural-natural landscape in its complex and multi-scalar contemporary context.

An integrated architectural conservation methodology was proposed, with six interconnected and interdisciplinary research blocks:

- Documentation and analysis of the bridge in its current state

- Historical and comparative research

- Hypothetical reconstruction of the structure

- Statement of 'significance' of the monument through time and today

- Construction of an appropriate, balanced and sustainable conservation and heritage management strategy together with the key stakeholders

- Conservation and management plan

Figure 26.9 Repairing the foundations of the bridge at Tello

The first campaign of the Girsu Bridge Project (October 2018) was dedicated mainly to the first three blocks of this methodology, focusing on the necessary research. The architectural documentation of the structure was essentially completed, and the characteristics of the building materials with regard to the structure of the bridge, the environmental conditions and the causes and processes of deterioration were studied and mapped. An area was selected to test some preliminary conservation measures. Some appropriate capping and masonry repair solutions were implemented using locally available materials. On the site-wide level, some urgent measures on water drainage were also taken.

In the 2019 season, the performance of the previous year's interventions was evaluated on-site. Judging from the results of the year-round monitoring carried out, a major aim of the season was to come up with more substantial drainage solutions. Due to changing climatic conditions Tello experiences heavy storms and rainfall. The bridge site, enclosed within a basin, suffers dramatically from repeated flooding and subsequent evaporation processes. Another priority was to continue with the capping and pointing interventions. For this purpose, a team of masons was trained. In addition to the capping, pointing and masonry repairs, in 2019 some structural support solutions were also devised. At selected areas where serious basal erosion can lead to structural failure, some physical support and fill solutions were designed and implemented. The interventions did not undertake reconstruction of missing parts of the masonry, but was rather designed to re-establish the load distribution and stability using reversible and inert materials.

Figure 26.10
The bridge at
Tello following
conservation
work

Chapter 27

Report writing

A very important part of the archaeologist's work is writing reports. Without a report, the information will be lost and all the great effort wasted. Over the course of the season, and the project as a whole, multiple levels of reports will be needed. You can think of these like tree rings, each level building on the one before it.

Supervisors' daily logs

At the start is the daily log. As discussed above, this is the basic building block of the written record. It is an entry written by supervisors in their notebooks and/or on the computer, summarising the day's proceedings in their excavation areas. This should cover new contexts assigned, with ample notes on material, measurements and stratigraphy; new small finds and sample numbers assigned; and any thoughts on the interpretation of the trench. Very frequently, when writing final reports the director will come back to examine the daily logs for the testimony they give on what was thought at the time.

Figure 27.1
Writing up the day's work

Weekly/fortnightly summaries

It is common to ask area supervisors to write a report at the end of every week or fortnight summarising the progress in their trenches. As in Iraq it is mandatory to submit a report to the State Board every fortnight, it may be that the director will want to establish a two-week cycle, using these reports to input into his/her own submissions to the State Board. These weekly (or fortnightly) summaries flow out of the daily log. They do not necessarily need to give all the very detailed context-by-context commentary from the daily log, but should cover the major areas of progress in the period under review.

End of season report

At the end of each season the director needs to complete a full report on the fieldwork. This will serve as an important record both for the excavation archives and for submission to the State Board. For the description of the excavations the director will rely on the end of season reports from the supervisors and other specialists. The supervisors' reports therefore need to include a full account of the excavation in each area with a description of all features, including context

Figure 27.2
Checking
details on-site
for a weekly a
report

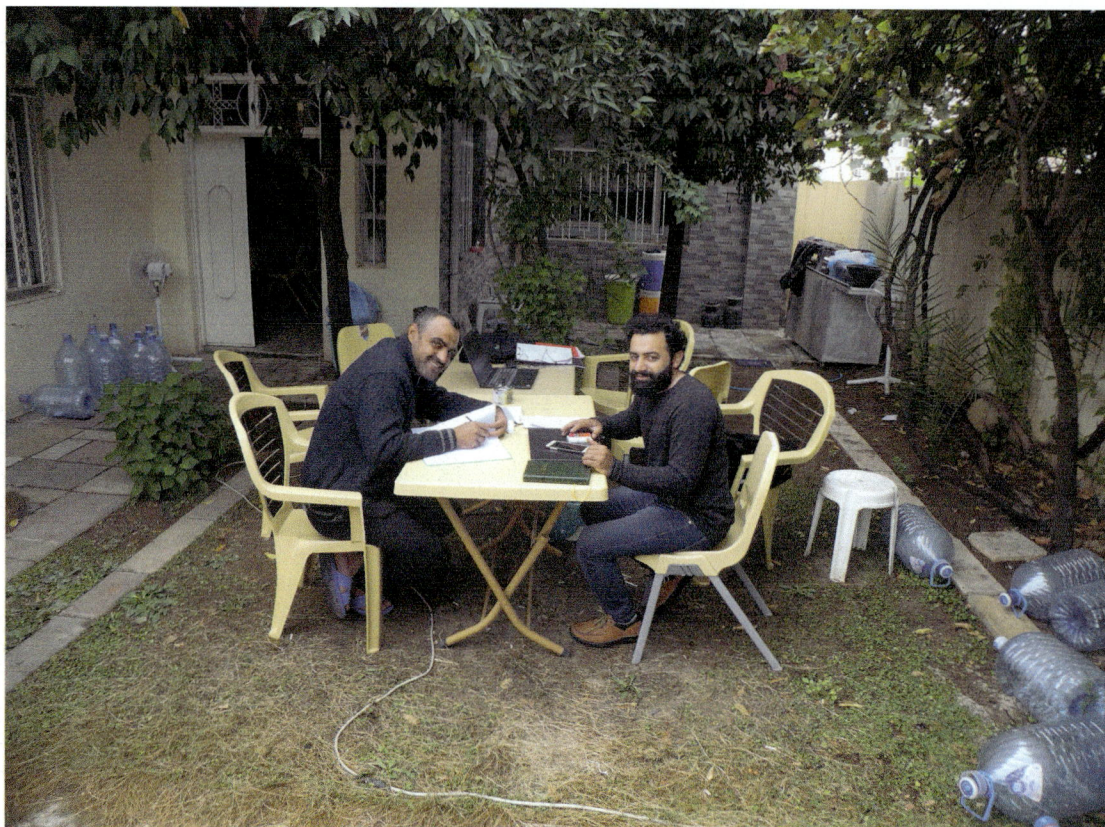

Figure 27.3
Working on
end of season
reports

numbers and dimensions, a list of all contexts assigned, a list of all small finds and field numbers assigned, plans and sections (ideally digitised), a folder of photographs with an accompanying Excel file listing the details of each image, and a Harris matrix. All of this material needs to be formatted and named in accordance with the excavation protocol. In addition to this, the director will need full end of season reports from the conservator, ceramicists, archaeozoologist, archaeobotanist, physical anthropologist, and any other specialists present on-site.

Preliminary and interim articles

The next stage will be the preparation of a preliminary report on the season for publication as a journal article. The end of season report forms the basis for this, but there is in addition the opportunity to compare the results of the season to those of previous seasons and from other field projects, to research individual finds, to include editions and discussions of epigraphic material, analysis of numismatics, the results of radio-carbon dating and to incorporate preliminary interpretations of ecofactual (environmental) datasets. All of this can be done in a more polished academic manner, with references to published sources, than is possible at the time of the end of season report when the workload is so intense (and the resources may not be to hand).

► Figure 27.4
The end of a
demanding
but rewarding
season!

This post-excavation period is also the time when specialists can work on their materials and publish articles on their analyses and interpretations. Typically, this might include studies of archaeobotanical and archaeozoological datasets, coins, seals, sculpture, ivories, inscriptions, ceramics, and others. All of these contribute materially to the understanding of the site and will in turn feed into the final report.

Final published report

This report, which will normally be published as a monograph, covers the full record of the project in as comprehensive a manner as possible – an introduction to the site, geographical setting, historical background, aims, methodology, topographic survey, ceramic surface collection, geophysics, a detailed phase-by-phase description of the excavation results, analysis of small finds and epigraphic material, the results and interpretation of archaeobotanical and archaeozoological datasets, physical anthropology, and anything else generated by the field research. To reach this stage there will have to have been enough time to evaluate phasing and dating, and for the specialists to finish their work so that their findings can be incorporated into the final report and the implications for the overall interpretation of the site assimilated. While the final reports will also appear in Arabic or Kurdish, it is important that a summary in English is prepared in order that the results of the project can fully and properly reach the international community.

Appendices

Surface survey record sheet

Surface survey record sheet

Site   Date

Grid Square   Supervisor

Sketch plan (indicate direction of north)

Notes

Levels recording sheet

Levels recording sheet

Site   **Trench**   **Date**   **Supervisor**

Level no.	TBM = Backsight	Instrument height	Plan no. Foresight	Reduced level

Context sheet

Context no. رقم الوحده الاثريه	Site الموقع Area المنطقة Trench الحفرية	Supervisor المشرف Start date تاريخ بداية التنقيب

Context type نوع الوحده الاثريه	O Primary رئيسية O Tertiary ثالثية O Clear واضحة O Merging مدمجة O Secondary ثانوية O Mixed مختلطة

Date (period) التأريخ (الفترة)	Phase السويّة	Room no. رقم الغرفة

Description الوصف

Measurements القياسات

	length الطول	height/depth الارتفاع /العمق	width العرض
max. الحد الأقصى			
min. الحد الأدنى			

Elevations الارتفاعات

max. الحد الأقصى	
min. الحد الأدنى	

Stratigraphic Relationships العلاقات الطبقية

Above فوق	Cuts نقطع	Fills تملأ	Abuts تتاخم	Part of جزء من	Equals مساوية لـ
Below تحت	Cut by مقطوع بـ	Filled by مملونة بـ	Bonds with مرتبطة بـ	Consists of تتكون من	Associated with ذو علاقة بـ

Finds اكتشافات

Find or Sample Nos. رقم المعثر/العينة

Pottery فخار O	Sieved? منخلة O	%
Bone عظم O		
Glass زجاج O		
Metal معدن O		
Slag خبث معدني O		
Lithics صوان O		

1.   6.
2.   7.
3.   8.
4.   9.
5.   10.

Additional records أرقام إضافية

Plan nos. أرقام المخطط	
Section nos. أرقام المقطع	
Photo nos. أرقام الصور	
Notebook p. رقم صفحه المدونة	

Burial sheet

Burial sheet

Context Number	Site Area Trench	Start Date Supervisor

Description and comments

disturbed/undisturbed (robbing / natural processes / other later activities)

evidence of matting or textiles

Measurements

mm / cm / m	Length	Width	Depth
Maximum:			
Minimum:			

Elevation

Maximum:	
Minimum:	

Stratigraphic Relationships:

Above	Cuts	Fills	Part Of	Equals
Below	Cut By	Filled By	Consists Of	Associated With

Finds:

Pottery ○	Sieved? ○	% Sieved:		Mesh Size:	Find or Sample No		
Bone ○	Finds Comments:				1.		6.
Glass ○					2.		7.
Metal ○					3.		8.
Slag ○					4.		9.
Lithics ○					5.		10.

Representations:

Plan No:	
Section No:	
Photo No:	

Burial context no. .... **Skeleton find no.** ....

Skeleton processed on .... **by** ....

Preservation of bones
well preserved ☐
partially decomposed ☐
badly decomposed ☐

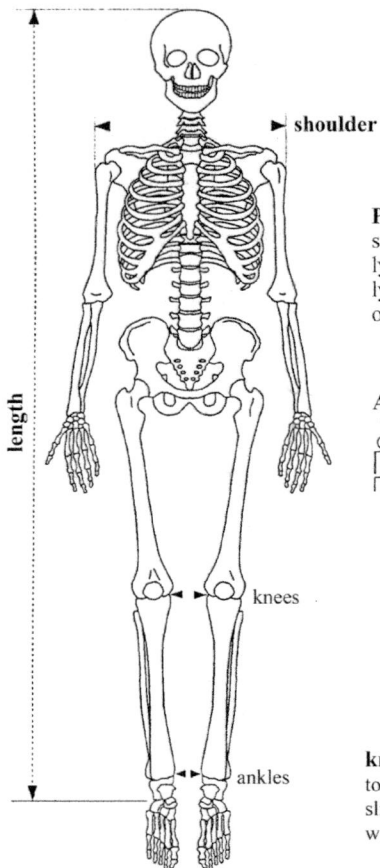

► shoulder

Position		**Skull**		**Mouth**	
stretched out	☐	frontal	☐	open	☐
lying face up	☐	facing left	☐	closed	☐
lying face down	☐	facing right	☐		
on left / right side	☐	supported	☐		

length

Arms
1 2 3 4 5 6 7 8 9 10 11 12 13 14

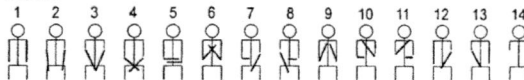

left over right ☐   right over left ☐

knees

Hands	right	left
palm up		
palm down		
resting on edge		

Legs	right	left
straight		
flexed		
fetal		

ankles

knees	
touching each other	☐
slightly apart	☐
wide apart	☐

feet	right	left
out to each side		
pointing forwards		
turned to the left		
turned to the right		

Sex

Age

Height

Other comments

Key to indicating bones
in situ   shade fully
dislodged   hatch
missing   leave blank